D0894292

The GREAT FLOWING RIVER

巨流河

The GREAT FLOWING RIVER

巨流河

A MEMOIR *of* CHINA, *from* MANCHURIA *to* TAIWAN

Chi Pang-yuan

齊邦媛

EDITED AND TRANSLATED
BY JOHN BALCOM

WITH AN INTRODUCTION BY
DAVID DER-WEI WANG

Columbia University Press
New York

Columbia University Press
Publishers Since 1893
New York Chichester, West Sussex
cup.columbia.edu

Library of Congress Cataloging-in-Publication Data
Names: Qi, Bangyuan | Balcom, John, editor, translator.
Title: The great flowing river : a memoir of China, from Manchuria to Taiwan / Chi Pang-yuan ; edited and translated by John Balcom with an introduction by David Der-wei Wang.
Other titles: Ju liu he. English
Description: New York : Columbia University Press, 2018. |
Includes index.
Identifiers: LCCN 2017055946 (print) | LCCN 2018013656 (ebook) |
ISBN 9780231547819 (electronic) | ISBN 9780231188401 (cloth : alk. paper)
Subjects: LCSH: Qi, Bangyuan. | Sino-Japanese War, 1937–1945. |
China—History—Civil War, 1945–1949 | China—History—1949– |
Taiwan—History—1945– | Authors, Chinese—20th century—Biography.
Classification: LCC PL2892.3.B36 (ebook) | LCC PL2892.3.B36 Z4613 2018 (print) | DDC 895.18/5103 [B]—dc23
LC record available at https://lccn.loc.gov/2017055946

Columbia University Press books are printed on permanent
and durable acid-free paper.
Printed in the United States of America

Cover design: Lisa Hamm
Cover image: (digital composite) Photograph of Chi Pang-yuan provided by the author and river photograph © plainpicture/Kati Kakamo

Contents

Preface to the English Edition

CHI PANG-YUAN

Since I came to Taiwan in 1947, the memories of the twenty-four years of my life lived in war-torn China have haunted me like a second reality. I came of age during a historic time when my country was united to resist the Japanese invasion.

The twentieth century is not too long ago. Gigantic human griefs were buried with it. Its indescribable sufferings have lingered for three generations now. There still are some middle-aged grandchildren looking for the graves or bones of the missing soldiers. After the 1949 national divide, remembrances were mostly smothered; the blood of the martyrs and the tears of the exiled have gradually become untraceable.

All these seventy years I spent my time reading and teaching, trying to push the overbearing nostalgia to the corner of my mind, but my heart rebels. It still bears the invisible scars of war. My soul sometimes still trembles with the fathomless sorrows of a lifelong exile.

When I finally determined to write down my memories to ease my heart, it was quite late. I was convinced that I could only start from the limited scope of my own experience, with my lifelong respect and tribute to those who fought so that I might live. I had to write the book for the millions who died in the war and the tens of millions who became exiles, like my own parents. I cannot leave this world without commemorating the many unsung heroes who lost their lives for an unprecedented national cause. Through them, I saw how the human spirit, with fortitude and grace, can soar despite the darkness.

How fortunate I was when my young friends Shan Te-hsing, Chien Chen, and Li Huei-mian miraculously appeared as angels and extended their timely encouragement and actual help. Without their steady conviction and cheer, I might have escaped again when things looked too overwhelming for me to handle.

I am deeply grateful to Professor David Der-wei Wang for being my tireless proponent and the best taskmaster one could ask for. Without his avid support and direction, the English version of my book would have been interminably delayed. Based on his profound understanding of the background of our long exile, his introduction to this book is the most lucid and sympathetic guide for readers fortunate to have been born during the peaceful second half of the twentieth century.

I must also commend my translator, Mr. John Balcom, for giving my story the equivalent of an English voice. I am aware that translation is an interpretative act as well as a creative one, and he has done a fine job on both accounts.

My heartfelt thanks also go out to my dear friends Leung Yanwing and Nancy Du for helping me review the English manuscript. I would also like to thank Ms. Jennifer Crewe, Christine Dunbar, and Leslie Kriesel of Columbia University Press for their editorial expertise.

Since my book was published in 2009 in Chinese, letters from readers all over the world have flooded my desk, telling me that I have also told their story. These emotional letters, many handwritten in shaky script, describe in great detail places I should have known as a child in northwest China (though I never had a chance to go back to my homeland). Some talk of the people we knew in common and their cherished memory. Together our tales become a tapestry of interconnected destinies and kinship. As I pore over these familiar stories line by line from people I have never met, I feel the veil of sorrow I have carried all these years begin to lift. It is a homecoming of sorts.

Chi Pang-yuan
Spring 2018

Translator's Acknowledgments

Professor Chi Pang-yuan's autobiography stands out among a number of recent popular autobiographies from Taiwan. Her personal narrative provides a fascinating overview of wartime China and postwar Taiwan. For me personally the book has additional importance because I have known and worked with the author for what is now decades.

I would like to thank Chi Pang-yuan for her assistance throughout the long translation and editing process. Chapters 8, 9, and 10 of the original book have been abridged, primarily in accordance with the recommendations made by Professor Chi, and combined to form chapter 8 of this translation. It was felt that the abridged passages were often too detailed with the minutiae of government, politics, academia, and other areas to be of much interest to readers outside Taiwan.

A number of other people who have been involved in the project over the last few years also deserve mention. I am grateful to David Wang for his support for this project and for the introduction he has provided. Peter Bernstein has also been instrumental in moving the project forward.

Several chapters of this translation originally appear in *Renditions*, the prestigious Chinese–English translation journal published by the Research Centre for Translation at the Chinese University of Hong Kong, which I am pleased to see reprinted here. I wish to express my sincere thanks to Ted Huters and the folks at *Renditions* for their invaluable input.

In Taiwan I would like to thank Nancy Du and Yanwing Leung, who read several of the chapters and provided comments and suggestions.

At Columbia University Press, I wish to thank Christine Dunbar for shepherding this book through to publication. Leslie Kriesel, my editor, also deserves thanks for another fine job with her usual keen eye and attention to detail.

Last but not least, I wish to thank my wife, Yingtsih, for her assistance and support.

John Balcom

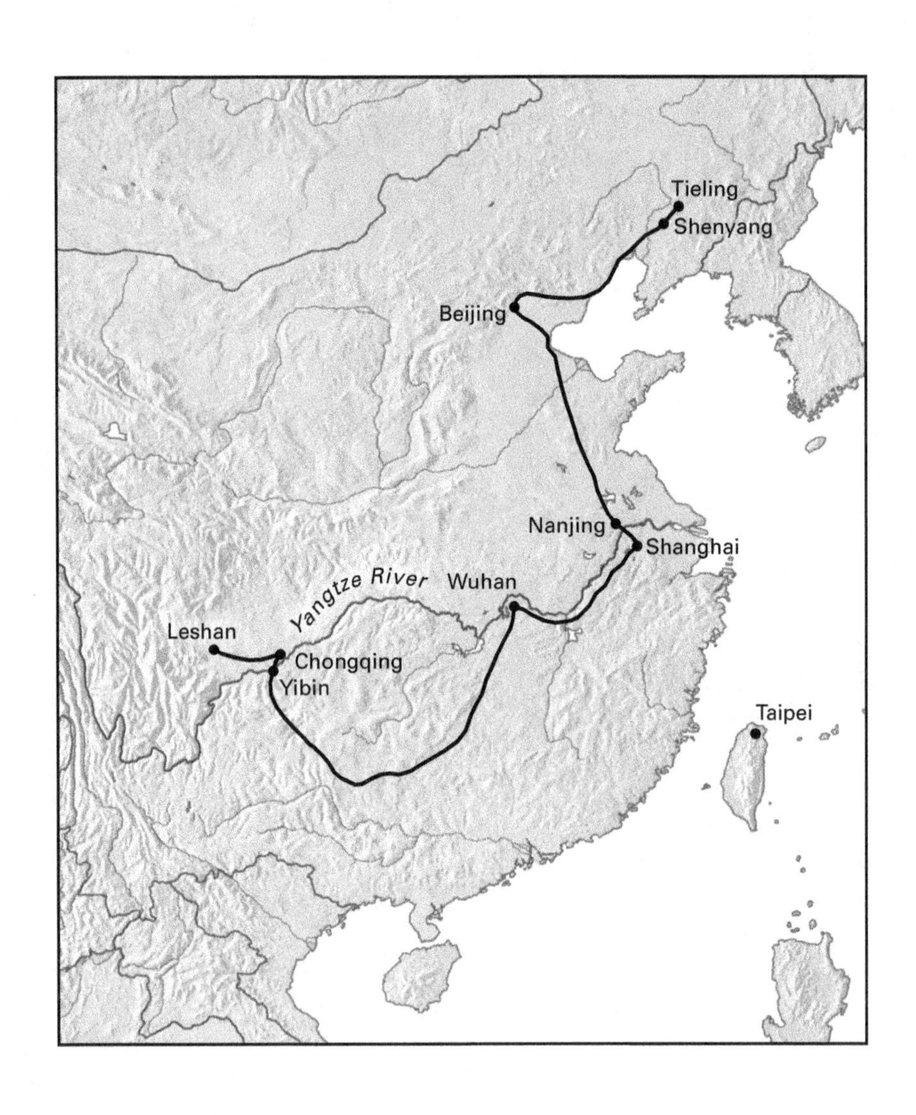
Tieling
Shenyang
Beijing
Nanjing
Shanghai
Wuhan
Yangtze River
Leshan
Chongqing
Yibin
Taipei

Introduction

Professor Chi Pang-yuan is a highly respected scholar, educator, writer, and translator in Taiwan. Her memoir, *The Great Flowing River*, first published in the summer of 2009, was a best-seller that won critical acclaim both on mainland China and among overseas Chinese communities. Its publication was regarded as a major event in Taiwan's literary scene. In her 250,000-word memoir, Chi recounts the ups and downs of her remarkably eventful life—beginning with her exile from northeastern to central and southwestern China, then from the mainland to the island of Taiwan. She grew up with war, death, and exile at her heels, casting shadows over her life. Her life in Taiwan, spanning more than sixty years, stands testament to how a generation of "mainlanders" exiled from China managed to put down roots there.

Memoirs similar to *The Great Flowing River* have been published on both sides of the Taiwan Strait, and some of the experiences recounted are just as storied as Professor Chi's, if not more so. Why has this particular book received so much attention? I believe *The Great Flowing River* is so readable because Professor Chi has written a book that is more than just an autobiography. Through the telling of her story, she touches upon various ineluctable turning points in the contemporary history of China: the dramatic and turbulent changes in northeastern China and Taiwan—her two "homelands"; the Chinese intelligentsia in diaspora and their all-consuming sense of upheaval; as well as the frustrations and courage of women in academia. More significantly, as a teacher of literature, Professor Chi asserts over and over again why we must insist on the importance of literature, especially that created during this woeful period in history.

Can *The Great Flowing River* not be considered a literary masterpiece too? Many readers were deeply touched by the chapters of her life recounted in the book. Professor Chi's descriptions of people and events are indeed touching, but the key might really lie in her narrative style. The period of time covered by *The Great Flowing River* was short on happiness and long on sadness. Professor Chi says that she grew up "in a vale of tears." Yet, so many years later, she has chosen to write about those heartrending events in the most restrained way. The emotions run deep, yet she holds them at bay. This is only possible if you have seen it all. *The Great Flowing River* starts in northeast China and ends at the Yakou Sea in Taiwan. From the roaring waves to the calm currents, Professor Chi tells the story of her stalwart life with dignity and literary finesse.

The Great Flowing River is a sad story. The sadness isn't just a projection of Professor Chi's personal sentiments. Rather, it is an emotional reflection of her entire generation. Professor Chi is one of the lucky ones, thanks to her family background, education, and accomplishments. Yet under the surface of her life story, she outlines the pursuits and regrets, the hopes and bewilderment of her contemporaries. Professor Chi was born in Tie-ling in Liaoning Province. She left her homeland when she was six years old, and during the seventeen years that followed, she traveled all over China. In 1947, by coincidence, she became a teaching assistant in the Department of Foreign Languages and Literatures at National Taiwan University, and she ended up settling in Taiwan for over sixty years. From northeast China to Taiwan, from six years to sixty years, these two places have affected her heart and soul—one is where she was born, and the other is where she has built a life. The subtle interaction between these two places and the huge sense of tragedy embodied in history contribute to the tour de force of this book.

There is a great distance between northeast China and Taiwan. The geography and demography of the two regions differ significantly. Yet both share similar fates in contemporary Chinese history, and the fate of one is actually the mirror reflection of the other's. Northeastern China was originally the territory of the Manchurians, vast and sparsely populated. It wasn't until 1870 that the Han Chinese were allowed to settle and cultivate the land in its three provinces. Taiwan is an isolated offshore island, and it wasn't until the nineteenth century that immigrants from the coastal provinces of China started to arrive en masse. These two places were targeted by the imperialist forces in the East as well as the West at the onset of the twentieth century. After the first Sino-Japanese War in 1895, Taiwan and the Liaodong Peninsula were ceded to Japan. Later, jurisdiction over the Liadong Peninsula was a point of contention among imperial Russia, France, and Germany, and after many rounds of negotiations, China "bought back" the peninsula from Japan. With the intervention of so many forces, these two places experienced a lot of strife and commotion. In the fifty years that followed, Taiwan became a colony of Japan; the northeast experienced the Russo-Japanese War (1905) and the September 18 Incident (1931), and under the orchestration of Japan, it became the Kingdom of Manchukuo (1932–1945).

Culturally and politically, both the northeast and Taiwan have tense and complicated relationships with their "motherland." The people in both regions were often immigrants, who tend to be bolder and more rebellious in nature. They were also accustomed to oppression by those in power. This gave them a sense of dolor, and they often felt wronged. *The Great Flowing River* doesn't deal much with the history of these two places, but if readers cannot comprehend the complicated sentiments that the author has toward them, then they will not be able to appreciate what she tries to say in the book. The life of Mr. Chi Shiying (1899–1987), Professor Chi's father, provides a historical and political context, linking the narratives of the northeast and Taiwan.

Mr. Chi Shiying was a member of the elite who studied in Japan and Germany on scholarships provided by the warlord Zhang Zuolin. This was a tremendous privilege, considering the insularity of the northeast during that time. Mr. Chi Shiying had lofty ambitions. In 1925, he returned to Shenyang from Germany and was introduced to General Guo Songling (1883–1925). The Russians and Japanese were invading the northeast, and yet the local warlords were at each other's throats. This greatly infuriated General Guo, and he attempted to stage a coup against Generalissimo Zhang. Mr. Chi joined the movement as a scholar, but luck and circumstances were not on General Guo's side. He was defeated at the Great River and killed. Mr. Chi went into exile.

The Great River that couldn't be crossed: this became a significant moment in the history of China, ushering in years of pain and suffering to the northeast. If General Guo had succeeded in crossing the Great River, if the coup had been successful, could the September 18 Incident and the Xi'an Incident have been averted? Could the northeast have been modernized sooner? If the central government had paid more attention to the region, then Manchukuo might not have been set up, and the Sino-Japanese War might not have happened, not to mention the war between the Nationalists and the Chinese Communists. But history is not a presupposition; nor can it be rewritten. Chi Shiying's exile had just started. He went into the heartland of China and joined the Nationalists. They put him in charge of party affairs in the northeast. He also founded the Sun Yat-sen Middle School for students in exile from the northeast. At the end of the war, Chi Shiying received orders to rebuild his homeland and coordinate personnel in the region. To his dismay, the Nationalist officials responsible for the handover were corrupt and inept, controlled by the Russians who made life miserable for the people living in the northeast. Later the Chinese Communists rose to power, and the northeast was the first region to fall. The Nationalists lost the war, and Chi Shiying went into exile once more.

In the oral history that he dictated in his later years, Chi Shiying described his long-held disagreements with the Nationalists' central committee. But he did not accuse the Nationalists outright, and the oral history recorded only up to 1949. *The Great Flowing River* is essentially a daughter's recollections of her father, and the angle adopted is of course very different. The book narrates what happened to Chi Shiying after he arrived in Taiwan. In 1954, Chi Shiying made Chiang Kai-shek very angry because he was opposed to the policy of increasing the price of electricity in order to feed the army. His penalty was expulsion from the Nationalist Party. In 1960, he was almost imprisoned for forming a new political party with Lei Zhen, a recalcitrant liberal, and others. In the second half of his life, Chi fought for the livelihood and rights of people in Taiwan. His innate anti-Chiang sentiments stemmed from his identity as a northeasterner. The northeast and Taiwan were both pawns of Chiang's regime.

The Great River that couldn't be crossed. In his old age, Chi Shiying's days were filled with loneliness and remorse. Nevertheless, he remained steadfast and true to himself and his convictions until the end. The karma between this man of honor from the northeast and Taiwan was to be inherited by his daughter.

Chi Pang-yuan came to Taiwan after the retrocession. At that time, Taiwan was still heavily influenced by the Sino-Japanese War, and the February 28 Incident—a bloody crackdown launched by the Nationalists on local rioters in 1947—had just happened. Civil war raged on in China, and there was a lot of uncertainty. Against this backdrop, a young lady from northeast China embarked upon her new life.

Professor Chi has always had a strong affinity with Taiwan. This happened long before the 1990s, when it was considered to be politically correct. She was the first scholar to pay attention to Chinese-language literature produced in Taiwan and pushed vehemently for its translation into English. Many of the writers she was close to were opposed to the Nationalist Party and even the "mainlanders." Regardless of how the political landscape changed, their friendships remained steadfast. Professor Chi's magnanimity stems from an I-know-what-you've-been-through kind of empathy—she understood that in the minds and hearts of the Taiwanese people, there too was a Great River that couldn't be crossed. Taiwan has had much to lose and has lost much in the currents of history. Books such as *Orphan of Asia* and *Wintry Night*—masterpieces available in English through Columbia University Press—describing the fate of Taiwan found an avid reader and supporter in a northeasterner from China.

The war at the Great River in 1925 has long vanished into the dusty corridors of history. The man with shining eyes in the photograph is now resting in peace after a lifetime of turmoil and strife. But his daughter, who left home when she was six years old, became the "guardian angel of literature in Taiwan," in the words of Kenneth Pai, an internationally renowned overseas Chinese writer. Looking back, Professor Chi once lamented that after embracing Taiwan all her life, she had yet to chronicle the blood and tears of the people from her homeland who struggled and fought so valiantly. Thus *The Great Flowing River* is a book late in coming. It is a dialogue between a daughter and her father spanning both sides of the great river of life; it is also Professor Chi's confession to the northeast she can no longer return to and to Taiwan, the island she can no longer leave.

The Great Flowing River chronicles the history of China and Taiwan in the twentieth century, a period filled with epic events. Yet Professor Chi chose to reminisce in a straightforward and composed tone, exercising restraint and humility even when dealing with the most poignant moments. Many readers in Chinese point out that this is the allure of the book. But besides the narrative style, the historical perspective adopted by the writer is also attractive. Who and what contributed to this particular style?

Among the many protagonists described in the book, I think four stand out and have influenced Professor Chi's attitude: Chi Shiying, Zhang Dafei (1918–1945), Zhu Guangqian (1897–1986), and Qian Mu (1895–1990). As mentioned, Chi Shiying's life is the subtext of this book. Before arriving in Taiwan, he was a very important military and political leader. But after he offended President Chiang, his political career came to an abrupt end. In Professor Chi's eyes, her father was a proud and honorable man who never made it into the inner circle of power. Yet she thought that what really distinguished him was not his stubborn pride, but more important, his being an authentic person, "gentle and pure."

Professor Chi recalls when her father joined the family in Wuhan after the Nanjing Massacre (1937): "His white handkerchief, which was gray with dust, was soaked through with tears. He said, 'Our country is lost and our family shattered!'" The Chi family lived a meager life in Chongqing during the war. Once after the bombing when it rained hard all night, "my mother was sick and had to lie in her own bed, over which was spread a large oilcloth to keep the rain off. My father sat at the head of the bed, holding an oilpaper umbrella in one hand to cover his head and my mother's, waiting for day to break." During his twilight years Chi Shiying was often melancholy, and whenever the fall of the northeast was mentioned, he would weep inconsolably. Those were tears of remorse and regret, tears of integrity and dignity.

Chi Shiying's was a turbulent life, yet his daughter, Chi Pang-yuan, learned gentleness and purity from him. Heroes are often made during chaotic times. Some win, some lose, but how many can retain gentleness and purity throughout their lifetime? This sets the tone of *The Great Flowing River.*

With quiet dignity Chi Pang-yuan narrates the story between herself and Zhang Dafei. He was also from the northeast. His father was Shenyang's police commissioner when Manchukuo was established. Because of his involvement in anti-Japanese activities, the Japanese killed him by pouring varnish over him and setting him on fire in public. Zhang Dafei escaped to inland China, enrolled in Chung-shan Middle School, and got to know the Chi family. He joined the air force after the Marco Polo Bridge Incident in 1937 and died in air combat in Henan the day before victory in 1945. His courtly love for the young Chi Pang-yuan left an indelible mark on her heart and soul. His fateful and untimely death is violently tragic.

Under Professor Chi's pen, Zhang Dafei is a dashing hero who is devoted and loyal. Young and romantic, he is probably the most unforgettable protagonist in the book. Readers will remember how he stood in the pouring rain waiting for Chi Pang-yuan, his devout Christian faith, and his moving farewell letter.

At the end of the last century, seventy-five-year-old Chi Pang-yuan traveled to Nanjing to visit the cemetery for war heroes. Among the thousands of names on the memorial monument, she found Zhang Dafei's name. The question that had haunted her for fifty-five years was answered. Ashes to ashes, and dust to dust. Professor Chi described Zhang Dafei's all-too-brief life as a night-blooming cereus, a flower "blossoming deep in the night and quickly closing to fall to the ground: such glorious purity, such unspeakable nobility."

Zhu Guangqian was contemporary China's most renowned philosopher and aesthetician. While teaching at Wuhan University during the war, he acknowledged Chi Pang-yuan's talent and encouraged her to transfer from the Department of Philosophy to the Department of Foreign Languages and Literatures. Most people know Zhu for his books such as *Twelve Letters for the Young* or *The Psychology of Tragedy*, but he was also an important member of the Beijing literary circle during the 1930s. Both he and Shen Congwen (1902–1988), the most important lyricist and nativist in modern China, advocated a scrupulous and authentic approach to writing. This gave rise to future contention over his writing. In 1935 Lu Xun (1881–1936), the founding father of modern Chinese literature, criticized Zhu's "solemn and tranquil" approach, creating quite an uproar. Indeed, talking about the aesthetics of quietude during an age full of sound and fury was out of sync with the times.

Zhu's aesthetics had a melancholic undertone, however. When he emphasized a solemn and quiet approach to literature, he was not oblivious to reality. It was a dignity and calmness born out of intense reflection and introspection under pressure, the Chinese spirit of tragedy. Yet in those roaring times, Zhu Guangqian was doomed to be misunderstood. In the 1950s, when his student was in Taiwan reminiscing about her professor's class in British Romantic poetry, Zhu was undergoing more and more vicious pressure from the Communist Party.

Qian Mu is arguably the most respected scholar of traditional learning in twentieth-century China. Qian Mu and Chi Pang-yuan's friendship is another highlight of the book. The two first met when Chi was working at the National Institute of Translation and Compilation. By then, Qian had already retired to his studio in Waishuangshi, the suburbs of Taipei. Both of them were swept into a debate over whether the newly compiled textbook of contemporary Chinese history was blasphemous in its depiction of Yue Fei, a historical figure who had been deified as the god of war. Qian Mu, the master of Sinology, was criticized for having endorsed an academic textbook that was considered a "threat to national security." During those days, everything was politicized, even history. Despite the criticism, Qian Mu stood firm, unwavering, because he had to remain true to his historical and cultural heritage.

At that time, Qian Mu's eyesight was deteriorating, but his mind was clearer than ever. The Cultural Revolution took mainland China by storm, and Taiwan would soon face the Native Soil Movement that would sweep over the island. Qian Mu must have lamented then that time wasn't on his side. Chi Pang-yuan relates movingly those afternoons when she visited the master, chatting about everything from the humanities to contemporary circumstances. Their friendship marked one of the most charming moments of Taiwan before it was engulfed by national identity politics.

From the 1930s until the 1990s, Chi Pang-yuan found her place in schools either as a student or as a teacher. She describes her life as climbing up a staircase constructed of books, sentences, and words. Ultimately, she admits, this was actually a staircase to heaven; furthermore, it was dismantled just as she had started her upward climb—not solely because of the war but also due to restrictions imposed by gender and identity.

After the Marco Polo Bridge Incident, masses of students from the northeast became refugees. Chi Shiying mobilized resources to establish the Sun Yat-sen Middle School in 1934, and 2,000 students were admitted the first year. For the first time in her life Chi Pang-yuan witnessed how the fate of a nation was closely linked to education. Most of the students at Sun Yat-sen Middle School had no home to return to. It was no wonder that the teachers and students saw each other as family. They were committed to one goal, and that was to win the war and recover their homeland from the Japanese. When the Sino-Japanese

War broke out, the students followed their teachers from Nanjing to Wuhan, passing through Hunan and Guangxi, and ended up in Sichuan. They were threatened by war all the way, and there were injuries and casualties, but their studies continued without interruption. This was indeed a legendary page in the history of education.

Sun Yat-sen Middle School was established because of the war. Nankai Middle School and Wuhan University, the alma maters of Chi Pang-yuan, were evacuated because of the war. Nankai Middle School was founded in 1904, and its alumni include two PRC premiers (Zhou Enlai and Wen Jiaobao) and two presidents of Academia Sinica (Qian Si-liang and Wu Ta-you) as well as many scholars and writers. Wuhan University was founded in 1928, and it was one of the best universities in central China. When the war broke out, Nankai Middle School was evacuated to Chongqing and Wuhan University was evacuated to Leshan, Sichuan.

Chi Pang-yuan was exceptionally lucky that her education was not interrupted by the war. Even when conditions were extremely unfavorable, Nankai insisted on the quality of education. During her six years there, Chi developed strength of character and set high expectations for herself. When she attended Wuhan University, she was able to study literature under the tutelage of renowned professors.

When recollecting the student movement that took China by storm half a century later, Chi Pang-yuan is solemn and cautious. She was once humiliated in public for not being progressive enough. She knew that there was only a very thin line between idealism and extremism, naiveté and fanaticism. What saddens her is the fact that many of her more progressive classmates in the 1940s later faced harsh prosecution. The price that they paid for what they did when they were hotheaded and idealistic revolutionaries was far too heavy. It is not fair for anyone to judge others with the hindsight of history, but we cannot help recognizing the difficult struggle between intellectuals and the state apparatus.

Through Professor Chi's description of her experience as a student and teacher, it is clear that her self-awareness as a woman has always stood out. In the 1930s and 1940s it was already quite common for women in China to receive an education, but not at all easy for them to pursue a career after graduation. After graduating with a bachelor's degree in literature from Wuhan University, Chi Pang-yuan also grappled with uncertainty. She considered going overseas to pursue further studies, but the threat of war in China between the Nationalists and Communists sent her to Taiwan, where she eventually married, became a mother, and started a new life.

Professor Chi never gave up her dream of pursuing an academic career. She reminisces about her days as a teaching assistant in the Foreign Languages and Literatures Department of National Taiwan University, describing how she was mesmerized by the stacks and stacks of books the moment she stepped into the office. She remembers her time as a teacher at the Taichung First Boys' High School pensively; she "felt fortunate at being able to 'steal' a few hours from the market, the coal stove, baby bottles, and diapers and once more talk about knowledge, precious knowledge." It wasn't until twenty years after graduating from college that she got to go back to school, and by then she was already forty-five years old.

In 1968, Chi Pang-yuan attended graduate school at Indiana University in the United States, where she took advantage of every single "stolen" minute to study. She claims that that was the most exhausting yet most rewarding year in her life. Yet, with her master's degree almost within reach, she had to give up everything and return to Taiwan for her family. Even her father urged her to make that very difficult decision.

For Chi, this was the Great River that she couldn't cross throughout her life. She had regrets, because she knew that she had the ability and opportunity, but even though she could see the other side, it was still out of reach. For Chi Shiying the river was filled with waves of epic proportion, whereas for Chi Pang-yuan, it was totally different. Her "river" consisted of meeting the obligations of a good wife and mother, day in and day out. The quotidian trials of life were so trivial and arduous, yet as daunting as any battle or political struggle. In the temple of knowledge, Professor Chi and her generation of women often worked very hard for compromised results. It took her many years to come to terms with that.

The Great Flowing River looks back upon the people and events swept up by the tides of modern Chinese history. Having witnessed the chaos and death caused by war, Professor Chi was sustained by poetry, which brought order and dignity to life with rhyme and reason. During her sentimental teenage years, Shelley's lines, "I die! I faint! I fail!" from "The Indian Serenade" were so different from the more constrained traditional Chinese poetry, yet the wailing lines resonated with her. She wrote, "Not only did I dwell on the life and death of the solitary individual, but I felt that a person's life and death were inextricably yoked with the world, life, and time that stops for no one. We were so young, but we were drawn into a vast war, one seemingly without end."

In 1995, fifty years after the end of the war, Chi Pang-yuan went to Shandong Province in China to attend a conference. Standing at the edge of the Bohai Gulf, she looked to the north, toward the Liaodong Peninsula. Farther north was her homeland, Tieling. Yet she was there attending the conference as a delegate from Taiwan. Due to return theren soon, she exclaimed, "I had been in Taiwan for fifty years, married, had children, and had a career, but I was still a 'mainlander,' and like the 'Flying Dutchman,' I could never go home." A line from Du Fu's poem brought tears to her eyes: "gazing sadly, a thousand years, shedding a few tears." And E. M. Forster's concluding lines in the novel *A Passage to India*, "No, not yet, no, not there," came to mind. When there is no road ahead, literature can bridge east and west, opening up new horizons and offering new perspectives.

Fortified by this broader perspective, Professor Chi has dedicated forty years of her life to the promotion of Chinese literature in Taiwan. Taiwan is small, but historical circumstances have given the island an opportunity to rival continental China in the breadth and scope of its literature. Taiwan was thrown into the throes of modernization after the First Sino-Japanese War; in 1949 after the fall of China, two million soldiers and civilians moved to the island en masse. While reading literature in Taiwan, Professor Chi was able to appreciate the pondering of writers like Ssu-Ma Chung-Yuan and Chiang Kuei, who came from mainland China, as well as the sorrow of native writers such as Wu Chuo-liu, Cheng Ching-wen, and Li Chiao.

The two sides of the Taiwan Strait are no longer at the brink of war. Years later, 1895, 1947, and 1949 might become mere froth in the tides of history. But Chinese literature from Taiwan might very well be the sole survivor that has witnessed a century of suffering. This is what Professor Chi believes in. If Shelley and Keats were able to move a Chinese high school girl during the war, then Wu Chuo-liu and Ssu-ma Chung-yuan might also transcend time, space, and linguistic barriers to move readers in the West. She spent forty years translating Chinese literature created in Taiwan into English, putting Taiwan on the world's literary map, because she sincerely believes that literature has the potential to overcome historical ambiguity as well as national and cultural hegemonies.

The Great Flowing River chronicles a woman of letters' perspective on history. As she reminisces, Chi Pang-yuan evolves page by page, becoming older and wiser. Yet, through her narration, we sense that even though time flows by and people and events sink and float in the currents, there is a voice that doesn't fade. It is a "pure" voice, transcending history, glistening with emotion and clarity, distilled from a thousand years' worth of tears.

Guided by this voice, we readers can reminisce along with Professor Chi and get to know her tall, handsome, and ambitious father; her kind and gentle mother; her selfless husband who dedicated himself to public service; the students in exile from the northeast who sang songs of home; the young girl at Nankai who discovered the joy of literature; the professor who recited the poems of Shelley and Keats with tears in his eyes; the blooming peonies of her homeland in the northeast, the roaring waves of the Great River, the deep and bottomless Yakou Sea, and the young Zhang Dafei who kept looking back over his shoulder in the twilight as he was leaving the girl he loved. . . .

David Der-wei Wang

Introduction based on an essay in Chinese, "So Sad, So Happy, So Unique," by David Wang, adapted by Chi Pang-yuan; translated by Michelle M. Wu; edited by Nancy Du.

The GREAT FLOWING RIVER

巨流河

1

MY HOMELAND IN SONG

In the year before the arrival of the twentieth century, my parents were born in a village twenty *li* (1 *li* = .3 mile) from the Liao River basin in China's northeast. The vast and fertile grassland was their inheritance, the homeland of straightforward and carefree herders, where "blue, blue is the sky, vast, vast is the land, where the sheep appear when the wind blows low the grass." But much of the two thousand years of Chinese history has been the history of war fought on that grassland. How many Han heroes has it produced since the great Han and Tang dynasties? How many Mongolian and Manchu horsemen have spurred their horses over that grassland, founding the great Yuan and Qing dynasties, which together lasted over four hundred years? The Chi family was of Han Chinese ethnicity and originally from Taiyuan in Shanxi Province, and later settled in Tieling County, Liaoning Province. The family home was near Hetu'Ala, birthplace of the Qing dynasty, and less than an hour from Shenyang by car. I grew up at my grandmother's side, and I often heard the older generations say that construction on the Great Wall ceased at Tieling. In the seventeenth century, after the Qing entered Beiping, the Kangxi emperor issued an edict stopping construction on the Great Wall. From the Qin to the Han, Tang, Song, and Ming, concern about frontier troubles had never ceased. When the Manchus entered at the end of the Ming dynasty, the Great Wall extended for thousands of miles, but did it stop them?

At the end of the Qing dynasty and the beginning of the Republican period, the three provinces of the northeast, which contained 1,230,000 square miles of grassland, were, in fact, in China's domain. Owing to troubles within and without, the country grew weaker by the day, giving rise to border troubles over thousands of *li* shared with Russia and aggression on the part of the Japanese. The very resources and abundance of her land brought disaster down upon her, but throughout the ages, the indomitable spirits of the grassland had never been conquered.

I was born in a difficult age and spent my life wandering with no home to return to. All I had was a homeland in song. When I was young I heard my mother sing "Su Wu Herds Sheep" with a hidden bitterness. Twenty years later, having arrived in subtropical Taiwan from a land of ice and snow thousands of *li* away, in Taichung, which is a hundred *li* from the Tropic of Cancer, she actually sang while sitting next to my son's cradle: "Su Wu herds sheep at the edge of Lake Baikal . . ." I said, "Mom, can't you sing something else?" Sometimes she would sing "Lady Meng Jiang." She said that at the age of nineteen she married into the Chi family, only to have her husband leave a month later to study, returning home a few times during the summer breaks, and when he did finally come home for good, he became involved in revolutionary work. Since then she had lived a wandering life and had never been able to return home. Looking after the young children, she felt like Su Wu, who looked at his lambs and was filled with hope that they would grow up and also bear lambs, waiting while sustaining almost impossible hope.

At thirty she finally crossed through Shanhaiguan on the three-day and two-night train trip that would reunite her family. From then on, as she followed her husband, her homeland grew ever more distant. Other than "Su Wu Herds Sheep," she never sang a real lullaby.

Before I turned twenty, I had crossed the Liao River and gone to the Yangtze River, and had gone up the Min River to the Dadu River. In the eight years of the War of Resistance against Japan, my homeland continued to reside in song. During the war, people from all parts of China hastened to the wartime capital of Chongqing. Wandering homeless on muddy roads, amid falling bombs, everyone sang, "The Great Wall, the Great Wall, our home lies beyond the Great Wall." But what was that home like? When we sang "My home is on the Songhua River in the northeast," everyone thought of their own home, on the Yongding River, the Yellow River, the Han River, the Huai River, the Gan River, the Xiang River, the Gui River, the Yi River, or any of the other beautiful rivers of China: "Every night the rivers sob as they flow by, all as if flowing through my heart."

THE BEGINNING OF MY LIFE

I was born on the day of the Lantern Festival in 1924 in my home province of Liaoning. At that time of the year, the temperature is often minus five to twenty-five degrees, or even as low as minus forty. My mother was ill during her pregnancy, so I was born weak. One day when I was about a year old, I developed a high fever that would not abate and my breath grew so faint that it seemed suddenly on the verge of stopping altogether. Sitting on the *kang*, a brick bed heated by the kitchen fire and used in northeast China, my mother held me close to her and refused to let go. A relative who had come to the house to celebrate the festival said, "The child is dead; there's barely any breath left in her. Why do you cling to her so? Let her go." My mother kept crying but refused to release me. By then it was already midnight and my grandmother said, "Okay, have one of the hired hands ride to town and find a doctor who can ride a horse, and see if he can come and save the girl's life." The hired hand went to town, which was about ten *li* from where we lived, and actually found a doctor who could ride a horse and was willing to brave the subzero temperatures in the middle of the night and come to our village. He came into our courtyard, and I was revived. The lifeless child my mother refused to part with became a child filled with vitality, which lasted all her life.

Statistics have it that the infant mortality rate was around 40 percent in those days. My life was like a small oil lamp in the wind, and the protection of my mother and that of my "guardian angels" was like a glass surrounding it, preventing it from being snuffed out.

Shortly thereafter, the doctor returned to our village to treat a patient. Carrying me in her arms, my mother went to see him and said, "You saved this child's life. Her father is studying in Germany and hasn't yet named her. Please do give her a name to mark your predestined affinity!" The doctor chose the name Pang-yuan and thus bestowed a double blessing on me at the beginning of my life.

Growing up, I learned that my name was derived from a line in the poem "She Who Is to Grow Old with the Lord" from the *Book of Songs*: "Oh, bright are your eyes, well-rounded your forehead! Truly a person like that, she is the beauty of the country." A few years ago, a reader sent me a photocopy of a page from an essay in Fan Chengda's *Clear Lake Collection*, from the Song dynasty, that contains this line: "Chi Pang-yuan, a woman of virtue. . . ." I actually possess the same name and surname as a virtuous woman who lived several centuries ago, something both an honor and a bit terrifying. In this new world of ours, in which I have spent half my life struggling between family and career, I often think of that doctor in the mountain village of my old home. I hope he knows how hard I have worked to be worthy of his blessing in an age when a girl's life was considered a mere trifle.

THE CHI FAMILY OF TIELING

My childhood was a world without a father. At the age of two, I caught a fleeting glimpse of my father returning home at night during a snowstorm, and then fleeing once again early the next morning. Two days later, my grandmother and my mother took my older brother and me to a nearby village, even smaller than ours, to hide there at the home of a relative for several days. We fled because the troops of Zhang Zuolin were trying to capture Chi Shiying, who had participated in Guo Songling's mutiny. They wanted to apprehend and execute his entire family. While we were there, I cried and shouted every day when it got dark, "I want to go home! I want to go home!" This compounded the difficulty, and fearing lest others be dragged in, everyone decided that we should go home and accept our fate.

The Chi family of Tieling arrived in Fengtian (Shenyang) from Xugou County (now incorporated into Taiyuan City), Shanxi Province, in the eighteenth century, first serving as civil officials there and then settling down. By my father's generation the family had been there for eight generations. The family estate was situated on Little Western Hill west of Fanjiatun, about five *li* from the Luanshi Mountain Train Station on the Chinese Eastern Railway. The family property consisted of about four thousand *mu* (1 *mu* = 733 1/2 square yards) of farmland, which made us an average large-scale landowner.

My grandfather Chi Pengda had four brothers. As a young man, he had no desire to stay in the countryside and farm the family land, so he left to study at a military academy and graduated from the former Baoding Army Accelerated School. Later, he began as a battalion commander in Zhang Zuolin's Fengtian Army, then rose from regimental commander to brigade commander. He served Zhang Zuolin loyally for more than twenty years. My father was his only son, and after studying abroad in Germany, he returned home with his head full of new thought and of saving the country and the people, so he took part in Guo Songling's revolutionary activities against Zhang Zuolin. It was only one month from when Guo's troops were deployed from Tianjin to when they were defeated outside Shanhaiguan. At that time, my grandfather was garrisoned at Baoding in Hebei Province, unaware of what had happened. Everyone in the Fengtian Army thought Marshal Zhang was certain to have my grandfather executed, but to everyone's surprise, he told his subordinates, "The father is of one generation, the son another, and I'm not interested in settling any score on that account. Chi Pengda has been with me many years and is loyal. His son is a scoundrel who went overseas to study and came back muddleheaded, but that doesn't mean I should kill his father." Later, my grandfather suffered minor wounds during a skirmish, caught a chill, and died. He was only fifty years old when he passed away. Zhang Zuolin was of humble origin, but he had the gallantry and the spirit of righteousness of the rough-and-ready woodland heroes of his time, and refused to appease the Japanese. He was killed in an ambush when they blew up his train at Huanggutun, and so ended the legendary age of the warlord, leaving the northeast in a perilous situation. His son, Zhang Xueliang, assumed his title, power, and wealth, but lacked his intelligence or sense of honor. Northeast China's hopes for soverign prosperity were never to be realized.

My grandmother Zhang Congzhou was Manchu. She married into the Chi family from a neighboring village at the age of eighteen and bore a son and two daughters. In the early days of my grandfather's military career, she accompanied him to wherever he was garrisoned, but later, because someone had to look after the family property, she came back to settle down, all alone taking care of the big estate she called home. She and my mother, two lonely women who kept watch all year long, along with three young children and twenty hired hands, passed their days with the spring plantings and the autumn harvests. I ran all over the mountains with my older brother, picking self-heal on Little Western Hill and cucumbers and blackberries in the back garden. In winter we would play on the frozen stream, impressions still vivid today. My grandmother was a dignified, generous, gentle, and benevolent person, who had much sympathy for and took pity on my mother, her daughter-in-law, who had married her only son. But in that age, she too had become a mother-in-law through enduring life as a daughter-in-law, and thus knew which rules were unalterable; so although she treated her daughter-in-law well and would never go out of her way to cause her trouble, and always spoke to her in a tender voice, rules were still rules. Even though there were a number of hired hands and servants in the house, when a husband's mother sat down to eat, the daughter-in-law would stand attentively to one side, her hands at her sides. That's how things were done in a family of position. My grandmother had a most tender regard for me, and it was she who had actually saved my life. Later when I went to the Western Hills Sanatorium in Beiping, she was reduced to tears, the memory of which makes me feel guilty to this day.

It was a big event whenever Grandfather came home. He was a powerful official in those days and had four guards standing at the door. Dress codes and table manners were of particular concern, and if something was not up to his standard, he'd throw a fit. No one in the family could breathe easy until he returned to the garrison. My father said that Grandfather was quite open to the new thinking, but was a person of such authority that no one dared argue with him. Shortly after I was born, my grandfather came home from the garrison and took a glance at the infant wrapped in a quilt on the *kang*. With an imposing manner, he took a seat in the main hall and said, "Grab that little kitten and bring her here so that I can have a look!" For some unknown reason, the little baby who didn't even weigh five pounds and wasn't worth being "carried" had aroused fierce protective instincts in him. He ordered, "No one shall bully this granddaughter of mine!" (This meant especially my older brother, that sturdy grandson of his.) Although it was an age when men were valued over women, the Chi family was small and all children were treasured. That military order only enhanced my position at home.

While in the military, my grandfather received a gift for his fortieth birthday: a delicate and graceful twenty-year-old concubine. Whenever he was garrisoned someplace new or went to war, he'd send her home. It wasn't long before she developed tuberculosis and died. My grandmother treated her well and raised her newborn son (who was named Chi Shihao). I was the same age as this little uncle, so we often played together and were teased by my older brother and cousins. My little uncle grew up under the blessed protection of my grandmother. After north China fell to Japan, he graduated from high school and was conscripted, and one day, while walking down a village lane dressed in a Japanese military uniform, he was shot in the back by the anti-Japanese underground.

Grandmother was sad and lonely her entire life. Her only son left home at thirteen to study in Shenyang, then went to Tianjin, then Japan, and then Germany, and only came home during summer breaks. After returning from studying abroad, he joined the revolution and thereafter lived a life on the run to the far corners of the earth, to be parted from her until she died. After the Mukden Incident in 1931, she took two of my aunts and my little uncle to live in Beiping. Later, in her middle age, she was often ill and confined to bed. My two aunts were well after they got married. The older, Chi Jinghuan, who was called Fourth Aunt according to the ranking of the entire family and accompanied her husband, Shi Zhihong, to study in Japan, was intelligent and brave. After 1933, my father returned to the north to organize and lead the underground resistance against the Japanese. During that time until just before the Japanese were defeated, she went to the Beiping train station and other locations many times to help members of the underground get in and out of Shanhaiguan. Every time she met or saw off someone from the resistance, she would say they were a cousin. Once the people at the railway station got to know her better they asked her, "How come you have so many cousins?" In all likelihood, they probably knew what was going on, but since everyone hated the Japanese, no one revealed what she was up to. Moreover, she was usually carrying a small child, and surreptitiously gave out gifts on New Year's Day and other festivals. Later, in Taiwan, many of these "cousins" remembered my aunt with gratitude and admiration. My two aunts' husbands couldn't remain in Japanese-controlled territory after the start of the war because of their anti-Japanese activities and so accompanied my family to the rear. Later they both fell ill and died in Chongqing, while my two aunts stayed behind with their seven children in Beiping, where they lived with my grandmother and performed their filial duty. My grandmother died of cancer. She was only sixty-four, in the first year of the War of Resistance. We fled to Hankou twenty days before Nanjing fell into Japanese hands, and after catching our breath a little, we were off to Xiangxiang in Hunan, where we stayed for half a year. From there we trudged thousands of *li* over the Hunan–Guizhou Road, overcoming great difficulties to arrive in Sichuan. Only after we made it to Chongqing did we hear about Grandmother's passing the year before, and for this my father felt great remorse his entire life.

THE CRYING IN THE FORAGE GRASS

My maternal grandfather, Pei Xincheng, was Han Chinese; my maternal grandmother was Mongol. They lived in Xintaizi, a small village twenty *li* from our home. My grandfather was a wealthy gentleman who owned a mill and lots of land. In 1904, he accompanied a prefectural educational inspector by the name of Jiang to inspect Fanjiatun Primary School. He was deeply impressed by the Chi boys from Little Western Hill Village, Chi Shichang (my father's second cousin) and Chi Shiying. The two of them were determined to advance in school and serve their country when they grew up. That day they were studying civics, and my grandfather and Mr. Jiang heard small, thin Chi Shiying ask his teacher why the Japanese and Russians were fighting in our homeland. When he was young and in a tutorial school, he saw the artillery action on Southern Mountaintop in which the Russians were routed and the Japanese victorious. Before the fighting ceased, the Japanese bivouacked at our estate for one or two months, until my grandfather sent the men back home. Several years later, the Pei family and the Jiang family requested a respected local person to propose marriage. Educational Inspector Jiang Xianxue's daughter and my second uncle were the same age, while Miss Yuzhen of the Pei family was the same age as my father. The boys were handsome and the girls beautiful and their family backgrounds were well matched, so the heads of the families agreed and made the engagements. At that time, my father and my second uncle were in high school in Shenyang, so they had no opportunity to express their opinion. During the summer break, my father accompanied the family elders to the village of Xintaizi ostensibly to see the grapevines planted by the Pei family, something rare in northeast China. It was then that he saw my mother, who was only fourteen. She was favorably impressed by her fiancé, whom she saw only once, and thought he would make a far better husband than someone from the country. She probably had fond dreams and saw only the good side of things and from then on imagined the outside world with longing.

My second uncle had a huge influence on my father from an early age. He was four years older than my father and filled with new ideas. When news of the Revolution of 1911 reached Shenyang, he cut off his queue, and his envious nine-year-old brother followed suit. He went with his brother to the governor general's office, where they knelt for several hours as part of an effort to petition for the establishment of a parliament.

Dissatisfied with the curriculum in junior high school, the two brothers went to Tianjin without permission, where they took and passed the entrance exam for Xinxue College, run by English missionaries; from there they went to study in Japan. My father, owing to his brilliant test scores, was awarded official funding and entered Tokyo First High School, from where he was assigned to Kanazawa Fourth High School the following year. During the summer of the year he turned nineteen, he was called home to marry, because Grandmother was sick and someone was needed to run the household. My father refused to return, so my grandfather dispatched an uncle to Japan for the sole purpose of bringing him home. My father always told us that he had several conditions to be met if he were to be married: no kowtowing, no red clothing, no face covered with red cloth, riding a horse instead of being carried in a palanquin; moreover, he wanted to take his wife abroad to study with him. If these conditions were met, he'd go home; if not, he would not return; the family agreed. After his return, however, everything was done according to tradition save his riding a horse. One month later, he returned to Japan.

After marrying into the Chi family at nineteen, my mother never stepped beyond the tangible or intangible entrance of the estate compound for the next ten years. My father was the only son, so my mother had to do all the things expected of a daughter-in-law; if she had any free time, she had to sew clothes, stitch shoe soles, embroider shoe tops, and, most pleasantly for her, embroider pillowcases in patterns of her own design. She had no friends, nothing of what we call a social life, and was immensely grateful to be allowed to go home twice a year to her parents' house twenty *li* away. As I recall, my mother's life at home was spent standing respectfully attending my grandparents when they ate, and crying in the forage grass. In those ten years, my father came home during four or five summer breaks and stayed at most two or three months. Once when my mother was pregnant, she had a craving for cherries, but there was only one harvest a year in July or August, and countryside peddlers carried baskets of them on their shoulders, selling from town to the villages. One day a peddler arrived at the entrance to our village, and my twenty-one-year-old father ran out to make a purchase.

Not having a bag with him, he wrapped the cherries he bought in his long scholar's gown and carried them home. That bunch of cherries, carried all the way from the village entrance to our house, supported my mother through nine years of loneliness.

That year he came home from Japan during summer break and said that her name, Yuzhen, was too common and so changed it to Chunyi.

Later he went directly from Japan to Germany. Letters and photos sent home were addressed to my grandparents and always began with "Greetings Dearest and Respected Parents" and ended by mentioning my mother's name and sending his regards to her as well. In those days, a man was either embarrassed or did not dare to write a private love letter to his wife. And so two people of the same age were taking two entirely different paths in life. Women stayed at home and were busy with the unending household duties at the estate—cooking three meals a day; polishing the sacrificial vessels for the New Year and preparing for the endless festivals; washing an unending stream of pots, pans, and dishes; and sweeping up the dust that was always blowing in from beyond the Great Wall. In October she watched the hired hands place cabbages and carrots in the cellar, and another year passed. All the while that young man of nineteen out in the wide world devoted himself to books and ideas, taking part in the society and activities of young people. Their paths diverged ever more, and she was no longer capable of imagining how vast and broad was the world that beckoned him. Even if the two of them had wished to pour out their feelings to each other, they no longer shared a common language with which to recount their vastly different life experiences.

The principal support for my mother in the loneliness of life was the birth of my older brother and me. My father returned every year during the summer break, and afterward a baby would be born, as if it were a token of pledge or a double of himself. The second spring after Father came back home, my older brother, Zhenyi, was born; two years later in the spring, I was born; and the following spring, my little brother, Zhendao, came along. In the small Chi family, our births took on a great deal of significance. In those days of undeveloped medicine, the child mortality rate was high. When my little brother was three years old, he was cavorting inside the house when he burned his hands on the stove. He was taken to Shenyang for treatment and while staying with our aunt, he caught meningitis from our cousin and died two weeks later.

My mother could not accept the fact of the death of her youngest. She cried and blamed herself and gradually slipped into a state of mental confusion. In traditional society, a young daughter-in-law crying for "no reason" was looked upon as inauspicious, so all she could do was avail herself of the time after serving dinner to hide in the forage grass as the sun was going down and cry. The empty yard behind the house was overgrown with grass as tall as a person. From when it grew a tender green after the snow melted in the spring until it became a vast expanse by snowfall, it provided refuge for her suppressed sobbing. After the snow melted, she took me to the family cemetery one *li* away, where she fell atop the small mound of my brother's new grave and cried bitterly. I recall that the cemetery was planted round with pine trees that swayed violently in the spring wind. Pink flowers blossomed all over the cemetery. I went and picked a big bunch amid the sound of my mother's grief-stricken weeping. When we returned home, my grandmother told me they were herbaceous peonies. Later, when I grew up, every time I saw peonies I would seem to hear my mother's suppressed weeping. That large expanse of petals, semitransparent and seemingly fragile, possessed a noble and delicate beauty so different from the other wildflowers thereabouts. Later in life, they came to represent for me images of the unending, undying beauty and sadness of much of life, especially the sufferings of the women of that past age.

After returning home from the family cemetery, my mother would sit listlessly on the *kang*, staring blankly out the window, and sometimes even when Grandmother called her, she failed to hear. Every year after Tomb-Sweeping Festival the ice would melt and the ferns would sprout. There was one kind called "fiddleheads" that were bitter but fresh and tender, and the village women all went to the vacant land by the riverbank to dig them up; naturally I was happy to go along. When we got to the vacant land, we would see flocks of geese in their V formations flying back from the south, their calls bleak and sorrowful.

My mother would frequently stand and stare for a long time, returning home only after everyone else had left.

LEAVING HOME

One morning, my maternal grandfather paid a sudden visit to my paternal grandparents. Someone had gone to Xintaizi and told him that his daughter Yuzhen had become so absent-minded and out of sorts that when she was cooking breakfast for her in-laws she had felt no pain when she thrust her hand into the wood-burning stove when adding firewood, and that she had been in this state for some time. Moreover, he had heard someone from Nanjing say that my father had taken up with some fashionable students studying abroad and was living with them, men and women together. My maternal grandfather finally obtained my paternal grandparents' permission to have my mother and us two children sent to Nanjing to be reunited with my father. If Father wouldn't have us, then he'd take us all back to his place. I clearly remember the autumn of that year—the trees had shed nearly all their leaves, the sorghum had been harvested, and two hired hands readied a horse-drawn carriage and took us to the Luanshi Train Station five *li* away; the stones from that area were used in laying the Chinese Eastern Railway. For the trip to Nanjing, I wore a long cotton padded gown with blue flowers on a red background that had been specially made in Shenyang. I was extremely excited.

Not long after our horse-drawn carriage had left the village, we saw the rows of barren hills just outside it, stony and rugged, where not a single tree grew. I asked, "Ma, what is this hill called?" My mother, who had been listening to my noisy questioning all morning, replied, "This is called the Hill of Weeping Ghosts and Howling Wolves." The name of the hill along with my mother's look left an indelible impression on me.

Now she was setting off with two small children to rejoin her husband, who had been away from home for years, in a big, unimaginable city thousands of *li* away, where she had no family or relatives. Wouldn't she have been confused and fearful, exactly like entering a world of weeping ghosts and howling wolves? She knew the future remained uncertain, but she was no longer willing to return to that small village out in the middle of nowhere, where she had been lonely and cut off for a decade, living the life of a widow. My passion and sense for literature actually came from my mother, who had never received an education above middle school. She turned the natural phenomena of the vast earth, the threats of wild beasts, and the unspeakable loneliness of life into many a story on a summer night, providing me with instruction and inspiration for a lifetime. Some of her rural tales were of gentle longings and sorrows; others were filled with terror, like the Hill of Weeping Ghosts and Howling Wolves, unembellished, powerfully symbolizing her fear of a big southern city as well as her anxieties about her fate.

The clearest memory I have from childhood is my maternal grandfather taking my brother by the hand and my mother taking me by the hand, and riding the train from Shenyang that traveled without stopping day and night. Outside the train window, there was no end to the fields, long harvested and cleared of wheat and sorghum stalks. In addition to the sparse windbreaks of trees, there was the dark brown soil stretching all the way to the horizon. My maternal grandfather said that plowing would commence the following year only after the thaw in the third month.

Arriving in Beiping after passing Shanhaiguan, we switched to the Tianjin–Pukou Railway to get to Nanjing, a trip that lasted three days and two nights. As we pulled into Xiaguan, my mother looked out the window and through the thick white steam saw him, a stranger, handsome and confident, with spirited eyes, standing ramrod straight on the platform. Even late in life his back was always straight and he never stooped. As the steam slowly dispersed, the wife he had been forced to marry at nineteen stepped off the train, her footsteps hesitant and her hand that held mine trembling like an elm losing its leaves. A shy look on her pretty face masked her joy. Standing beside her on the platform were two country kids dressed in brand-new padded cotton gowns.

My maternal grandfather stayed in Nanjing about ten days before getting back on the train and returning to his home beyond Shanhaiguan. At his departure, my mother cried, reluctant to be separated from him. My maternal grandparents had four boys before they had a girl and she was much cherished as she grew up, and now he had to leave her behind in this vast southern sea of people, with no family. In those days, my mother often told my brother and me, "If you don't study hard, your father will leave us."

From a very young age I had learned to worry and never slept soundly. Sometimes I would awaken at night and hear my father talking softly to my mother. His voice was warm and steady, and I would peacefully go back to sleep.

Soon after arriving in Nanjing, I was sent to the local elementary school for first grade. Recently arrived from rural northeast China, I was very skinny and rustic and could not understand the local dialect. The only thing I understood my teacher say on the first day of school was, "Drinking one moment and peeing the next is not allowed." I found going to school frightening and had a hard time making the few friends I did. One classmate who liked me gave me a colorful red and green eraser, something I had never seen in the countryside, which made me happy. Two days later he got upset and demanded the eraser back, which made me feel terribly sad. To this day I can still remember that eraser; when I began to travel, I always bought pretty erasers.

One other thing that left a deep impression happened early one spring when the snow was melting. To get to school, I had to walk down an alley called "three alleys," which was all mud save for two dry strips on either side that had to be treaded upon with caution. Having always been curious, I looked at everything as I walked. That day, as I was walking to school with my brother, I stepped into the mud by accident, and my cotton shoes sank into the muck. My brother, afraid of being late, hit me, and I started to cry. At that moment a car pulled up and stopped, and my father was seated inside. He told the driver to pull my shoes out of the muck and help me put them on, after which they drove away. When he returned home that night, he said that children were not allowed to be taken to school in a government car, nor were we allowed to use paper with an official letterhead. This was because we had to distinguish between public and private, and also because a child shouldn't develop a desire to show off.

When I was spanked for the first and probably only time, he informed the six-year-old me in the same tone of voice that I shouldn't run wild as I had in the countryside, I shouldn't pick flowers in the parks, and even if I did, I shouldn't lie about it. He said, "The reason I spanked you is so that you will remember." This very early impression made me rarely ever tell a lie. Even if I told a small white lie to make someone happy, I always felt guilty.

THE GREAT FLOWING RIVER THAT COULD NOT BE CROSSED

My father, Chi Shiying, as I remember, was a gentleman of mild temperament his entire life. He said that was the real wellspring of his ideals—to be a man, you had to comport yourself like one.

In his youth, he had accompanied my grandmother to stay where Grandfather was garrisoned and got a taste of barracks life as well as the chance to see many northern villages, thereby becoming profoundly aware of how blinkered most citizens were, almost entirely ignorant of the fate of their country, and themselves. Behind the façade of pure and simple virtue was indifference and foolishness. When he was fifteen years old he began to attend the Tianjin Anglo-Chinese College and for three years he received an English-style education for the cultivation of a courteous gentleman. In Tianjin he often heard the people from Shanhaiguan mock the roughness of Zhang Zuolin's Fengtian Army. As regular as the flag-raising ceremony at the Anglo-Chinese College, every day there was a morning class devoted to Bible reading. Although the students were not forced to convert, it did lead my father to begin considering questions of the soul and the meaning of life.

Obtaining official funding to study in Japan at eighteen, he got to know more about a modernized country. People there were generally brought up to be sanitary and law-abiding, and those who had a higher level of education were concerned about civility and manners, encouraged the pursuit of learning, and pledged fierce loyalty to their country, which was why Japan, despite its small size, became a powerful Asian country.

He entered the preparatory course of Tokyo First High School to study Japanese. A year later he was assigned to the School of Natural Sciences at the Kanazawa Fourth High School, one of only eight high schools in Japan back then, which was rich in artistic and cultural tradition. Kanazawa, located in central Japan overlooking the Sea of Japan, was referred to as Kaga Hyakumangoku after the sixteenth century. All the departments of that school were strong, and language instruction was emphasized. In addition to Japanese, every week there were eight hours of instruction in English and German. In his three years there, he laid a solid foundation for a lifetime of reading. Initially, he frequently attended church where he read works on Christianity, but finding them wanting, he began reading works of philosophy. The teacher who had the greatest influence on him in those days was Nishida Kitaro, who first taught at Kanazawa Fourth High School but later taught philosophy at Kyoto Imperial University. He guided my father's reading in works of philosophy, economics, and socialism, especially *The Tale of Poverty* by Kawakami Hajime, and others that permitted him to see that society was filled with various kinds of inequality. He didn't have much money to buy books, so it was arranged with the bookstore that he could return the books if they were still in good condition after he finished reading them and have 80 percent of his money back to buy other books. It rained frequently in Kanazawa and snowed heavily in winter, so he spent a good deal of time indoors reading. With the passage of time he went from being a smart and active youth to a deep-thinking, well-read young man.

At twenty-two, he followed in the footsteps of his cousin and went to Berlin to study economics and philosophy, earnestly reading Marx's *Das Kapital* and other works about socialism. But he felt he still had too many unresolved doubts, such that he could not establish an ultimate intellectual foundation, and he was rather hesitant. That was just after

Germany's defeat. Inflation was bad and Chinese and Japanese silver money was worth a lot, so he and his classmates lived comfortably and frequently got together to enjoy themselves, learning more about German society while neglecting their studies. The following semester, he transferred to Heidelberg University where he studied under the great philosophers of history Heinrich Rickert and Alfred Weber, the younger brother of the recently deceased Max Weber. He went there because he was attracted by their reputations, so he listened eagerly and often asked questions after class. The Philosophy of History school analyzed the phenomenon of life through the history of political and economic thought, elucidating the necessity of rational thinking in the process of research while reminding him that regional realities were different and that one cannot with impulsive enthusiasm force a theory onto general policy, as in *Das Kapital*. This provided him with a lesson for a lifetime and the firm belief that only true knowledge and rational education were capable of saving a weak China by a subtle and gradual process, not via some impassioned mass movement. Arriving at the goal of class revolution by means fair or foul would leave many social and cultural problems that could only be resolved through even more rational solutions.

During those two years, he would cross the bridge and think while pacing along the banks of the River Neckar. Those would be the best days of his life. The rapid flow of the river in spring made him think of the turbid Liao River at thaw, as his youthful ambition rose and surged like the water. He recalled a scene when he was five in which he wore a new pair of cloth shoes and walked along the bank of the Liao River, where he jumped and gamboled quite happily around his mother. He then heard a voice in his heart say: *Go back to set up a school in my vast, beautiful homeland. I must dedicate myself wholeheartedly to acquiring a skill, and go back to set up a school in the most rational way. There will come a day when I will pay you back for your kindness to me in raising me with everything I have learned and know today.*

The greatest setback for him was his cousin dying of tuberculosis in Freiburg in southern Germany. At first he concealed the truth, but shortly thereafter his uncle died, and as he couldn't explain away why the son didn't hasten home for the funeral, he had to return home with his cousin's ashes. After his return to Shenyang, the family was steadfast in not allowing him to leave again, so his dream of an education came to a halt. He was twenty-five that year. After the funeral, he left the estate and returned to Shenyang to find another way of continuing his studies. In Shenyang in those days, for a student with official funding to return from Germany was taken very seriously. General Guo Songling, who was a classmate and good friend of his father's at the Fengtian Military Academy, felt that it was inconvenient for him to stay at a hotel, so invited him to stay at his house. On the northern frontier in January, snow and ice made the roads impassable but perfect for staying in and talking through the night, and they discussed everything from local to national and on to world events. When General Guo had important guests, my father would be invited to join in the conversation. The newly returned student thus had the opportunity to look at the local situation from a broader perspective, whereas the guests also found what he had seen in Japan and Germany to be of great interest. This was especially the case when he talked about Germany after its defeat in World War I, with its economy on the verge of collapse and the people living in difficult circumstances. But the people demonstrated in every way their national dignity and firm determination to overcome the difficulties. In their old houses with stone foundations, the columns still in good order, and the trees out front along the cobblestone streets, one could feel the stability provided by firm cultural roots. But northeast China in those days, coveted by both Japan and Russia, was in a dangerous situation, so in what way could the tangled conflicts of warlords make any sense? When would the people of China enjoy universal education and extricate themselves from the condition of being simple-minded and ordered about by others? He had no idea that those long conversations on snowy nights and those chance meetings, during which everyone was filled with indignation and a sense of a mission to reform, would change the course of his life.

Since ancient times, the legendary people of the frontier have all been heroes, brave archers on horseback good at fighting, who guarded the nation and built its strength. General Guo Songling was born in the ninth year of the Guangxu Emperor (1883) in the late Qing dynasty in East Village in Shenyang County, Liaoning. His family was poor, and after he had studied for a few years in a tutorial school (when he was fifteen years old) he entered the Fengtian Military Academy. Upon graduation he went to Sichuan with Zhu Qinglan's (1874–1941) army, and in the New Sichuan Army he joined the Revolutionary Alliance (Tongmenghui). At thirty-three, after graduating from the Army College and at the recommendation of Zhu Qinglan, who was serving as governor of Guangdong Province, he served as a guard in Sun Yat-sen's Constitutional Protection Military Government and as a military instructor at the Shaoguan Military Academy. He had knowledge and ideas, and in his classes, he urged that young men became democratically minded patriotic officers. In the state of chaos after the Revolution of 1911, he fully experienced the turmoil and suffering throughout the country and had a broad view of the situation. He became military tactics instructor at the newly established Northeast China Military Academy. At that time, Zhang Xueliang, the young marshal of the Fengtian Army, was his student and greatly admired Guo, asking him to join the Fengtian Army in order to reform it and set up a new army. They worked earnestly together in everything. In two of the Zhi–Feng wars, Guo's distinguished military exploits were the result of his tactics and strategy. But what was the point of entering China proper to fight? There was not enough manpower to till the fertile land at home, and the young soldiers ended up as casualties far away, leaving their families to a pitiful fate. The fighting had to stop and education be revived.

In the eyes of the young people who returned from Europe, the idea of a new army was attractive. General Guo was already the head, his position prominent, his appearance imposing, and he was decisive and a man of action. His wife, Han Shuxiu, was a graduate of Yanjing University. They were deeply attached to each other, fond of reading, and open to new thought; good at making friends; and when they talked, they took the world and the country as their own responsibility. General Guo and Zhang Xueliang along with others planned to set up a middle school for the education of the surviving children of soldiers who had lost their lives, doing everything they could for their comrades-in-arms. The school was called Tongze Middle School. Knowing that since returning from abroad my father had set his mind on education and fostering new ideas among the young at home, they appointed him the school principal. Following the examples of schools in England, Germany, and Japan, they set out good rules and regulations, laid a solid foundation, and hired excellent teachers from all over the country. Before the establishment of Manchukuo, politics had no influence on the school, and it was always well run. Later Tongze Middle School for Girls was established. At the same time, there were also plans to set up a real research university that would not be controlled by the authorities and did not have the training of government officials as its goal.

After Tongze Middle School was established, but before the school buildings were finished, they borrowed some newly remodeled barracks at the Dongshanjuzi Military Camp at Shenyang, the remainder of which was used for military officer instruction. In the summer of that year three classes of students under fourteen (one of the students was Song Changzhi, who later served as Commander-in-Chief of the Republic of China Navy in Taiwan) passed the entrance exam and were admitted. Such a promising undertaking was the realization of a young man's dream. The young principal was in high spirits, busily doing his job wholeheartedly—attending to teachers and class schedules, and instructing students. The barracks at Dongshanjuzi Military Camp were about twenty *li* from Shenyang and there was a small train to town used for the construction of the barracks. The state of his mind was like the locomotive of that little train—full of drive to advance.

In less than a year, these happy days came to an end. One night early in November 1925, General Guo telephoned him and asked him to come to town to talk. The coal fire of the little train had been shut down by that hour, but after a little discussion, it was fired up again to take him into town. General Guo said that he had received orders to lead troops back through Shanhaiguan, going first to Tianjin. He asked my father to join his troops; the director of school administration could handle everything for a short while, as they had to leave the next day. Several days after arriving in Tianjin, General Guo stayed in the Italian hospital in the Italian concession and told him that the purpose of entering

Shanhaiguan this time was to fight the Five-Province United Army assembled by Sun Chuanfang after the Second Zhi–Feng War and secure the territory under the control of the Fengtian Army in Hebei, Shandong, Anhui, and Jiangsu. The army of General Guo was ever triumphant, but he was tired of this policy of constantly waging war in which casualties were high and there wasn't a good reason for fighting. After garrisoning Tianjin, he called a meeting of his core cadres and all officers above the rank of regimental commander. Those willing to return with him to the northeast would sign their names to the plan of peacefully developing the region; those unwilling would stay in Tianjin as part of Li Jinglin's troops. Most signed their names, except for a few leaders who had served Zhang Zuolin for many years and found it inconvenient to "rebel."

General Guo charged my father with obtaining foreign support when they returned. First of all he had to obtain assurances that the Japanese army stationed along the South Manchurian Railway would remain neutral. A number of important political figures from Shanhaiguan were also in attendance in Tianjin, including Rao Hanxiang (who served as secretary-general to Li Yuanhong), Yin Rugeng, Gao Xibing, Yang Mengzhou, Su Shangda, Fan Guang, Lin Changmin (Li Huiyin's father), and Lu Chunfang. Since Wang Zhengting, who had been appointed department head for foreign affairs, had not yet assumed office (he later served as Minister of Foreign Affairs in the ROC government), Chi Shiying acted as deputy in charge of foreign affairs. Everyone had a great deal of confidence in General Guo's innovative idea of returning to Shenyang and not becoming involved in a civil war among warlords. The evening before returning, General Guo said to everyone, "If we succeed, great; if we fail, everyone will pay with their life."

On November 22, General Guo marched his troops toward Luanzhou in Hebei and cabled Zhang Zuolin to cease fighting, resign, and hand control of the army and government over to Zhang Xueliang. The cable said that the casualties among the officers and men who entered Shanhaiguan to fight were very high, the surviving families had no means of support, and the lives of the people were difficult. Japanese and Russian ambitions to invade the northeast were growing stronger by the day, so the Chinese must recuperate and build up reserves to deal with the foreign aggression and never again become embroiled in a civil war. They had to revitalize education and wholeheartedly dedicate themselves to the development of the homeland, whose resources were the richest in the entire country. After receiving the cable, Zhang Zuolin sent a telegram the following day in which he never mentioned ceasing hostilities or passing on his authority, but rather asked Guo Songling to return to Shenyang to discuss matters face to face. It was clear that the murder of an invited guest was planned. Guo waited a day before sending another telegram from Luanzhou, but not receiving a reply, he set out to attack. Going out of Shanhaiguan and north from Qinhuangdao along the coast to fight at Lianshan, they encountered a once-in-a-century snowstorm. The temperature fell to five below zero (twenty degrees Celsius) and the sea froze, over which both man and horse could walk. That night, Guo's vanguard, the Second Corps, broke through Zhang Zuolin's defending troops in a surprise attack over the ice and captured Huludao and three days later garrisoned Jinzhou. When the news arrived in Shenyang, the entire city was shocked. Marshal Zhang urgently mobilized ten large trucks, which were filled with wealth amassed in office, and sent them to the warehouses of the Japanese along the South Manchurian Railway, where this wealth was stored; more than ten trips were required to remove it all. The marshal's residence was surrounded by wood and drums of petrol so that when it came time to flee, it could be burned down. The Provincial Legislative Assembly and the various chambers of commerce sent a telegram to General Guo, saying that after he entered the city, "the demands, aims, and future of our Revered Sir can be assured . . . we hope that there can be a temporary cessation of the fighting." At that time, the Fengtian Army and the Japanese garrisoned along the South Manchurian Railway had reached an agreement to keep Guo pinned down and the Jilin and Heilongjiang garrisons were hurriedly dispatched to help, being deployed along the eastern bank of the Liao River to meet the approaching enemy. On December 20, Guo's forces took and occupied Xinmin City and prepared for battle on the western bank of the river. The vanguard troops could already see the lights of Shenyang and they only awaited the arrival of the main group in Xinmin City, after which they would cross the river in force. But the troops, who had marched a long way in extreme cold without proper provisions or clothing, stopped several days in Jinzhou to rest, giving Zhang sufficient time to move his troops. This delay also gave the other side a number of opportunities to infiltrate and divide Guo's army. The difficulties increased and the soldiers grew conflicted. The morale of Guo's brave and skillful troops was shaken when they heard the other side shouting: "Those who eat at Zhang's table shouldn't fight Zhang's people." The armies confronted one another across the river for three days. Guo's forces could have crossed the river with one vigorous push to fight to Xinglongbao, ten *li* from Fengtian Army headquarters, but at the critical moment, the shells fired by Guo's army failed to explode because someone had removed the fuses. On the morning of the 24th, Chief of Staff Zou Zuohua and two others, who had become agents of the Fengtian Army, forced Guo to capitulate and sent a telegram offering to surrender.

General Guo, leading a guard of more than two hundred, left Xinmin City. Riding fast horses should have made it easy to escape and attempt a comeback later, but the general's wife and the scholar Rao Hanxiang didn't know how to ride. Unwilling to flee alone, General Guo rode south in a wagon with them. The enemy horsemen caught up with them and had been ordered to execute them on the spot to avoid any further problems.

General Guo's final words before execution were, "I started a righteous cause but failed to eradicate the traitors, so death is what I deserve. If there should happen to be in the future those who share the same ideal, please follow this trail of blood."

General Guo's wife, Han Shuxiu, said, "My husband dies for the country, I die for my husband; neither of us has any regrets." Guo Songling was forty-two; Han Shuxiu, thirty-six. Their corpses were transported to Shenyang, where they were put on display in a square by the river for three days before the family was allowed to collect them. Their bodies were still on display when on Christmas Day, snow fell and covered them, forming a pure and peaceful coffin. No one dared to go and pay their respects; the tears of the family and friends lamenting at a distance froze immediately.

Guo's followers should also have been put to death, but Zhang's brother Zhang Zuoxiang, a wise, kind man who had been with Zhang Zuolin from those early days (the initial greenwood) until his ultimate seizure of power, said, "This is no way to do things. They are brothers from our homeland, reprisal breeds reprisal, so where will it end?" It's hard to say how many lives were preserved with these words. When the rebellious soldiers returned to their posts, they were more loyal and worked even harder, thus extending the political life of the Fengtian Army.

Later it was learned that Lin Changmin, who offered his services to General Guo, had been killed by a stray bullet as he was on the run. Rao Hanxiang was apprehended on the road to Shenyang and was questioned by the guards: "What do you do?" He replied, "I write." The soldiers said they had no use for his sort, so they pushed him off the wagon and he lived to return to Li Yuanhong's house in Tianjin.

But the Zhangs, father and son, made a point of offering a reward for the capture of Chi Shiying, because he had gone abroad to study with their support and had come home to oppose them, stirring up the mutiny of Guo's troops, and therefore had to be apprehended and executed. In those days, they believed that northeast China was theirs and that all students selected through exams to study abroad with official funding were from the Zhang family and should be loyal only to them.

On December 24, just after daybreak, Chi Shiying went to the temporary headquarters in Xinmin City to prepare for the full-scale crossing of the great flowing river, having no idea that General Guo had been forced to flee in the middle of the night. In the midst of the chaos, he took with him five people from the foreign relations office—Yin Rugeng, Liu Youhui, Yang Mengzhou, Su Shangda, and Lu Chufang, who had caught up later—to the Japanese consulate in Xinmin City to seek temporary refuge despite the risks. Two days previously Chi Shiying had negotiated with the Japanese about the Japanese military garrisoned along the South Manchurian Railway. He had met them a number of times, so this time political asylum was granted without much ado.

The Fengtian Army surrounded the Japanese consulate and demanded that the six be handed over. In order to protect the political offenders, the Consul General in Shenyang, Yoshida Shigeru (1878–1967), sent ten policemen to Xinmin City and told the Fengtian Army that it was not to set foot inside the consulate. To protect the political offenders, he himself also came to negotiate, while even sending luggage and whiskey to show the refugees his respect.

This humanitarian decision of Yoshida Shigeru not only saved the lives of the six men but also displayed the political courage in acting and shouldering responsibility that marked his whole life. His father, Takeuchi Tsuna, was the leader of the foreunner of the Liberal Democratic Party in Japan, and left his immense family wealth to his son as capital so that he might involve himself in politics. His father-in-law, Makino Nobuaki, was in the first generation of important government officials after the Meiji Reforms and cultivated a macroscopic political wisdom that lasted for generations to come. As the Shenyang Consul General, Yoshida Shigeru was in charge of investigating the political situation in north China and had a low opinion of Zhang Zuolin, because he held the rich land of the northeast but did nothing to foster the well-being of the people and society or elevate culture and education, and considered his frequent recourse to war ignorant and shortsighted. It was said that in the consulate, he never referred to Zhang Zuolin by his title or name but simply called him "horse thief." He had nothing but respect for Guo Songling's reformist thinking. With a background in foreign affairs, he deeply believed that in a normal international situation, if Japan could maintain close relations with a modernizing neighboring country, it could benefit appropriately. Yoshida served as Japan's first prime minister after his country was defeated in World War II and, using the liberal assistance of America's occupation forces, not only saw the reestablishment of Japan's politics and economics from the rubble but also helped it grow into an economic superpower. During his term in office he also fostered a large number of talented cabinet ministers, a group later known as "Yoshida's School."

Chi Shiying and his companions in misfortune slept in an eight-*tatami* spare room in the consulate. They were besieged by the Fengtian Army day and night for six months, and during the day dared not even enter the courtyard for fear of being shot. They learned from the consular officials that General Guo had died and that his body had been displayed for three days in a square by the small river in Shenyang, and moreover that the army had been reorganized and incorporated into the Fengtian Army. The six of them lived in confinement, where setting one foot outside meant death. They had followed General Guo in his earth-shaking heroic return. But it was like smoke and clouds passing before the eyes—everything had been blown away and scattered outside the imprisoning walls.

Through the long days and long nights he repeatedly wondered: *We were victorious the whole way, so why on the night when the lights of Shenyang were already within sight did we fail to cross the great flowing river? If on that night in the temporary headquarters at the inn, when the chief of staff had sent a telegram offering to surrender to the Fengtian Army and forced General Guo to flee, I had dispatched someone to escort the general's wife to the Japanese consulate in Xinmin City for asylum, then I could have accompanied General Guo and his guard to dash back posthaste to Jinzhou. The west bank of the river was controlled by Guo's forces, and by retreating to Jinzhou, we could have preserved our forces and staged a comeback.* Pondering this, he couldn't help but feel chagrin about the battle by the river that ended in defeat when success was so close at hand. Oh, that great flowing river, that great flowing river that could not be crossed, could its water be the severe cold of reality, with foreign affairs and innovative thought frozen up within?

When the thaw came and it was time for spring planting, the Fengtian Army once again entered Shanhaiguan and fought with the warlord armies of Hebei, Shandong, and Henan. The Beiping–Liaoning Railroad ran about five hundred and fifty yards from the Japanese consulate, and judging from the sound, the trains carrying troops and the train tracks were all worn due to constant friction. The Fengtian Army made life impossible for the people. Even if he weren't pursued and killed, Chi Shiying couldn't return home. His only hope was to escape and find another way to survive. "But even if I'm the only one left alive, I will fight this evil to the end!"

On a night of the waning moon at the beginning of July 1926, with the help of Consular Secretary Nakata Chiyoda, who was sympathetic to General Guo, and the police officer Kanei Fusataro, the six were finally able to leap over the wall and in disguise made their way through the siege, which had been somewhat relaxed. They followed the railroad tracks on foot for sixty *li* to Xinglongdian where, with the aid of Japanese friends, they reached Huanggudun. For the first time, twenty-seven-year-old Chi Shiying and forty-eight-year-old Yoshida Shigeru spent a whole night talking in a meeting of the minds. Yoshida admired Chi Shiying for his education and opinions and found him a candid young man; although Yoshida carried out Japan's policy of neutrality at that time, his action of protecting political offenders and helping them escape showed a bit of romanticism. The young man was grateful to him for the helping hand he extended in such a timely fashion, and when they met again after the end of World War II, though the experience of each had been quite different, he grew to admire Yoshida even more for his international perspective and his farsightedness in fostering talented political people after the war.

Chi Shiying went from Liaoning to Pusan, Korea, in disguise, where he took a steamship to Japan. Upon arrival he took a train to Tokyo, and as the train arrived in Kyoto he was pursued by reporters. The following day, the newspapers were filled with wild surmises, so he decided to see the reporters and explain the truth of General Guo's innovative ideas and what happened before and after he decided to return home. The news quickly spread to all parts of China. Arriving in Tokyo, they found that a play about Guo Songling was being staged in the Asakusa District and they were invited to attend as honored guests. A good part of the drama involved Chi Shiying. What was originally a daring act meant to change the fate of the northeast remains today in the human world as just a play.

When he returned to Tianjin from Japan, the tangled emotions of love and hate among old and new figures in the Beiyang government had yet to settle. He couldn't go home and had neither the means nor the inclination to go back to study in Germany. In the foreign concession in Tianjin, he met General Guo's friend Huang Fu, who had provided timely help by sending money to the consulate in Xinmin City (when the Northern Expeditionary Army took Shanghai, Huang served as mayor of the city and later served as premier of the Republic of China). Huang encouraged him to first travel to Shanghai and assess the situation before deciding where to go. From Shanghai he went to

Wuhan because the revolutionaries in the south were sympathetic to Guo's cause. Drifting alone with the mind-set of one banished, he reconnected with his former classmates in Japan and Germany, and they talked to their hearts' content. During that first period of cooperation between the Kuomintang and the Communist Party, he met and talked with communists such as Li Hanjun, Zhan Dabei, and Geng Bozhao and attended the mass outdoor rallies they organized. He listened to the speeches of the various parties, read their publicity booklets, and, after much consideration, decided that the Nationalist Party and its Three Principles of the People—nationalism, democracy, and people's livelihood—represented the steadiest course for China's actual situation. He also found the party members to be of a high caliber, and the most appealing. Thus, he joined the Kuomintang in Shanghai at the end of 1926 with no intention of seeking anyone's protection. The first time Chiang Kai-shek met him at Nanchang, Chiang said, "You don't look like someone from the northeast," something he never forgot. This was in the days before Chiang became the sole holder of power. Thirty years later, when he stripped my father of his party membership in Taipei, it was probably because the consummate politician from Zhejiang discovered that mild-mannered and handsome Chi Shiying had indeed the intransigent and unbending nature of a real northeasterner.

After joining the Kuomintang, he traveled between Shanghai and Hankou a number of times and accompanied Huang Fu to KMT headquarters in Nanchang. Chiang Kai-shek and Huang Fu were quite close, and when they ate together my father was often invited as well. It was in those days that he met the brothers Chen Guofu and Chen Lifu. After the Nanjing–Hankou split between the Kuomintang and the Communist Party, he met a number of influential people at Nanchang, Jiujiang, and Hangzhou, and came to understand the state of the Kuomintang and its relationship to the Communist Party. That year, he also went to Japan a number of times to observe and do research on that country. During the revolutionary rising of Guo's army, he had experienced political rise and fall and profoundly understood that in politics one could not be ignorant of military matters, and hoped that he could conduct systematic research on the modern military. Consequently, in 1928, with the rank of first lieutenant in the army conferred upon him by the government, he formally tested into the Japanese Infantry School for serving officers (it took three years to graduate). Before the start of school he was assigned to the Takada Thirtieth Company, where he served as assistant company commander. He attended class during the day and served with the company at night. On weekends he took the night train to Tokyo, where he met with the military officers sent by the central authorities to study in Japan (most were from the first class of the Whampoa Military Academy). Since he had graduated from Kanazawa, his spoken and written Japanese were excellent and he was considered an expert on Japan and was often able to help others. He had a wide range of contacts and would sometimes get together with his old Japanese classmates to reminisce. The Japanese were generally interested in northeast China (which they called Manchuria), and because he took part in the revolution led by Guo Songling and was fond of conversation, he frequently heard a lot of frank talk about Japan coveting the northeast, which left him inwardly apprehensive about his home. During this period he progressed in his study of Japanese military history, the samurai spirit of the shogunate, the modernization of the military since the Meiji Reform, and the stirrings of expansionism in the twentieth century.

In those three years, a twenty-seven-year-old young man from north China had seen military defeat and fled to the ends of the earth. From conversations around the fire at General Guo's house to the Yangtze River, he had met many people engaged in the creation of China's modern history. Brought together by fate, they had long conversations on their ambitions and ideals and found that they were of the same cast of mind. Those long conversations shaped his political disposition and the strength of his character for the rest of his life.

THE MUKDEN INCIDENT

In June 1928, the Japanese Kwantung Army killed Zhang Zuolin by exploding a bomb at the Huanggutun Station on the South Manchurian

Railway. On September 18, 1931, the Japanese occupied Shenyang in one night, which marked one of the most painful moments in recent Chinese history, the Mukden Incident. For my mother, who thought happy days were coming after all the suffering she had endured, this came as a bolt out of the blue. That frozen land full of lonely memories she had just bid farewell to now became a homeland to which she could not return, making it difficult to see her parents, who loved her deeply, ever again.

For my father, it was a day that he had expected to arrive sooner or later, after having witnessed the shells of the Russo-Japanese War falling on the mountain behind his home when he was five years old, after Guo Songling's fight to alter the fate of northeast China ended with his body displayed in a Shenyang city square following his defeat, and after Zhang Zuolin was blown to bits and his son Zhang Xueliang immediately assumed power as warlord. Zhang Xueliang was neither able nor bold enough to protect such a large territory; all he could do was watch wide-eyed as it became a vast land without a master. The homeland was lost for good due to ignorantly "ruling the country like a family," and it was enough to fill a person with grief and indignation.

The Japanese, who at the beginning of the century had constructed the South Manchurian Railway through half of northeast China, had waited patiently for thirty years for that day. After the Mukden Incident, the Japanese Kwantung Army controlled all outgoing information, and the railroads, roads, and telephone communications were cut off. But all the way from Shenyang to Heilongjiang they met with defensive resistance, and it was a year before the entire land was occupied. Manchukuo was established in 1934, marking the start of what would become the Greater East Asia Co-Prosperity Sphere in 1940 and in preparation for opening the full-scale invasion of China. Where was Zhang Xueliang during that one long year? What had become of the Fengtian Army that had once swept the country with such ease?

In one night, China was like a giant who, while sleeping, had his feet lopped off. Awakening suddenly, the whole country was engaged in protest marches and shouting slogans such as "Down with Japanese imperialism!" and "We pledge our life to recover our territory!" but the shouts were heard only by ourselves. The world in those days was still under colonialism, in which all strong countries with the power of sanctions had colonies (England's colony India only became independent in 1947, and France's colony Annam became independent in 1945 as Vietnam. This was accomplished in exchange for millions of souls lost during World War II.) The League of Nations formed the Lytton Commission because of the Mukden Incident, but to no avail, as there was never any real justice in the world.

In the year following the Mukden Incident, my father repeatedly thought things over, considering the various possibilities for practical work. In the two years since he had gone to work for the central government, most of the people he had contacted or assigned to work in northeast China were involved in education. After the fall of Shenyang, they all retreated to Beiping, where they set up an office in exile; some went to Nanjing to report on the situation at home, calling for the central government to effectively aid the volunteer armies that had vigorously arisen in Jilin and Heilongjiang provinces. The cream of the Fengtian Army, now under young Marshal Zhang Xueliang, had withdrawn to Shanhaiguan under his declaration of "nonresistance." But locals, who were not content to sit around and wait to fall into enemy hands, rose up as long as they had guns. The more prestigious became known as the Volunteer Army to Resist Japan.

Countless young people were unwilling to receive a Japanese education and fled to Beiping and Tianjin. Some sought refuge with friends and relatives; others wandered about from place to place. At that time, the central government didn't understand the situation in the northeast and had no way to deal with it. My father knew the only thing he could do to comprehend the actual situation was to return to the lion's den himself. This was to risk everything on a single desperate venture with "one's head on the line," as people from the northeast would call it.

He quit his job in the central government and with utmost secrecy (only Chen Lifu knew) took a ship from Shanghai with the passport of a Germany-bound businessman named Zhao to Kobe, Japan, where he boarded another ship for Vladivostok, Russia, and then traveled by train, which ran once every two days, and crossed the Suifen River to

Harbin. In Harbin he stayed at a hotel owned by a White Russian and contacted comrades who were still struggling with the critical situation in Jilin, including Xu Zhen (director of the Telephone Office, who became chairman of Liaoning Province after victory over Japan; withdrawing to Taiwan in early 1949, he and his entire family lost their lives when their ship, the famous *Taiping*, sank in the Taiwan Strait), Zang Qifang (director of the Land Office), Zhou Tianfang (director of the Office of Education), and other comrades engaged in secret activities, from whom he obtained a detailed picture of recent anti-Japanese actions in his homeland since the Mukden Incident. Nearly all of Liaoning Province had been occupied by the Japanese. Only Jing Kedu, Xu Junzhe, and Shi Jian (style name Mo Tang; he was captured by the Japanese near the end of the War of Resistance and sentenced to death. His trusted lieutenant, a young lawyer by the name of Liang Surong, who was sentenced to fifteen years in prison, luckily regained his freedom after the war and withdrew to Taiwan for yet another struggle.), under cover in their capacity as civil officials, developed the the volunteer army.

Han Qinglun and Ge Wenhua had been the most active and effective people in Jilin before it was taken by the Japanese. They planned the integration of military and civilian armed forces in northeast China into the volunteer army, which resisted Japanese efforts to advance north with an impressive display of power. The bloody battle for Changchun lasted a month before it was occupied by the Japanese. Ge Wenhua and eight other comrades were captured and decapitated, and their heads were hung on a tower on the city wall.

Chi Shiying departed Harbin and went via the northernmost base of operations at Hailun, the temporary provincial capital of Heilongjiang, which was the responsibility of Wang Binzhang, Wang Yuzhang, and three other brothers, to meet the most famous leaders of the volunteer army, Ma Zhanshan and Su Bingwen. He learned of their shortage of gunpowder and their already precarious situation with regard to equipment and food. The remnants of the Zhang family army had already stopped resisting. The central government was thousands of miles away and communications had been cut. The volunteer army, with nothing but their bare hands, patriotic fervor, and the bone-piercing north wind, was unable to stop the Japanese Kwantung Army. The general situation was hopeless, and the only thing Chi Shiying accomplished with the trip was to convince the leaders not to surrender, that the enemy must not be allowed to make use of their armed force, and that they should not recklessly sacrifice themselves. They had to do their utmost to help the volunteers return home and keep their patriotism under cover so that they could answer the next call. After the Japanese occupied Heilongjiang in 1932, he helped arrange for Ma Zhanshan and Su Bingwen to enter Shanhaiguan, where they were given a hero's welcome in Nanjing and Shanghai, giving a huge boost to the people of China in their later resistance against Japan.

Since it was impossible to go directly to northeast China to work, after completing his liaison effort in the enemy's rear, he returned to Nanjing. Chairman Chiang Kai-shek told him that once the government set up a Northeast China Association in Shanghai, he would be in charge of liaison between the central government and the anti-Japanese underground in the northeast, along with the arrangements for helping people who entered Shanhaiguan from the northeast to settle down. He would plan for the long term and never give up.

HEADS ON THE CITY GATE TOWER

Then my grandmother brought my two aunts to Beiping from the northeast. My father had already entrusted someone to take my mother, brother, and me from Nanjing to Beiping, and told friends that his wife was going to look after her mother-in-law. After my father returned to Beiping from Harbin, he decided to do his utmost to stay in north China and use all possible means to make contact with the anti-Japanese underground resistance fighters in the northeast, to facilitate command over the situation there. In those days, Beiping wasn't very safe and there was little protection. Japanese spies were frequently at work collecting information, so we moved to the French concession in Tianjin. My brother stayed in Beiping with my grandmother, and my mother went to visit them from time to time. At this time, my mother began to play a new role in her life, hosting the families of the revolutionaries and students from our homeland. I remember one day an Aunt Ge and my mother were crying together in our house. My mother told me to take the two little boys into the courtyard to play. The Ge brothers said, "We have no idea why our father's head is hanging on the gate tower." In 2001, at the opening ceremony for the Chi Shiying Memorial Library at the reactivated Zhongshan Middle School in Shenyang, someone gave me a copy of a commemorative album titled *Don't Forget the Mukden Incident* in which there was a full-page and very clear photo of bloody men's heads with angry eyes and clenched teeth, suspended from the tower. The sanguinary hatred felt by families and the entire country was still there, confirming my youthful memory, one that would be forever indelible.

But even in the foreign concession it wasn't very safe and the surname Chi attracted a lot of attention, so my father often changed his surname.

I recall we most frequently used the surnames Wang and Xu. When we used the surname Wang, I was a third-grade student at Laoxikai Primary School in Tianjin. Since my parents didn't dare let me run around on the streets of a big city on my own, they hired a yellow rickshaw to take me to school and bring me home. I remember when leaving school in the rickshaw, sometimes the naughtier students would shout "Wang Bayuan! (son of a bitch), Wang Bayuan!" It made me furious, and I would be in tears by the time I got home.

After a while, my father changed his surname again, this time to Xu, and I had to change schools on account of this. At that school there were some English missionaries who taught oral English, but I was only in the third or fourth grade and did not usually use English, so it was soon completely forgotten.

After bearing the surname Xu for a while, I was renamed Zhang. Because my father kept changing his surname, my mother kept changing from Mrs. Wang to Mrs. Xu, and so on. Often before going to class, I would ask, "Mom, what's my surname today?" It was oddly funny for a seven- or eight-year-old child to be asking her own surname.

In those days, surrounded by danger and owing to our frequent moves, my mother no longer cried. In those uncertain times, the relationship between my parents deepened and grew stronger, my mother being happy to be able to share my father's troubles, and that kind of wholehearted acceptance and support provided me with the greatest sense of security growing up. Shortly before she died at the age of eighty-three, we talked about a woman's right of choice in marriage in the new age, and I asked her if she still would have chosen my father. At the time, she smiled without answering; in a few days she said, "I'd still marry him. Although he wasn't a man who put family first, he was a real gentleman, warm and untarnished."

Returning to Nanjing from Tianjin, we rented a house on Fuhougang Street. It was a small new house facing a large open space of empty land filled with locust trees that were covered with racemes of fragrant yellow blossoms in early summer. I have loved them more than anything else all my life, and like herbaceous peonies, they give me a strong sense of family happiness.

Every morning, I would follow the newly laid tracks of the Jiangnan Railroad to the Drum Tower Elementary School, along with Duan Yonglan from the neighboring lane and her cousin Liu Zhaotian. Along the way there were always dandelions and an assortment of other little flowers in bloom.

Right after the start of summer vacation in 1933, my mother gave birth to my younger sister. My father chose the name Ningyuan for her in memory of our homeland, Liaoning Province.

She was a plump, cute, and extremely healthy baby, who smiled all day long but would often cry when night fell. My mother was afraid she'd wake my father, so she would hold her and walk around the house.

Mama Li, who had just arrived to help look after the children, was concerned about not being sufficiently helpful, so one day she asked a comrade in the underground resistance named Yang Mengzhou, who had come to Nanjing to report on his work (he was living with us at the time, waiting to set off for Xinjiang to offer his services to Sheng Shicai) to help her write an edict from her hometown in Fengyang, Anhui: "Lord of Heaven, Lord of Earth, my home has a child who cries at night;

passersby and gentlemen, please recite this three times, and the child will sleep till the sky grows light." She asked my older brother to paste it on a telephone pole on his way to school.

As we passed it every day, we looked to see if anyone had stopped to recite it three times. We were also afraid lest our father see it and get angry. While in the Nanjing central government, his greatest ideal was to get rid of superstition and corrupt customs so that all the populace could found the new China.

During the time I was attending Drum Tower Elementary School, Nanjing was filled with a new spirit. I was nine years old and I remember the slogans of the New Life Movement, which elementary school students helped paste up; the slogans included "No Spitting" and "Stir Oneself to Be Strong."

No one mentions these nowadays, but I remember when I had just arrived in Taiwan, "No Spitting" was still an object of struggle. On the streets were slogans such as: "Be Hardworking and Thrifty," "Don't Drink," Don't Gamble," "Eliminate Superstition," and so on.

From 1928 to 1937, China, with its capital in Nanjing, was filled with hope, and there was new construction everywhere. Some call it "the golden decade" in modern history. Official Japanese records mentioned that their military advocated war as soon as possible, because if they didn't strike now before China became strong, they would never be able to strike at all.

LIME-SCATTERED CHILDHOOD

I became sick quite suddenly in the summer of 1934.

Ever since I was little, my trachea and lungs had been in poor shape. That summer I suffered from pneumonia twice, with my life in the balance, and many times it seemed to hang by a thread.

My parents were deeply concerned and a doctor told them, "With lungs like hers, she should be in the dry north if she is to improve." My grandmother was still in Beiping then, and when she learned of my condition, she wrote saying, "Send her here to Beiping." My grandmother herself was not well, and owing to my father's connections, she frequently went to the German hospital there.

I remember taking the Tianjin–Pukou Railway with my father to Beiping without knowing the real reason for the trip, but because my father himself was taking me, I was extremely happy.

The train traveled for about two days and two nights. On the second day, when we crossed the steel bridge over the Yellow River, I ate in the dining car for the first time. My father cut the steak into small pieces for me, showing me how to hold a knife and cut with it. Amid the steady, vigorous rumble of the train as we crossed the long steel bridge, I sat facing my father for the first time, and I still clearly remember the happiness I felt.

After the German doctor at the hospital in Beiping examined me, he said to my father, "If the child continues in this way, you will most likely lose her. It would be best to send her to a sanatorium."

My father took me by the hand and took me to the Western Hills Sanatorium twenty *li* from the city, which was a German–Chinese joint venture located at the foot of the Western Hills. The German doctor had assured us that I would receive excellent treatment there.

The sanatorium was run in Western fashion, with each patient having an individual room. Even though I was the only child there, I too lived alone. Every night when I went to bed alone in the room I was frightened. I stayed for one year and was frightened the whole time.

In those days, pulmonary tuberculosis was a serious illness, and some people were cured while others were not. For this reason, people often died at the sanatorium, after which lime would be scattered in their room. At first I didn't understand; later I knew that if lime was scattered it meant that someone had died. I didn't understand what death was, but as soon as I saw lime being spread, I'd start to cry.

There was an Old Wang there who brought meals to everyone. He was stout, had a pale complexion, and was probably thirty or forty years old. He had a daughter about my age and always called me "Little Girl." Every time I cried, Old Wang would say, "Don't cry, Little Girl. I'll go boil a potato for you."

I loved to eat potatoes more than anything else when I was little. Even today when I go out to eat with friends, whoever has a round boiled potato will give it to me. Every time I think about this, I feel an irrepressible sadness.

Every Saturday, my grandmother, who was over sixty, would take a sedan chair for twenty *li* to visit me at the sanatorium. Each time she left, I would tearfully try to climb out of bed and go after her, but I was not allowed out of bed, so I just shouted, "I want to go home with you! I want to go home with you!"

Far away in her sedan chair, my grandmother could still hear me crying, but she couldn't take me away. Once when she was about to leave, she also cried, her tears flowing sideways along her wrinkles. I only realize now what the ancients meant in their writings by "tears flow sideways."

In the sanatorium was a female patient by the name of Zhang Caiping, who was probably twenty-five or twenty-six. I called her Sister Zhang. Old Wang said she had become sick on account of having been disappointed in love. She was very interested in me because she thought I was a clever child and I understood everything she said to me, so she often secretly invited me to her room (the sanatorium did not permit us to visit the rooms of other patients). She had many volumes of new literature, most of them translations from around 1935. I read all of her books, of which I still remember Lin Qinnan's translation of *La Dame aux Camélias*; his was a style I really enjoyed in those days.

I remember very clearly one afternoon, lime was being scattered in her room, so I asked Old Wang, "Why are they scattering lime in Sister Zhang's room?"

Old Wang said, "Little Girl, I'll boil a potato for you."

Although I really didn't understand what death was, I knew she had died. That was the first time in my life that I perceived death's relationship to me, all on account of lime being scattered in my friend's room.

I think I was probably pretty distraught and cried all day, making it hard for my grandmother to bear. Throughout my life, I have often thought of my grandmother, who worried about her granddaughter from the day I was born until she herself was old and ill. I often feel that I owe her too much. A few years later, we roamed for quite some time from Hankou to Chongqing, where we received news indirectly that she had passed away. I couldn't believe that that warm body that had held me in the winter could ever become cold.

When my parents reached seventy, they moved to Neihu and lived there peacefully until they died. That period of time was when we most frequently got together and were happiest, it also being the time my father and I talked most closely. One day after dinner, he saw me to the edge of the lake to wait for the bus, and I mentioned to him how I had felt at the Western Hills Sanatorium and that it had made me timid and afraid of the dark for the rest of my life.

"You were very cruel to send me alone to that hospital on that barren mountain."

He sighed and said, "No one knew anything about child psychology in those days. I was involved in the revolution for many years and constantly in danger, and didn't know a child's psychology could be so complicated. I spent one-third of my monthly salary for you to stay in the sanatorium, and my only hope was that you would live. Friends and relatives all said I was a good father!"

We sat on the bench at the bus stop without saying anything for a long time, and only came back to ourselves with the arrival of the bus.

I'm sure he was thinking, *If I had known this at the time, what would I have done?* But I knew how very fortunate I had been: my parents bore me, raised me, and strove to keep me here.

Without much of an alternative during my year in the sanatorium, reading became my sole pastime, gradually becoming a lifelong interest. Books were like a magnet that drew me toward them. Sometimes when I think back on my attachment to books that was so deeply rooted, I could describe it as a lifetime of happiness rising out of misfortune.

I remember after leaving the sanatorium, I saw a Chinese edition of Adam Smith's *An Inquiry Into the Nature and Causes of the Wealth of Nations* at the house of an uncle who had studied abroad. Naturally I didn't understand it, but read it with great pleasure. I read practically everything I could lay my hands on, all the while reading *Little Friend* magazine, despite scorning the cat and dog cartoons inside. I still remember connecting the numbers to draw a dog.

A year later, the doctor declared me cured and my father came and took me back to Nanjing. My younger sister was already nearly two years old.

Initially, I returned to Drum Tower Elementary School, but none of my classmates would play with me. I understood later it was because their elders had heard that I had contracted tuberculosis and had spent time in a sanatorium. A classmate by the name of Wanfang, who, I remember, had been my best friend and who was quite a charming little beauty, suddenly blurted out to me, "My mom told me not to play with you." I didn't have any idea what I had done wrong and didn't understand that people were simply afraid of being infected.

Later we moved to Ninghai Road in the Xinshe District, where I attended the Shanxi Road Elementary School. Because I was a transfer student, most of my interaction was with other transfer students and marginal students who had been held back, and we all got along well. My essay writing was excellent, and the teacher lavished attention on me. Gradually, my health improved and I graduated from elementary school without a care or worry, and a lot of nice memories from that year.

MOTHER AND HER RELATIVES FROM HOME

After Zhang Zuolin, who controlled northeast China, was assassinated with a bomb by the Japanese army in June 1928, that part of China seemed leaderless. Zhang Xueliang had negotiated a settlement with the central government in Nanjing and the flag of the Republic was raised before the New Year. This grand changing of the flags eliminated the greatest obstacle to the Northern Expedition.

That fall, the Whampoa Military Academy (after it moved from Guangzhou to Nanjing, the name was changed to the Central Military Academy) began recruiting students from all over the country for its eighth class, and the party asked my father to assist in the recruitment from the northeast. When my father met with Chairman Chiang

Kai-shek, he suggested that the hundred-plus students from there who passed the first exam should be accepted so that these young people, who for so many years had possessed only a concept of region, could develop a concept of nation and thereby become the seeds of revolution, possessed of modern military knowledge. For this reason, from the ninth class to the twelfth, Zhang Zhizhong, who was the dean of instruction at the academy, entrusted my father to appoint someone to go to the northeast every year to recruit a hundred high school graduates. After the Mukden Incident, students from the northeast accounted for almost one-quarter of the whole academy. These young people whose homeland had fallen to the Japanese were assigned to all branches of the armed services after their graduation, where they became a vital force in the War of Resistance. Few of them were able to return to their homeland.

In addition to students recruited for the military academy, another twenty or thirty came to Nanjing to enter the Central Political Academy and the Central Police Academy. Every Sunday, my parents took turns entertaining this group of young students who ventured so far from their homeland. One of the reasons we moved from Fuhougang Street to Ninghai Road in the Xinshe District was to have more room to entertain, but also because my mother was expecting again. Soon thereafter, Jingyuan, my youngest sister, was born. That was certainly the happiest time for my mother—at thirty she had become the head of her own household.

That newly built, cream-colored house had a big courtyard, and my mother quickly planted all sorts of flowers. Her bedroom window on the second floor faced Zijin Mountain, the highest point in Nanjing, and Sun Yat-sen's mausoleum sits at the foot of the north side of the mountain. The hue of the cloud mist that circles the peak is an indicator of the day's weather.

One of my father's jobs was looking after the students who had come to Nanjing from the northeast, and it was a joy for my mother to invite them over to the house to eat every week, her greatest comfort in her nostalgia for her homeland. We had a cook from Shandong by the name of Old Song (who was with us through ten years of exile in Sichuan).

Every Sunday, we'd invite a table of students from the Whampoa Military Academy and the Central Political Academy for some northern fare and in my mother's heart, each one of them was family. She enjoyed listening to them talk about the seasons at home, their relatives, and their crops.

After moving to Ninghai Road, she discovered a fairly large courtyard behind the house. She bought various sized jars and, with the exception of the hottest days of summer, she and Mama Li were always busy pickling vegetables (after the cabbage was blanched, it would be fermented in the jars for more than a month, after which it became a crispy, white pickled vegetable). She also had someone buy a copper hot pot in Beiping. Before the Marco Polo Bridge Incident, more homesick hearts than I can say were warmed by the Chi family's pork belly and pickled vegetable hotpot!

My mother also believed that soybean paste from northeast China was the best. In Taiwan it's known as sweetened soybean paste, but in fact it isn't sweet. Soybeans are good and plentiful in northeast China, so most families make their own paste. Mother wanted to make the paste, but the process is a little scary because the soybeans first have to become moldy. My father found out about this and was opposed: "What are you doing in the yard?" My mother replied, "I put everything in the backyard so no one can see it." My father found it dirty and disgusting and forbid her to do it, but she was determined and made a vat in secret. When the Whampoa students arrived, my mother gave them cucumber slices dipped in soybean paste and then served the pickled vegetable hotpot. Some wept as they ate because they were reminded of home. They never had a chance to return for the rest of their lives.

During the bombardment of Quemoy (starting August 23, 1958), my father and other legislators went to Quemoy, where the commander, General Wang Duonian, told my father that he had been one of the students recruited for the tenth Whampoa class and would never forget my mother's home cooking. In battles fought from Nanjing to Sichuan, a number of Whampoa students looked after the students from Sun Yat-sen Middle School, as well as my family, as a token of gratitude to my mother. At my mother's funeral, Zhao Jinyong, who had served as ambassador to the Republic of Malawi, recalled when he was a student at the Central Political Academy how my mother always showed concern for him and gave him spending money after our homeland fell to the Japanese.

That year my maternal grandfather managed to come to Nanjing to visit his beloved daughter and saw that she was in high spirits, busying herself with flowers in the front yard and various sizes of vats in the back, which finally set his mind at ease. Two years after he went back home, he passed away in peace, with nothing more to trouble him.

Mother was happy running her household, and she often hummed something while she was at work. I don't know what it was, but whenever she held my little sister, I clearly heard her singing "Su Wu Herds Sheep." When she got to the lines, "Sitting upright in severe cold, hearing a Tartar reed pipe makes him sad of heart," she would sing it over and over again without missing a line until my sister went to sleep. Sometimes she would sit alone for a while.

More than a decade later, after victory over Japan, she went back to northeast China to pay her respects at her parents' graves and return to the Chi family house on Little Western Hill where she had spent ten lonely years. Following this, she was forced to flee the north for an even farther destination: Taiwan. Twelve years later in Taichung, she again softly sang "Su Wu Herds Sheep" as she sat by my son's cradle. Su Wu still herded sheep at the edge of Lake Baikal for nineteen destitute, sad years. In the thirty-eight years before she was buried at Tamshui, Taipei, my mother never again saw the Lake Baikal in her heart.

A LARGE FAMILY GOES INTO EXILE

My father believed that founding National Northeast Sun Yat-sen Middle School was something he was meant to do.

In 1932, he left Nanjing for the north, risking his life exiting Shanhaiguan and secretly returning to his homeland, only to see the underground military forces like the volunteer army fighting against the

Japanese in complete desperation. His comrades in the underground felt he should go back to Nanjing because he could more effectively assist his homeland from his established position in the central government and through the Northeast China Association.

And so he went first to Beiping, where he set up the Office of Educational Relief for the Young People of Northeast China, in which exiles from cultural and educational circles looked after young people who had fled to Beiping and Tianjin rather than become abjectly obedient Japanese subjects after the puppet state of Manchukuo was established. Some wandered destitute on the streets, suffering from cold and hunger by the roadside when winter arrived. The Office of Educational Relief put up some tents, fed them, and looked after basic needs.

At the mass celebrations of the Nanjing government at New Year's in 1934, my father got to know the Vice Premier of the Executive Yuan, Peng Xuepei. Knowing that he was also from north China, he persuaded him to allocate fifty thousand silver dollars, with which he immediately, with his friends in Beiping, Li Xi'en, Huang Henghao, and Zhou Tianfang, proceeded to set up a school. On March 26, 1934, with space borrowed from Baoguo Temple, the Shuntian Government Administration Building, and the former Advanced School for Police Officers, they set up the National Sun Yat-sen Middle School, admitting two thousand exiled students, from junior high freshmen to high school seniors. Thus China's first national middle school came into being, because my father convinced the Ministry of Education that only the state could securely guarantee the continuous existence of such schools that aimed at saving the country from extinction.

Li Xi'en, the former president of Jilin University, became the first principal of the school. (He had been a classmate of my father's eldest cousin in Germany. He and my father shared similar political ideals, and my father looked upon him as a brother.) The teachers were almost all university professors in exile in Beiping. My brother, who had been studying at Chongde Middle School in Beiping, took the exam at the Sun Yat-sen Middle School and was admitted to the second year of junior high.

By the autumn of 1936, the situation in northern China was as tense as the turbulent wind before a storm. The people and undertakings directly supported by the central government were gradually becoming difficult to maintain due to the hidden threat of Japan and the infiltration by the communists. Therefore my father, Huang Henghao, Gao Xibing, and other anti-Japanese comrades from northeast China purchased a piece of land in Banqiao Village, twenty *li* outside Nanjing, where they built some basic school buildings and living quarters for the teachers, then moved the school from Beiping to Nanjing.

After getting settled there, the students themselves set to work and leveled the ground for a playing field, and built the school walls and gates. On the mud brick wall at the front gate a huge motto could be seen from afar: "Though Chu has only three families, it will be Chu that destroys Qin." Every morning at the flag-raising ceremony, the teachers and students sang the school song (lyrics by Hao Lengruo; music by Ma Boshui) that reflected their shared fate:

> High are the white mountains, long are the black rivers;
> truly beautiful is the country, the hatred and suffering cannot
> be forgotten.
> There are young people drifting in misery.
> The Three Principles of the People provide guidance, take
> them as the country's ideal and bear the hard tasks.
> School serves as home as shelter where the students thrive,
> a bracing shelter where Taiye, Qinhuai look on.
> Learning to know shame so as to know uprightness, only the
> people of Chu have upright men;
> with merely three families to destroy Qin, I come from the
> north and to the north I will return.

In the early days at Banqiao everything was difficult, not to mention that everyone was quite young. My father always thought optimistically of the long run. Thus passed a year and a half of poor but settled days filled with hope, until Nanjing could no longer shelter us. After we left Nanjing, the days were much harder over that long journey than in Banqiao; we wandered in a desperate plight and suffered hunger and cold over half the land of China.

ZHANG DAFEI: THE STORY OF HIS FAMILY BROKEN UP AND DISPERSED

My brother moved with Sun Yat-sen Middle School from Beiping to Nanjing, and he would bring five or six classmates home with him every Saturday. After dinner, they would take the Jiangnan Railway train back to Banqiao, while my brother would spend the night at home.

In her happiness, my mother felt that every child without a home from northeast China was her own. After we moved south and during the eight years of the War of Resistance, every student at San Yat-sen Middle School was homeless, and almost every one of them had a heartbreaking story.

The first time Zhang Dafei came to our house, no one really noticed him. He sat quietly, saying very little and not taking part in any of the games. When it came time to eat, my mother insisted he sit beside her and kept putting food in his bowl.

Prior to this, all I knew was that Father had asked my brother to locate a student surnamed Zhang; his father had been the chief of police in Shenyang County right after Manchukuo was established. Because he had assisted and released many anti-Japanese comrades, the Japanese had doused him with varnish and burned him to death in a public square.

My brother finally found him among his classmates. He was three years older than my brother, took part in no extracurricular activities other than playing basketball, and seldom spoke. My brother only found him when he heard Zhang's story through Fu Baolu, a national pole-vault champion (all the girls idolized him in those days) who had graduated that year and who had played basketball with Zhang.

On New Year's Eve that year, the students stayed at school ands prepared dumplings to celebrate the New Year. Two days later, Zhang Dafei came home with my brother. It started snowing that day and it was very cold, so we made a fire in the house, and after eating we sat around the fireplace. My mother asked him about the circumstances surrounding his leaving home.

He said that after the Japanese burned his father but before they came in pursuit to kill the rest of the family, he and seven other family members fled in all directions. He and a younger brother and sister took flight that night to seek refuge with an aunt in Yingkou, where they attended a church-run middle school; they had morning prayer service every day, which started with the Lord's Prayer: "Our father who art in heaven, hallowed be Thy name. Thy kingdom come, Thy will be done on earth as it is in heaven. Give us this day our daily bread. . . ." In this way he could entreat the protection and love of a father to his heart's content, and as a result he became a Christian.

In the second year after Manchukuo was established, the Japanese began a policy of assimilation through education. At fifteen he entered Shanhaiguan on his own and went to Beiping to seek refuge with an uncle; he had missed a year of school and couldn't stay long with him. There were at the time a huge number of homeless young people from the northeast on the streets of Beiping and Tianjin, and by winter, many had died of cold and hunger.

One day when he was at the end of his rope, he wandered by Baoguo Temple and noticed several tents pitched in the courtyard, and on the gate was pasted a notice that National Sun Yat-sen Middle School was recruiting exiled students from northeast China. He tested into the third year of junior high school. After being admitted, all students were provided with food and accommodation at government expense, so from that point on he had a home where he could settle down.

The academic standards of the school were high, and he felt like he had a future, but with the Japanese pressing on north China from Manchukuo, the situation became precarious and gradually so untenable that the school was forced to move south. When it came time to leave Beiping, he could only send word indirectly to his mother, who was homeless in their native land, that he would follow the school south. After arriving at Banqiao in Nanjing, he never received news of her.

I'll always remember that icy cold evening. I saw him muster all the dignity an eighteen-year-old could to keep from crying as he sat beside the fireplace in our warm house, narrating the story of his family broken up and dispersed. It was as tragic as that little boy telling me about his father's head hung above the city gate a few years before.

Outside the window, several small trees my mother had planted swayed in the snow and bent as if they would break. From that moment, I could never forget his name—after he had fled to Yingkou, he changed the auspicious name his parents had given him, Zhang Naichang, to Zhang Dafei (fly).

From then on, I would look forward to seeing his gentle and melancholy smile among my brother's noisy classmates every Saturday afternoon. He really liked to take my three-year-old sister out to play in the courtyard and would sometimes help my mother by carrying my baby sister, who was still in swaddling clothes. Occasionally he'd go over to the chair I often sat in and read the books I had recently bought. One time he brought his small copy of the Bible with its gilt-edged pages to show me and my mother, saying it had been his only source of support since leaving home. At the time I didn't understand, but many years later it became clear why in his gentle loneliness he had a peace and serenity about him. I seemed to have encountered another profound book waiting to be understood, to which I was attracted, but he took it with him when he left.

Early that spring, the school built several small wood-framed bungalows with mud walls outside the gate. Mother went to these and stayed four or five days each week because she was pregnant again and she liked living a rural life and could raise some vegetables. In addition, there were a number of teachers and their families from northeast China who could better comfort her in her homesickness.

I went to Banqiao every weekend, where I could run wild in the mountains and fields as if I were six years old again. Zhang Dafei often showed up, and what he enjoyed the most was holding my two little sisters as he watched my mother do her household chores, but still, he seldom spoke.

One day after lunch, my brother and seven or eight of his classmates said they were going to climb a small nearby mountain called Mount Bullhead. I had long had my eye on that mountain, so I caught up with them and followed them there.

At four in the afternoon when we started down the mountain, the wind suddenly sprang up, and as I walked slower than the others, I soon found myself left behind. My brother and the other big boys had already descended the mountain while I was stuck halfway down, holding onto a small rocky outcrop, unable to proceed or go back. The mountain wind whistled sharply, and, filled with fear in the cold wind, I began to cry. Just then I saw Zhang Dafei look back at me from a narrow defile.

It was getting dark, but he walked back up, took me by the hand, and led me down the mountain. At the mouth of the defile, he wrapped my sixty-odd-pound body in his cotton student's coat and said, "Don't cry, don't cry, everything will be fine when we get to the main road." The sympathy and concern in his eyes were something a twelve-year-old marginal person like myself, who frequently changed schools, rarely encountered.

Upon returning home, my brother said to my mother, "She should never come with me again! She was so slow going up the mountain and then couldn't get down, crying at the drop of a hat. What a pain!"

At the beginning of summer, we moved back to Nanjing in readiness for my mother to give birth.

Our lives and the fate of China soon changed completely: I was fated never again to set foot in that small house.

In all my travels around the world in the decades since then, every time I saw a friendly little mountain, I would always think of him looking back at me from the defile in the wind.

2

A JOURNEY OF BLOOD AND TEARS

The Eight Years of the War of Resistance

DENSELY SPREAD THE CLOUDS OF WAR

The Northern Expedition was successful in 1928; the country was united; Nanjing became the capital of the Nationalist government; the best from each province gathered together to establish the new China. That decade was not only the nation's ten golden years but also the ten golden years of my father's life.

Chi Shiying, who arrived in Nanjing from outside Shanhaiguan, was given a hearty welcome. Although Guo Songling's military remonstrance of Zhang Zuolin was defeated and he himself perished, his demand that the Fengtian Army remove itself from the contention among warlords in the central plains, return home and build up local strength, and resist Japanese and Russian aggression had spread throughout the country. Thus, the Nationalist government formed by the revolutionary party that had overthrown the imperial system welcomed this first young revolutionary from the northeast to take part in the work of building the nation. His Kuomintang Party membership card number was 1, Liaoning Province.

But when Chairman Chiang Kai-shek met him, he unexpectedly said, "You don't look like someone from the northeast!" which meant something quite complicated. During the Northern Expedition, the impression most people had of the Fengtian Army soldiers was that they were brave and warlike, fierce, and even crude. But this twenty-seven-year-old revolutionary from the northeast was gentle and refined, graceful as a jade tree in the wind (a comment by Lu Chunfang). Knowing three foreign languages—English, Japanese, and German—and having studied historical philosophy at Heidelburg University two years before, he was very hard to classify. He informed Mr. Chiang that he was willing to work in foreign affairs, culture, or education; Mr. Chiang replied that there was too much to do in a huge country like China; therefore, he dispatched him to the Central Policy Committee (at the time it didn't have a fixed name) to serve as an appointed legislator, working with Niu Yongjian, Huang Fu, Chen Guofu, and Chen Lifu. He thus made friends with people of note in the country and became the expert on Japan in the central government. He was also sent to Japan with the rank of first lieutenant to study at the Japanese Infantry School for a year.

Japan's ambition to encroach upon China had grown stronger with each passing day since the Treaty of Shimonoseki after the First Sino-Japanese War of 1894–1895, which had ceded Taiwan to Japan. In 1905, the Japanese defeated the Russians in the northeast and obtained control over the railroads there, after which they never ceased causing trouble throughout China. In 1915 they forced China to accept the unequal treaty composed of the Twenty-one Demands; in 1928 they fomented the Jinan Incident; and in 1931 they occupied Shenyang in the Mukden Incident, then a year later established the puppet state of Manchukuo. The Nationalist government was clearly aware of this string of aggressions, but before catching its breath, it could only quicken the pace of building up the army, establishing industry, and organizing the people. In those ten years, it was as if Nanjing were racing to build up the strength of an old man who had been gravely ill for a hundred years. It was such hard work, but filled with hope and good faith. The Xi'an Incident launched by the coarse and impetuous Zhang Xueliang hurt the image of the northeast army while providing the Communists in Yan'an with a new lease on life to later grow in strength, and thus focused the ardor of the people even more to fight the Japanese under the leadership of Chairman Chiang Kai-shek.

In 1930, my mother took my brother and me and traveled thousands of miles to Nanjing in search of my father. There was construction everywhere in the flourishing capital. My father and his young friends were busy buying time, promoting all sorts of modernizing construction to strengthen the country, because they knew that the Japanese militarists were quickening their pace to invade. As the Japanese army said: "If we don't act soon, China will stand up!"

THE MARCO POLO BRIDGE INCIDENT

On July 7, 1937, the flames of war at the Marco Polo Bridge changed modern China's destiny and laid the foundation for my own lifelong attitude of hard struggle.

The sanguinary blade of war severed me from my sickly childhood—on the elementary school playing field newly laid with gravel, just as I finished singing the song of farewell at graduation, the lyrics of which no longer fit the situation: "Beyond the pavilion, beside the ancient road, the fragrant grass extends to the sky. . . ." My childhood came to a sudden end.

Before the summer in Nanjing—one of China's three great furnaces—had passed, Japanese planes began bombing. On August 15, the first bomb was dropped on the Ming Palace Airport.

Three days before, my mother had given birth to my little sister Xingyuan at the Central Hospital across from the airport. The strong blast broke the doors and windows of the hospital and everyone ran for their lives. Barefooted, my mother clasped her infant daughter and followed everyone to the basement, where she had a bout of metrorrhagia. Two days later, after everyone else had left the hospital, she was carried home, where all she could do was take styptics and wrestle with death.

A month after the shots were fired at the Marco Polo Bridge, the Japanese army entered Beiping (Tianjin had already fallen). On August 13, troops dispatched from the Japanese concession in Shanghai started the battle of Shanghai, and Suzhou, Wuxi, and other cities were soon lost and the Beiping–Shanghai Railroad cut. The Japanese troops in north China followed the Tianjin–Pukou Railroad south, leaving Nanjing isolated; after the Northern Expedition, the residents of Nanjing, which was the capital and symbol of modern China, had to withdraw.

The air-raid sirens sometimes started in the morning and stopped only after the sun had set. The Japanese planes came in wave after wave to bomb mainly Pukou, important military targets along the railway, and government organizations. The government had already started to urgently transport personnel and documents to the southwest, with those who remained working in temporary air-raid shelters. Setting out each morning, no one was certain if they would be able to make it safely back home.

In August, the Military Committee was renamed the Supreme Command Headquarters for the War of Resistance, to prepare for full-scale resistance. My father was remitted to serve as Secretary of the Sixth Bureau, headed by Chen Lifu.

By September, Nanjing was half deserted and by October, we were the only ones left on Ninghai Road. The neighbors had left in such a hurry that they didn't even properly close up their doors or windows, which banged in the autumn wind. Scraps of paper and clothing blew through the streets, and the air was filled with an empty menace.

From our doorway, I'd watch my father set off for work in the morning. Then I would ride my bike for a while, but before I'd gone very far, the frightening silence would send me quickly home. The air-raid sirens would go off every day at daybreak. There were quite a few of us at home, but with no air-raid shelter, we boosted one another's courage as we listened to the bombs falling, feeling lucky we didn't live in the center of town.

At night, I slept alone in the room next to my parents'. When the moonlight was bright, the enemy planes would come and the air-raid sirens wailed even more shrilly. After one long and two short bursts of the siren, the planes could be heard ponderously approaching, followed by exploding bombs and the light of fires on the horizon. Alone in bed, I listened to the latches of the window screens creaking in the autumn wind, and seemed to see white lime raining down out of the sky, falling over the interminable steps at the Sun Yat-sen Memorial on Zijin Mountain, between the waves in Xuanwu Lake, on Dongchang Street Park, on the locust tree flowers in front of our house on Fuhougang Street, and on the seesaws at Drum Tower Elementary School. Death had already found its way to my window and rained down on the starlike cypress vine flowers growing on the newly built bamboo shed.

I'll never forget how every day at dusk, my mother, distressed and weak from illness, would force herself to get out of bed to greet my worried-looking father, comforted then at having us all together again.

My father was always positive and optimistic. But even so, he still had not only to face the national crisis but also to find, through his own efforts, a way to solve the difficult problem of getting the teachers and students of Sun Yat-sen Middle School from the outskirts of Nanjing to Hankou, and then farther to the southwest.

FLEEING FROM NANJING TO HANKOU

In the middle of October, my father arranged first to send the seven-hundred-plus girl students and junior high students via the Jiangnan Railroad to Anqing, where they would board a riverboat to Hankou. They were to be led by the teachers and members of the Northeast China Association who had family dependents. The second group, three hundred plus high school boys, would remain in Banqiao until the next train and ship arrangements could be made. Only Huang Henghao, who had come from Beiping to establish the school, and Wang Yuzhang, the new principal, remained in Nanjing. Principal Wang was the second of five Wang brothers who were working for the anti-Japanese underground in Heilongjiang and who taught at the Central Military Academy after entering Shanhaiguan. Facing the present crisis, he had been ordered to take the more than one thousand teachers and students to the unoccupied rear. Our family left Nanjing with the second group of teachers and students.

A month before departing, my father was worried about safety in the remoter areas, so he requested one hundred rifles for the school from Wu Keren, Corps Commander of the Sixty-seventh Army. He also gave the students military training to ensure their safety and that of the teachers along the way.

We saw scarcely a soul on the way from home to the train station, and only upon arrival did we realize everyone had flooded into it. Thousands of people in large, dark cotton-padded coats pressed toward the platform, supporting the aged while leading the young. Bedding and luggage were everywhere, the station becoming a boiling cauldron of cries and shouts.

The seniors from Sun Yat-sen Middle School, shouldering rifles and wearing leggings, did their best to protect and move the more than two hundred students and teachers onto the carriages reserved by the Ministry of Education. My older brother, my cousin Pei Lianju (my uncle's son, who was also studying at Sun Yat-sen), and nineteen-year-old Zhang Dafei had wrapped my mother in a quilt and carried her aboard to a corner where she could half lie, half sit. After that they passed my three little sisters and me through the window into the carriage. A small cloth bag fastened at my waist contained two gold rings and some money, along with a contact address in Hankou.

On the train, people were pressed together, some sitting and standing while others squatted, without an inch of free space. The top of the train was full of people clinging to it, and no one would come down regardless of how forcefully the stationmaster shouted. All anyone could think about was getting on the train and out of Nanjing.

Around noon, my father stood in the cold autumn wind outside the station, his heart filled with worry as he watched the train filled to bursting, its roof covered with clinging refugees, ponderously pulling out. Twenty days later the city would be the ghastly scene of the Japanese massacre. Day and night the Japanese planes bombed along the Yangtze River. Would these people, who were constantly on his mind, come though the five-hundred-*li* journey unscathed?

When the train passed through the first tunnel, crying and shouting were heard coming from the roof: "Someone got swept off! Someone fell!" But the people inside the carriage couldn't extend a helping hand.

The train seemed to crawl along, and when planes were heard, the train hid in the next tunnel. By the time we got to Wuhu, where we would change to a ship, it was already dark.

In order to avoid being bombed in daylight, the ships sailed at night, but with no lights on the wharf and just a few small lamps on the gangplank to light the way. We finally made it onto the wharf and stumbled aboard ship. Too many people swarmed forward and some fell into the water, and even though the boat couldn't carry any more passengers, people still pushed forward on the gangplank. There was a sudden cracking sound as the gangplank broke and even more people plunged into the water.

On that perilous and dreadful night, the cries for help of the people who had fallen into the water and the sound of those who were drowning rose from the surface of the black river, along with the shouts of the people already on board calling out to their children. The sounds, mixed with the cries of the people who had been swept from the roof of the train during the day, often came back to me through the rest of my life. Those piercing screams reverberated through many a sleepless night and were the beginning of my compassion, which began from what I read in literature and gradually broadened to encompass all the people of my country and humanity.

In those days, Yangtze troop ships were one of the lifelines in the defense of the capital, and from the upstream city of Hankou, the farthest they could go was to Wuhu. Shanghai had fallen ten days earlier, and after the last defending soldier had pulled out, the Japanese planes focused on bombing the Yangtze River shipping, so the shipping channel beyond the wharf at Xiaguan in Nanjing was full of sunken craft. After the reinforcing troops from upstream disembarked at Wuhu, the empty ships were soon filled with government officials and documents (including treasures from the Forbidden City) before sailing back to Hankou at night. If the skies were clear after daybreak, the ships would draw near to the riverbank where there were overhanging trees and proceed slowly under cover, the tops of the ships camouflaged with tree branches. We took what was probably the last group of troop ships. In order to impede the Japanese ground offensive, Chinese troops destroyed the steel bridge as well as the road bridges at Wuhu on December 1, which meant that the ships could only get as far as Anqing, farther upstream. Trains from Nanjing to Anqing could no longer operate, as they had nearly all become bombing targets, and whether a person lived or died was solely a matter of fate.

The trip upstream to Hankou from Wuhu should have taken two days and a night. We hid on the banks of the Yangtze during daylight for two days. Fortunately it was the start of winter, so the days were short, and after three nights, the ship arrived at Hankou wharf in the first glimmer of dawn. The students sitting in the hold of the ship took another ship to a middle school in Wuchang and were temporarily housed in the auditorium, where they rejoined their classmates of the previous group. We stayed at a hotel that my father had entrusted a friend to book and where we were to wait for him, lest we lose contact.

THE COUNTRY DESTROYED, THE FAMILY SHATTERED

At that point, however, my family faced an even greater life-and-death challenge.

Although there was someone to carry my mother from the Nanjing train station to the military wharf at Wuhu, she had still suffered greatly, and once on board ship she began to bleed heavily. By the third day of the trip, the styptics could no longer stem the metrorrhagia, and all our underclothes were placed under her lower body after the bedding was used up.

By the time the boat reached Hankou, my mother was in a coma. She seemed to be breathing her last when she was carried from the wharf to a Catholic hospital that morning. My eighteen-month-old sister

Jingyuan was carried to the hospital at the same time. She hadn't been fully weaned and, having just learned to walk, was very cute. On board ship, when the adults were doing everything in their power to attend to my mother, she would walk around alone and people would sometimes feed her things. On the third day of the voyage, she began vomiting constantly and when we sent her to the hospital, she was placed in the pediatric ward. The doctor diagnosed her as having acute enteritis. She was in the far right end of the hospital and an aunt took me along to to see her; my mother was in the intensive care ward at the far left end of the hospital, where my uncle looked on as the doctors did everything to stabilize her in her severely weakened condition. My uncle Pei Shuqing had been an elementary school principal who had fled northeast China after Beiping and Tianjin fell and managed to get to Nanjing to join us in our flight to the rear.

On the fifth morning, as I slept leaning against my sister's bed, I was suddenly awakened by the sound of my aunt crying. My sister had become nothing more than a bag of bones, and her small sweet face had turned snow white. She had died. Just before I had drifted off to sleep out of weariness, she had opened her eyes and said, "Sister, hold me." But now she was already cold.

A Catholic nun who served as nurse came and closed her eyelids and said, "With your tears falling on her face, she won't be able to go to heaven." My aunt told me to go out and wait in the hall for a while before coming back in. When I came back, they had already wrapped her tiny form in a white blanket and carried her out.

It was already daylight but still raining. It was a unfamiliar steel-gray winter sky over an unfamiliar city. Thirteen years old and filled with trepidation and grief, I seemed to crawl to the doorway of my mother's room at the left end of the hospital.

She no longer recognized me. Several doctors and nurses stood around her bed, and although they had just given her a transfusion, she had not yet revived. The oldest doctor motioned my uncle to the doorway and said, "You should prepare yourselves. We'll continue doing everything we can, but there's not much hope."

My uncle, accompanied by his students, found a coffin maker in that unfamiliar city and ordered a coffin for an adult, along with buying a small one. He also had to order mourning clothes for me and my sixteen-year-old brother. When he returned to the hospital, my mother's heartbeat was very weak.

Rushing to my mother's bedside, my uncle shouted to my barely breathing mother, "Yuzhen, wake up! You can't die. Your children are so young, you can't die!"

Many years later, my mother still remembered that morning, when wrapped in a shroud of gray clouds and fog, she heard my uncle shout her name. She seemed to see my older brother and me carrying or holding three little ones by the hand, standing in the snow. She struggled to grab hold of us, stumbling forward. . . .

I stood alone in the doorway of my mother's room, listening to my uncle shout her name, feeling cold, alone, and frightened. At that moment, I saw Zhang Dafei enter through the main door and run over to us. My tears began to pour down once again as I said to him, "My sister died, and now Mom is dying!"

He entered her room, knelt before her bed, bowed his head, and prayed.

When he came out of the room, he said, "I've already enrolled in the military academy. I changed my name to Dafei. I have to assemble at the wharf at eleven o'clock, but I had to come and see Mom before I left. Tell your brother that I'll write as soon as I can."

He then took out a small package and placed in my hands, saying, "Take good care of this. It is what I want to say to you." Then he strode quickly out the door of the hospital.

Later, he told me in a letter that he had run almost all the way to the wharf and reported on time. He wept all the way because for over a year he had received motherly love and warmth from my mother, and he didn't know if he would ever see her again.

The little package he placed in my hand contained a small Bible, identical to his own, brand new, bound in leather with gilt pages. From that day on, I carried it with me on every rough journey in all sorts of vehicles and boats. Today, more than sixty years later, it is still clear and legible.

On the flyleaf, he wrote:

To little sister Pang-yuan:

This is the life of mankind, the soul of the universe, as well as the spiritual granary for all Christians. May eternal God always love you and always be with you, and see that your sweet future is always bright, that you might always reside in the garden of happiness. Amen!

Zhang Dafei, your fourth brother in God
November 18, 1937

Before that day, no one had ever blessed my weak and troubled life with words like "sweet future."

THE NANJING MASSACRE

On December 7, my father arrived in Hankou. He and several dozen members of the Supreme Command Headquarters for the War of Resistance, who were the last to leave Nanjing, went first with Chairman Chiang Kai-shek to Yichang, where they boarded a military ship for Hankou.

Our father had finally returned to us, dark and thin, for it had been difficult to procure food and drink in the last few days in Nanjing. It was the first time in my life that I had seen a grown man cry—tears streamed down his face as he looked around at his frightened children. His white handkerchief, which was gray with dust, was soaked through with tears. He said, "Our country is lost and our family shattered!"

Mother, who hovered between life and death, was relieved at seeing her husband rejoin the family. Her worried heart now settled, she went on to live.

Every morning, my father would cross the river from Hankou to the garrison Supreme Command Headquarters for the War of Resistance, which had been moved to Wuchang Garrison Headquarters, where he would review battlefield reports and manage the overall strategy. The war had already lasted five months, and the Japanese army that once boasted it would occupy all of China within three months now found itself confronting an awakened country.

Japanese firepower, which had been aimed at Nanjing, Shanghai, Wuhu, and Nanchang, was now redeployed to bomb Wuhan day and night. All that remained of the once densely populated city center were the broken walls of tall buildings. All night long, firelight burned without ceasing along the river. The number of enemy planes increased, and our air force met them head on, shooting many down. The people, though living under the threat of death, still stood amid the rubble, cheering the air force that had become the biggest hero of New China.

On the afternoon of December 13, the newsboys on the street shouted "Extra!" My uncle ran downstairs to buy a paper, which said: "Nanjing falls. Japanese troops drive through the Zhonghua Gate into our capital, burning and pillaging, and massacring."

On the front page of the paper the following day was: "Nanjing falls. In the first two days, fifty thousand defenders are killed and wounded; more than one hundred thousand women, children, old, and weak are brutally massacred. Japanese abominations include even a killing contest."

On the same page was printed a foreign dispatch reporting that Albert Einstein, Bertrand Russell, Romain Rolland, and John Dewey had issued a joint declaration calling for the people of the world to band together and boycott Japanese goods, and not cooperate with Japan, so as not to give strength to the Japanese invasion. At the same time it called for lending full support to China until Japanese troops were completely withdrawn and had put an end to all savage acts. The declaration was supported by nongovernmental groups and unions from all nations. But in any age, the voice of international justice is often drowned out by the gunfire of the mighty. Three months later, Hitler's troops marched in and swallowed up Austria. Thinkers and scholars watched as their European homelands fell under the frightful control of totalitarianism. How could their sympathy for China have any practical effect?

After Wuhu fell, in order to delay the Japanese advance upstream, the Chinese army scuttled eighteen ships and a large number of sailing vessels, blocking the river at Madang, forming a second blockade line so that our full force could be brought to bear at Jiujiang City and protect Wuhan. The evil and savage acts of the Japanese in Nanjing made the entire country determined to fight a protracted war of resistance. The southwestern provinces all cabled to say that they were joining the front line in the war and on December 26, the Chinese Communists announced their support for Chiang Kai-shek to fight a war of resistance to the end.

FLEEING FROM HANKOU TO XIANGXIANG

The government ordered the dispersal of all residents and refugees in Wuhan; all factories, military and government facilities, and schools were to move southwest to Guizhou and Sichuan. Chongqing was officially now the capital, and all people fleeing were to follow the Hunan–Guangxi Road southwest as expeditiously as possible.

My father ran all over and managed to find an ancestral temple called Huangbi Hall in Yongfeng Town in Xiangxiang, Hunan. The locals acceded to his request to allow the one thousand students to be housed there.

It was another five hundred *li* from Hankou to Xiangxiang in Xiangtan County. The students and teachers who located vehicles rode, while those who did not set out on foot from Hankou. It took about one month to make the trek to Yongfeng Town.

My father found a car to take my mother, the mother of a teacher, a married woman, and my two little sisters and me, and we set off for Hunan as well. Halfway, we caught up with the contingent of students, at the rear of which walked my brother. My uncle told my brother to get in the car, and a place was made for him to squeeze in beside the driver.

The following day we arrived at a stop, where my father caught up with us. He asked my brother why he was riding in the car.

My uncle replied, "There is space in the car. You have only one son, so let him ride in it!"

My father said, "Many of the students with us are only sons, and their families entrusted them to us. So why do they walk and my son gets to ride?" He ordered the car to catch up with the contingent, where he dropped my brother off to walk with the others.

This moving contingent took to the road at daylight and stopped at night. We stayed in countless inns along the way. It was arranged for the students to stay in different school auditoriums, classrooms, or playing fields, while the local garrisons would provide some straw and a little rice. Everyone slept on the straw, and each meal there was also some boiled turnips or cabbage.

After my brother was forced out of the car and rejoined the others on foot, I raised a ruckus every day to be allowed to join him: "Why does he get to walk, and I don't? Why do I have to ride in the car?" So they let me out to walk with the others.

I only walked part of the day and that night, while sleeping on the straw, I developed a high fever. Early in the morning on the next day, I was returned to my mother and dared not broach the subject again.

Just prior to the lunar New Year, we reached Xiangxiang and discovered that Hunan alone was rife with different dialects, and that of Xiangxiang was different from other cities in Hunan.

Qi Baishi was from Xiangxiang, and it had a good deal of local color. Huangbi Hall was another ten *li* from Xiangxiang and located in Yongfeng Town. It was the ancestral temple of the Ming dynasty imperial family. The temple actually did have nearly a hundred rooms, which meant that there was enough room not only for the students but also for classrooms. Meanwhile, my family moved into another temple: Fujia Hall.

This was the first time since fleeing Nanjing that we had the semblance of being a family again. It was only then that we dared tell our mother the truth, that Jingyuan had died. In Hankou my father had told her that Auntie Han had taken Jingyuan and left with the first group of students and teachers dispersed to Hunan. And it was only then that we dared to tell her that cousin Pei Lianju and Zhang Dafei had enlisted. After she learned of this, she wept, deeply sorrowful, whereupon her illness returned and she remained sick in bed for a long time before recovering.

MY HOME IS ON THE SONGHUA RIVER IN THE NORTHEAST

After the school was settled in Huangbi Hall, a sense of calm returned, and then the lunar New Year soon arrived. On the stormy night of New Year's Eve, the entire school assembled and made dumplings, a tradition since the establishment of Sun Yat-sen Middle School. The children, who had not had a hot meal in some time, on New Year's Eve ate the authentic food from their native place with joy and alacrity.

After the meal on the Lantern Festival, some went down to a clearing by the riverside outside the temple and lit bonfires, with hundreds sitting around the fires.

Someone said we were getting farther away from home with each passing day. The Japanese had occupied half of China, and they were still killing. When would we ever be able to go home? Soon the sound of weeping was heard on the riverbank, and a few of the younger girls actually began to wail.

Amid the tears, Hao Lengruo, a Chinese teacher, led everyone in singing "On the Songhua River" (lyrics by Zhang Hanhui), a song that had been handed down to later generations:

> My home is on the Songhua River in the northeast,
> where there are forests and coal mines,
> and where soybeans and sorghum grow all over the mountains and fields.
> My home is on the Songhua River in the northeast,

where my compatriots live,
and my aged father and mother too.
The Mukden Incident! Starting from that tragic date,
The Mukden Incident! Starting from that tragic date,
I fled my home, abandoning its countless treasures.
Wandering! Wandering! Inside Shanhaiguan, days on end
I wander!
When will I ever return to my beloved home?
When will I ever recover those countless treasures of mine?
O Father, O Mother!
When will we ever be reunited under one roof?

After this song was written, it was taught in the music classes at Sun Yat-sen Middle School by our music teacher, Ma Baishui. We sang this song from Hunan to Sichuan, accompanying about a thousand students who had wandered from the northeast to the southwest. Eight years later, the same group of students would sing the same song while traveling from the southwest back to their decimated homeland. A wanderer's trilogy for this tragic age: a song amid tears bespoke the pain of wandering children in exile; it was sung across the vast land from the time of fighting the Japanese and then the Communists; it was sung accompanying the tears of countless people for nearly a decade after arriving in Taiwan.

ZHOUNAN GIRLS' MIDDLE SCHOOL

I had only finished elementary school, so I had to continue my studies, but I was not accepted by Sun Yat-sen Middle School because they were afraid that I might frequently be sick and become a burden to them. On account of this, my parents sent me on my own to Zhounan Girls' Middle School in Changsha to start my first year of junior high. Zhounan Girls' Middle School is a famous school with a history, and there is still an alumni club in Taiwan.

The class tutor, as I recall, was our teacher Li Shifen. Almost twenty years after I arrived in Taiwan, I moved from Taichung to Taipei and frequently came across his name in the paper, as he was serving as the chairperson of the board of the Broadcasting Corporation of China. When I went to visit him, he still remembered me. My schoolwork was good, but I was often sick and would frequently faint or suffer from a high fever and then have to be sent to the hospital. It was a boarding school and the families had to entrust their children to the school, which thus was responsible for taking care of them. In his Hunan dialect, he said, "You were such a troublesome little girl."

In that one short semester, I was a very good student and quite diligent. When the Japanese attacked and entered Hankou, our school participated in a huge patriotic march in Changsha, and the whole city seemed to boil. I joined the school band and the teacher asked me, "What do you want to play?"

I said, "I want to beat a big drum."

Since my anti-Japanese feelings were running high at that time, I could only express myself by beating a big drum. But I weighed a little more than sixty-five pounds and was as thin as a monkey, nowhere big enough to carry a drum, so Mr Li, helped me to fulfill my wish by having a bigger student carry the drum while I walked alongside and beat it. During the march, I led the band, beating that large drum. This also demonstrated the kindness and sympathy with which the school treated the refugee students from the northeast.

Later, in Taiwan, I still held on to a small autograph book in which my teachers and classmates had written their good wishes for me. Amid dramatic changes in real life and during the free time between raising my children and cooking three meals a day, I would still think of that frail thirteen-year-old and the whole city of Changsha boiling over with patriotic fervor in the march, and my own fear and anger amid the sound of a beating drum.

Two months after we arrived in Xiangxiang, my brother received a letter from Zhang Dafei written at boot camp and sent to the school. A number of their young instructors were Whampoa graduates from the northeast from the eighth through the twelfth classes, who knew that

Sun Yat-sen Middle School had made it to Hunan and had put up in Yongfeng Town in Xiangxiang.

His letter opened by asking about my mother's health (he dared not ask if she was still alive). He asked us to be sure to let him know. He addressed his letter to both my brother and me, perhaps fearing my brother would not reply.

In his letter, he also explained his reasons for joining the army: "I'm already nineteen and at graduation will be over twenty, with no guarantee that I'll be admitted to a public university. The Japanese have forced us to our current situation, putting me in no mood to study or await some unknown future. I have three brothers, and having gotten into the Air Force Officer Candidate School as I wished, I can really do something for the country and avenge my father."

He said that shortly after joining the army, he tested into the officer candidate school and that the training was very arduous, but he had enough to eat: "I haven't had so many good meals since leaving home, except at your home in Nanjing." He was in good shape and could get through the training. He asked me if I had been reading the Bible, suggesting that I start with the New Testament. My brother was very busy in school, so he told me to write back right away.

Before I went to Zhounan Girls' Middle School in Changsha, I wrote a reply, telling him clearly about our family and my mother's health. I also said that I carried the Bible he had given me in my waist pocket and that I took it with me even when I was running for my life as the warning sirens sounded, but that I didn't understand why Jesus said that if someone struck your left cheek you should offer him the right.

On the eve of two conflagrations in Changsha, the situation became more difficult by the day, so my parents had me return to Xiangxiang in order to get ready to flee once more.

To this day, I still remember the good days we spent in Yongfeng Town. Hunan is abundantly productive, the people are sincere, and the literary heritage is time-honored. On account of their persistence and self-confidence, people from Hunan are often called "Hunan mules." It is a land of rice and fish, and, while I've been to a lot of places in my life, I have rarely seen such beautiful turnips and cabbages as I saw there.

Before the fires of war arrived, the days were quite peaceful and quiet as if the place were cut off from the world, like Cuicui's lovely world in Shen Congwen's novel *Border Town*.

In the *National Northeast Sun Yat-sen Middle School Golden Anniversary Commemorative Album*, many people noted that the nearly one year's time spent amid the beautiful scenery of Xiangxiang with sufficient food and clothing constituted a beautiful memory, even though they were still on the run as refugees.

FLEEING FROM XIANGXIANG TO GUILIN

On October 21, 1938, the Japanese landed at Dapeng Bay and took the city of Guangzhou, which was engulfed in flames. In November, Chinese troops mistakenly thought the Japanese army was about to reach Changsha, so the order was given to burn the city, resisting through a scorched-earth plan. On December 21, Chiang Kai-shek, Chairman of the Military Commission, released "A Letter Informing the People and Soldiers of China of the Withdrawal from Wuhan," in which he vowed that the entire nation should be united as one, continue to fight in the southwest, and never surrender.

By now, it had been a year and three months since the Japanese military made its crazy guarantee to the emperor and the people that it would occupy all of China within three months. And the southwest was more mysterious than the Japanese ever imagined—the mountainous territory would tie up hundreds of thousands of invading Japanese troops for eight years, many of whom were to die in a foreign land.

Mother took us and went with Sun Yat-sen Middle School, which my father had arranged to leave Hunan, which had been surrounded by a Japanese pincer movement, and take the Hunan–Guangxi Railroad to Guilin and then on to Sichuan via Guizhou.

We thought we could pause and catch our breath after reaching Guilin, so my parents sent me to the Guilin Girls' Middle School to continue my first year of junior high, as even one day of schooling was better than none. My family stayed in an inn while I boarded at school, studying for a little more than a month of the fall term.

Two things that occurred at that time that are difficult to forget.

If the skies were clear during the day, the Japanese planes would bomb, the air-raid sirens would wail, and we'd have to run to the outskirts of town. Several of the older high school girls, probably as arranged by the school, would take me to a place on the river where there were a lot of willows under which we would hide. As the planes flew overhead, we watched as they dropped strings of shining bombs, followed by black smoke and flames rising from the city.

Sometimes a dogfight would seem to begin right overhead, with the Chinese and enemy planes exchanging machine-gun fire. When we saw a plane with a rising sun on it begin to smoke from the tail and fall toward the earth, we would applaud excitedly despite our fear. One time an enemy plane crashed nearby and lots of people ran to have a look, cheering without end.

While waiting for the all-clear signal, I remember hearing one of the older girls sing in a soft voice, "Every day I go to the Huansha River . . . and foolishly count the days till you return." Although I was old enough to understand it, I felt pretty uncomfortable listening to that sort of "decadent" song under a sky like that.

One other thing that left a deep impression on me was that through the long night, with the lights out from nine o'clock until the following morning, you had to take a long walkway in the open air from the dormitory to get to the toilet. The walkway was supported by columns like those of the temple, on which hung two or three large oil lamps that flickered in the night breeze, casting dark, wavering shadows. I always waited for someone else to get up and went with them. My feelings of fear are still vivid today.

After lights out, sometimes someone would tell a ghost story. I would just tightly cover my head, and my fear of the coming dusk was similar to what I had felt at Western Hills Sanatorium. Fortunately, we soon left Guilin with Sun Yat-sen Middle School and set off for Guizhou, and only then was I set free.

FROM GUILIN TO HUAIYUAN

All too soon the situation grew more unstable as refugees from Shanghai and Nanjing who had fled to Wuhan and Hunan now surged toward Gulin. All the places to stay were bursting at the seams.

Of the Sun Yat-sen Middle School students and teachers, the boys lived in a cave on Qixing Crags, while the girls lived in temporary thatch shacks. My father went on to Sichuan to find a place to house the school. With the assistance of the local government, he found the Jingning Temple near Ziliujing in central Sichuan where the students could live and take classes.

Once again we embarked on the road to refuge, which became ever more difficult. The students and teachers in Guilin divided into three groups and set off for Liuzhou in Guangxi. They then went on to the prearranged meeting place of Huaiyuan Town in Yishan County, Guangxi, and after getting a clear picture of the situation, set off for Chongqing in Sichuan.

In Guilin, the local command helped my father by lending three military transport trucks to carry the basic school equipment, and my mother took the rest of the family to Liuzhou by long-distance bus.

My uncle and I rode in the baggage truck on top of suitcases and trunks piled as high as they would go. We had to be tied in place so as not to fall off. I felt "honored" to be allowed to ride in the baggage truck and not sit with the little children on the bus. I had no choice but to grow up after the separation and deaths in Hankou.

We stayed in Liuzhou for a few days. The commander of the newly garrisoned armored regiment, who was from the northeast and a graduate of the eighth Whampoa class, delivered my family and those of the last group of teachers and their families (most had already gone to Sichuan) to Huaiyuan Town, where we were to stay.

Every morning my mother went to the highway in front of the town to wait for the Sun Yat-sen Middle School students who had proceeded on foot, including my brother. After 27 days and 760 *li*, the first students appeared. The moment my mother saw Dong Xiumin (the only son of my father's good friend Dong Qizheng) shouldering his luggage and in his tattered clothes and shoes approach and call her "Auntie Chi," she broke into tears.

It had been days since the several hundred teenage students had washed their khaki uniforms. Since leaving Xiangxiang, they hadn't slept in a bed and had walked all the way; their hair was mussed and their faces were dirty. She couldn't recognize her son among them.

In that age of suffering, being bullied and insulted by foreigners and fleeing the spreading flames of war, I had the chance to see the majesty and beauty of the land of China. On the Tianjin–Pukou Railway we crossed the steel bridge over the Yellow River, and from Nanjing to Wuhu, again from Wuhu upstream to Hankou, on to Changsha, then to Xiangtan and Xiangxiang, and in the paradise of Yongfeng, we saw the beautiful land and its culture. After reluctantly setting off from Xiangxiang, I saw the actual Xiang River during the bumpy trip from Xiangxiang to Guilin and crossed the river to Zhuzhou, then to Hengyang, heading ever south through Chenzhou. (No wonder that since I read Qin Shaoyou's *Tune: Treading on Sedge* in Nankai Middle School—"The Chen River should be meandering around Chen Mountain, / Why does it flow into the Xiao and Xiang rivers?" tears well up in my eyes whenever I think of it, even to this day). You could say that I crossed the entirety of Hunan, and when I read that Mao Zedong had advocated the independence of Hunan back in 1920, it didn't seem all that crazy for something from back in that hermetic age. Going from Hunan to Guilin in Guangxi, the refugees took the precipitous mountain road toward Guizhou, where everywhere you looked were natural barriers, and when you looked back, you couldn't see the road by which you had come.

Huaiyuan was a beautiful place, and just like Yongfeng in Xiangxiang, it glows brilliantly in my memory.

There is a river (a tributary to the Yi River) at Huaiyuan that at the time I believed to be the clearest in the world. The river flowed past the entrance to the town, and a lovely pavilion stood there, where I sat for a time each day, reading one of the few books I had or watching the small flat-bottomed boats crossing the river.

The boats ferried in the vivid outside world. Sun Yat-sen Middle School stayed at Huaiyuan for about three months with classes officially resumed, and after the New Year in 1939, finals were rigorously conducted.

TWISTS AND TURNS DOWN INTO SICHUAN

The situation in Guangxi was growing tense, so we followed the school along the Sichuan–Guizhou Road to Sichuan, seeking the shelter of Chongqing, the capital during the War of Resistance.

The teachers' families rode in military trucks and students rode in buses if there were buses, and walked if there were none. From Guilin to Guizhou and then the switchbacks of Oumuping into Sichuan, I saw precipitous peaks and the difficulties of the people who used their two humble feet to surmount them.

General Sun Yuanliang, who had graduated from the first Whampoa class, a commander in the regular army during the Northern Expedition and the War of Resistance and now the commander of an even larger military unit, had fought throughout China for half his life. Before his death he was interviewed by Hu Zhiwei and recalled the situation of refugees during the War of Resistance. In the interview, he gave accounts of the big events and examined the mistakes of our own side:

> At the beginning of the War of Resistance, we implemented a scorched-earth policy, encouraging retreat and dispersal, but failed to make appropriate arrangements for our loyal compatriots; nor did we extend a helping hand to those who became refugees, just letting them run helter-skelter as they might and abandoning them to their fate. This was perhaps when we started to lose the hearts and minds of the people on the mainland. When I returned to Guizhou after a long military march from Hanzhong, I saw that the mountain wilds were filled with an army of refugees—railroad and highway workers and their families, wandering teachers and students, industrial

> workers and miners and their families, and nearly a million military families; defeated and dispersed soldiers, hot-blooded young people unwilling to become slaves, men and women, young and old, all became a surging flood of humanity, growing larger as more territory was lost. They lacked the capacity to fight the enemy troops, but they got in the way of our own forces. The tail end of this flood was just ahead of the enemy, but its head was always blocking the advance of our army. All sorts of vehicles, from wheelbarrows to cars and everything else, clogged the roads; the agricultural fields along the way were crowded with people, trampling everything underfoot until there was nothing left, save for long stretches of mud. Vehicles either broke down or got stuck behind those that did. Wherever the army of refugees went, the food would immediately run out, and the locals would panic and soon join the column of refugees. On cold nights, people would light fires to stay warm and the moans of the old, the weak, and the sick could be heard amid the many fires, along with the sad cries of cold and hungry children. Along the way were bloated corpses of those who had fallen and died, and there wasn't a house left intact as far as the eye could see. What sort of world was this? One couldn't help feeling sad and frightened, and soon despondent, and the effect on the hearts and minds of the troops can't be underestimated.

It took an entire year to travel from Nanjing to the Jingning Temple in Ziliujing, Sichuan. That life on the road was filled with untold hardships, but whenever a place could be found for a few dozen people, indoors or outdoors, that was where the teachers would hold class. The school always carried enough textbooks in all subjects, lab instruments, and basic school equipment along.

Today, when I think about how our teachers could hold class at any time, I deeply feel the hopes and faith of China's intellectuals that they represented. They genuinely believed that "though Chu has only three families, it will be Chu that destroys Qin"; in addition to the courses in various subjects, they also taught sacrifice and love, but especially dignity and self-confidence.

After Sun Yat-sen Middle School arrived in Sichuan, the proportion of graduating students who tested into university put the school among the top ten nationwide (after the school arrived in Hankou, several hundred students were admitted from Jiangxi, Hubei, Hunan, and Sichuan). Most of the graduates who entered the workforce went into the military, government, or cultural circles.

With victory over Japan in 1945, most students went back to the homes they had been separated from for a decade, no longer willing to live a wandering life. During the fight between the Kuomintang and the Communists, most decided to stay in their battered homeland to rid it of the residual poison of Manchukuo and reestablish national confidence and education, but they never ever forgot the love, which went beyond blood relations, that they experienced in adversity at Sun Yat-sen Middle School.

The 1990s saw the reestablishment of Sun Yat-sen Middle School in Shenyang, the principal impetus for which came from the students who had returned home after years away, including the provincial governor of Jilin, the secretary of the Liaoning Provincial Party Committee, and the mayor of Shenyang. In those days, they all trudged along the Hunan–Guangxi and Sichuan–Guizhou roads, singing with tears in their eyes, "My home is on the Songhua River. . . ."

In 1984, the Taiwan Sun Yat-sen alumni club published a *National Northeast Sun Yat-sen Middle School Golden Anniversary Commemorative Album*. It was written and compiled by an editorial committee composed of Li Xingtang, then principal of the Police Academy; Liu Shaotang, founder of *Biographical Literature*; and Zhang Linde, executive director of China Airlines; along with Xie Zhonglian, Chen Mingren, Jin Shiguang, Ling Guangwu, Long Shiguang, Shi Shengjiu, Li Guangbi, and Zhao Shumin. The book consisted of sixty recollections of blood and tears, and whoever read it couldn't help but be moved.

Among the pieces, "Fifty Difficult Years" by Zheng Peigao provides a detailed narrative of that rootless decade. It opens:

> The National Northeast Sun Yat-sen Middle School was born amid suffering, and its closing was particularly heartbreaking. From its

founding to today, fifty years have passed; in all that time, has there been one day we could be happy about ourselves? The local worthies surmounted hardship, tasted all kinds of bitterness, busied themselves appealing for the cause of education, and abandoned their personal happiness in order to bring our school into being. Most of them, as far as I know, have left us, and their great ideals have, as of today, still not been fully realized; knowing this, their souls cannot help but feel deep regret. Prior to the school moving south, the upperclassmen from Tianjin and Beiping received less than a month's military training before the Japanese demanded that the Chinese Army remove to south of the Yellow River and cease all anti-Japanese and resistance activities; they also demanded that all student military training cease, among other unreasonable requests. The following morning after raising the flag, General Guan Linzheng, the commander of the Twenty-ninth Army, stepped up to the flag-raising platform and with tears in his eyes announced that training was disbanded, adding, "Our country has been brought to the point that it no longer resembles a country. This anger and hatred must be avenged; otherwise, can we call ourselves men? Can we call ourselves the children of China and descendants of the Emperors Yan and Huang?" Everyone was immediately moved and choked with tears, all anxious to finish off the enemy immediately, even to die the cruelest death without regret. After they were dismissed the ground was covered with tears, clearly visible in rows and columns. . . . The northeast fell; many students and teachers were captured and killed; those who fled to Taiwan had escaped death by a hair's breadth. Recalling the past, who cannot help but feel caught up in the ceaseless quaking of the world?

Zheng Peigao appended a note at the end:

Written on the eve of the fifty-second anniversary of the Mukden Incident. Writing this, I seemed to feel the artillery fire of the Japanese passing overhead while the Northern Military Camp was in a sea of fire.

In addition, whenever anyone mentions Sun Yat-sen Middle School, my clearest impression from that long course of flight is of my father, who, after seeing us safely on the road, would hurry to the next stop to meet the garrisoned troops and arrange for room and board for the students.

Stop after stop, he would rush past my sick mother and my baby sister. By then, I had been "promoted" to riding on the baggage truck, careful at all times not to be jolted off, while my brother joined the troops on foot. Sometimes we would see our father from afar as he rode on a military truck hurrying to the next stop. He seemed not to notice us, as at that time, his mind was filled with those thousand or so students, who were all his children and all had to be taken to a safe place of hope.

3

WITH ME, CHINA SHALL NOT PERISH

Nankai Middle School

ZHANG BOLING, PRINCIPAL OF NANKAI MIDDLE SCHOOL

From the time I left my home on Little Western Hill while still a child, I was often ill, changing schools, or subject to misfortune. Although we passed happy days by the Nanjing fireside, those blissful moments, the birth of my sister and the contentment of my parents, were fleeting and things changed all too quickly. My family followed the displaced students, suffering hardships as we drifted our way over half of China. We arrived in Chongqing via the mountain roads of the southwest and had only just entered the city when five Sun Yat-sen Middle School teachers and students died in the Japanese bombings. The threats of war and death followed us like shadows. In the following seven years, the bombings never ceased and seemed to come with the sunrise and the moonset. But Chongqing was the end of our peregrinations. Sun Yat-sen Middle School had moved five hundred *li* and settled at Jingning Temple near Ziliujing, where school recommenced. Not only did the teaching go on uninterrupted but also new students from Hunan, Guangxi, Guizhou, and locally in Sichuan were taken in.

My father rented a house in Sideli in Chongqing and restarted the Northeast China Association (financed by the government and responsible for training the anti-Japanese underground in northeast China, and disbanded in 1946 after the northeast was returned to China). Shortly after we settled in, however, the house was destroyed by a bomb. My father entrusted someone to find two bungalows outside Shapingba Town—one to live in and one to house the association office. Later the editorial office of *Time and Tide* was also housed there.

Early one morning in November 1938, after making our way across half of China in the year since leaving Nanjing, my father put me in a car, set off from Shangqing Temple, and took me to school.

We drove along the Jialing River, heading upstream for about fifteen miles, and soon after passing Xiaolongkan we saw off in the distance on a yellow earth embankment a group of large reddish buildings. Set amid scattered trees and shrubs, the buildings looked quite imposing. That was Nankai Middle School at Shapingba. In the six years I was there, I matured into a healthy young person, broadened my mind, and developed my lifelong character of positive thinking and aspiration.

After the Japanese occupied northeast China, they used the foreign concession in Tianjin as a base to aggressively extend their evil clutches into north China. For several years, students and teachers at Nankai Middle School and Nankao University engaged in protest marches and called for self-strengthening, patriotism, and fighting the Japanese. Zhang Boling (1876–1951), the principal, knew that the situation was desperate and it was only a matter of time before war would break out. Therefore, as early as 1936, he went to Sichuan to find a place to set up a branch campus. The local gentry of Shapingba contributed the land while all sectors contributed money to build the school. The first year, 160 students were admitted. After the Marco Polo Bridge Incident and the start of war, Nankai Middle School was the first school to be bombed by the Japanese as well as the first school reestablished in the rear with a conviction to maintain a long-term resistance against the Japanese. In 1937, after Shanghai fell, the Nationalist government moved to the wartime capital of Chongqing on December 1. In the eight difficult years of the War of Resistance, Nankai Middle School educated tens of thousands of young people, nearly all of whom continued in the spirit of Zhang Boling.

Principal Zhang's pioneering work was entirely based on his unswerving patriotism. He was the embodiment of "imposing is our Nankai spirit" in our school song, and he left an indelible impression of warmth during those years as I grew up. He was very tall—over six feet—large and robust, but not fat, and broad shouldered. All year round, he wore a long gown and tinted glasses. Almost every day we saw him striding across campus, tall and strong, his shoulders squared. Regardless of how distressing the reports from the front lines or how fierce the Japanese bombings, under Principal Zhang's leadership, we all firmly believed that China would not perish.

Imagine how difficult his life must have been 120 years ago, when he was still young and following his father, who traveled extensively to teach in various old-style private schools while he would study in community-run schools along the way. Because of this, he early on understood the importance of education.

At thirteen, he was awarded government funding to attend the Beiyang Naval Academy. He understood the ideals of enlightened thinkers for founding schools. In those days, reformers in the Qing court like Yan Fu and Wu Jiandeng, as well as a number of young military officers who had studied in England, introduced Western ideas and new thinking in the hope of establishing a strong, modern navy to wipe out the country's humiliation. This will to rejuvenate the nation through hard work made a lasting impression on him.

When Principal Zhang attended the Beiyang Academy, he was the same age as I was when I attended Nankai. I was there for six years and heard him tell many stories at our weekly assemblies, all of which were indelibly etched in my memory.

He graduated from the Beiyang Academy in 1894, just in time for the First Sino-Japanese War. The Beiyang Navy was utterly wiped out—there wasn't even a ship left for the students to use for training. A year later, he had a chance to train on board the Tongji steamship and saw with his own eyes the battleground of Weihaiwei in Shandong turned over by the victorious Japanese to the English for them to occupy. He watched from the territorial waters of his own country as the national flag was changed three times: first down came the Qing banner and up went the Japanese flag, and on the following day it was replaced by the English flag.

Later in life, he would recall, "My breast was filled with anger and sadness and I was deeply pained. Thinking of how feeble the country had become, was there any other choice to survive but self-strengthening? And the means to self-strengthening, after all, came down to education" (*A Look Back at Forty Years at Nankai*, 1944). With anger, he recalled, "The soldiers wore vests, on the front of which was written 'soldier' and on the back of which was written 'brave.' Their clothes were either too big or too small, nothing fit. Their faces were sallow and they were thin and listless. They held large knives in their hands and opium pipes at their waists. They slowly walked out and lowered the dragon banner of the Qing court. Shortly thereafter, the English troops marched out in strict formation and in grand spirit. With one look you could tell the victors from the losers."

He was deeply pained by the shame, and even more so by the lazy and ignorant masses. Without discipline or dedication, they had no idea the country was in imminent peril. He thus believed that the only thing that could bestir the people was education and the teaching of modern knowledge and patriotism. He left the navy resolved to put all his energy into education and establishing schools. In 1908, the Yan family school was expanded into Tianjin Nankai Middle School (the donated land, known as Nankai Hollow, was located in the southwest corner of Tianjin). Before establishing the school he made two trips to Japan to observe various sorts of schools, especially private ones. He was not yet thirty and, full of patriotic fervor, he vowed to dedicate himself to the education of the youth of a new China.

Even more unexpected was that in 1917, at the age of forty-one, he decided to go to Columbia University in the United States to study Western theories of education. Many people tried to dissuade him: "You are already successful and famous. What's the point of going to study with those foreign kids?" Others even said, "Even if you don't mind losing face, we do." But leave he did, studying diligently and working as an intern, engaging in many exchange activities. James Dewey, the father of pragmatism, was his teacher. Upon returning home, he set up Nankai University.

At the start of the War of Resistance, he was loathed by the Japanese for all the patriotic activities he initiated, so they destroyed Nankai. At the time, Chairman Chiang Kai-shek announced, "Nankai sacrificed itself for China; as long as there is a China, there will be a Nankai." And thus Nankai University joined Peking University and Tsinghua University to form National Southwestern Associated University, located in Kunming, which became the most outstanding university during the War of Resistance.

After the victory over Japan, Columbia University awarded Principal Zhang an honorary doctorate in 1946. In 1948, Hu Shi and eleven American scholars jointly authored *There Is Another China*, celebrating his accomplishments at age seventy. The book was compiled and edited by John Leighton Stuart, the president of Yanching University, and published by Columbia's Crown Press. The book was translated into Chinese, with the title meant to point out that, amid the political and military chaos, the Nankai spirit represented a different China, progressing daily and filled with the highest ideals.

From 1904, when there were only seventy-five students, until his death in 1951, Principal Zhang delivered fervent speeches all over the country, promoting the idea of "With me, China shall not perish" and popularizing the ideal of saving the nation through education. So he spoke for over half a century! In those fifty years, disasters in China took on a variety of novel forms, foreign aggression and internal strife in equal measure. Returning home to Tianjin from Chongqing after Japan was defeated, and despite his old age and frail health, he continued to call for peace and cooperation in building China as the Communists and Nationalists fought each other. At seventy-five, as he approached the end of his life, the thing that gave him the greatest comfort was seeing Nankai Middle School and Nankai University reestablished in their old locales in Tianjin.

The figure of Principal Zhang will remain forever in the hearts of the students. In his eight years at Shapingba, he lived in a dorm, and every morning, cane in hand, he would go out for a walk and inspect the campus. Seeing a student studying by the road, he would walk over and pat him on the shoulder, rub his head, and ask if he had enough to wear and to eat. The students at Nankai were all required to live on campus, and he felt that their parents had entrusted them to him, so he had to take good care of them. He had no way of knowing it at the time, but his struggles were not in vain. All of the tens of thousands of students remembered his words regardless of where we ended up in the world, and in our own fields transmitted that undying flame he had ignited.

RECOLLECTIONS OF CARING TEACHERS

I am most grateful for the schoolwork I did while at Nankai, as those six years helped lay the foundation for furthering my studies later in life. In addition to the academic standards it always possessed, Nankai was able to attract quite a few outstanding faculty who had come to Chongqing from Beiping and Tianjin. They heeded Principal Zhang's call and took up residence in Jinnan Village on the Shapingba campus. In the eight years until victory over Japan, very few people left.

Jinnan Village was the first faculty housing I ever saw. Living in those rows of small detached concrete dwellings were many legendary personages the people of Nankai relished talking about, such as my unforgettable Chinese teacher Meng Zhisun, memories of whom I have cherished for decades, and Zhang Yali, the stunning but aloof math teacher who struck fear in the students' hearts. There were also the two daughters of Yu Chuanjian, the head of the school administration. They both had studied abroad in the United States and taught at Nankai after returning to China. "Yu the elder" taught English and "Yu the younger" taught science.

Nankai always emphasized its internationality, and therefore the English-language teaching materials were very advanced. The school was also strong in physics and chemistry, and the students who went on to study those subjects in the university were in a class of their own. The teaching of mathematics was also very solid, and it were probably the first middle school at that time to teach calculus. My schoolwork was pretty good in those days, with the exception of mathematics, especially geometry. For the life of me, I couldn't grasp why some lines were imaginary and some real. For me, there were only real lines, no imaginary ones.

Old Zheng, who taught chemistry, was an oddball. Very few people called him by his name, Zheng Xinting. He didn't teach the middle-school girl students, but every time we heard the boys mimic his Shandong accent when reciting chemical formulas or how, after a few drinks in the dorm, he would tell the boys stories from the *Romance of the Three Kingdoms*, we were all very envious. In addition, he also had many heroic words to encourage the "real men."

Geography teacher Wu Zhenzhi taught junior high Chinese history. In mentioning Taiwan, she told us to remember *Ji* (chicken) *Dan* (egg) *Gao* (cake) (Jilong, Danshui, Gaoxiong). We called her "chicken egg cake" behind her back. In senior high, she taught world geography and often lugged around several large, thick foreign tomes from which she would show us pictures of various places in the world, expanding our perspective. One year at the beginning of summer, her fiancé was on a small steam launch on the Jialing River when the boat capsized. When the terrible news reached us, several of us girls went to her room in the singles dorm and slid a letter under her door in which we had written, "Miss, we weep with you. . . ." After that, no one ever referred to her by the nickname again. Early in 1948, I ran into her on the stairway at the College of Liberal Arts of National Taiwan University as she was on her way to see the dean, Shen Gangbo. We stayed in touch until she retired from the College of Liberal Arts at National Cheng Kung University. I also went to see her one last time in the hospital at the end of her life.

I recall there was a math teacher with the surname of Kang, who was the son of Kang Nairu, one of the founders of the school. He was a good teacher and well known among the girl students. I forget his first name, but everyone called him Kang the Junior. He was tall and single, and all the girls thought he was handsome, except me. During the war, everyone wore cotton-padded jackets and straw sandals, but he was unique in that he often wore a white Western-style suit.

At the time, he was fond of one of the girl students in our class, who was also the class belle. She sat only a seat away from me. We frequently had quizzes, at which time Teacher Kang would walk between our seats, pacing back and forth while proctoring. Occasionally he would bend over to see if the student knew what to write or had any questions. Each time he bent over that one girl, the entire class would make faces, giving each other a nudge and a wink. We wrote with brushes in those days, and we each had an inkstone. One classmate was really angry and found it annoying that he only looked at her, so she rubbed a good deal of ink in her inkstone and put it on the edge of her desk so that it hung over a bit. When Teacher Kang passed by, he bumped against it and the ink spilled all over his white suit. Angry, he blurted out in his Tianjin Mandarin: "What's the meaning of this?" The girls played such pranks on their male teachers, and sometimes it could get pretty nasty.

The teacher who had the greatest influence on me was my Chinese teacher, Meng Zhisun. The celebrated Nankai Chinese textbooks—twelve volumes for six years from the first year of junior high to the last grade of senior high—were edited by Mr. Meng. The texts selected for the junior high years went from the easy to the difficult, with an equal emphasis on both the vernacular and classical language. Excellent works from the May Fourth period and after inspired us to the creation of new literature. The textbooks for the senior high years were a veritable anthology of the history of Chinese literature, beginning with the *Book of Poetry* and continuing up to the Republican period. The developments in each period were elucidated and the selections were all the choicest.

During my second year of high school, Mr. Meng not only taught my Chinese course but also introduced a set of elective courses rarely seen in middle school curriculums, which included a junior-year class on poetry offered to all levels, both boys and girls, and a senior-year song-lyric class. I was all grown up, and in addition to the other required classes and preparing for the National Joint College Entrance Exams, I spent my time, day and night, memorizing poems. Calmly recollecting it today, I realize I must have memorized most of the important works of Chinese literature in those two years.

In addition to teaching classes, Teacher Meng was like a father to me. He loaned me all the books he felt I would be able to read, and sometimes he would say, "Today we're having fried bean sauce noodles at our house, why don't you come and join us?" That was one of the tastiest things I remember eating.

Nankai teachers, regardless of what period they are judged against, were all knowledgeable and sought to inspire creativity, just like so many of the teachers at Sun Yat-sen Middle School fondly remembered by their students. Amid the flames of war, they fled from the north to Sichuan, heeding Principal Zhang's call for education, sharing both the bitter and the sweet.

In 2004 in the fiftieth anniversary souvenir book of the class of 1943, the most memories were about Teacher Meng and Teacher Zheng (the boys said that 40 percent of the graduates chose chemistry and related fields because of Old Zheng). One piece titled "Calling for the Education of Man" by a classmate named Fu Guoyong tells the story of the famous physics teacher, Wei Rongjue: Xie Bangmin, who was in the class of 1941 and one of Mr. Meng's prize pupils, handed in a blank exam, on which he instead composed a poem recounting his aspirations, but assumed that he wouldn't be able to graduate. When Mr. Wei evaluated the exam, he wrote four lines: "A blank paper it is, but the poem is good. Each has his own ambitions—so a bare pass for you too." Xie tested into the Law Department at National Southwestern Associated University and later taught at Peking University. Many such stories circulated on campus, and it comes as no surprise that Nankai teachers are so fondly remembered.

Physical education at Nankai was also famous throughout the country. Every day at 3:30 p.m., all classrooms were locked and everyone had to go to the playing field and join in some ball game. Sports practice and competition were mandatory except on rainy days; there was no evading it.

At first, I thought softball (there was little baseball in those days) was less rough and suitable for me because I was so thin and not very strong. Who knew that running the bases required great speed? After much ridicule, I discovered that, in actual fact, I could run very fast. My friend Cheng Keyong was not very tall, but she ran surprisingly fast and was thus nicknamed "Jeep Car." With practice, I went from being a reserve player standing on the sidelines to first baseman in six months, and in my third year of junior high, I actually became a member of the girls' track and field team and competed in sprinting, high jump, and long jump. One teacher praised my high and long jumps, saying they appeared so effortless, I seemed to float through the air.

My parents were incredulous with regard to my athletic performance. One day my mother worked up enough courage to come and watch me compete, probably a one-hundred-yard dash. Worried as she could be, she was prepared to pick me up and take me home when I collapsed. Sixty years later, I still remember the wind whistling through my short hair as I made the long jump and landed in the sand pit. It was the first time that a spindly fifteen-year-old girl felt that life was great and was confident of her existence.

But in fact, physical education did entail one nightmare—tap dancing.

Teacher Gao was my physical education instructor for several years. She was of upright posture and had a graceful figure. Tap dancing was required, and all the students all danced according to the instructions, but I could never keep up. The teacher held a little baton and often struck my ankles and said, "Your schoolwork is so good, but how come your feet are so clumsy?" Later she came to Taiwan and my classmates went to see her. Not me, because I had been struck by her so many times. I really couldn't dance and didn't know why I was so incompetent. I just couldn't tap dance, and she really did hit me with the baton and in all sincerity called me stupid. I was ashamed of myself, but in no way did I ever blame her.

A ROOM WITH EIGHTEEN BEDS

Throughout our years in middle school, we all earnestly looked forward to going home each Saturday at 3:30. Decades later, I always wait for something good to happen on that day at that hour.

All students were required to reside on campus because Nankai was located in the suburbs. Althouh my family lived some two *li* from school,

I too had to live on campus. In those days transportation by car was virtually impossible. The wartime slogan was: "A drop of petrol, a drop of blood." I never heard of any family having a private car.

Every room in the girls' dormitory had eighteen plank beds, three rows of six beds each, between which there was only enough space for one person to walk. Beneath each bed was a small wooden trunk for each girl to store her clothes. Self-study time morning and evening was regulated the same way as regular classes. Every Saturday at 3:30 p.m. you could go home, but you had to be back by 6 p.m. on Sunday.

I lived in the dormitory for six years, and it was like growing up in a huge family, filled with memories of conflicts between group discipline and individual interest. The most interesting times were in the morning and in the evening after the lights went out.

During the war, in large organizations and schools, bugle calls announced the time for rising and retiring and the start and end of class. This was because we could not afford large clocks while we moved around, and electric clocks were beyond our wildest dreams. Every morning at six o'clock, before it was fully light, the shrill and persistent bugle call indicated it was time to rise and shine. We would struggle to climb out of our bedbug-ridden plank beds, which was especially hard on winter days. When we would line up on the playing field, often the mist would be so thick that you couldn't make out the faces of the next class. The time preceding morning calisthenics was devoted to a lecture by Wang Wentian, the director of the middle school girls' section. For the rest of our lives, few of us would forget what she said to us, "Your minds grow grass and your heads emit smoke!" For some reason, many years later when recalling this, everyone would laugh happily.

In those days, the girls were not the only ones afraid of her; the boys were very much afraid of her too. While they were in school, the more timid of the boys never dared enter the gate of the girls' section. To this day it remains a mystery to me how such a serious woman (we called her the Sphinx behind her back) like her, who graduated from the first girls' class and studied overseas in Germany, could marry after the age of forty (she married famous scholar Li Shuhua after his first wife died). Some years later, when I was past forty, I went to see her in New York.

When she opened the door I asked her, "Do you still remember me?" She replied with tears rolling from her eyes, "Oh my, why wouldn't I remember you and that class of mischievous imps?" In those years, as soon as she spoke through the morning fog, we'd immediately forget our dreams from the previous night. Her voice was like a small cannon, and in her Tianjin Mandarin she would berate us for being beyond hope. How could she now have such a warm image of us as mischievous imps?

An even more interesting part of dorm life came after the lackluster bugle call for lights out. Sleep did not necessarily follow upon darkness. On moonless nights we knew there would be no air-raid sirens, and it was the only time the girls in the eighteen beds could have heart-to-heart talks. Naturally seventeen- and eighteen-year-old girls had a yearning for love. They were able to find hints of love in the words and between the lines (such things wouldn't have been expressed clearly in those days) in all books, whether textbooks or casual reading. All poems were filled with the fever of spring and the melancholy of autumn. But in the middle school of those days, no one would bill and coo, much less admit to having fallen in love. If anyone did admit to being in a relationship, she probably would have been expelled.

The worst thing about dorm life was the bedbugs, and they were particularly active in the Nankai dorms. When we went home we were not permitted to take our luggage indoors but had to first put it out in the courtyard under the sun. Our duvet had to be opened and washed and if a bedbug was found, it had to be thrown away. Sometimes bedbugs were even found in our books. Zhang Zhongmei's autobiography also mentions the bedbugs at Nankai Middle School and the student protests about them to the school administration.

In order to deal with the bedbugs, every few weeks three or four of us girls would carry the plank beds to the steam room next to the boys' dorm and steam them, managing to get rid of some of the vermin at least. Later we discovered it was relatively ineffective because the bedbugs would secret themselves in the floor or the ceiling, and there was no way to scald the whole room. On nights before exams, the lights would stay on an extra hour or two. Battling the books at night, we'd see a frightening scene of a column of bedbugs descending the electric wire from which a naked bulb without a shade hung. Even from the floor countless bedbugs could be seen crawling beside our feet. We could do nothing but scratch the itch of the bedbugs as they climbed on us while we tried to sleep. None of us would forget this for as long as we lived.

Nothing could be done about the bedbugs. The school couldn't solve the problem because there was no system of sterilization. DDT didn't exist during the war; if it had, it would have been something magical. Only after we graduated and left school did we escape the menace. As for the mosquitoes and the flies, they hardly require mention. Despite this, Nankai was considered quite hygiene conscious—the cafeteria windows did have screens. But regardless of how conscious it was, it was impossible to resolve all the hygiene issues in those difficult surroundings. Thinking back on our younger days, all of us were badly bitten, and it really wasn't easy. The bedbugs, as hateful as the Japanese planes, engulfed and plagued us in the same way as yet one more nightmare. If I start writing about them, I will never stop. In those years we resisted with our young flesh and blood.

GENERAL LI MI'S WAR HORSE

I was skinny and not very robust the first two years of junior high. I even became the butt of jokes for my classmates because I sometimes fainted during the long morning flag raising and speech. When it was too hot or too cold and we had to stand for any length of time, someone would say, "Watch, Chi Pang-yuan is going to faint any minute." I was often a disappointment to myself and really did faint.

Toward the end of the first semester of the second year, it suddenly became extremely cold and most of us developed chilblains on our fingers and heels. Having stood for a time at a weekly meeting in the fog on the playing field, I grew faint and was about to collapse when I heard Li Xin'e, a classmate standing to my left, quietly say, "Give me your hands and I'll rub them, it will make you feel better." She pressed my wrists a few times and then the left side of my forehead. It hurt a lot, but I did grow steady and my breathing became smoother. Back in the classroom, she took out a small bottle from her desk, poured out a few pills, and told me to take them. I actually went against my father's warning never to casually take medicine, and I felt quite well all day after taking her pills.

Li Xin'e enrolled late, joining our class two months after the second year began. Refugees were pouring into Chongqing from all the provinces of China in those days, and owing to wartime needs, Nankai allowed qualified students to enroll late and enter at any time. I myself took the exam and was admitted to my first year in November.

However, in order to maintain teaching standards, the school mandated that if at the end of the semester, a student failed one third of his or her classes, they would be held back, and if they failed one half, they would be expelled, regardless of who their parents were. After summer break, grades for the entire school were posted publicly at the administration center in the Fansun Building, and those with more red marks were held back. This was the infamous "Red Roll" that made everyone tremble. I remember one year everyone was so squeezed together to get a glimpse that the floor gave way.

The day Li Xin'e joined our class, the teacher in charge brought her to the door and said loudly, "This is Li Xin'e, a new student." She was very small and was given the seat to my left. I, too, was skinny and short back then and sat in the first row. She looked both shy and frightened standing there in the doorway, the way I must have looked the six times I enrolled late and entered a strange new class before coming to Nankai. Since she was seated next to me in class, she also stood beside me at flag raising and morning calisthenics. I tried to help familiarize her with everything at school, especially where we were in the coursework and what homework had to be handed in the following day, and so on. She didn't say much of anything but just smiled and listened with gratitude. Then just before the New Year on a Saturday afternoon, when the dormitory was nearly empty, I saw her sitting on the edge of her bed, crying.

That afternoon, it was my turn to be the student on duty. After sweeping out the classroom, I returned to the dorm to get my small bag before returning home. Passing through the neighboring room, I saw her all alone, and in all earnestness I took her home with me.

Ever since we lived on Ninghai Road in Nanjing, where my parents entertained the Whampoa students from northeast China, they had always entertained guests with the simple but abundant food and drink of the northeast; they did this for nearly a half century until they passed away. After arriving in Shapingba, my brother tested into the Medical School of National Central University, but all he really wanted to do was be a diplomat, so he tested again and got into the Foreign Affairs Department at the National Political Academy. My mother encouraged him to bring his classmates who had no home of their own to have dinner with us. She couldn't stand for a child to be homeless or to go hungry.

Li Xin'e was the first guest I ever brought home. She was puny and weak like me, which only made my mother all the more concerned about her. All we knew was that she was from Yunnan and that her father was a soldier garrisoned at Chongqing. He brought her with him to attended Nankai, but her mother hadn't come. From then on I invited her home almost every weekend. After learning that she was stunted because she had suffered from malaria, my mother showered her with affectionate concern, providing her with extra nourishment and treating her like her own daughter.

After the spring of 1939, the Japanese intensified their bombing of Chongqing. They came every day except when it rained; they even came on moonlit nights. The air-raid shelters hastily built by the people were sufficient to protect against shrapnel but not against a direct hit. Air defense observation posts were located on the high mountains all around Chongqing, and when there was an air raid, a red lantern would be hung from a tall pole in front of the observation post accompanied by a siren, which sounded alternately long and short. When the enemy aircraft advanced a certain distance, another red lantern was hung, which was followed by the siren resounding within and without the city. That shrill, woeful sound pierced our hearts and souls, resembling a harbinger of death. That was particularly the case when you were awakened with a start in the middle of a moonlit night and had to immediately jump out of bed, fasten your belt, put on your shoes, and run for your life. The confusion and anger, together with the air-raid sirens that kept howling for many years, etched a deep wound on my heart that has never healed.

Nankai couldn't build air-raid shelters on level ground. The only thing we could do when the air-raid siren blared was to scatter. At every weekly meeting, the students were led in reciting the following mantra: "One air-raid sounds; two pairs of clothes, three people make their way together, four sides all checked. . . ."

Behind the girls' classrooms were lots of little sand dunes like countless foxholes, and when fleeing, three people would run together and crouch against a sand dune. When the sky was clear, you could see the red suns on the wings of the Japanese bombers; once the wings tilted a string of cone-shaped silver bombs would fall from their bellies. Sometimes we would see our pursuit planes arrive from the opposite direction to engage them in battle with machine guns blazing loudly in midair. Other times we'd see black smoke pour from a plane as it fell, a fireball, to earth. Our hearts burned with hatred for the Japanese, a feeling built on my own flesh-and-blood experience through the years of my growing up and impossible to erase. Eight long years spent wandering over my country with no feeling of security, with even the blue sky violent. How can it be forgotten?

In June of that year, the government ordered that after July all students, the old, the infirm, women, and children should disperse to the suburbs where there were more trees, so as to lessen the casualties. One day Li Xin'e came and told my parents that her father had invited us to come and take shelter at his garrison in a place called Huangjueya and that we could return when classes resumed after the summer break. My father asked her father's name and military region and learned he was a division commander of the Yunnan Army by the name of General Li Mi.

At the start of summer break, my mother and I and my two younger sisters crossed the Yangtze River. Crossing, a crewman shouted, "They've hung a warning! Pull harder, come on! Pull to the shore." On shore, we boarded a military car and drove about thirty *li* to a temporary military base outside a village surrounded by mountains. Li Xin'e's father came out in military dress to meet us. I never expected that someone as puny as she would have such a handsome and imposing father. Three days later, he left for another defense zone and didn't return until the end of August, by which time we had returned to Shapingba.

At the Huangjueya military area, I had another experience to make me proud. Three days after settling in, Li Xin'e took me horseback riding in the morning. During my childhood days in the northeast, my grandfather had horses, and most men rode horses between villages, but for me it was an unattainable dream! That morning, the orderly led out two huge horses. We didn't even reach the height of the horses' backs. The horse soldier said that the horses had to be taken out for a run each morning and if he put us two "dolls" on their backs, they "wouldn't even know it!"

Leaping onto her horse with ease, Li Xin'e clearly knew how to ride. But I stood beside my horse—they were giving me the commander's horse as a special treat—simply at my wits' end and only thinking to escape. But the horse soldier just smiled and placed my left foot in the stirrup, then helped me onto the horse. Then he told me to just straddle it and put my right foot in the stirrup. Sitting securely astride the tall horse, I tightly grasped the reins in both hands. From a trot to a canter, the horse soldier never took his hand off the bridle. Several days later, surprisingly, I dared to let the horse gallop. Thirty *li* away, Chongqing was still undergoing the bombardment of vicious Japanese planes as the sirens wailed day and night. But living at the base, I finally got to enjoy some temporary security. Every morning as I galloped the horse on the dirt road among the trees, I felt the cool wind blowing through my short hair.

I couldn't have imagined that feeling even in my wildest dreams. On horseback, Li Xin'e was self-confident, steady, a completely different person from at school. She said that at home in Yunnan, if she accompanied her father for redeployment, being able to ride was a must. And there I was, through some predestined chance to ride General Li Mi's war horse! Her description of the lofty and precipitous peaks on the Yunnan–Burma border and the rapid waters through narrow gorges roused my boundless imagination. In those years, I often wished I was a boy so that I could join the army when I grew up and be in the cavalry, like the broadsword group in the Twenty-ninth Army who went from Xifengkou on the Great Wall to Nantian Gate, or like the Mongolian ancestors of my maternal grandmother, who would leap on a horse and travel thousands of *li*. There was no way I would cower beside a sand dune and let the Japs, those dwarf pirates, bomb me right over my head. Two girls, one from the extreme north and one from the extreme southwest of China, became good friends under the enemy bombings. The affection gained by sharing adversity together is something those who grow up in peacetime can never imagine. This was especially true during nighttime attacks, when we were halfway to the shelter and, urged on by the air-raid sirens, tried to find a sheltering sand dune by the light of the moon, holding and pulling each other along, calling each other's names, and then after sitting down, listening to the bombs near and far and seeing the light of fires thirty *li* away in the city. Two fifteen-year-old girls huddled together, shouldering the same incomprehensible terror. When the sirens ceased it was generally two or three in the morning. The slow, extended all-clear siren sounded, as if it were a prolonged sigh of relief rejoicing in the fact that we were still alive. Several hundred people who fled in the night and didn't get a wink of sleep staggered back to the dorms, and very few had any interest in looking up at the skies that had just brought the threat of death. The moon was setting, the stars twinkling, but I did not find the starry sky at all beautiful.

After graduating from junior high, Li Xin'e returned to Yunnan with her father. The war had pressed close to the southwestern provinces and the newly constructed Burma Road along the border needed strong defense. The last time she visited my house, she brought a jade bangle wrapped in brocade and asked my mother to keep it for her, saying it was a souvenir of her mother, who was no longer "around." To this day I am not really sure what she meant by that, as she hardly ever brought up her family life in Yunnan. Save for one letter she wrote just after returning there, we lost touch after she left Chongqing and the War of Resistance ended. Ten years later, my family once again having fled a few years before, this time to Taiwan, and amid the call to counterattack mainland China, the newspapers printed a major story about how the last holdout on the Yunnan–Vietnam border, the Nationalist general Li Mi, had been ordered to retreat to Taiwan. After fighting in one place after another for ten thousand *li*, he had rejoined his unit to a hero's welcome. When he appeared before the Legislative Yuan to make his report, my father arranged to meet with him and asked that he give the bangle to Li Xin'e. It was only then that we learned she had married and was living abroad. General Li was surprised to see the bangle. The two of them talked about Chongqing as the center of the War of Resistance, their confidence and fighting spirit in those days, and the current situation in which they had retreated to a remote corner of the ocean. Filled with so much emotion, all they could do was sigh.

THE GIRL SCOUT DREAM OF DOING ONE GOOD DEED A DAY

One of my happiest memories of my three years in junior high is of scout training. In wartime, young people are more courageous because they really are innocent, and in matters of patriotism they never lag behind.

After the fire resulting from the worst bombing of Chongqing, we selected a group of representative scouts to walk into the city to contribute to the effort to save the country. We had gone more than halfway, and all we encountered was countless charred corpses removed from the still burning city by the soldiers. With a Sichuan accent, the commanding officer asked the teacher leading us, "What are these little girls here for? Hurry up and take them back."

We stood by the roadside crying our eyes out and singing, "We, we are the little soldiers of the Chinese people; though small, our aspirations are high. . . ." It was said that upon returning to the school, the teacher was given a major demerit. But that ten-*li* stream of blackened corpses remained a nightmare for the better part of my life.

To this day I still remember going to the foot of Gele Mountain and practicing with signal flags. I diligently transmitted information on the enemy situation and felt myself more than useful. And because a scout was expected to perform one good deed a day, I always hoped to chance upon someone in need of assistance each time I passed through Shapingba on my way home. But Shapingba was already well known as a town of culture because of the tens of thousands of students and teachers there at Central University, Chongqing University, and Nankai Middle School. There wasn't much chance for a scout to do a daily good deed, which made us feel there was no way to show ourselves off.

Not long after the start of my third year in junior high, some foreigners paid a visit with Nankai as their first stop. A classmate and I were sent to the main gate to stand as sentries. I had just been promoted to junior squad leader and thought I was performing some really important function as I stood there in my scout uniform with an epaulette that resembled a braid on my shoulder, baton in hand, and a scarf sporting the purple and white of Nankai.

By coincidence, Zhang Dafei arrived at our house from Chongqing that very day—he had started flying pursuit to fight with the Japanese planes. He had passed the front gate of Nankai and, after arriving at our house, said to my mother, "I just saw Pang-yuan standing sentry outside the school gate, and her arm is as thin as the baton she was carrying."

I didn't think anything about it because everyone said I was too skinny. I, on the other hand, said that fat people were tacky. In those days, I had no awareness of my appearance, pretty or ugly. My hair was cut like a boy's and I never looked in the mirror, never really paying any attention to the differences between boys and girls. My cousin Bao Gang was the exact opposite. She was very pretty and in her junior year at Sun Yat-sen Middle School, it was said that she was the belle of the school. When she came home during summer break, she spent all day in front of the mirror and, displeased with my carelessness about my appearance, she said, "Why are you still such a child?"

In point of fact, my years in junior high did feel like an extension of my childhood. I, who had changed schools all over the place from an early age, now entered a period of steady growth. In the fine atmosphere for study at Nankai and under the salutary influence of my teachers, I established the basis for a lifetime of study and good conduct.

Before the start of school that year, my mother had several light blue long-gown uniforms made of indanthrene (a material you could wash over a lifetime and it wouldn't fade; I never saw the material after I got to Taiwan) made for me in the town, because I was going to start senior high and a scout uniform was no longer acceptable. One morning, wearing a short-sleeved, light blue uniform, I walked up the slope in front of our door, following the ridge separating the fields. You had to be nimble and have good balance to walk the narrow ridges covered in tall grass. The fields on either side of the path were full of water due to the recent rains, and looking down for a moment, I caught sight of a girl's reflection in the water—it was me in my long gown! I extended both arms to keep my balance, and my face was filled with concentration and radiant with happiness. The sky above was so high, so blue, with the white clouds that never stopped changing floating overhead. At sixteen, I for the first time had used that huge mirror between the heavens and the earth.

The signal fires burned intensely and the sound of bombs accompanied our studies. When we weren't fleeing on account of the air-raid sirens, we buried ourselves in our studies; when the air-raid siren sounded, we carried our textbooks with us to prepare for the following day's test. Children who grow up in such an environment are more conscious of potential threats even in times of peace and mature more quickly than those who grow up in today's happy surroundings, but their souls age more quickly as well. In such difficult conditions, we ate poorly, dressed poorly, were eaten alive by bedbugs at night, and had to flee air raids by day and were not spared on moonlit nights. But precisely because of this, what little time remained was even more precious. Our teacher said, "If you don't make an effort to be a good person, you'll just end up being put aside." It had the same admonitory and frightening effect as not taking proper cover during an air raid and being blown to bits. At flag raising each morning, the teachers would always give us a pep talk, and this "percussive education" provided by Nankai influenced us deeply. As the flames of war burned over time, our teachers joined hands to protect this pure land of learning, and with perservance and diligence lifted us from being immature children to becoming sensible young people. We grew up properly in adverse circumstances; just as Principal Zhang Boling said, "Even if you don't wear the school badge outside, you must still let people see that you are from Nankai."

A LITERARY YOUTH UNDER FALLING BOMBS

In the summer break of 1940, looking at the publicly posted roll of students, I knew that I had successfully graduated from junior high and had been admitted to senior high, which gave me temporary relief from the pressure of schoolwork. During the long days of summer, I frequently cut across the Central University campus on my way to the Jialing River, where I'd sit on the corner of a rock beside the water and read. That place, to which no path led, was suspended above the river where the water ran very clear.

I read classical Chinese fiction voraciously. I read *The Water Margin* twice and I had read *Dream of the Red Chamber* six times without growing tired of it, mainly because the male and female characters were all beautiful and endearing, living in a completely different world from one of war and flight. The characters in *Journey to the West* were all ugly, and as for *Romance of the Three Kingdoms*, well, probably only my father understood it.

After advancing to senior high, I took off my scout uniform and put on a long cheongsam. The cheongsam for spring and summer was light blue and made of indanthrene in autumn and winter. This affected me psychologically and I even walked differently, conscious that I was a sixteen-year-old girl. From then on, schoolwork was more than just schoolwork (with the exception of math)—it was knowledge. I felt that all topics, from the simplest to the most profound, began to enlighten me in some way.

I was happiest in my junior year. Miss Wu Zhenzhi was assigned to teach world cultural geography to my class, which brought together all the most important currents and changes in world history. Miss Wu placed particular emphasis on history and current trends and developments and she would sometimes draw a world map on the blackboard: Greece, Rome, and Carthage; she would lecture on Queen Elizabeth I and the Spanish Armada; the voyages of Columbus; the exploration of the North and South Poles, India, and the Middle East; as well as the backwardness and mystery of Africa. Each class would hold us spellbound like some legend of the high seas. The textbook was already full of information, but our teacher would frequently bring large foreign books and pictures rarely seen at the time to show us. Her voice was deep and full of feeling, as if she were often examining the vicissitudes of the vast globe. Perhaps that class of girls understood that the depth of her voice was a result of her having recently suffered the greatest bereavement a young teacher of twenty-three or twenty-four could suffer. Taking this class when growing up led me to look forward to reading and traveling later in life. With such youthful knowledge and longing as a basis, one could explore the depths of other cultures and not be satisfied with superficiality and blindly making one's way forward.

That happy year, Mr. Meng Zhisun taught our Chinese class. I also elected to take his first poetry class, so all together I had class with him seven times a week.

He must have been around fifty, which made him incredibly old in our eyes. Wearing a light- or dark-colored serge scholar's robe all year round, he was neither handsome nor elegant (although occasionally he would wear a black or white tunic suit). He had a rather harsh Tianjin accent, but as soon as he started to lecture, everyone was immediately all ears. His words were not a stream but a river, broad, endless, and deep, which here and there would pick up speed depending on what poems or essays he was discussing. Fifty years later, in a commemorative volume by Chongqing Nankai students, the most memories recorded were about Chinese class, almost all of which were about Mr. Meng. (More than thirty years ago, Lu Qiao penned a long remembrance in his book *Repentant Love Letter.*) One piece in particular by a male classmate named Zhu Yongfu, titled "The Enthusiasm of Master Meng," recorded in detail how the success of the teaching materials in our Chinese class stemmed entirely from the editorship of Mr. Meng and also how his lectures were "lively, brilliant, and filled with enthusiasm. Anyone who listened to his class would be spellbound as he guided our echoing emotions through the world of Tang and Song poetry. Only when the bell rang indicating the end of class was everyone brought back to reality as if waking from a dream." He also said that the girls' classes were unfortunate in that they never saw Mr. Meng express his feelings, the scintillating and passionate expression of joy and anger.

Although such was the case, I was grown up at that time and in the middle of the national calamity and could certainly understand why Mr. Meng said there wasn't enough time to read the entire *Records of the Grand Historian*, but if one still wanted to read the best parts, one could start with Sima Qian's biographies of unlucky individuals; "The Basic Annals of Xiang Yu" was altogether superior to "The Basic Annals of Liu Bang." The experience of fleeing thousands of *li* from Nanjing to Sichuan allowed me to clearly understand why Mr. Meng, when teaching the poems of Du Fu, would be unable to contain his tears as he spoke, with silent resentment and sadness pervading the classroom, lingering on and on.

I was immersed in Mr. Meng's classes on poetry for two years. Like one intoxicated, I memorized, recited, and appreciated all the poems, and they remain as clear as ever in my mind even today. Later, at Wuhan University, I took Zhu Guangqian's English poetry classes, where I memorized and recited another hundred or more English poems. For four years, the similarities and differences in meaning and mood evoked by Chinese and English poetry stirred and reverberated in my mind; their fusion, in the early morning of life, made me who I am, much like the line in Qin Zihao's poem "The Golden Mask": "So sad, so happy, so unique."

TIME AND TIDE MAGAZINE AND THE DEBATE COMPETITION

In high school I edited the girls' wall newspaper and even took up the writing brush to write some parts of the whole page (my clear, stiff hand in the print style and later my writing in English on the blackboard show that I have never been able to write in an elegant cursive style); later, in the debating society, I bowled over the opponents with well-founded arguments, much of which came from the latest materials at the *Time and Tide* magazine editorial office, many of which were internationally authoritative works written in English.

Time and Tide was established with money raised by a couple of young intellectuals from the northeast in the dark days of 1938 after they retreated to Hankou from Nanjing and Shanghai. They asked my father to run the magazine, which, aimed at introducing the current international situation and familiarizing people with trends and global events, became quite successful upon publication. Shortly after we retreated to Chongqing in 1939, the street on which the print shop was located was bombed. My father located an old machine and set up a print shop and the editorial office outside of Shapingba, after which publication became regular.

It could truly be said that during the war years Chongqing was the cultural center of the country. In addition to members of the government, most intellectuals and students employed whatever means possible to get to Chongqing, not simply to avoid being the subjects of the invader but to come forward and contribute their own strength to the protracted War of Resistance.

Time and Tide established its reputation shortly after publication began in Hankou, and after it moved to Chongqing, the editorial staff increased and production became smoother. At the very beginning most of those involved were brilliant students from the foreign language and literature departments of the country's elite universities. Some, such as Liu Shengbin and Deng Lianxi, already had writing experience and were recommended by the Northeast China Association (after the fall of the northeast and north China, my father's work shifted from organizing underground armed resistance against the Japanese to culture and education). Owing to the convenient location at Shapingba, Professor Jia Wu (Linan) of National Central University was engaged to serve as chief editor, and most of the translators and editors were professors at National Central University and Chongqing University. Four or five years later, quite a few talented translators were hired, and among the youngest of the editors were Wu Xizhen, He Xin, and Wang Yiding. They made significant contributions in cultural education and economics after coming to Taiwan, but working at *Time and Tide* was their first job out of university. Later, Mr. Wang was sent to Taiwan by the Relief and Rehabilitation Administration of the U.S.-Sino Cooperation Agency. I arrived at National Taiwan University in 1947, and he often borrowed a jeep on weekends to take He Xin and me to visit various scenic spots outside of Taipei. They reminisced about when they worked at *Time and Tide*, the challenges, the joys and sorrows of life during the War of Resistance, and the various changes after the war, both abroad and in China. There was no end to the topics we discussed, and decades later we often got together; there was never a dull moment.

In order to obtain the latest information on World War II, *Time and Tide* dispatched Liu Shengbin to London and Deng Lianxi to Washington, DC, to collect and read all the dailies (the magazine had translation rights to *The London Times* and *The New York Times*) as well as the latest magazines and books. They would send the most useful clippings, discussions, and analyses of major events to India, where Shen Xuyu, special correspondent to India, would send them by airplane "over the hump" of the Himalayas. During the war, military and daily supplies sent to China by the British and the Americans all arrived in Chongqing via India. In his early days as a pilot, Zhang Dafei was often sent to India to fly the American aid planes back to Yunnan or Sichuan in China. It took about seven days for the materials to get to Chongqing. After the editorial staff received them, they would immediately begin working around the clock to translate them into Chinese, thus allowing *Time and Tide*, as a fortnightly, to stay up to date.

In those days in that far-off city in the hinterland, a publication like *Time and Tide* was very welcome, valued by the government and the general public alike, and it almost always sold out immediately after publication. Many people said it was like an open window in the abyss of suffering behind the battle lines, allowing them to see the outside world. Before and after the United States entered the war, each issue was reprinted four or five times; the presses were so hot as to burn the hand.

The shrewd and perspicacious selection of materials, the fine translations, and the high level of discussion all served to make *Time and Tide* a publication to which few others could hold a candle.

The office of *Time and Tide* was nearby, only about fifty yards from our house, across from a paddy field, and we could see the office lights from the house. Prior to the publication of each issue, my father would simply sleep in the office in order to spend long nights going over the manuscripts until late. My mother would always watch the lights when he was there; as long as the lights were on, she would not sleep either. That was probably an expression of love for their generation! I remember that the lights would only go off around one or two o'clock in the morning.

I ran out the school gate every Saturday at 3:30, walked down the only big street in the town, and took a small path to the right that led to that small white house. I always went to the editorial office to see if my father was there. On weekends he would come home from Chongqing, but would first go to the office to examine the new information and translated manuscripts, hold meetings, and decide on the table of contents for the next issue. Passing through Shapingba to his small director's office, I'd buy a big bag of peanuts and go into his office and sit on the single bed he had there, the one on which he slept during those nights spent reading manuscripts, and shell and eat peanuts (his desk was filled with manuscripts, which he wouldn't let me touch). If he wasn't there, I shelled a big handful of the best peanuts and put them in a little earthen jar for him. In those days, shelling peanuts was probably something men in their forties, especially those working in the government, would never voluntarily do themselves. One day he told me that I could no longer sit on his bed and eat things, because the night before a rat had come and bitten his nose.

At some point after I started high school, my "uncles" in the editorial office decided that my knowledge should go beyond eating peanuts, and having also formed a better opinion of me because my questions were getting more and more profound, they would lend me interesting English articles they had already used or were not going to use to read, including some on different customs and cultural trends. Later when I accompanied the magazine staff to the air-raid shelter at the sound of the siren, chief editor Uncle Jia Wu always liked to say, "Come along and I'll test you." The sentences and phrases he quizzed me about and the important points of the English writings he guided me through were far beyond the scope of high school English (even though the level at Nankai was already well above that of other schools). Thus for days and months my knowledge of English accumulated until I took the National Joint College Entrance Exams. The topic of the English-to-Chinese translation was the story of how the soldiers of the British Thirty-eighth Division met up with the Chinese army deep in the forests of Burma, which for me was a piece of cake, and if I dared to take liberties, I would have given three big laughs on the spot.

Liu Shengbin, the special correspondent to England, taught me many things about England and its manners. After coming to Taiwan, he became a legislator but died shortly thereafter. Deng Lianxi, special correspondent to the United States, died in a tragic accident while taking a steamship from the Chinese mainland to Taiwan. His wife had arrived first and his luggage had also been shipped previously. After his death, his wife opened his luggage and finding it filled with books, asked me to come and choose what I wanted. Because he was in the foreign language and literature department, I took several of his books. Seeing them reminds of him and the days and nights they spent in that office going over manuscripts, and I weep, overwhelmed with grief.

In my second year of senior high, I was chosen to be part of the school's debating society. Not long after the start of school, I had to compete at the end of September, representing the second-year class.

The topic for debate originally was the reading preferences of male and female students. After the posters went up, Principal Zhang saw them on his walk and said, "Can't anyone see that it's wartime? The kids run for the air-raid siren every day, so why make them debate such a lame topic?" The teacher in charge immediately changed the topic to: "Will America enter the war?"

Once the topic was announced, it attracted a great deal of attention in the cultural center that was Shapingba. How could high school students debate such a serious and weighty question? Originally six students were selected (three each for the pro and con positions), but they were all afraid and wanted to back out. The teacher said that the Nankai spirit was one filled with public spirit and ability, bravely accepting all challenges, and there was no backing out, so they had to intensify their preparations.

It was a huge topic well beyond our abilities, so both sides mobilized their parents. On the con side, arguing that America would not enter the war, one student's father was an editorial writer for a major wartime newspaper; I was on the pro side, arguing that America would enter the war, and had access to the *Time and Tide* archives, which specialized in analyzing the international situation. Both sides actually had informed sources backing them up, which was an open secret among the students. My father, who felt that the topic was too serious for a bunch of kids, smilingly said to me, "Just so long as you don't cry if you lose." All the uncles in the editorial office had varying opinions, but instructed me to summarize nine points from the original material and divide them among the three on our side to master. For a whole month, the three of us collected a lot of material but had to maintain secrecy, for, as our teacher said, surprise was the key to victory. The debate is still vivid, and I recall to this day my nervousness standing at the podium in the auditorium and the calm and confidence I possessed during the question-and-answer session in the second half. My memory for what I read has always been very good, and I was always able to use printed material at the appropriate time. At the time, I debated with assurance and after a bitter battle, victory was ours. In my life up to that point, it was the first time I realized that I didn't have to be a crybaby. It was also the first time I realized that victory didn't necessarily come at the cost of happiness.

The weekend after winning the debate, I walked from the Shoutong Building in the girls' section and was passing the Fansun Building, the administration center, on my way to the main gate to go home. The windows of the high school boys' classrooms were filled as usual with teenage boys looking at the girl students, and when they saw me approaching, they began singing the lyrics of Liu Bannong's "Skilled and Able," which they had slightly altered: "I remember when you were young, you wanted to go to war, I didn't . . ." Then they shouted:

"Quick march, left, right, left, right. . . ." I almost ran for the gate. Later, each time I passed there, I would walk quickly because they would shout: "Pick it up, fast feet!"

Three months later, on December 7, the Japanese launched a surprise attack on Pearl Harbor at one in the morning our time. America declared war on Japan, the Western allies all joined in declaring war on Japan, and at that moment the situation in the world was clarified, with China no longer standing alone. Having waged a war of resistance alone for five years, Chongqing, which was nearly exhausted, suddenly found itself the center of the biggest alliance of nations in Asia. Everything was hopeful again, and my high school student's arguments were all confirmed, so, young as I was, I couldn't help but feel quite pleased with myself for some time.

One day at the dinner table my father said, "Your winning the debate was no small matter, and it shows you can find the main point when you study something. But what is most important is not what you say but what you think." Each time I was feeling self-satisfied in life, my father was there to say, "That was no small matter, but . . .", which guided me to think more deeply. Despite being angry at the time, whenever I faced adversity in life and was unwilling to submit, I would always calmly examine myself afterward as my father had enjoined me.

The track record of *Time and Tide* became ever more impressive. In addition to the fortnightly political commentary, a monthly *Time and Tide Literary Supplement* was added that introduced the latest on living, medicine, and society, as well as a *Literary Bimonthly*, both of which sold really well. At the same time the U.S. ambassador to China, on behalf of *Reader's Digest*, gave rights to *Time and Tide* to publish it in Chinese. It too was widely popular.

In addition, the magazine contracted numerous famous writers and academics as special or part-time contributors to translate many English, American, and French works into Chinese, for example, works that analyzed the current situation and history such as *The Tragedy of France*, *Two Women of the French Underground*, *Roosevelt: World Statesman*, *Inside Latin America*, *India in the Midst of War*, and dozens of other books on special topics, all very popular at the time. The best-selling purely literary work was *This Above All*, the story of a British nurse and a soldier and their love in wartime. The story was quite moving, and it sold so well that everyone seemed to possess a copy. I had the pleasure of reading the book as it was being translated. I often went to the office just for the fun of it and when they were taking a break, they would lend me the original to read. There was only one copy, which had arrived from India over "the hump" and was therefore considered quite precious, so like a vulture, I would wait until they took a break and then would swoop down and read the book. Several nights I took the book home with me and would hurry to return it the following day, because someone would need it for their work.

In addition to publishing, my father opened Time and Tide Bookstore in the best location on a large street in Shapingba in early spring 1941. It was spacious and bright, and in addition to displaying their own publications, there was also a comprehensive selection of the classics and all other publications that could be obtained from around the country during wartime. Since profit was the principal motive for the store, students were welcome to read there, so some books ended up in tatters from being read so much and had to be repaired. During the war, many students had no money to buy books, so many went to Time and Tide Bookstore with no qualms to go through book after book, absorbing knowledge. Some called it the most "up-to-date" library around; others, Zhao Shumin, for example, recalled that for her it was her school of enlightenment.

Every weekend on my way home, I'd stop at Tide and Time Bookstore to return books, and on my way back to school, stop and borrow some more. As long as there was a book to read, I rarely missed it. During the years of Nationalist and Communist cooperation, many Russian works were translated into Chinese. In addition to reading the works of Turgenev and Tolstoy that I worshipped, I was deeply impressed by Gorky's *Mother*; another title that attracted me was *Lucia in Love*, but other than the title, I can't remember the author's name or the story line. Of left-leaning literary works, the most respected at the time was *How Steel Is Tempered* by Nikolai A. Ostrovsky, which is the autobiography of a worker during the Russian Revolution in 1917. At the time, I really couldn't understand such strong political ideology, but around 2002, I stumbled on a copy in the used book market in Taipei; it was like encountering an old friend, so I bought it and took it home to reread. The political fanaticism of the Communists that I hadn't understood sixty years earlier had driven us out of mainland China, and they themselves, prompted by their own fanaticism, ended up killing one another over many years, through the Great Leap Forward and the Cultural Revolution. Thinking of all that has happened, one can only feel the unspeakable tragedy of it all. I'm sure the rational basis for my opposition to communism was rooted in me early on, and that sort of book formed the basis for my judgment.

Having the large and up-to-date library at the Time and Tide Bookstore, I read the Chinese translations of famous Western literary works. Most of those who dared to translate for publication in those years were from literary or education fields, with a solid foundation in Chinese and a thorough grounding in the the study of Western literature. In the days before television, there was no threat to the survival of the publishing world, there was little competition in it, and publishing a book was one way to gain recognition and a true position in society. Editors had broad vision and a good deal of authority and thought it unworthy to be motivated solely by sales. But the vernacular writing in those days was more restrained, not as natural and fluent as it is today.

Some books that I found moving began to wear out after a few readings because of the poor-quality paper and and the difficulty of printing during wartime. After graduating from high school and waiting for the results of the National Joint College Entrance Exams, I purchased a notebook of the highest quality paper, in which I respectfully copied out Andre Gide's *The Pastoral Symphony* and *Chinese Garden*, a collection of poems by He Qifang, Bian Zhilin, and Li Guangtian. I still treasure the volume today, though the poor-quality ink has faded over the years. Dayan Publishing, founded by Jian Zhen, published a string-bound version of He Qifang's *Painted Dreams* in 1989, a copy of which I treasure, also with the feeling of reencountering an old friend.

At a key time as I was growing up, the impact of *Time and Tide* on me was profound and far-reaching. Not only did it provide the foundation for a lifetime's pursuit of knowledge, it also opened my eyes to the world and helped me learn to examine things from a macro perspective. I am most grateful to my father for precisely this, that he took education so seriously, even though I was just a girl.

THE MASSIVE BOMBINGS

Life is full of irony, and as I think about it today, there are indeed many things that leave me not knowing whether to laugh or to cry.

I started to discuss literature when we were taking cover during the air raids on those clear days and moonlit nights. In junior high, my thinking was quite simple, talking about difficult points in the textbook or about the little joys and sorrows of my classmates as we dispersed to the suburbs. Although it was frightening, sometimes missing class (especially mathematics in the morning) and getting out and running around was also quite interesting. But missed classes had to be made up, often in the evening when we were fighting off sleep.

The bombings were particularly bad in my first year of senior high and the casualties were heavy. Responding to the government call, *Time and Tide* constructed a pretty sturdy air-raid shelter on the mountain slope. The shelter could hold about twenty people; inside were a small desk and a number of wooden stools, electric lights, and water and dried food. This allowed the editors to work on manuscripts while taking shelter. My parents told me to go there immediately in the event of an air raid via the small path through the paddy field. The school encouraged the senior high students to take three to five junior high students along when they took shelter. I usually brought Hong Chan and Hong Juan, the daughters of my father's friend Uncle Hong Lanyou, with me. After the all-clear signal, we'd pass by my house and eat our fill before going back to school. The threat of death was always present outside the air-raid shelter, but every living moment listening to the grown-ups discuss the current political situation and analyze current events was precious and inspiring for me. In those days, the sound of bombs reverberated in our ears, but the books read in the shelter also stirred my heart. On the way back to school, I'd often retell what I'd read in a book. This was probably the only way to assuage the fear in those days.

I was fortunate (or perhaps unfortunate) to have been born into the household of a revolutionary, so the tragic historical scenes I heard about and saw as well as personally experienced were all branded on my mind. The peace and happiness of the second half of my life were not sufficient to erase them. The most profound and lasting of all occurred between the ages of thirteen and twenty—the relentless and violent bombings by the Japanese throughout the years of my growing up. Every day the sun would rise as usual, but in the sunshine, survival was a luxury.

When I recall all the frightening scenes that took place during those dark nights sixty years ago, they are just as vivid today. Rereading the history of the War of Resistance, even the simplest such as *Daily Record of the Major Events of the Republic of China* (published by Biographical Literature, Taipei, 1989), which contains just a few lines for each day, for August 1940, in addition to important international news and reports from the front lines, there is also recorded the following:

August 9: Sixty-three Japanese planes attack Chongqing.

August 11: Ninety Japanese planes attack Chongqing, five of which are shot down.

August 19: One hundred ninety Japanese planes bomb the urban district of Chongqing.

August 20: One hundred seventy Japanese planes again bomb Chongqing. A huge fire burns in the urban district and civilian losses are massive.

August 23: More than eighty Japanese planes attack Chongqing.

September 13: Forty-four Japanese planes attack Chongqing, six of which are shot down.

September 18: The ninth anniversary of the fall of northeast China. Li Du reports that in the first half of the year, the volunteer army of the northeast fought more than 3,200 times, which amounts to attacking the Japanese bandits on average twenty times a day.

October 7: Fierce air battle over Kunming.

December 29: President Roosevelt, in a fireside chat, proclaims that the fates of China, the United States, and England are closely linked and that America has taken upon itself the duty of being the arsenal of the democratic nations and will be sending large quantities of military supplies to assist China.

In his famous fireside chat, Roosevelt said there was no Shangri-la left in the world. This was the famous place name in the English writer James Hilton's book *Lost Horizon*, published in 1933, a place still world famous today.

On June 5, 1941, the Japanese bandit planes attacked Chongqing at night. A tragic incident of suffocation occurred in the large tunnel at the entrance of Jiaochangkou, and more than thirty thousand city residents were killed or injured. The report points out that the Japanese bombed the various exits of the tunnel, cutting off all escape routes. Amid the conflagration, rescuers were able to open two or three exits. Most of the people trapped in the tunnel had torn open their clothes and clawed their chests before suffocating, and their faces were etched with the struggle and suffering; there were few survivors. The brutality of the Japanese is evident throughout these blood-soaked pages, but such cruelty served to further unify resolve to fight them. The national hatred that cannot be omitted from the historical record still fills me with anger and grief to this day.

On August 7, 1941, the Japanese planes began around-the-clock bombing of Chongqing, with the goal of breaking the Chinese people's resistance. Almost every day more than a hundred planes would bomb different parts of Sichuan, and several small cities were half destroyed. Until the thirteenth, they attacked for one week, day and night, with less than six hours between bombings. There was no drinking water or light in Chongqing and people had no food and no place to sleep, but under such maltreatment, the will to fight was even stronger. On that day, eighty-six planes attacked Commander Chiang's troops stationed at Zengjiayan, dropping bombs three times without hitting the target. On the thirtieth of the same month, they attacked the war council's meeting place at Huangshan, killing many guards and destroying the Nationalist government's auditorium.

Throughout August, bombs fell on Chongqing, which is called one of the three great summer furnaces along with Nanjing and Hankou. In the high heat of midsummer, residents of the city were besieged by bombings and countless fires caused by the incendiary bombs. Not a single street in Chongqing was undamaged, and the residents seemed to live in a purgatory, tasting all sorts of tortures.

One day the Japanese planes bombed Shapingba, intending to destroy the spiritual bastion of the cultural center. Half my house's roof was blown off, and the neighboring farmer was killed; his mother sat on the ridge between the fields and cried for three days and three nights. Hong Chan, Hong Juan, and I bravely returned to the still-standing dining room, found the rice still warm in the wooden rice bowl, and even ate a bowl before the two of them returned to school. That night, a torrential rain fell, and our entire family, half sitting and half reclining, squeezed into the half of the house where the roof remained. My mother was sick and had to lie in her own bed, over which was spread a large oilcloth to keep the rain off. My father sat at the head of the bed, holding an oilpaper umbrella in one hand to cover his head and my mother's, waiting for day to break. . . .

That was one of the earliest scenes from my youth. Death could fall from the sky night or day, but the life force of the survivors grew ever more resilient. Even at seventeen or eighteen, a fiercely unconquerable spirit was fostered, along with a yearning to roar with anger.

A THOUSAND PEOPLE SINGING TOGETHER

Winter break in 1941 was spent amid the bombings. After classes resumed, the Nankai chorus practiced "A Thousand People Sing Together" each day for one hour under the direction of our teacher Li Baochen. The first performance was held in the auditorium on March 12. Later, another performance was held under a makeshift shelter amid the ruins of downtown Chongqing (later referred to as Spiritual Bastion Plaza). Twenty choruses from throughout the city joined together to sing patriotic songs, hoping that all the suffering compatriots in the city would hear, that all of the world would hear, and that all the lost souls would hear. We sang:

> China is certainly strong! China is certainly strong!
> Look at the eight hundred warriors, an isolated force rising to guard the eastern battlefield. . . .
>
> Arise, those unwilling to be slaves, and build a new Great Wall with our flesh and blood.
> The Chinese people are in great danger; each person is forced to roar in anger.

That night, the sound of singing shook the sky, everyone's blood boiled, and the tears were never dry, as we loudly sang out the suppressed grief and indignation of national emnity. Many years later Mr. Li recalled, "When I stepped up to the podium to conduct, I saw the buildings burned and destroyed by the Japanese planes behind the chorus and heard in the singing of a thousand people the magnificent sound of the Chinese nation." The power of that singing is unimaginable in a time of peace.

When we came out after the performance that night, there were several large military trucks to take us back to Shapingba. As our truck was going around a curve, the tailgate was forced open by the overload of people inside and we all spilled out onto the road. Falling down into a pile as we did, no one was really hurt, but all we heard was shouting, after which we picked ourselves up and set off in pursuit of the truck. A boy surnamed Hu, who ended up on the bottom of the pile, was a genius on the piano at Nankai and had played a piano concert on campus. I quickly got to my feet, helped him up, and asked with some urgency, "Are your hands okay?" Over the years I have occasionally thought about him, but I can't remember his name or if he ever became a pianist.

That evening we laughed as we pursued the truck over the damaged highway. The Jialing River flowing along the road as the moon was rising created a beautiful scene like a fairyland. Youth finally had a moment to catch its breath under the shadow of death amid the flames of war. That temporary respite of happiness is unforgettable.

In addition to the academic atmosphere at Nankai, there were also many artistic and social activities, with concerts and choruses frequent on campus. Among the solo performers was the mezzo-soprano Zeng Hui'en, who sang "A Flower Is Not a Flower" and "I Live at the Head of the Yangtze," which spoke directly to the heart. Some called her "Voice of the Angel," and she was able to intoxicate us. Fifty years later, while attending an alumni meeting for the class of 1943, I learned that she had been teaching vocal music all along at the Hangzhou College of Music. Another memorable figure was Zhu Shikai, a tenor. He was the toast of the school because he sang "Brindisi," the drinking song from *La Traviata*. Some were simply crazy about him, and each time he sang "Duna" even more girls came to think of him as their Prince Charming. Forty years later, I ran into him in Taiwan at a gathering of Nankai alumni. Old as I was, I still felt a fan's admiration for him, telling him how all the girls were captivated by him back in the day. After he returned to the States, he sent me a handwritten copy of the lyrics of "Duna." I sighed, lamenting over the dreamlike past. He had long been suffering from high blood pressure and died before he reached seventy.

Another unique feature of Nankai was the Drama Society, which was set up by Principal Zhang shortly after the school was established. The original purpose was to arouse patriotism by performing patriotic plays, as art and culture were also ways to save the country. In the beginning Principal Zhang wrote and directed the plays. In the 1920s, Zhou Enlai studied at the school and worked on the stage settings and played a female role (as men and women could not perform together in a play back then). When I attended the school the society no longer limited itself to performing patriotic plays, and one year the graduating class performed Oscar Wilde's *Lady Windermere's Fan*. Lu Qiaozhen, who played the leading role, was one year ahead of me. Normally she wore a uniform and was lively and refined, but on stage her every movement was filled with the charm of a mature, elegant lady, leaving everyone amazed.

Stage performances, concerts, and all kinds of ball games at Nankai were great occasions at Shapingba and earned the support of National Central and Chongqing universities. There were some recognized stars who attracted a good deal of attention walking down the only street in town. One year the Nankai basketball team and Northeast Sun Yat-sen Middle School's basketball team, both of which produced players of national caliber, had an exciting match, which Sun Yat-sen won by a whisker. Fortunately, I had already graduated; otherwise I would have had a difficult time deciding whom to root for.

FAREWELL, ALMA MATER

In addition to studying, friendship was something else that I cultivated and harvested during the three years of high school. As a person grows, aspiration gradually becomes an important factor in friendship, and from my first year in junior high to my last year in senior high school, only a little more than thirty people with whom I shared joys and hardships remained the whole time. Most of the others opted for the sciences when they were in their junior year, while I and around ten others selected the liberal arts.

In general, the people in the liberal arts were not suited for the sciences, but that didn't mean they were good at the liberal arts either. My Chinese and English scores were very high, and I was always selected as chief editor of our wall newspaper and won several writing contests. In the dormitory, where there were no academic divisions, I would tell stories from books or movies after lights out, which were always welcomed, and in this way I maintained my friendships with some old friends who studied the sciences.

Every month or two, I would go into town to see a movie, such as *Camille*, *The Thief of Bagdad*, *Bathing Beauty*, *The Wings of Morning*, *Heaven Can Wait*, and others. One time we were discussing Robert

Taylor, Greta Garbo's boyfriend in *Camille*. I said he was nothing but a pretty face, which made all his fans angry. They asked me, "Well, who do you think is the most handsome?" I replied Henry Fonda, whom they later referred to as "your not-so-pretty face." Years later in Taiwan, I saw him in *On Golden Pond* playing an old man, which saddened me greatly. On account of him, I have always liked his daughter Jane Fonda, who has brains.

One time, as I told them the story of *Heaven Can Wait*, I had them in tears. More than fifty years later, when we got together again during a trip of mine to Beiping, some brought it up again. After half a century, and having endured the joys and sorrows of this world, they still recalled that dreamed-of love from high school. I never dared ask the details of how the young girls from the dark dormitory of those days endured all the political tempests and managed to survive the Cultural Revolution.

Just at that time, when we would spend nights talking with the person in the neighboring bed, Yu Yuzhi and I would alternately recite the lines of the poems and lyrics from Mr. Meng's course. Occasionally I would add the lines from He Qifang's famous poem "Wreath": "The most fragrant flowers are those that blossom and fall in a deep valley, the brightest morning dew is that not remembered by a soul. I say you are fortunate, Little Lingling, the clearest stream is the one that has never seen a reflection." Sometimes I would recite Bian Zhilin's "Fragment": "You stand on the bridge looking at the scenery, a person upstairs looking at the scenery watches you. The bright moon adorns your window; you adorn another's dream." From the moment I knew He Qifang was a philosophy graduate from Peking University and that Bian Zhilin was a foreign language and literature graduate from the same university, I was even more fascinated by their verses.

Thinking about it today, I realize that those lines, like the words of an otherworldly divinity that so pleasantly surprised several of us seventeen- and eighteen-year-old students, such as this line written about a young girl's tears, "flowing with an unnamed sadness," had perhaps been inspired by the first line of Tennyson's "Tears, Idle Tears": "Tears, idle tears, I know not what they mean." Chinese poetry, of course, contains such conceptualizations, but modern poetry expresses them in pure and fresh language and in an uncommon fashion, which in those difficult times was like the music of heaven to us.

During my senior year, preparations for the National Joint College Entrance Exams intensified, as did the gradual feeling of imminent departure. Countless are the memories I cherish from Nankai, especially of my classmates and teachers. Having lived on campus, we all had feelings for one another, and I don't know how many days I cried when I thought about leaving.

Just before graduation, my teacher asked me to write a class song. I wrote: "The blossoming plum trees and the morning sun; the western pool and the evening clouds . . . the wind of 1943 is now far away; farewell, alma mater, we know not when we'll return." It was a sentimental, childlike poem, the outpouring of a high school girl who had devoted herself to the study of classical poetry for the preceding two years. Our music teacher wrote music to accompany it, which was tasteful and pleasant to listen to, so it was soon sung by all the girls and liked by all, and I was widely looked upon as some sort of hero. No one foresaw that since there were more teachers in the boy's section they would choose a song written by one of the boys instead: "Several years of studying and reciting will now end, we'll be like birds flying in different directions. . . . We cut though the wind and waves on our ways ahead and shall spare no effort." When it came time to sing the class song at graduation, many girls refused to sing it, and a few of my sworn followers even cried. At the time only we were aware that our mood was only half sullen, and the other half was sorrow due to our imminent parting. After half a lifetime spent teaching, I am well aware that a class song at those times had to be grave and sedate, because graduating from Nankai was such a serious event. Fifty years after graduating, I never expected to see in the *Newsletter of the Class of 43* that a student by the name of Wang Shize still remembered everything and wrote a recollection titled "On the Class Song."

After graduating at the beginning of summer, most students remained on campus to make the final preparations for the National Joint College Entrance Exams. The school didn't provide any tutoring, as the teachers were off for the summer. We lived in the dorm and abided by the same rules, and getting up with the bugle and lights out at night no longer posed any difficulties. By the sixth year of the war, only Guizhou, Sichuan, Xikang, Qinghai, Xinjiang, and Yunnan had not fallen into enemy hands. Every day, the battlefield reports spoke of territory lost and the obstinate seesaw of the battle. We had no other hope but to get into a university, and the minuscule dreams of high school girls contained no scene of "cutting through the wind and waves." At night after lights out, we lay on our wood-plank beds and talked about our reluctance to leave, but uttered not one word of encouragement to each other about the future.

I woke one night and was unable to go back to sleep. I went and stood by a window in the dorm hallway and suddenly heard singing drifting over from the music classroom: "The moon hangs high in the sky, its light shining in all directions . . . deep is this silent night, I think of my home." It was so sad that I wept as I listened. After half a century, the sadness brought on by that song, the suffering of the country and countless families, and the uncertainty of my own future are still indelibly scored on my heart. Later, when I studied, engaged in advanced studies, taught, and wrote criticism, the sadness of that song on a moonlit night would still faintly shine through.

THE NATIONAL JOINT COLLEGE ENTRANCE EXAMS

During my final year, I decided to choose only three colleges of preference for the National Joint College Entrance Exams: my first choice was philosophy at Southwestern Associated University; my second was philosophy at Wuhan University; and my third was foreign languages and literatures at Southwestern Associated University. National Central University was at my doorstep, so I didn't choose it, because for college, I hoped to live far away from home and be independent. It was said that some boys at school even listed only one choice, as in those days the

Nankai spirit gave people excessive self-confidence but seldom led to failure. I chose philosophy because I childishly wanted to challenge my father: you studied in Germany; I can at least study in Kunming, Yunnan, and explore the profound meaning of life. After I made up my mind, I put all my heart into preparation for studying philosophy, and even when Mr. Meng Zhisun, whom I most respected, tried to persuade me to study Chinese, I would not be dissuaded—I even tried hard to justify my superficial views.

Our preparations for the exam were just as arduous as those of students today. Some Nankai students were worse off, because their homes were not in Sichuan or Chongqing and they had to make the school their home. Every day the study rooms were open until 9 p.m., and those who wanted to could remain at school until after the exam. My home was at Shapingba, but I also went to school to study. That year the National Joint College Entrance Exams were held in July, and Chongqing, being one of China's three furnaces, was extremely hot. I remember that the backs of the metal chairs were hot enough to burn, but still we sat in them and studied strenuously, sometimes even wanting to doze off.

With English and Chinese scores to compensate for my appalling math score (it was only 48), I was qualified for my second choice—philosophy at National Wuhan University. However, not long after the results were posted, my third choice, the Department of Foreign Languages and Literatures at National Southwestern Associated University, sent me a letter saying that given my high English score, I would be welcome to study there. But I was not well informed at the time and, bent on "the pursuit of truth and the contemplation of life," I opted for philosophy. Who could have foreseen that a year later, after receiving advice from Professor Zhu Guangqian, I would switch to foreign languages and literatures anyway? It is as if my path had been decided by fate. Throughout my life, matters concerning life and truth have seemed forever beyond my grasp.

The alumni of Nankai are the ones who have made her famous. Nankai alums, starting with Mei Yiqi and Yu Chuanjian (who was in charge of school administration for decades) in the first class of 1908 and later alums such as Zhou Enlai, Wu Dayou, Cao Yu (Wan Jiabao), Wu Nesun (Lu Qiao), and others, compose a mile-long roster. In 1949, the year the Nationalist government moved to Taiwan, more than ten ambassadors and four or five ministers had all graduated from Nankai. In recent years Zhang Zhongmou and Premier Wen Jiabao of mainland China have both commented on how Nankai Middle School influenced their lives. The alums of Nankai University and National Southwestern Associated University are even more numerous, but this is beyond the scope of my feelings as I recall my growing up and education.

I believe that in the hundred years of Nankai Middle School history, the roster of famous student parents is perhaps even more illustrious and would constitute a veritable modern history of China. The earliest include: Liang Qiqiao, Yuan Shikai, Li Yuanhong, Duan Qirui, Hu Shi, Zhang Xueliang, Zhang Zizhong, Weng Wenhao, and Wang Jingwei. During the War of Resistance, Ma Yanchu's youngest daughter, Ma Yangfeng, and I were classmates for three years, and more than half the famous generals (most in their forties and fifties) during the War of Resistance sent their sons and daughters to Nankai. Since they lived on campus, their fathers didn't need to worry about leaving them behind. No one really paid much attention to anyone else's family background because we were all pretty much the same. I still remember discussing literature in the dorm with Fu Dongju (she was one year ahead of me), the daughter of Fu Zuoyi, the famous general from north China. After victory in the War of Resistance, the turning point in the war between the Nationalists and the Communists was that Fu Zuoyi, who had been in Beiping resisting the Communists, supported their call for "an end to the civil war and peaceful unification" in January 1949. Later, I was shocked to read that his daughter was one of those who had urged his capitulation. Back in those years, when I was crazy about poetry and literature and had little conception of politics other than resistance against Japan and patriotism, another storm was already brewing.

LETTERS FROM THE CLOUDS

In that age when letter writing was the only means of communication, Zhang Dafei became my steadiest pen pal during the six years I lived at Shapingba.

When I entered junior high, he was already flying pursuit aircraft, and over the two previous years he had been flying out of Chongqing and probably visited our house five or six times. Ningyuan, my younger sister, was already attending Nankai Primary School and Ningxing, my youngest sister, would accompany her every day for "fun" (she could recite all her sister's textbooks from memory). In those days, I was the only member of the family who really loved to write letters, and when Fourth Brother Dafei (he was the fourth child in his family) was away from the base in Chongqing, he'd send me a letter on light blue airmail stationery every week. He had not been able to get in touch with his family and said that we were the only family he could send a message to and tell that he was fine. He wrote as if he were writing home, and I was so touched that I would always respond. If those letters were around today, they would constitute the precious history of two young people coming of age during the war.

We were like two parallel lines that could never intersect in the simple and pure way in which we shared our experiences growing up. He grew up at the edge of the clouds, in a life-and-death struggle amid a net of machine-gun and antiaircraft fire, while all I did was run for cover at the sound of an air-raid siren, cry over the catastrophe, or join in the chorus singing "China shall not perish." Perhaps the one thing we shared in common was that we wanted with all our might to drive the Japanese out of China.

His life was so glorious, while I was just a junior high school girl living in my own little world. In junior high, I often copied essays of concern for our country from our Chinese textbook for him, works such as *Li Ling's Letter in Reply to Su Wu*, Sima Qian's *Letter to Ren An*, Han Yu's *Funerary Message to Nephew No. 12*, Yuan Mei's *In Memory of My Sister*, and Shi Kefa's *Letter in Reply to Duoergun*. Gradually I came to write about the things I was reading outside of class, works that enchanted every girl, such as Pierre Loti's *An Iceland Fisherman*, Charlotte Brontë's *Jane Eyre*, and the very sentimental poetic prose of Lamartine's *Graziella*. Dafei always seemed interested in discussing these things with me, but would always end his letters by telling me to look after my health, not to worry my mother, and similar exhortations.

By the time I entered senior high, he had already fought numerous battles, and the content of our letters was much broader than the junior high school world of before. I wrote about all of the meaningful activities at school—famous speakers at the weekly assembly, the wall newspaper I edited, writing letters to comfort the soldiers on the front line, and fund-raising activities for rebuilding after the bombings, among other things. He was interested in it all. Sometimes I would send him a book or two from Time and Tide Bookstore. My letters, he said, were his only letters from home and the greatest comfort to him.

Gradually, he wrote more about the Bible. He also liked the poems that I copied from my teacher Meng Zhisun's textbook of selections of classical poetry and lyrics, saying they were one more comfort for his soul (in all those years, he was the only person who often spoke to me about the soul).

He virtually studied my teacher's textbook of classical poetry and lyrics along with me. Of course he liked Su Dongpo and Xin Qiji, praising their heroic, masculine spirit. He agreed with the great boldness of vision in the ending lines of Qin Shaoyou's "Tune: Treading on Sedge": "The Chen River should be meandering around Chen Mountain / Why does it flow into the Xiao and Xiang rivers?" But he disapproved of a girl my young age enjoying the bleak tone of Huang-Fu Song's "Dreaming of the South of the Yangtze": "The candle burns low / The banana leaves on the screen dark red / She idly dreams of the ripe plums in the south of the river / On a boat, a flute plays in the night as the rain sighs / Voices carry from the post station bridge."

His letters, from the very first one he sent from Hunan describing how his training toughened him up after joining the army to those written upon his return from the United States and his being selected to join the Flying Tigers, were often accompanied by photographs, from early ones in which he marched quickly in cotton-padded military garb to later ones of him standing in his airman's uniform in front of a shark-faced Flying Tiger P-40. Over a period of seven or eight years, I ended up with quite a number of his photos.

He grew up amid the flames of war and began his rich life (if it can be called a life) all as a result of his having been chosen to join Claire Lee Chennault's Flying Tigers and serving alongside the American volunteers. In 1941, he met the American military chaplain at the base in Yunnan. For years he had suffered a psychological conflict between his religious beliefs and fighting in the war, but by talking with this Presbyterian chaplain he gained a modicum of relief. When he was in the States for training, he frequently met with the base chaplains, who believed that fighting in defense of the country was just and that it was the bound duty of a soldier to reduce the casualties of innocent people. This provided Dafei with an outlet that allowed him to attain a spiritual peace, caught as he was between killing and spiritual redemption.

Gradually, he wrote less about the war and started talking more about how afterward he wanted to become a military chaplain, but the war had to be successfully fought first and the Japanese could not be allowed to win. His words were filled with a heroic spirit like that of Principal Zhang's rousing speech, "With me, China shall not perish!"

Chennault's connection with China's air force, it seems, could only be explained as predestined. Once when he was flying a stunt plane as part of a small performing U.S. Air Corps group, he attracted the attention of Mao Bang, a Chinese Air Force representative among the spectators. Chennault, who was forty-five in 1937 and did not have a particularly successful career, had retired from the military due to illness. In May, having accepted the invitation of employment as an advisor from Song Meiling, Secretary of the Air Force Committee of China, he arrived by steamship in Shanghai, one month before the war with Japan broke out.

In China's most difficult hour, he helped train the newly established air force. The group of American volunteers he put together attacked the Japanese from their muddy airfields in Kunming, becoming the world-renowned Flying Tigers (despite the fact that a shark head with its mouth open was painted on the nose of each plane). Their small numbers shot down large numbers of a vastly superior Japanese force, significantly reducing the casualties suffered by Chinese troops and civilians, and during the war years their marvelous story was widely known. Some called Chennault a daredevil, but he emphasized strategy, strict training, and living side by side with the pilots through thick and thin; in this way, they developed the superior skills needed to fight the enemy in the sky.

Two years later, he returned to the States for leave, but sitting in front of the warm fireplace at home, he couldn't help but think about the Chinese cities in flames as well as the old-fashioned fighter planes flown by the Chinese pilots and how they were being shot out of the sky. Looking at the table full of good food, he couldn't help but think about the poor Chinese farmers who were barely eking out a miserable existence, and he started having trouble seeing eye to eye with his fortunate compatriots. Two months later, he returned to China and with the full confidence of Madame Chiang Kai-shek and the Chinese air force, he began to intensify the training of young Chinese pilots in order to increase their combat readiness.

After the surprise attack on Pearl Harbor, the American Volunteer Group was officially made a part of the Army Air Corps. In March 1942, Chennault was made commander of the Fourteenth Air Force based in China under the leadership of Generalissimo Chiang Kai-shek with headquarters in Kunming. Their mission was to support the joint British–American force in Burma, with their main theater of action in the southwestern provinces of China.

Zhang Dafei joined the military at the end of 1937 and due to superior performance during basic training was selected for the twelfth class of officer flight school. After graduation, he took part in the defense of the skies over Chongqing, and owing to his outstanding performance, he was chosen to be among the first group of pilots sent to the United States for training. In the summer of 1942, after receiving flight training in Colorado, he returned to China and joined the Fourteenth Air Force of Chinese and American pilots. The noses of the planes were still painted with an open-mouthed shark's head, but the papers persisted in calling them the Flying Tigers.

When he visited us at Shapingba, my mother said that the food in America must have been good because he looked stronger and seemed a little taller. Newly promoted to the rank of first lieutenant, he sported flying-eagle insignias on his collar and two stripes on his sleeves. How spirited his stride was! When he left us, he immediately reported to Kunming. According to newspaper accounts at the time, the U.S.–China joint force was victorious in nearly every battle. At that time, Chinese ground troops were engaged in bitter fighting, with Hunan and Guangxi almost completely fallen into enemy hands. The air force heroes were the only thing giving us much hope.

His letters, carefully written in his elegant, fine hand on blue airmail stationery and posted in blue airmail envelopes, were filled with strange place names: Yunnanyi, Gujiu, Mengzi—place names extending all along the Burma Road. In one letter he said he could see the street from one end to the other and a small store with a glass jar containing the round candies that my younger sister liked so much when she was four years old during our flight inland. Most of the pilots when they were off duty liked to drink; however, because he did not drink, the others laughed at him. One time he got a little drunk after only a few drinks and started dancing on the table singing "Hallelujah," and after that no one pressed him to drink again. Nor could they prevail upon him to go dancing; in their eyes he was an oddball who wouldn't join them in seizing the day and making merry while they could in such uncertain times. To his mind, being able to be on the ground and read the Bible, books, and newspapers, or write to his young, understanding friend made him happier than all other forms of merriment.

In one letter he told me that two days previously he had taken to the skies to track the enemy when suddenly, through a break in the clouds ahead, he saw a plane on which was emblazoned the rising sun! He clearly saw the face of the pilot in the cockpit, a face filled with fear. He didn't have time to think—all he knew was that if he didn't shoot first, it would be all over for him. Since returning, he couldn't forget the face of the pilot he had shot down. I never saw it, but I couldn't erase that face in flames from my memory either.

Yes, no matter how he expressed it in his letters, the conflicts in his mind, his sufferings, or his longing for home, amid the flames of war in an age when life was as short as that of a mayfly, he was the sort of hero young girls yearned for. The very image of the hero who defends his country, he far surpassed the common man, and he was that larger-than-life image no young girl like me dared desecrate with her personal feelings.

During summer vacation in my second year of senior high, after we had lunch, I took him through the Central University campus to that small rocky lair of mine above the bank of the Jialing River. The sun shone brightly and the river water was clear as we sat there discussing the things I had read outside of class and what he had seen from the air. On that riverbank beyond the ken of human affairs, time passed quietly. We never spoke a word touching upon what was in our hearts, much less of love. Then he returned to Yunnan, and it was nearly a year before I saw him again.

In April 1943, I was preoccupied with my approaching graduation and the National Joint College Entrance Exams. One day around sunset, as we returned to the dorm to get ready for dinner, a junior high school girl ran up to me and told me that someone was waiting for me on the athletic field.

I came out and saw him approaching from among the plum trees in a large military raincoat. Halfway over, he suddenly halted and said, "Pang-yuan, how you have grown and how pretty you have become in a year." It was the first time I ever heard him offer me praise, a feeling I'll never forget.

He said that they were changing planes in Chongqing en route for redeployment and that he had to be back at Baishiyi Airfield before half past seven. He only wanted to rush over and see me for a second. A friend was waiting for him at the school gate in a jeep, the engine still running, so I followed him toward the gate, but halfway there, the rain came pouring down. He ran, pulling me to the Fansun Building, where we stood together beneath the eaves. He pulled me to him, covering me in his raincoat, and pressed me close. Under his uniform and belt, I could hear his heart beating like a drum. In a moment he released me and told me to hurry back to the dorm, saying, "I have to leave." In the rain I saw him trot to the gate, get in the jeep, and speed off.

That summer, I said good-bye to the most wonderful days of my life and headed up the Yangtze River to western Sichuan. The spring wind of 1943 was now far away.

It was the last time I ever saw him in this life.

4

AT THE CONFLUENCE OF THREE RIVERS

University Life

GOING UPRIVER

The Yangtze River is 3,964 miles long, the third longest river in the world. Two major turns in the course of my life occurred when I left home in tears, making my way up that river. The first time, I had just graduated from primary school when I took a military transport ship from Wuhu and fled to Hankou; and now, at the end of August 1943, having just graduated from high school, I was going upriver from Chongqing to Jiading (formerly known as Jiadingfu) in western Sichuan.

I boarded the boat at noon that day, and my father, who was always so busy, unexpectedly came to see me off in person at the wharf at Chaotian Gate, about thirty *li* from home. As the car passed Xiaolongkan Station, lightning flashed in the sky and it started to rain. I was carrying the standard luggage for a long trip in those days, a small suitcase and a bedroll that consisted of clothes and bedding rolled up in a blanket and bent in an oval shape, on which was fastened an enamel washbasin outside of which was an oilcloth, all tied off with coarse hemp rope. In 1976, at a baggage claim area in an airport in Europe, I saw the same sort of bedroll from Pakistan, which struck me as possessing a universal wisdom—all you have to do is unroll it and, voilà, a home.

From the wharf at Chaotian Gate to shipside there was what seemed like an interminable series of slippery stone steps. It was raining buckets and when we got on deck, the water was pouring over the gunwale from the awning, so an umbrella was of no use. My father's white summer scholar's gown was soaked through, and the water flowed like a column from his head to his shoes. I have no idea what I looked like; all I remember was doing everything possible to stifle the sobs that shook my body as I listened him express his gratitude to my elder schoolmates, then watched as he disembarked from the ship and quickly vanished behind the curtain of rain.

I have never been able to recall the entire trip by river. All I remember is the rain, my father soaked to the bone, and recalling with emotion that "Alas! Alas! My parents, with what toil ye brought me up!"

I did as everyone else did and placed my luggage on the half-dry floor in steerage, where we opened our suitcases and took turns concealing each other so we could change into dry clothes. When the bell tolled, we went forward to get our food and then sat on our belongings and ate. Night soon fell and the lamplight glowed faintly, the darkness inside merging with that outside. Gradually everyone fell silent, and the only thing that could be heard was the laboring engine of the steamship on the river. Where was I on that immense river?

Before daybreak the following morning, I awoke, having dreamed that I had heard a robust male voice shouting: "Head toward the trees on the right, as fast as you can, the Jap planes are coming!" I had just finished helping my mother change the bloody mats beneath her and had left the cabin but was not able to find my little sister, who was eighteen months old and had just learned to walk. Before I had let go of her hand, she had been walking unsteadily from my brother to Zhang Dafei to the troop of students and to the wounded soldiers in their seats. . . . I woke up to see the unfamiliar faces of those sleeping around me. Six years later, on the same river, I would once more shed tears of parting.

At dusk the ship tied up at the Yibin Wharf, and the Min River followed its course south to join the Yangtze.

My elder Nankai schoolmate Feng Jialu was from an old, influential family in Yibin, and she invited the six of us to dinner and to spend the night at her house. It was the first time I ever experienced the plentitude and stability of Sichuan, commonly referred to as a land of abundance. After dinner, we took a stroll in town and to the Protestant church. The local gentry and businessmen I saw all had cultured taste that seemed to have been handed down for generations, with a level of self-confidence that was greater even than that seen in Hunan before the flight of refugees began.

From Yibin we continued our boat journey upriver, but the river was appreciably narrower and there were fewer boats on the water. In August, the rivers were surging at their fullest, and at several points the boat made no headway and was in fact was pushed back, which set the passengers to screaming. I leaned against the gunwale and shed tears of homesickness for quite some time, thinking I was unseen. I had never been very robust and always had someone to look after me. Nankai Middle School was only three *li* from my home, and I had never for one day been "free." When it came to choosing universities, I didn't select one near Chongqing, because I thought one could become strong by facing life in the vastness of the world. But all I could think of now was Shapingba, and I regretted leaving home, but it was too late to do anything about it. At that moment Lu Qiaozhen silently walked up to me and said, "A boy student just said to me, no wonder the river is swelling, given the way that new student keeps crying." She continued, "Last year, on the way, I also cried for a while. This is my second year, so I'm okay." In the three years before she graduated in 1946, she was my best friend. We were of one mind and of the same views and talked about everything; there wasn't a thing that we didn't understand about each other.

THE GIRLS' DORM ON WHITE PAGODA STREET

What I remember of university life doesn't begin with beautiful Leshan City, but with the girls' dorm.

I spent about ten years of my life living in dormitories, eight years in wartime and two years in the early period of demobilization after victory. In those days, dormitory facilities were quite simple and crude, and lights went out at 9 p.m. But there was a huge difference in atmosphere, as university dorms were freer, and one could come and go freely before the lights went out. The girls' dormitory on White Pagoda Street in Leshan was nicknamed the "White Palace." It was a four-story wooden structure originally built by a Christian church for training missionaries in the hinterland and was able to lodge a hundred people. With its own courtyard, it was quite safe. Repairs were impossible during wartime, so it seemed rundown and was neither white nor a "palace," but it was far better than any of the six places in temples and temple halls that served as dorms for the boys. It probably owed its name to its location on White Pagoda Street (though I never saw a white pagoda).

The single dorm supervisor was a woman by the name of Zhu Junyun. Unlike Wang Wentian, a very strict teacher at Nankai, who was always present, she seldom meddled with us and was rarely seen. I thought she was the wife of the famous playwright Xiong Fuoxi, now divorced. Being aloof and mysterious, she didn't need to "mix with the rabble" and get involved with trivial matters of clothing, food, housing, or our behavior. As I recall, the only person who got involved in our lives was Old Yao, a worker who sat at the door to the dorm (it was said that the boys called him Gramps or Master Ye). He was more than an impartial and incorruptible old man who locked the door with a large metal key and bolted it every night; he also looked after everything inside and outside the dorm and clearly understood everything. He had the personal information of each of the more than one hundred girls in his head and was like some very sharp character out of a Shakespearean comedy. He was very short and almost entirely bald—I don't recall him having any hair—and all year round he wore a blackish gray cotton-wadded jacket. In summer we went home, so I don't know what he wore then. Whether he was smiling or not, his top row of teeth always protruded from his lips.

When my elder classmates and I carried our ridiculous bedrolls through the front door of the dorm, we seemed to be reporting to Old Yao. He told Lu Qiaozhen and the others to go to the second floor, and he led me through a small courtyard to a small room on the left corner and, pointing to the upper bunk of the innermost bunk bed, said, "That one's yours." The bed was next to the only window in the room, so I was in luck, but I soon discovered that the window opened onto White Pagoda Street and had been boarded up for security reasons. That night the sky never grew light from moon or stars and if it had, I wouldn't have known.

Zhao Xiaolan, a math student who was in the lower bunk, had arrived three days before me. She showed me the toilet and the nearby cafeteria. On the right side of the small courtyard was a row of bathrooms, each of which was subdivided into eight smaller stalls; inside of each was a wooden frame to hold a washbasin. Near the door was a huge metal cauldron. Every morning water carriers would haul water from Shuixi Gate, fill the cauldron seven-eighths full, and light a fire underneath. After the water was heated, we would walk up the small stone steps to scoop out some hot water to fill our basins.

Our room was the last choice in the entire dorm (that is, if we had a choice). The bunk beds were pretty flimsy and had been hurriedly installed by the school, because all the local carpenters were busy making desks, chairs, and beds. However, the girls were a lot better off than the boys. Neither one of us weighed much, but when you rolled over or got in or out of bed, the whole thing would sway. The upper bunk had no railings, and I was always afraid of falling out of bed in the middle of the night. One night I noticed that the bed had been trembling lightly for some time, so I leaned down and asked, "Can't you sleep, either?" Zhao Xiaolan replied, "Every night I hear you lie there and cry and I start feeling homesick. . . ." From then on, the two of us relied upon each other. Every day after dinner, we would go out to White Pagoda Street, turn onto Shaanxi Street and then onto County Street to "explore" and try to find something to fill up on. On rainy days, we'd carry an umbrella and walked supporting each other on the slippery cobblestone streets, especially at the corner to Shuixi Gate, where, from morning till night, countless people went to fetch water from the Dadu River. A third of the water in the wooden buckets carried on shoulder poles would end up on the cobblestone streets before it got to anyone's home.

On the first day of class, Lu Qiaozhen, who was a sophomore in economics, led the way. Classes in the College of Arts, Letters, and Law were held in the Confucius Temple; the main library was also located in the temple. When Wuhan University was moved to the rear, it proudly moved more books than any other university. In those four years, most of our class materials were borrowed from the library by the class representative and were shared out and copied by the students before class. The first thing everyone did after coming out of the Confucius Temple was to go and buy notebooks.

Taking the stone steps up Yue'ertang on the left-hand side led to Dingdong Street and to Fu Street and Purple Cloud Street, and after walking for some time you would hit Jialemen Avenue, where the store of the Jiale Paper Factory was located. One's first sight upon entering was unforgettable—the paradise among paradises! Spacious and wide wooden shelves along four walls were filled with all sorts of notebooks with elegant and immaculate covers, large and small, light blue, lake green, butterfly white, light yellow, thick volumes, side by side, in all the colors a person could dream of.

Jiale paper, famous throughout the rear, came in hundreds of varieties—from *xuan* paper treasured for calligraphy to notebooks used by students—and all were works of art, produced by ingenious handiwork using the bamboo and wood from Emei Mountain and steeped in the flowing waters of the Min River at the foot of the Giant Buddha on Leshan, Jiading. A museum expert said that even after a few hundred years, the paper would retain some faint fragrance. I was so lucky to live in this mountain city for three years with such an auspicious beginning.

Coming out of Jiale Paper Factory, my classmates led me through Anlan Gate down the stone steps to Xiaogongzui to see the rapids where the Dadu River and the Min River converged, a broad and magnificent space that impressed me even more than the Giant Buddha carved in the Tang dynasty from 713 to 803. Owing to its history and value to tourism, it was so modernized after the Cultural Revolution as to be unrecognizable.

THE NEW STUDENT IN THE PHILOSOPHY DEPARTMENT

In my freshman year, university work wasn't really very challenging. The introduction to philosophy and economics required listening to lectures, but the class handouts were simple and we had no assigned reference works, and even if we had, the books wouldn't have been available because the specialized works in the library were allotted to various departments. The professors at Wuhan University all seemed to have a tacit practice of giving low grades—no matter how well you did on an exam, you'd never score 90 percent. Freshman Chinese and English were easier than at Nankai, and the classes progressed slowly. I remember the English teacher spoke the word "blackbird" with a heavy Hunan accent in class and thenceforth was known by that name. The required physical education class was a joke, and I don't remember there even being a playing field.

That year I had plenty of time to think about my situation and frame of mind. I seemed to float around without direction the whole year, and my space seemed limited to the upper bunk and a small wooden desk. On the second floor of the dorm was a study room that was made bright by a big window, and at night there was plenty of lamplight. The thirty or so seats were always occupied by the upperclassmen since the light in the dorm rooms was particularly dim and during the day there was no sunlight. After the lights were turned off at nine o'clock, people with homework to do would light their own small oil lamps (the primitive, shallow indented porcelain ones filled with paulownia oil and two or three rush stalks lit with a match). Before an exam, one would splurge and light a small candle by which to study.

In winter when it was cold, the one door to the room had to be kept closed, so the air would grow stuffy. Eight of us lived that way seven days a week, and all we hoped for was the coming of summer break when we could go home and eat our fill and sleep a little better. Later we'd exaggerate and say that we survived that year and returned home because next to the dorm there was a little building with Mr. Zhan's home-style cakes and breads, which I still think had the best bread ever made. In the dorm, Old Yao sold peanuts for five *yuan* a bag—small paper tubes holding a handful of peanuts, fragrant and crisp, with which to stave off hunger and keep up one's health. Fifty years later, every female classmate recalled it fondly in writing.

Shortly after arriving at Leshan, I slavishly imitated Lu Qiaozhen and Yu Xianyi and became familiar with that small town. The first extracurricular activity I attended was the Nankai Alumni Association, whose activities for new students included not only food and drink but also a number of outings: twenty- and thirty-*li* walks to scenic spots to go to teahouses such as Nanmulin, a high-class, private garden, which I was even more reluctant to leave than the famous Wuyou Temple or Lingyun Temple.

To this day I admire teahouse culture, probably because it was a male student monopoly. The "White Palace," as it was referred to by the boys, was more comfortable than the six boys' dorms scattered throughout the city, or so it was said. Most of the boys' dorms were located in temples that didn't have many worshipers, and most consisted of a few wide beds for several people. The names of the temples were actually quite imaginative—Dragon Spirit Temple, Dingdong Street, Dew Benefits Temple, and Speckled Bamboo Bay, among others. The self-study rooms were too small, but there were teahouses nearby and you could get a pot of tea and sit there half the day. The teahouses hosted homework, theses, friendships, chess games, mahjong, and political debates, the sort of life that was more than a girl could hope for. In those days, no girl would dare go out on the street alone, or go to a teahouse. Among one thousand students, the male students outnumbered the female students ten to one, which naturally meant two distinct worlds. Many years later I read Virginia Woolf's *A Room of One's Own* and learned that women all over the world encountered the same problems in the pursuit of knowledge. Different times had different expectations, different difficulties, but seldom was there equality between men and women.

PALE BLUE AIRMAIL LETTERS

Under the guidance of an elder classmate from Nankai, I joined the Luojia Christian Fellowship the following semester.

The night we stopped in Yibin during the boat trip from Chongqing to Leshan, we met Chen Renkuan, the son of Pastor Chen, a missionary with the Inland Mission, at Feng Jialu's house. He was a senior in the law department at Wuhan University and boarded the ship with us the following day. He wasn't handsome, nor was he tall, but he possessed a youthful intelligence and self-confidence that made him stand out in a crowd. Someone must have told him that I cried on the ship all the way to Yibin, and like a missionary, he came and sat down next to me and tried to comfort me by saying that when he had gone to Chongqing to study at Nankai, he had really missed his family in Yibin. I took out the copy of the Bible I always carried with me and showed it to him. I don't know what he said at the time, but it almost brought me to tears and made me tell him that I not only missed my family but also missed and worried about the person who had given me the Bible, because he was in the air day and night in pursuit of enemy warplanes. No doubt fate works to make you spill the innermost secrets of your heart to someone you have just met. After the start of classes, he introduced me to Gui Zhiting, the advisor of the Luojia Christian Fellowship and the dean of the College of Natural Sciences at Wuhan University, who took me to join the fellowship and made sure that I was warmly looked after. In the four years at school, I played the part of Maria in the silent play *The Birth of Jesus* during the Christmas celebrations. All my friends in the fellowship said I was tall and thin and had a melancholy air about me, which made me suited for the part.

In the year before graduation, Chen Renkuan, who met me at the fellowship meetings but never once came to the girls' dorm, always maintained the attitude of a protective older brother. Upon graduation he set off immediately to study abroad in Europe and frequently wrote to me, encouraging me to maturely take part in university activities, and often wrote about his studies and ideas, and how Europe, like China, was in the earthshaking throes of a heated and divisive battle, and with a concern more mature than his age. Many years later he returned to Communist China and we lost touch, but about ten years ago, *Luojia*, the alumni newsletter, had an article by Yang Jingyuan that stated that in 1980 she had got together with Chen Renkuan, who had changed his name to Gong Chao, and that he worked in a translation company and foreign policy institute, so I assumed everything was going smoothly for him.

That year, my inner life was focused on writing letters to my Nankai classmates, writing about our different lives at different schools. The one thing we had in common was that we all missed Shapingba.

When I first entered the girls' dormitory and reported to Old Yao, the doorman, he saw my name and reached over to the sideboard on the left, took out a letter for me, and said, "This letter got here ahead of you." Then he looked at me as if making a special note. The handwriting on the envelope was Zhang Dafei's and the return address was a military box in Mengzi, Yunnan. It was again a light blue airmail letter. What was new was the heavy and oppressive concern it contained; he said nothing about it, but the letter was full of yearning. He had been worried about my trip on the Yangtze River, worried about my life after leaving home. "What kind of university student are you? I'm enclosing my contact address behind the lines. I'll wait to hear from you after you get to Leshan. Every day I take off and land waiting for your letter." My understanding over many years was that "landing" meant returning safely from battle.

Almost all his letters were written in the war room, in the hot, humid borderland in Yunnan, looking at the runway hastily constructed for the Flying Tigers. A twenty-five-year-old who had been through numerous battles, he wrote with the frame of mind of one writing a letter home to comfort a homesick nineteen-year-old girl, telling her not to cry, that in war-racked China, being able to go to the university was the beginning of a glorious future.

Every Monday afternoon when I returned from the Confucius Temple, Old Yao would grin and hand me a letter from Yunnan. In addition to remembering with longing, the letters contained even more encouragement. One also included a photograph of three fully armed fighter planes with shark mouths, with three handsome men full of self-confidence in their cockpits, which had been snapped just prior to takeoff. It was hard to imagine that "life is but a smile on the lips of death." Flying Tiger pilots were heroes of legend in those days. Chennault said, "I've never understood how the Chinese people of Kunming gave the name Flying Tigers to those P-40s with shark faces." After the United States entered the war, the Flying Tigers formally became part of the larger Sino-U.S. air corps.

He had received my wan and feeble letters, and probably not having much to say, we shared a fond remembrance of the poems from Nankai. Each time he took off to do battle in the sky, the wind whistling in his ears, the clouds rolling all around him, he had to be entirely focused because the enemy planes were around and he could have no other thoughts. But everything would pass and he would return and land his plane, and all his concerns would immediately come back to mind. At the base, the newspapers were three days old and the war had entered a period of difficult struggle. The western part of Sichuan was far from the war, so there was no news. He said, "I can't fly to that mountain city at the confluence of three rivers at the foot of the Giant Buddha to see you, but I love you so much and think of you constantly!"

Once I didn't receive any airmail letters for two straight weeks. During the day we were squeezed into that little room and at night the moonlight shone in, putting me in the mood to pace back and forth and worry about him. Stuck in a city among mountains and rivers, cut off from the world, the only thing that remained was thinking wild thoughts and suffering from nightmares.

Finally I received a letter from him, mailed from Kunming, in which he said he had been slightly wounded and would be well enough to rejoin his group the following week. From then on I never again wrote about my own vexations living in peace, nor did I dare bring up my own worries; I did my best to find interesting things to write about such as the debate over white horses and black horses in logic class, as well as the conflicting theories among schools of economics or how in the local Leshan dialect all measure words were replaced with one word, *kuai* (lump), for all objects—a lump of a week, a lump of a house, a lump of a notebook . . . or how two years before, the number 8 boys' dorm became a cemetery after it was flattened by bombs, for the students who suffered from prostration and died. The most romantic thing I told him was how I located the hollow tree on Dingdong Street that produced the ding-dong dripping sound. Ignorant as I was, I finally, in a terror, began to become acutely conscious, precisely because I had grown up, that it didn't matter how deep his love was: I couldn't touch his blood-soaked reality.

After he returned to his group, once again the postmarks on his letters were from places like Mengzi, Gujiu, Yunnan Station, and Tengchong, all of which I located on the map. I read about the war in the newspaper and knew that the Flying Tigers had been helping to protect the Burma Road with all their strength so as to maintain the lifeline of supplies for the Allied fight against Japan.

After he recovered from his wounds, he seemed on more familiar terms with death and never again mentioned his feelings in his letters. He just said that I was already twenty and that all the new things I had learned were useful and could help me make mature decisions.

I hadn't played my part well just after entering the university. All I had done over the last year was think about home and the past and complain about being isolated far away, with my head in a complete muddle.

IN THE MAIN HALL OF THE CONFUCIUS TEMPLE: MY FIRST MEETING WITH PROFESSOR ZHU GUANGQIAN

My feeling of being adrift underwent a rapid change near the end of my first year.

The exams for Chinese and English were the first given for all freshmen, and classes were based on scores rather than schools or departments. At the end, all freshmen were again tested and the results determined advancement or the criteria for changing departments. Wuhan University didn't have a medical school, and the most popular departments had always been foreign languages and literatures, economics, law, and electrical engineering, but they also had the highest failure rates. One day shortly after the exams, a classmate returned to the dorm and said she had seen an announcement posted at the Confucius Temple, and that I had the highest score on the freshman English exam. Hearing this, I wasn't especially excited, because I was thinking about how I was going to tell my parents that I wanted their permission to switch to the Department of Foreign Languages and Literatures at National Southwestern Associated University in Kunming. My mind was no longer on Leshan. I didn't know what to say and knew that permission wouldn't be readily forthcoming, which kept me awake much of the night. Everyone in the dorm was packing, because summer break would begin in a couple of weeks and we all would go home. I was facing the first really big hurdle in my life.

The following afternoon, Old Yao gave me a note handwritten with a writing brush from the office of the dean of studies, telling me to meet with the dean, Mr. Zhu Guangqian.

Professor Zhu was at that time already a world-famous scholar. Before he was fifteen, he had studied at home in Tong City in Anhui, and had spent ten years memorizing the classics and classical prose before entering Tong City Middle School. At twenty-one he earned a scholarship to study at Hong Kong University. After graduating he went to Shanghai to teach and along with Kuang Husheng, Zhu Ziqing, Feng Zikai, Ye Shengtao, Liu Dabai, and Xia Yan, founded and edited a magazine, *Daxueyuan*, and established the Kaiming Bookstore. At twenty-eight, with government funding, he attended Edinburgh University for advanced studies in English literature, and also studied philosophy, psychology, ancient European history, and art history. He also went to France to study literary psychology at the University of Paris, and in Germany he improved his German at the University of Strasbourg on the Rhine and penned his thesis, "The Psychology of Tragedy." During his eight years in Europe, he frequented the museums and libraries of Great Britain. He read and he wrote; his government stipend was often cut off, and for money he wrote for the periodicals *In General* and *Middle School Student* published by Kaiming Bookstore, articles later collected in a volume entitled *Twelve Letters to the Youth*. This book and his *On Beauty* were two "eye-opening" books that were required reading for any student beyond middle school.

Why would such a great scholar wish to see me, a first-year student? To tell the truth, it was with trepidation more than honor that I entered his profound and awe-inspiring office in the Confucius Temple. And the old gentleman, who was in no way large and robust, sat in a huge wooden chair (Professor Zhu was forty-seven that year; in my eyes at the time, anyone over forty was old) and did not smile in a kindly fashion.

He looked at me and said, "Your university entrance exam score got you into the philosophy department, but your English is very good—you are number one for the entire school. Why don't you change to the Department of Foreign Languages and Literatures?"

I said the reason was that my first choice was philosophy and that I hadn't applied for foreign languages and literatures at this university, not that I didn't have a sufficient exam score. When I graduated from high school, both my father and Mr. Meng had hoped I would study Chinese literature.

He asked me why I wanted to study philosophy and what sorts of philosophical works I had read. My reply must have seemed childish and ignorant to his ears (my father had already tactfully said as much to me). He thought for a moment and said, "Now that Wuhan University has moved to this remote location, it is very difficult to get teachers, and a number of the philosophy classes cannot be offered. Your Chinese teacher let me see your Chinese compositions, and they are too sadly sentimental, as if you had never penetrated the root of philosophical wisdom in your studies. You can sit in on the Chinese classes, or you can study on your own your whole life. But the foreign languages curriculum requires the guidance of a teacher as well as a solid base, if one is to make her way. You can think about it during the summer break and then make a decision. If you switch to foreign languages, I can be your advisor, and if you have any questions, you can feel free to ask whenever you wish."

That last sentence lingers in my mind to this day.

THE FIRMAMENT OF THE DEPARTMENT OF FOREIGN LANGUAGES AND LITERATURES

At summer break, my companions and I joyfully boarded the Min River steamer at Wutong Bridge for Yibin and then went down the Yangtze River, home to Chongqing, which had a more beautiful significance to me than ever. My middle school friends, who had been dispersed after the National Joint College Entrance Exams, were all home, and we had so many experiences to talk about since we had departed. The previous year, I had been the only one to go to far-off Sichuan; now, returning to Shapingba, I was like a solitary goose returning to roost with the flock, and there was no end to my happiness. As for the war, the Japanese had lost so many planes since the United States entered that they could no longer bomb Chongqing with any frequency and their main force had been shifted to the Burma Road. Each time they attacked, they were shot down in great numbers by the Sino-American 14th Air Force. Although Chongqing was as hot as ever that summer, there was a new atmosphere of rebuilding and repairing and, because we weren't fleeing for cover every day due to air-raid sirens, it was perfect for our group of first-year university girls to get together in each other's homes to chat. On moonlit nights we would go the banks of the Jialing River to sing and have heart-to-heart talks. That was probably the happiest summer of my life, and it was genuinely a carefree break.

Returning home, I naturally wanted to discuss switching departments with my parents. My father never came out and said, "I knew from the start that you wouldn't study philosophy," but he did say that my feelings were stronger than my reason, which made me better suited to study literature. Then, with a forced nonchalance, I mentioned that after posting the exam scores the previous year, National Southwestern Associated University had suggested that I join their Department of Foreign Languages and Literatures, that there were many Nankai students there, and that I hoped to go there too. If we were victorious in the war, I could go to Beiping University, Qinghua University, or Nankai University. . . . His expression hardening, he said that since the United States had entered the war the situation had changed significantly, but the battle lines in China were repeatedly changing due to setbacks. Hunan had fallen, Guangxi was threatened, and Guizhou couldn't be defended. "If you go to Yunnan, you'll be even farther from home. Although Leshan is far away, it's still in Sichuan. I can look after you if you are closer. Given your health, it would be a good idea for you to transfer to National Central University and stay in Shapingba. That way I wouldn't have to worry so much. If the situation worsens, at least the whole family can be together."

Shortly after returning home, I received a letter from Brother Dafei. He was firmly opposed to me switching schools to Kunming, since he moved from base to base at any time and couldn't be there to look after me. Given the current situation of the war, he didn't even have three days off, nor did he have time to go to Sichuan to see me. He hoped that I would return with peace of mind to study at Leshan. The only way out was victory. His tone was that of an older brother speaking to a little sister.

During that time, I also sought the advice of Professor Sun Jinsan, chief editor of *Time and Tide Literature and Art*, regarding Professor Zhu Guangqian's recommendation. Sun Jinsan was a well-known professor in the Department of Foreign Languages and Literatures at National Central University and was greatly respected by my father. Under his direction, *Time and Tide Literature and Art* had published works by Shen Congwen, Ba Jin, Hong Shen, Wu Zuxiang, Mao Dun, Zhu Guangqian, Wen Yiduo, Zhu Ziqing, Wang Xiyan, Bi Ye, Zang Kejia, and Xu Yu, writers who not only were widely popular among readers but also became important authors in the history of modern Chinese literature. *Time and Tide*also published the classics of many countries translated by Liu Wuji, Li Jiye, Fang Chong, Li Changzhi, Xu Zhongnian, Yu Gengyu, Fan Cunzhong, Chen Shouzhu, Dai Liuling, Yu Dayin, and Ye Junjian. The high level of attainment of the men of letters in those days is clear. Each issue contained information on literary trends and on art and literature in China and around the world, an extremely valuable record for the years 1942–1945. Unfortunately, soon after victory, the war between the Nationalists and the Communists started, and my father couldn't sustain the magazine for more than three issues, so *Time and Tide Literature and Art* ceased publication in 1945.

Professor Sun said, "Zhu Guangqian has an article entitled 'Bad Taste in Literature' in the May 1944 issue. It was written from the perspective of someone who teaches literature, and it is very clear and very pertinent. One would be very fortunate to take classes with Professor Zhu at Wuhan University. What's more, he himself urged you to switch departments and volunteered to be your advisor, which is more than anyone could hope for. The value of an education in literature is in the stimulation of the intelligence or the root of wisdom. Fang Chong, Chen Yuan (Xi Ying), Yuan Changying, and Chen Yanke all teach in the Department of Foreign Languages and Literatures at Wuhan University, and the foundation is quite substantial. The foreign languages department at National Southwestern Associated University isn't necessarily better, and they don't have someone like Zhu Guangqian, who has taken notice of you."

Mr. Sun's analysis helped me decide to return to Wuhan University. For some reason, that river town several hundred *li* upstream also attracted me like a secluded paradise.

At the end of summer break, I returned to Leshan a week early in order to do the paperwork to change departments. I had also arranged to meet Zhao Xiaolan to register early for a dorm room—the second-year students were advanced to a row of new wooden rooms above the cafeteria, and I hoped to get a desk by the window.

My father had arranged for me and a classmate to take an express mail truck to Leshan. For the convenience of civil servants and college students during wartime, every mail truck could sell passage for two people. An ID had to be produced to guarantee the safety of the mail. The two of us and a postal employee took turns riding in front with the driver or sitting among the dozens of bags of mail. We began to feel very important. Napping on the tightly bound bags, I imagined the innermost feelings contained in each letter and the joy of the recipient. Arriving at each stop, the postal employee would shout the name of the place and elegantly toss down a bag, while someone down below would pitch up another bag. Later I read a history of the Qing dynasty that said that the post office was the earliest modern government system and the postal employees were of the highest possible caliber. After the government arrived in Taiwan, the post office was still one of the stabilizing strengths. Over thousands of years letters had gone from being delivered by horse to being distributed by green mail trucks, and everywhere had inspired our rich imagination. I now had the good fortune to be taken like a parcel from eastern Sichuan to western Sichuan. Such a special experience deserves to be recorded.

The first night we spent in Chengdu at the dorm of a Nankai alum. During the war, Yanjing University, Nanjing Jinling Men's College and Jinling Women's College, and Shandong Jilu University, along with the local Huaxi University, moved to Huaxiba Station in Chengdu and made it a lively place. The following morning we again boarded the truck, which never broke down, securely making its way along the safe and reliable roads. Passing Meishan, mailbags were loaded and unloaded, but then all that could be seen were the trees going by as we sped along. We didn't stop the entire day and drove directly to the door of the Leshan post office. This time, I knew in advance what life was like and how I would face it. In Chengdu, I saw the true style and features of Sichuan's old capital, and I found myself in a far more relaxed mood than the year before.

PROFESSOR ZHU GUANGQIAN'S ENGLISH POETRY CLASS

Entering the Department of Foreign Languages and Literatures in my second year, I had Professor Zhu's English poetry class for one year. Although I was nervous facing the challenge, it did have the effect of calming me, so I immediately dived in and worked hard. Professor Zhu used *Palgrave's Golden Treasury*, the standard international anthology then. But after moving, the Wuhan University library only had six copies of the book, three copies for the female students and three for the male students, which were passed around in turn based on class progress and then copied before class. I went to the Jiale Paper Factory and bought three large notebooks of the finest quality Jiale paper, a dreamy blue inside and out. I filled them with lines of poetry under the dim lamp, along with my teacher's comments. A whole year of notes made while studying are still with me today on that now fragile paper.

Although Professor Zhu used *Palgrave's Golden Treasury* as textbook, he didn't follow the editor's order of chronological division: William Shakespeare, 1564–1616; John Milton, 1608–1674; Thomas Gray, 1716–1771; and the Romantic period. The poems for the first semester were chosen for their pedagogic value, to teach us what makes a good poem good. The first section was Wordsworth's sparkling Lucy poems.

Two hundred years after the fact, the identity of Lucy, the young girl of chaste and elegant beauty, is unknown, but those five short poems that attempt to recall that eighteen-year-old sweetheart who died young are gems in the history of English literature. Few have surpassed the depth of emotion with such simplicity. The last poem, "A Slumber Did My Spirit Seal," has been my best medicine for alleviating suffering over the last sixty years. When I recite it in a lecture or quote it in writing, I hope to show the efficacy of poetry in life. In those days, Professor Zhu certainly must have hoped to use this to indoctrinate us in Western literature. In the third poem in the group, "I Traveled Among Unknown Men," the poet says he will never again leave England, because the last thing Lucy saw was the wild green of England. For me, who put patriotism above all else at the time, this was the most beautiful and the most powerful poem about love of country.

Professor Zhu selected more than ten of Wordsworth's short poems, pointing out the directness of the language and the cohesiveness of scene. When he got to "The Solitary Reaper," the sound of her song as it diminished with distance reminded me of the excess of rhyme in Tang poet Qian Qi's verse: "the song is ended, no one is seen, / several green peaks above the river."

Another day, Professor Zhu taught "The Affliction of Margaret," one of Wordsworth's longer poems, which is about a woman whose only son left to make his way in the world; there has been no news of him for seven years. Every night, from the other side of a marsh, the poet hears the woman calling her son: "Where art thou, my beloved son. . . ." When she runs into someone, she asks if they have seen him, imagining all sorts of reasons for his absence.

Reading "the fowls of heaven have wings, . . . Chains tie us down by land and sea," Professor Zhu said that classical Chinese poetry contains similar ideas, for example: "Birds have roads in the wind and clouds, / the Yangtze and Han rivers, barriers without ferries." His voice caught at this point, and he paused before continuing to read to the last two lines: "If any chance to heave a sigh / They pity me, and not my grief."

Professor Zhu took off his glasses; tears rolled down his cheeks. He suddenly closed the book and quickly left the classroom, leaving everyone in the room astonished, but no one said a word.

Perhaps in such difficult times, the display of emotion was frankly a luxury. In the eyes of a university sophomore who still worshiped idols, this was something unexpected and difficult to discuss, and even something of an honor to see the tears of emotion shed by a famous scholar of literature.

Over twenty years later, when I was teaching the history of English literature, Palgrave's anthology had long been replaced by other anthologies, few of which included this poem. Different tears for different ages. However, most of the poems selected by Professor Zhu are still found in anthologies today.

The second part of the English poetry class emphasized the intellect. Reading some of Shakespeare's sonnets, we discussed transience and eternity. We also read Shelley's "Ozymandias," with the awe-inspiring visage of the Egyptian king half buried in the sand, "boundless and bare, the lone and level sand, stretched far away."

Professor Zhu commented that the poem was about how a thousand years of human history is no more than a moment to heaven, and that Chinese literature had countless similar lines, but we should listen to the stress on the words "boundless" and "bare" and the lack of stress on "lone and level." This is another sort of language, one different from the feeling of beauty.

As for "Ode to the West Wind," Professor Zhu commented that since the inception of vernacular literature in China, many people had intoned the famous line, "If Winter comes, can Spring be far behind?" to the point of making it tiresomely superficial. Shelley's odes sing the praise of a wild spirit, the inspiration of youth, the awesome power to overturn the old and corrupt. The entire work is composed of five linked sonnets, all seventy lines of which must be read at one go in order to appreciate the magnificent power of Romantic poetry through the cyclical process of the seasons and the palpitation of the human heart within. In that small room in a wing of the Confucius Temple, Professor Zhu usually lectured with a serious expression and seldom gestured, but on this occasion, he made large sweeping gestures as he read, and taught us to use "the mind's eye" to imagine the image of the west wind's roar. This was the first time I truly observed the imagery in a Western poem, the benefit of which I have enjoyed ever since.

BRIGHT MOONLIT NIGHT IN MEISHAN

Winter break began. Some of my classmates and I participated in a winter camp organized by the activity center of Wutongqiao Bridge District. After dinner on the first night, a Nankai upperclassman, then in the school of engineering, suddenly came looking for me. More than twenty of the students had been drafted to assist with a professional engineering project in Chongqing. The trucks would drive directly to Chongqing and I could get a ride home, and when school resumed, they would bring me back to Leshan.

What great news! Since there was no direct transportation between Leshan and Chongqing, I grabbed a small bag and went to join them on the truck, but I was so dizzy with excitement that I nearly fell into a pit by the roadside. Four upperclassmen from Nankai were on the truck, so it was very "safe." The plan was to arrive in Chengdu before midnight and drive straight to Chongqing the following day. Who could have foreseen that after ninety *li* the truck would develop engine trouble just outside of Meishan? Not one of the expert engineers on board could fix it, so we had no choice but to split up and look for lodging for the night.

Eight male classmates and I spent the night in the best hotel, which was, in fact, a teahouse with a few plank beds, mainly for travelers who had trouble on the road. On a winter's night, with no streetlights, the room was large and cavernous, gloomy, cold, and clammy. The owner arranged for me to stay in a room next to the one used by the owner and his wife. Just as we were making up the plank beds, someone shouted from outside: "Hurry! Hurry up and get packed!"

Alarmed, he told us that since the end of the year things had been difficult because a group of bandits in the mountains came down at night to rob and loot. They had already been there several times and giving them a little money would probably pacify them, but with a female student present, things might be a little dicier. What was to be done?

The wife suddenly hit upon a way out of the predicament. She dragged a huge old wooden cabinet out from behind the counter and said to me, "Hide in our cashbox!" She had me lie down inside at once and closed the huge wooden lid. She then had a short, fat student unroll his bedroll on top of it and lie down to sleep. Most of us were undernourished in those days and pretty skinny, so I remember him, a handsome, broad-minded, and outspoken young man.

Fortunately, there was a hole under the handle on each end of the cabinet, so I could breath while inside. I heard shouting and confused noises, tables and chairs being pushed aside and turned over, which almost made my heart stop but also didn't give me any time to think about being afraid of sleeping in a box. Finally things quieted down and I heard the sound of the heavy door closing; then an elder classmate by the name of Yu opened the cabinet and said, "It's over. You can come out."

When I stepped out of the cabinet, I saw that all the bedded-down students had several books under their heads, because they knew bandits in Sichuan wouldn't steal books: the word for "book" was homophonous with "lose" in the local dialect. Moreover, the respect for culture ran deep in Sichuan, and even thieves respected those with an education.

Among the students in the group was one who had been with me on the boat from Chongqing to Leshan the previous year and had seen me crying all the way up the Yangtze to the Min River. He was surprised that I didn't cry upon encountering such a frightful situation that night and even asked if any of them had been injured. Actually, after I grew up, I never again cried when I encountered danger or was threatened.

The following day, we left as soon as it was light. We didn't go to Chengdu but took a shortcut and drove straight to Chongqing. Someone was going to Shapingba, so they took me right to my door. As the truck drove across the Meishan County line, it suddenly occurred to me that Meishan was the home of Su Dongpo! It was none other than the Meishan in his poem "To River Town," in which he mourns his wife: "Ten years have we been parted / the living and the dead—hearing no news, / Never tried to remember, / still hard to forget." During the dramatic situation of the previous night, I had set foot in Su Dongpo's beloved home, but I had no idea if it had been a bright moonlit night or not. I hadn't even thought about Duansonggang, the burial place of Su's wife, or if I was destined to see the Hall of the Three Sus. I thought at the time how easy it would be to visit those places if I were in school in the Min-E area. In truth, however, in those days, it would have been very difficult, because it would have been quite a luxury for a young woman to go traveling.

Unexpectedly I had the good fortune to spend the winter break at home. My parents were concerned and my little sister amusing. Every day I dressed well and had enough to eat, and slept under a thick, warm quilt, my heart always filled with gratitude. This was to be the last New Year's season I would spend at home with my parents. We would only be together again after arriving in Taiwan.

WHEN THE FLAMES OF WAR PRESSED NEAR: READING KEATS FOR THE FIRST TIME

Upon returning to school, I most looked forward to resuming my English poetry class.

During the winter break, I sought Mr. Sun Jinsan's advice on English Romantic poetry, especially that of Shelley (that was before I read Keats). From the books he loaned me, I copied out some secondary information, which kept me fully absorbed and blocked out the threat of war.

Then slowly the tide began to turn in favor of the British and American allies in the Pacific and they went from the defensive to the offensive, and the United States recovered the Philippines (MacArthur had uttered those famous brave words of his when they retreated: "I shall return!"). After the allies landed on Iwo Jima, the bloody battles from island to island began. But the battle lines inside China were more worrisome. With no way back, the Japanese forced their way along China's Guangzhou–Hankou Railway, and the educated youth of China heeded Chairman Chiang Kai-shek's call for "100,000 young people for 100,000 troops." Two hundred thousand young people joined the army. Nankai alum Wang Shirui, who was in the school of engineering while I was at Wuhan University, took the test for the air corps officer school. At a time when the army was suffering defeat in battle and the critical front gradually shifted from Guizhou to Sichuan, only the air corps showed glorious military success, but unfortunately their numbers were too few and losses had been great. The Chinese and Americans of the 14th Air Force became everyone's heroes of hope.

It had been quite some time since I last received a letter from Zhang Dafei. I couldn't tell anyone that those light blue letters mailed from places with strange names were like a miracle that had vanished. Only old newspapers with battle news came from the world outside the three rivers.

Returning to English poetry class, Professor Zhu lectured on the special features of English Romantic poetry. He had us copy out eight poems by Shelley. All young readers of Shelley are roused by his unbridled passion, and the premonition of love and death frequently appears in a line of verse with three exclamations. That sort of pure and candid outcry is something I never encountered in Chinese poetry. In his "The Indian Serenade," we read: "I die! I faint! I fail!" The most resonant line to my young dejected mood was the opening of his poem "A Lament": "O World! O Life! O Time!" (later editions omit the exclamation points), which were the very pent-up emotions I was unable to utter. Not only did I dwell on the life and death of the solitary individual, but also I felt that a person's life and death were inextricably yoked with the world, life, and time that stops for no one. We were so young, but we were drawn into a vast war, one seemingly without end. Professor Zhu said that the poem wasn't that good, but it did reveal Shelley's true colors. Young people are troubled by feelings and wish to break free and shout aloud, but poems written purely to vent feelings always tend to be a little shallow and can't withstand the test of time. Since I first read this poem in February 1945, my country and I have faced tremendous changes; decades of "O World! O Life! O Time!" have left my heart in continuous turmoil, a state of confusion that cannot be more suitably or succinctly expressed.

At seventy-five, Bertrand Russell, the English philosopher, completed *Fact and Fiction,* in which he recounts the growth of his mind from age fifteen to twenty-one, and the books that most influenced him. In a chapter titled "The Importance of Shelley" he describes how deeply obsessed he was when as a young person he read Shelley's poetry, in which the real seemed unreal. Later in life, with more experience, he did encounter deeply tranquil states of mind and have similar sensations. He was thoroughly familiar with Shelley's short lyric poems and hoped to produce the same kind of infatuated, though bitter love—"I liked the beauty of despair, the isolated and illusory scenes"—that became the fountainhead of feeling and the power of his imagination. It is said that Marx and Engels liked nothing better than to talk about Shelley and how they admired the antitraditional spirit of this brilliant and elegant poet who was born a nobleman.

Professor Zhu insisted that all good poems ought to be memorized, and every poem we studied with him, we had to memorize. Fewer than twenty people attended the English poetry class, and memorizing poems was an activity for which there was no escape, like in an old tutorial school. In the process from "memorizing" to "teaching," each poem went from being new to being familiar. With a few words of guidance from our teacher, we got at the true meaning of the poems. After studying a few short poems by Shelley, we turned to his "Stanzas Written in

Dejection—December, Near Naples," a poem filled with regret in which he blames and censures himself. In this poem he was also fairly accurate in prophesying his own death by drowning, so it has been treasured by later generations.

One freezing morning in February 1945, three of my classmates and I set out down White Pagoda Street, passing wet Shuixi Gate, which was already covered by a thin coat of water. Each of us carried our hand-copied English poetry textbook, trying to memorize "One Word Is Too Often Profaned" along with "Stanzas Written in Dejection," the first line of the third stanza of which aptly expressed my state of mind, for which we could not find the words: "nor peace within nor calm around."

The four of us recited the verses, sometimes picking up where another left off. We turned into Confucius Temple Square from the county government office and went up the broad stone steps through the Confucius Temple gate. Before us, on the stone column beside the Lingxing gate, was pasted a large brush-written announcement, the ink of which still seemed wet:

> On the morning of February 25th, 1,800 large American planes bombed Tokyo, turning the city into a sea of fire. Filled with trepidation, the Japanese prime minister entered the palace to apologize.

The several hundred university students standing around the notice had experienced eight years of war and survived through state expense; their clothes in tatters, their dark faces thin and lean, they stood in silence on the flagstones in front of the main hall of the Confucius Temple, reading the news of revenge, their hearts surging with complex feelings of joy.

Finally the Japanese, who had violently bombed us for eight years, got a taste of the suffering of their country being destroyed and knew the terror of destruction falling from the skies. Since invading and occupying Manchuria, they had found glory in conquering others and had grown self-satisfied and self-confident. The cherry blossoms and fall leaves in their homeland were always resplendent, but as a people they drove others into the abyss of wandering for years on end!

I too was silent, standing there before that stone column, filled with a mixture of joy and pain, visualizing those 1,800 bombers approaching and blotting out the sun. I could almost hear the sharp whistle of a thousand bombs just before they hit the ground, the red-hot gust just prior to explosion, buildings toppling and burning, the cratered ground with earth and stones thrown up all around. . . . Ah, the unforgettable time of youth! Death circled in the light of the sun and in bright moonlit skies, and then it fell. There was no place to hide.

How could those men, who were arrogantly self-conscious on account of the chrysanthemum and the sword, protect those women with their swept-up hairdos, their faces covered with a thick layer of white powder, their flowery kimonos tied up with an even more flowery *obi*, fleeing on high wooden clogs? Some of these women strapped the ashes of their boyfriends or husbands who had died in battle in China on their backs, only for them to be incinerated a second time.

The class bell brought us back to reality. From the stone column we walked to the second classroom in the right-side hall of the temple and continued with that beautiful "Stanzas Written in Dejection," written in a peaceful world so different from our own. All of us knew how beautiful it would be to die amid the sounds of lapping waves.

Professor Zhu always started class on time. He stood behind a small rostrum, about two feet from the first row of students. After he entered, the small stone-paved room inside the hall of the temple was no longer a classroom, but rather a secret room between the blue sky and me. In addition to the unvarnished desks and chairs, there was just a small blackboard and four bare walls making for a solemn environment, like some modern or postmodern studio. Resonant of the soul, music seemed to flow from the walls, accompanying Professor Zhu's British English with an Anhui accent, carrying us into a magical realm. Perhaps for me, whose imagination is first piqued through sound via the ears, in turn leading the eyes to the mirage of the floating clouds outside the window, my lifelong love for the rhythms of English poetry, like mountains rising and falling or the surge of waves going on and on without end, began at that time. For me, English and Chinese poetry are both a kind of emotional utopia, and even the most despairing of poems possesses a vigorous life force. This is a fate of sorts—at some point in life, a few sounds are heard, a few images seen, all of which take hold of one's heart, binding one inextricably for life.

Of course, the strongest reason for this is that I first read Shelley's "To a Skylark," then Keats's "Ode to a Nightingale." I didn't notice Professor Zhu's Anhui accent, I just saw the infinite differences in human life. Reading these poems again years later, standing at the rostrum teaching, reading them through till they reverberate, I deeply feel that all the differences in life arise from the joy of "To a Skylark" and the melancholy of "Ode to a Nightingale." Fate, character, talent, and the reality of life go round and round, linked together. Shelley's unrestrained soul soared and sang, like silver starlight and the splendor of the bright moon, like the seasonable rain, like a firefly, like a vernal downpour moistening the earth. And we mortals are forever cautious, and even our sincerest laughter hides some pain. The poet says, "If I could sing with but one half of your joy, the world would surely listen!"

LEIBO, MABIAN, PINGSHAN, AND EBIAN

As we were reading and reciting "To a Skylark," school president Wang Xinggong appeared in the square in front of the Confucius Temple and had the teachers and students assemble to hear an important announcement: defeat might allow the Japanese army to invade Sichuan. The Ministry of Education had ordered that when things became critical, all schools should be prepared to retreat to safe areas. The Headquarters of the Jiading Division Regional Command was assigned to protect Wuhan University, and if necessary, we were to retreat to the Yi Autonomous Region of Leimaping'e in the Liangshan area on the border between Sichuan and Xikang. We were told that as adults we should not be alarmed, but we should be mentally prepared.

In the university we seldom saw the president, and even more seldom heard him give a pep talk. I remember President Wang, one of China's first chemists and one of the founders of Wuhan University, standing in the square on that cold windy day in early spring, in his old scholar's robe, his face lean and his voice sad. His brief conclusion was, "We've hung on through eight difficult years, and we won't give up for one day. Everyone has to do their utmost. The Ministry of Education has ordered that until the very last day it will be business as usual at every institution."

Sixty years later, having traversed the entire country, I still hear the four words Lei-Ma-Ping-E with a tragic ring in my heart; they signify a sort of final safety. In life there is always a way out under any circumstances, and the belief that schooling must go on without interruption has always kept me alive.

I wrote to my parents and asked if Chongqing fell, how would I find my home if I had to go to Leimaping'e? Ten days later, my father replied by express mail. Simply and forcefully, he said, "The battle lines in China are spread too far, and truly great efforts are needed in the present situation. However, the situation for the allies in the Pacific and Europe is improving by the day. My child, your safety will be ensured by staying with the school. Regardless of the changes in the tide of war, I will find you as long as I have a breath of life left in me."

Those were truly terrifying days. Nights on my wood-plank bed were spent thinking about how difficult it would be to trudge 300 *li.* Among the upperclass girls in the dorm it was rumored that the soldiers in the Jiading Division Regional Command said the female students were all so proud, but where would their pride be if they had to follow the troops into the mountains? Others said that it was just a divisive rumor spread by the advance elements of the left. A number of the male students among the upperclassmen suggested to the school that two hundred male and female students should accompany the troops into the mountains.

At the beginning of April 1945, in those fearful, uneasy days, at the Confucius Temple where schooling went on without interruption, I read Keats's "On First Looking Into Chapman's Homer" for the first time. It is probably the first poem by him that everyone reads. It is a sonnet, a formal verse form likened to dancing in chains, which he wrote upon first reading the epic in a new translation and feeling a joy not unlike that of an explorer discovering a new mountain peak.

But I didn't understand his rapture. Bombs were falling around me. The scream of the bombs and the sea of fire that followed, going from near to far and far to near, surrounded me there in that mountain city at the confluence of three rivers in western Sichuan. Even there I didn't have a feeling of security, so I couldn't understand how he and his friends had "discovered" a new poetic form. Reading from nightfall till the sky grew light at dawn, he walked three miles under the starlight back to the cotttage where he was staying, and then, dashing off this sonnet of immortal joy, he sent it posthaste to his friend to read. After penning that poem, he would expend his life's genius over the next five years, dying at twenty-six, coughing up blood and dying.

Five years was a long time for me and twenty-six still a long way off. If I lived through that day, who knew what tomorrow would bring? In his letter, my father had said that as long as he had a breath of life left in him, he would find me. He was forty-six that year. What did he mean by "breath of life"? I had a bad feeling.

When we returned to class, Professor Zhu didn't say a word about our situation, but began to lecture on "Ode to a Nightingale," the second poem by Keats that we studied. He said that by reading "To a Skylark" by Shelley and then "Ode to a Nightingale" by Keats, one could see the two faces of Romanticism. The more you read, the less likely you were to apply simplistic terms such as "Romanticism." When Keats was eight years old, his father fell from a horse and died; when he was fourteen, his mother died from tuberculosis; when he was twenty-four, he sat by his brother's sickbed and watched his life ebb away. Inconsolable, he sought to escape the bitterness of life through art, and gradually conceived this poem. On a tender night listening to the song of the nightingale, he sank into a stupor as if he had drunk poison, grew intoxicated as if he had drunk good wine; the nightingale must not know the sufferings of men, "Here where men sit and hear each other groan." The poet sat in an orchard and "still wouldst thou sing and I have ears in vain— / To thy high requiem become a sod."

The poem was difficult to read and recite. The poet's mind moves between life and death, and the lines of verse are long and rich in imagery. Shelley's "To a Skylark" seemed as lively as a nursery rhyme by contrast. We read three more short poems by Keats after this one: "When I have fears that I may cease to be / Before my pen has glean'd my teeming brain," "Why did I laugh tonight? No voice will tell," and "Bright star, would I were steadfast as thou art." In two short months, I experienced another realm of human life through a spiritual resonance with the poems of Keats.

PROGRESSIVE READING GROUPS

For the first two years, my life at Leshan seemed divided between two worlds, with Shuiximen as the dividing line. Coming out of Shuixi Gate and turning left, I headed toward the Confucius Temple for class, to look at the notices, read the wall newspapers, and view various exhibitions (the works of famous artists such as Xu Beihong, Guan Shanyue, Feng Zikai, and Ling Shuhua were displayed, but of course prominence was given to the works of local personages, teachers, and students); turning right onto White Pagoda Street took me back to the dormitory, which was the real world of daily life that I shared with others.

Not long after Zhao Xiaolan and I moved to our new room, a law student in the same building invited the two of us to attend the "reading group" after dinner. I thought it would be wonderful to read some new books, so I set off with great enthusiasm.

More than thirty people were there, with boys outnumbering girls. That day they were discussing Maxim Gorky's *Mother*, which I had read when I was at Nankai Middle School and had found very moving. The book assigned for the next meeting was Mikhail Sholokov's *The Silent Don*. We passed the book around and took turns reading it. My roommate, Elder Sister Hou (she had returned to school after taking some time off, and was two or three years older than me), was in charge of the book in the girls' dorm. I attended three meetings with her, all of which were spirited, fiery, and politically charged. We also sang many songs, Russian folksongs and "The East Is Red," among others.

When I attended Nankai Middle School, we had no evening activities, and I returned home on weekends. I had never heard of reading groups, so this was quite novel to me, and I was very excited to write home about it. I soon received a letter from my father that said, "These days, all universities have reading groups. They are peripheral organizations of the Communist Party used to recruit intellectuals. Today the Nationalists and the Communists are cooperating for the sake of full-scale resistance against the Japanese, so all mass organizations are operating in the open. My child, you are naïve and interested in your studies. I suggest that you make full use of Wuhan University's famous library and read things related to your coursework. There is no need to get involved in political activities. The situation in China is still at a low point and you could say that the Nationalist troops are spilling their blood to preserve our territory. My child, you are alone and away from home. You must look after yourself so that you can handle anything that arises." (I still remember every word of such letters from those days.)

From then on, I was no longer willing to attend the reading group with Elder Sister Hou, telling her that I was too busy with my studies. I even showed her my notebooks—Keats's "Ode to a Nightingale," for example, was both long and difficult. I had just returned from the library where I had borrowed an academic book in English and was constantly flipping through my dictionary. After that she attended the meetings only with Zhao Xiaolan, and after returning from them, she would sing "Katyusha" and "The East Is Red" louder than ever. She no longer spoke with me, and when we met in the hall, she'd intentionally turn her head aside and not look at me. What saddened me the most, however, was that Zhao Xiaolan gradually began ignoring me too, and we ended up living like strangers in our small space.

Looking back today, there is clear evidence that the Communist Party recruited intellectuals through reading groups.

During the War of Resistance against Japan, the Nationalists and the Communists cooperated half the time, and both Mao Zedong and Zhou Enlai visited Chongqing. After Mao was elected to the National Political Council (Zhang Boling, Nankai principal, served as vice chairman, and Wang Jingwei, who served as speaker, concluded and signed a secret agreement with Japan betraying the country in 1940, and left shortly thereafter for Nanjing to set up a puppet government!), he went to Chongqing to show solidarity in the resistance against Japan. My father, who was also a member, met and spoke with him briefly.

The Communist Party's *Xinhua News*, after officially getting off the ground at Hankou in 1938, moved to Chongqing and only stopped being published when the war with Japan was nearly over. In an age when newspapers were the sole source of news, its position influenced many intellectuals and students.

Zhou Enlai was also a graduate of Nankai Middle School and often visited Principal Zhang Boling on campus; since he was an alumnus, he spoke many times at Monday assemblies. Everyone really enjoyed it when Zhang Boling, filled with warmth for this outstanding alum, introduced him with his Tianjin accent, "Now I'll ask Neng (En) to talk."

Caring only for the old principal's position, Zhou limited his remarks to strengthening the nation, throwing off the Japanese yoke, and becoming one of the great nations of the world, and never once did he engage in Communist propaganda. Actually, his own charisma was the best propaganda. His gentle and cultivated style and his erudition brought many people into the fold of the Communist Party. Young people didn't understand how, when the regular troops of the legitimate government were entirely focused on fighting the Japanese, the Communists were using every means to infiltrate the rear so that after victory, they would deprive the government, which was exhausted and had suffered casualties, of state power. Then later, through the Great Leap Forward and the Cultural Revolution and other totalitarian measures, they dominated and consolidated state power.

In 1943, when I was a senior in middle school, the bombings were at their height. Fu Qizhen transferred to the College of Natural Sciences, and she was always friendly to me in school. She was big and tall, pretty, optimistic, and always smiling; she was a good student and got along well with others. Later she tested into National Central University and remained in Shapingba, while I left for Leshan in Sichuan Province. When I returned home for the summer break, we met and talked; later I heard that she and Chen Chunming and four others as well as some male classmates from Central University went to Yan'an. I was shocked and saddened by this at the time. I always thought she was a close friend, as we often spent time together, reading books outside class, writing for the wall newspaper, and organizing activities. She took such a huge step without giving me the slightest hint of her intentions, and she never said good-bye before leaving. It wasn't until I encountered the reading group at Wuhan University that I gradually came to understand how unlikely it was that Fu Qizhen could have told me what she was planning. Perhaps she had early on attended an activity like a reading group and had been recruited by leftists, becoming a "progressive element," while I, an "immature" and infatuated student of literature, had ceased to be a "fellow traveler." Of course, the same could be said of my relationship with my new acquaintance Zhao Xiaolan.

At that time, the president announced the Ministry of Education's order that we had to be prepared in the event of an emergency to evacuate to Leibo, Mabian, Pingshan, Ebian at a moment's notice, everyone in the girls' dorm was alarmed. Fortunately, the teachers were a source of stability. They all had family and said that everyone was in the same boat and we shouldn't be afraid. Several of our Sichuan classmates asked for leave to go home (the school permitted classes and exams to be made up). The third floor of the dorm, owing to the slope of the roof, had two garret rooms in which two beds and two desks could be placed. Only one side of each room had a window, but there was a skylight. Classmates who preferred things a little more lively couldn't stand living in those rooms, and lowerclassmen couldn't move up. Those on the third floor shared the same stairway. One day I ran into Li Xiuying from the history department, who told me that her roommate had been taken home by her fiancée, perhaps for good, saying that marriage was more important in wartime. As a result, there was an empty bed in the garret room. She knew that I really liked less crowded rooms and asked if I'd like to share the room. I practically ran to the dorm supervisor's office and applied for and got the bed. That small plank bed, small wooden desk, and foot-and-a-half-square skylight were like a beautiful palace to me.

As I was packing my bags and gathering together my books, Elder Sister Hou, in her usual loud voice, without indicating who she was referring to, said, "Someone whose father has been in Chongqing for a while as a high official is receiving public funds and living off the fruits of the people's toil. She has no shame! All day long she does nothing but mumble about skylarks and nightingales without understanding how the people suffer. It's as if she has no soul." Everyone kept their heads down, pretending to read, without saying a word. I didn't know how to respond, so I just said good-bye to Zhao Xiaolan, grabbed my things, and moved up to the garret room.

After I made my new bed, I sat down and, quite upset, thought about what had just transpired. I recalled how when I had just moved in, she insisted that we address her as Elder Sister, and she especially looked after me, even saving a stall for me when we bathed and always saving a spot for me at the dinner table. How could she come to attack me so viciously in less than two months? That evening as I lay in bed, I looked at the stars filling the sky; it was the first time I thought that perhaps God was sending me a message. Was he telling me to look up at the dome of heaven and forgive those who had trespassed against me? But my young heart was unwilling to swallow such a heartless attack.

The following day when I went to class at the Confucius Temple, I paid a visit to the student affairs office and asked, "Which students are receiving a government stipend?" That work-study student replied impatiently, "All students attending public high schools and universities in war zones are receiving public stipends." I asked, "If the parent of a student in a war zone works for the government on a fixed salary, does that student also receive a stipend?" He scrutinized me before replying, "No one has ever asked that before. What's your name? What department are you in?" He wrote down my name, pulled a long face and said, "You go back and write a memo saying you'd like to give up your stipend, and the school will submit it to the Ministry of Education for you." Then he closed his information window.

Within three days, the students of the College of Arts, Letters, and Law were all saying that I had applied to give up my public stipend. Lu Qiaozhen asked me what was going on, so I told her that I had simply gone to inquire about the qualifications for a public stipend and hadn't said anything else. She said that the progressive (leftist) students wanted to use this to attack the Ministry of Education. After dinner that evening, as I went upstairs past my old room, that "elder sister" surnamed Hou said in a loud voice, "Some people are afraid that others don't know what a no-good bigwig they are, so they go around showing off! Daughter of a corrupt official, get the heck out of here! Don't get the idea that you are anything special!" This was the first time in my life that I understood how frightening politics and its lies can be. In my family, one would have braved untold dangers for revolution and patriotism, as a matter of love and honor, and what we most detested was heartlessness and the betrayal of one's friends.

In the sixty years since then, I've never gotten involved in politics, nor ever gotten involved even in school politics when I was a teacher.

AT THE CONFLUENCE OF THREE RIVERS

Living in that small garret room for one year and three months was a true delight of the sort seldom encountered in life, and my mood was brighter than the room. Li Xiuying had a steady boyfriend, who found a job in town while waiting for her to graduate. Every day after dinner, he'd come to the dorm to take her out. Every night the dorm super would come to take roll, and Xiuying would often come flying back around 9 p.m., just before the dorm was locked. So, every night I had three hours of peace and quiet to myself. It was the first time I felt free and unrestrained to read or sort out my concerns, a happiness I had not previously experienced. The small skylight opened toward the banks of the Dadu River, and in the quiet of the night I could hear the water flowing by, not a purling brook but the mighty and eternal surge of a large river. Gradually, above the sound of flowing water, I could hear a bird calling on the opposite bank and an echo beneath my window. Those two notes were so pure, clear, and pleasing to the ear, but nothing like the joy of the skylark or the melancholy of the nightingale in the poems. After singing briefly, the bird would fly off, to sing a little of its monotonous two notes farther in the distance. The first time I heard it I didn't sleep half the night, waiting for it to return. How was it possible? Although I was young but living in a troubled world, I unexpectedly heard a real bird singing to the sound of the river outside my window at night!

When day came, I asked my classmates if the bird singing on the opposite bank was a cuckoo. They said it was a *bugu* and you could hear it call "Bu-gu! Bu-gu!" urging the farmers to plant the rice sprouts. Lines such as, "Late spring in the third month, the grass south of the river grows tall, the various trees and bushes flower, flocks of warblers fly" were insufficient to describe the beauty of this river's banks. During the day, I pushed the window ajar and the songs of various birds flowed in with the sunlight, making me fidgety and anxious to get out of the small room and go in search of the sources of those songs. On the days when I had only half a day of classes, I would pick up my book of poems waiting to be memorized, go through Shuixi Gate and then down the stone stairs where the water carriers walked up and down, and set off to the right along the riverbank. On the riverbank overgrown with wild grass, there was a barely discernible path that led off below a ruined brick wall. If you had the courage to cross over, you'd find yourself in a small meadow facing the river. A small wood stood behind the meadow, behind which stood the dormitory, with my small garret room jutting out between the third and fourth floors. The little skylight shone in the sunlight, as if reflecting my pleasant surprise. If you continued on another twenty feet, a bend in the river occurred along which there was no path. It was my own private paradise that no one else knew about. Like the rocky lair on the cliff by the Jialing River, it was a pure land from which to escape the world.

I discovered that this place was destined only for one.

One morning in the second semester of my first year, I left that ugly room a little late and as I walked to the main door, I saw that an old water carrier had fallen on the stone step by the cauldron. His head had struck the step and his face was covered in blood. The other water carriers had lifted him up but couldn't stanch the blood. Immediately I ran back to my room and grabbed the first-aid kit I had brought from home. It contained cotton, iodine, gauze, and adhesive tape. Employing the first-aid training I had received as a scout in Chongqing, I managed to stop the bleeding and bandage him up. In the six years I was at Nankai, I was unable to apply my skills, but now I was able to do "one good deed a day" in this destitute state away from home. I was deeply moved.

I gave the iodine and gauze to the injured man, and two of the others standing there said the man was their headman, who was over fifty and had to carry water because his wife was sick and his son unreliable. Every morning I checked to make sure his dressings had been changed until the wound healed. In those days, medical care was fairly basic, and my scout training was considered pretty advanced. That morning, as I stood outside Shuixi Gate looking around, I saw that the old water carrier was in the river filling his buckets with water. When he saw me with my book, he came over and whispered to me that I could find a nice place to read if I followed the little path and kept on going around the bend. "There are a lot of people here; I'll tell them not to bother you," he whispered.

That was the best place! In my remaining two years at Leshan, I never told another soul about it. Like the rocky lair above the river, it was a sacred place for me. I was twenty that year and felt I could lose everything at any moment from life's various threats, which made me feel alone and helpless. The only thing that would remain was my soul, this mind of mine urgently pursuing admirable knowledge, seeking beauty and goodness. In that little paradise on the riverbank I could concentrate on collecting my soul.

When I first moved up to the garret and heard the cuckoo calling at night, it was really like Keats hearing the nightingale singing and building its nest in the garden of that cottage he rented. I wanted to find the tree and the bird's nest and looked several times on the riverbank below my window, but of course never found it. Late in spring, not only did the trees and bushes flower, the warblers flew and grass grew tall! Sitting beside the river on a clear day, I watched as the boats sailed down the Qingyi River from afar, where river and sky were joined in boundlessness. To this day, the thought of the Qingyi River produces reverie in me. A thousand years ago, Li Bai passed Leshan and wrote a poem titled

"Song of Emei Mountain Moon": "Emei Mountain moon half-full in autumn / shines on the Pingjiang River with its current flows. / Setting out for the Three Gorges from Qingzi at night, / I think of you, but no longer seen, sailing down to Yuzhou." The Pingjiang River is the Qingyi River. The Jiang and the Yi are indigenous people of western Sichuan. I don't know in which dynasty they were "pacified" by the Han Chinese, but the name of the river was changed to commemorate the conquest, and down through the ages, people with hearts like the clear river continue to call it by its original name, the Qingyi River. The river came from the snowmelt in the Qionglai Mountains in the mysterious west of Xikang and after pouring into the turbid, roaring surge of the Dadu River at my feet, it bent to the left and flowed into the Min River, through the rapids at Shanjiajiao, and just beyond Shuixi Gate, where the city got its water, it became clear and flowed past the foot of the great Tang-dynasty Buddha standing 230 feet high at the foot of mountain, purling as it flowed and never muddy. On a clear day at noon you could faintly make out a dividing line of clear and muddy in the river.

Facing the beautiful mountains and rivers, I couldn't help but always recite lines from Zhang Ruoxu's poem "Spring River, Flowers, Moonlit Night": "Who by the riverside first saw the moon arise? / When did the moon first shine on men by the riverside?" I knew I was insignificant, ignorant, anxious, and helpless, but I was perhaps the first Chinese woman to memorize Keats poems beside this river. I paced back and forth on my little stretch of riverbank and memorized his "Ode to a Nightingale," "Ode on a Grecian Urn," and "To Autumn," and the last few lines of "La Belle Dame Sans Merci":

> I saw their starv'd lips in the gloam
> With horrid warning gaped wide,
> And I awoke, and found me here
> On the cold hill's side.

I raced back to the dorm on account of the gloomy feeling I experienced while reciting these lines, but I went back to memorize another poem the following day. It was the first section of the long, difficult, and enchanting "The Eve of St. Agnes." The memorization of the lines and the poetic inspiration that burst forth in my youth, along with the season and the environment, combined to form a feeling toward life that would never become indifferent. Laughed at by my classmates in those days as one who was absent-minded and not of this world, I later, in a long life, sometimes became an eccentric who was unable to explain her discomfort with the status quo.

"To Autumn" is the only poem by Keats I like to share with others. It's a warm, mature, and perfect poem about resignation. The stubble wheat fields manifest the season's natural palpitations; the foolish bees in the last faded flowers of late summer think that summer will last forever, and the crickets sing softly and the swallows twitter as they fly through the sky. It's late autumn and a time of completion.

After reading a dozen poems by Keats, Professor Zhu returned to the first part of *Palgrave's Golden Treasury*, lecturing on a number of Shakespeare's sonnets, allowing me to experience another form of lyricism.

May was over by then and June beginning. On the days when we had English poetry class, three or four classmates and I would walk down White Pagoda Street past clammy Shuixi Gate, reciting poetry as we made our way to the Confucius Temple, but I knew that the world outside had changed completely.

ZHANG DAFEI GIVES HIS LIFE FOR HIS COUNTRY

The Allied forces occupied Berlin on May 2, 1945, and Japan was crumbling in the face of intensive American bombing. The kamikazes became Japan's final and most savage weapon. China was gradually recovering lost territory in Guangxi Province, and reports from the battlefront on June 13 were that the Japanese military there was isolated and that in the massive fighting in western Hunan, Chinese troops had been victorious, killing over ten thousand of the enemy, and were then advancing on Guilin. . . .

The dorm was filled with elation; everyone began unpacking the rucksacks they had made ready in the event we had to trudge off to Leibo, Mabian, Pingshan, Ebian, and began preparing for finals and the return home for summer vacation. Activities associated with the choir, concert, and farewell party heated up. Many of the students who had halted their studies came back with shamefaced expressions. On April 12, Roosevelt suddenly passed away, which came as a great shock to the Chinese. One day in English class, Professor Zhu read Whitman's elegy for Lincoln, "O Captain! My Captain!", in which the poet laments that the president had not lived to see the end of the war. Reading this poem at the time, I felt it had a resounding power, much like the beating of a funeral drum. But within the next one hundred days, I'd be called upon a second time to clearly remember that poem, which became permanently imprinted on my mind, heavy of heart and resigned to sadness as I was.

The last time I went out past Shuixi Gate to my spot beside the river was in June. Spring was over, and the grass grew so tall on the riverbank that it gradually had covered the trail. I went there to read my brother's letter, received two days before, of which I had already memorized every word, but I had to find a place to think. . . .

My brother's letter said that on the 18th of May, in the battle for Henan, Zhang Dafei, while covering a friendly plane, had perished in the skies over Xinyang, Henan. In Chongqing, my brother had read the news in a wartime report from the front lines. When I returned home on the weekend, there was a notification about him waiting from the 14th Air Force in Yunan, because our house was listed as one of Zhang Dafei's mailing addresses. He had left behind a letter for my brother and a large package—probably letters—for me in an American military canvas mailbag. My brother said that before I finished up and returned home for the summer, I needed to be mentally prepared. Inside his letter was a letter to him from Zhang Dafei.

It was a letter bidding final farewell; a farewell from a twenty-six-year-old to his short past. Although I no longer have the letter, each word he wrote is branded on my mind. He wrote:

Dear Zhenyi,

If you receive this letter, it means I have died. Seven of those with whom I tested into air training school have departed. Three days ago, my last friend did not make it back. I know my turn is next. I pray and I contemplate; I am at peace. Thank you for your friendship over the years. Thank your mother for her loving concern for me over the years, such that I have had a place to think of as home amid all this wandering. And please forgive me for laying aside Pang-yuan's feelings before even reciprocating them.

I have asked ground personnel Mr. Zhou to return all the letters Pang-yuan has sent me over the years to her. Please forgive me for making her so sad in this way. Since learning your address in Hunan, she has replied to all of my letters, standing in place of your mother. Over the last eight years, my letters to her have been my only letters home, and hers have been my greatest comfort. I can almost see how she has grown from a skinny little girl into a young woman. When I saw her that day, walking across the playing field at Nankai, I was so amazed and I spoke what was in my heart. How could I have finally come to tell her I loved her? These last few years, I have told myself that our affections should be those of brother and sister; otherwise, I would hurt her if I died, and I would hurt her if I lived. We have walked two such vastly different paths: these years I have only fought in the sky, concentrating on surviving or perishing in the sky or on the ground; she has spent her days amid poetry and books, proceeding down that path of light with my blessings. Knowing that I must die, how could I say to her, "I love you"? Before summer break last year, when she said she wanted to transfer to Kunming to be closer to me, I knew things had become serious. How could Mother and Father consent? How could I, someone who lived in constant danger and who was always on the move, look after her? I wrote to her strongly recommending that she remain in Sichuan and study hard. Now when I am off, I drink and dance. I am twenty-six years old and have never tasted life. Since joining the service I have maintained purity in body and mind, my one desire to become a military chaplain after the war. While stationed in Guilin in the fall, I met a middle school teacher my age at church. She came to Yunnan to find me, and we were married on base. When I die, half my pension will go to my younger brother, and I ask that he support and take care of Mother when he returns home after victory. Please ask Pang-yuan to forget me. All I have ever wanted was that her life be happy.

Final exams were postponed that year so that those students who had left school could make up their coursework. Along with many of my classmates, I took the boat back to scorching hot Chongqing. When I saw that green canvas military mailbag on my desk, even my mother would have had a difficult time telling whether it was sweat or tears running down my face. My heart was a turmoil of complex emotions, as if I had thrown myself into that confluence of three rivers. I didn't open the mailbag until two days later, and right on top was a letter in an unfamiliar hand:

Captain Zhang Dafei died in the line of duty in the skies over Henan on May 18. He always took this bag of letters with him when he was transferred elsewhere. Two months ago, he gave it to me and said that if one day he shouldn't return, I was to send it to you at this address. I work in maintenance for the squadron and was with him for two years. He was a very kind and considerate captain, and we are all deeply saddened by his loss. After finding your letter in his coat pocket, I'm enclosing it as well. I hope you can restrain your grief.

From Zhou XX

The letter had been folded a number of times; the pale blue paper had faded yellow. I had written it in the third year of Nankai Middle School. It was purely a letter written by a student interested in literary writing:

I envy you flying high in the sky, closer to God, because the "Valley of the Shadow of Death" does not exist among the white clouds in the blue sky. You said that flying back that night, the moon, huge and bright, suddenly appeared before your eyes from behind the clouds. You said it felt as if you were going to collide with it. If you did, poet Li Po would be jealous of you. . . . These days, I sit in class eight hours a day. Geometry is so hard that there is no joy in life. With Professor Meng's *Poetry and Song Lyric Selection*, there is thankfully more to life than just testing into a university. Today I saw the high school freshmen sewing skirts out of bedsheets to dance in at the unified city athletic meet. We all did that once, terribly childish. Right now I don't have much interest in reading books outside of class. Going home on Saturday I pass by the Time and Tide Bookstore. I walk by quickly so as not to be tempted. . . .

I wrote such letters for years, until I went to Leshan to study philosophy. These letters, no doubt, helped him forget a hideous reality the way smoking, drink, and dancing helped his fellow soldiers. When I contacted him while considering switching from Leshan to National Southwestern Associated University in Kunming, he had hurriedly replied, dissuading me. I remember one line in particular: "The less you know of my real life, the better; the less you know of the actual quality of my 'glory,' the better." When I first read it, I didn't understand, and felt he had "changed." Several years later, I came to fully understand him. As caring as he was, he had suddenly awakened, though it was a little late for him to back up and play the role of a caring older brother. But he prevented me from putting myself in a difficult situation, and in fact still protected me.

He had painstakingly arranged that huge bag of my letters by year. The first letter was mailed from Fujia Hall, Yongfeng Village in Xiang County, Hunan Province, and was a report on my safe and sound life when I graduated from primary school; the last letter was written when I was a college sophomore and literature major, in which I confessed that I didn't have the knack for philosophy and had thrown myself entirely into the Romantic poetry of Shelley and Keats. Looking up at the star-filled sky from my garret room, listening to the birds twittering in the trees, I wondered, where was he? How was it that he had miraculously showed his earnest love and then just as suddenly disappeared?

The more than one hundred letters recorded in detail the emotional development of a girl's heart amid the cruelties of war from 1938 to 1944. I had an even larger bag of his letters from that seven-year period in the closet, which stood as a complete account of how a nineteen-year-old young man went from fleeing difficulties to throwing himself into war. When he flew pursuit and shot down enemy aircraft, he sometimes thought: *How will God judge me for being a devout Christian while having spent years killing? Didn't he say, "I am the life and resurrection?" Didn't Jesus say that if someone struck your left cheek you ought to offer your right? But the Japanese not only struck my cheek, they also killed my father and exterminated my family and to this day have not left off killing the people of my country in their own land. Every time I shoot down one of their planes, I could save many people from dying under Japanese bombings. . . .*

I put the two large bags of letters together, but I didn't have enough strength to read them again that summer. Although I was conscious of his death, it still came as a shock because it didn't seem real.

By all indications, the war would soon end. MacArthur retook the Philippines, realizing his vow of "I shall return." On July 7, eight years after the Marco Polo Bridge Incident, the Military Council announced: "In the eight years of the war of resistance, more than 250,000 Japanese have been killed, wounded, and captured; we have lost over 130,000 troops with more than 170,000 wounded, but now we have turned the war to the offensive." At that moment the entire country began to live in expectation.

At the same time, General Chennault's resignation shocked the Chinese government and the public. Roosevelt died, and Eisenhower took command of the armed forces from Marshall. (The Marshall Plan for reconstruction after the war had a profound impact on the postwar world. Marshall also managed to broker a halt to the war between the Communists and the Nationalists, but most people felt he favored the "progressive reforms" of the Communists, and that is what led to the defeat of the Nationalists and the loss of mainland China.) General Stilwell, head of the allied forces in China, and Generalissimo Chiang Kai-shek did not cooperate well. When General Albert Wedemeyer took over, he received a directive from headquarters that said Chennault had waged a guerrilla war for years with minimal funding, but "the quickest and most effective way of waging a modern offensive war with modern technology was to replace the commander."

Nothing as enthusiastic and moving as Chennault's farewell at Chongqing was ever seen before or after. More than 200,000 people thronged the streets and windows, making it impossible for his car to proceed. People pushed his car all the way to the square and a variety of banners, many embroidered with the Flying Tigers emblem, hung from the city's damaged buildings. Generalissimo Chiang himself presented Chennault with the country's highest honor, the medal with the blue sky and white sun, and expressed the nation's gratitude for his years spent toiling to assist the Chinese. The U.S. government also bestowed upon him the Distinguished Service Cross and second oak leaf cluster. Chennault was fifty-two that year. He had come to China, a distant and mysterious place, departing from the regulations of the U.S. military, and through his shrewdness and charisma, had brought together similar fine men to use a strategy of pursuit aircraft to alleviate the sufferings of countless people on the ground.

Within a matter of four months, Roosevelt had died, Chennault had been dismissed, and Zhang Dafei had given his life for his country. The curtain fell on the war and the hatred of many people. Those powerful lines from Whitman's "O Captain! My Captain!" from across the Pacific expressed the mourning of all people in the face of war.

O Captain! My Captain! our fearful trip is done,
The ship has weather'd every rack, the prize we sought is won,
The port is near, the bells I hear, the people all exulting,
While follow eyes the steady keel, the vessel grim and daring;
But O heart! heart! heart!
O the bleeding drops of red,
Where on the deck my Captain lies,
Fallen cold and dead.

THE WAR ENDS

After the Allies were victorious in Europe, they were anxious to bring the war against Japan in Asia to an end. The Japanese army clearly knew that their superiority in China and the Pacific islands was gone, but they insisted upon fighting to the death like a cornered beast. Hundreds of thousands on both sides died on those forsaken islands, until thousands of U.S. planes conducted mass bombings of Japan, leaving Tokyo in ruins.

On July 26, the leaders of China, the United States, and England demanded the unconditional surrender of Japan at Potsdam in Allied-occupied Germany (on the same day, Churchill, who had led England to victory in the war, was not reelected to office and would not see the results after the war). The following day, the Japanese cabinet met from morning until late into the night, with the hawks advocated preparing to fight to protect Japan on Japanese soil. The people of Japan preferred death to surrender. The new leaders of England and America, Atlee and Truman, announced a joint declaration of war against Japan on August 3. Three days later, the first atomic bomb was dropped on Hiroshima, but the Japanese still refused to surrender; on August 9, a second atomic bomb was dropped on Nagasaki. On the front page of every paper in the world was a photograph of a mushroom cloud from the atomic blast rising above a sea of flame.

On August 14, the Japanese soldiers in the trenches, struggling to the point of death, heard a broadcast from the Showa Emperor telling them to lay down their weapons: "Japan has been defeated and has surrendered unconditionally and, in accordance with the Cairo Declaration and the Potsdam Declaration, returns Taiwan to China. . . ."

On August 15, Chairman Chiang Kai-shek broadcast a speech to China's soldiers and people: "After victory, we should be neither arrogant nor idle. We must work to build and not harbor old grudges or seek revenge on the Japanese." This magnanimous attitude became the generous reparations clause of "returning evil with kindness," which, to this day, has posed problems for the Chinese people. With the aid of the

Allied nations, Germany and Japan quickly recovered, but after the war the Chinese Nationalist troops, exhausted and with no time to rest, were forced into a civil war with the Communists for political power. Even the slightest happiness of an "ignoble existence" was not theirs to enjoy.

When Japan surrendered, Chongqing was ecstatic, the only time I have seen anything like it in my life. Following Chiang's broadcast, the miserable earth erupted in joy, as people dropped their accustomed reserve and embraced in the streets, and jumped, laughed, and sang patriotic songs such as "beautiful mountains and rivers, the national flag waves . . ." until they were hoarse. It was said that turning out en masse was not enough and shortly after sunset, a huge torchlight parade lit up every street.

My brother, cousins, and I ran with torches to the main street of Shapingba, then left to Xiaolongkan Station and right to Ciqikou. Everywhere we went it was brightly lit and people were singing, and their shouts of "Long live the Republic of China!" rose to the clouds. I walked with them to the gate of Nankai Middle School, with two extra scouts standing sentry, holding the same thick military baton I once held, their faces filled with young and simple self-confidence, exactly the same as when I accompanied Principal Zhang in reciting "With me, China shall not perish." All the lights in the Fansun Building were lit, and I recalled the time Zhang Dafei walked across the playing field toward me. At that moment, I suddenly felt everything go silent and could no longer stand being in the crowd. I actually cut through the campus to get to the small path home and gradually got to the empty raised paths between fields and continued on toward Yanggong Bridge. Before the small bridge on that slope there was an abandoned and forlorn cemetery, where my brother and his friends would often challenge one another to see who dared go there and pull out a half-exposed coffin. They also told a lot of will-o'-the-wisp stories to see who was the bravest. Normally I returned home via the main road; I occasionally had passed the cemetery, but with plenty of company during the day. Across the small wooden bridge on the slope was the home we had moved to in order to avoid the air raids last year. I cried as I ran; my torch had long since gone out. When I returned home I saw my mother's startled face. I said, "I can't stand this reveling." I spent victory night weeping bitterly in the dark.

Afterward, I never again mentioned his name. I put the large pile of his letters together with mine in the mailbag and placed them with my books and the few clothes I owned, thinking that one day I would be strong and read through them again. But the following summer I was unexpectedly "demobilized" from Chengdu and returned directly to Shanghai, while my mother and my sister returned to Beiping. In addition to the clothes she took a few photos of sentimental value, but those letters and all trace of them had to be left to the wild winds of those bitter years. I had a hard time imagining their fate in later years spent wandering.

In November of that year, eight full years after Zhang Dafei joined the military and gave me a copy of the Bible, Pastor Ji Zhiwen wrote a long letter to me from Chengdu in which he said he had heard from a friend at the Christian Fellowship that I was suffering a great deal. He urged me to pull myself together and wrote the last line from *The Revelation of St. John the Divine*: "For the Lamb which is in the midst of the throne shall feed them, and shall lead them unto living fountains of waters: and God shall wipe away all tears from their eyes."

A short time later, Pastor Ji came to Leshan to preach the gospel, and I was baptized at the Methodist Church. After much consideration, I chose this solemn way to remember him always: to remember his sad life, to remember his Christian goodness, to remember all those who, like him, had heroically sacrificed everything to take national and personal vengeance.

5

VICTORY

Empty, Everything Is Empty

THE NEW SITUATION AFTER THE WAR: A LOST BEGINNING

While the entire country greatly rejoiced, my father often frowned and said nothing.

One evening at the dinner table, my father said to some old friends that five days before the end of the war, Russia had hastily declared war on Japan and had crossed the border into Manchuria, driving over sixty miles into the northeast, and in a matter of ten days had occupied Harbin, Changchun, Shenyang, and other cities, and taken Pu Yi, the puppet emperor of Manchukuo, prisoner. On August 23, in complete disregard for the political authority of China, Stalin announced, "Manchukuo has been completely liberated." Zhu De, of the Chinese Communist Party, issued seven orders in the name of "Headquarters in Yan'an" for the full-scale mobilization of the Communist troops to take control of cities and territory; he also ordered Lu Zhengcao, Zhang Xueshi, Wan Yi, and other Koreans to lead the march and fight alongside the Russians to take the three provinces of the northeast.

One month later, Mao Zedong arrived in Chongqing on the anniversary of the Mukden Incident to participate in the National Political Council, where he expressed his gratitude to Chairman Chiang Kai-shek for the invitation in his speech: "For future peaceful development and to peacefully build a new age for the country, we must work together and put an end to civil war. Therefore, all parties should, under a single, fixed guiding principle and under the leadership of Chairman Chiang, thoroughly implement the Three Principles of the People to build a modern new China."

This was one of the biggest lies I ever heard in my life.

To effectively facilitate administration, the national government established the Northeast Military Headquarters of the Military Council and divided the three provinces of the northeast into nine: Liaoning, Andong, Liaobei, Jilin, Songjiang, Hejiang, Heilongjiang, Nenjiang, and Xing'an (after the Communists took over, the original three provinces were restored). The people who excitedly went to "take over" the nine provinces never dreamed that three and a half years later, after being defeated by the Chinese Communists, they would flee to Taiwan, a province one thirty-fifth the size of the northeast, and never return home.

Shortly after victory, when all schools were about to recommence, the Ministry of Education announced that the majority of schools in war zones had been damaged or requisitioned by the Japanese army and needed to be repaired, and those schools that had moved behind the lines would have to remain where they were until the following summer, when they would return to their original locations. Classes that year would start on schedule and students should keep their minds on their studies while the plans for moving the schools were drawn up.

My brother had graduated from the foreign affairs department of National Zhengzhi University and was awaiting a posting to an embassy abroad. His first posting was to be at the embassy in Uruguay, where he would serve as a third-level secretary (he was teased by his friends on account of the country's name, which, when pronounced in Chinese, sounded like "turtle"). He regretted never having been able to join in the revolution—his participation in the "100,000 young people for 100,000 troops" the year before had been blocked, and he had taken it to heart. He decided he didn't want to go to Uruguay, so he applied to the Central News to be a military correspondent; after passing the exam, he asked to be sent to the war zone in the northeast to experience the life of the soldiers there.

My younger sister Ningyuan had graduated from elementary school and was in her first year at Nankai, and loved to play softball. My youngest sister Xingyuan was in the third grade at the elementary school attached to Nankai. My parents decided to stay in Sichuan and wait until my summer break the following year before moving back to Beiping. The first thing that had to be done was to bury my grandmother, whose coffin had been housed in a temple outside of Beiping since her death in 1937.

REACQUAINTED WITH FAMOUS TEACHERS

Jiading is a hundred *li* from Emei Mountain, and the landscape has long been famous. Down through the ages, famous literati such as Su Dongpo from Meisan and Guo Moruo from Leshan have resided along the banks of the Dadu River, the Qingyi River, and the Min River. During the War of Resistance, those who taught at Wuhan University in Leshan included writers such as Zhu Guangqian, Dong Xiying, Ling Shuhua, Yuan Changying, and Su Xuelin. In 1941, Wuhan University engaged famous historian Qian Mu to lecture on Chinese political history. As the lectures were intended for the whole school, they were held from 6 to 8 a.m. in order to avoid being interrupted by air raids. (The previous year the Japanese had conducted massive bombings of Leshan, with half the city destroyed and an enormous number of casualties, which were followed by the rampant spread of Kashin-Beck disease and typhoid. The dead from Wuhan University were buried in a place known as Dormitory 8.) At the time, electricity had not been fully restored to the city, so the students from the various dormitories had to carry torches to illumine the way to the classroom to listen to Qian Mu's lectures. The torchbearers occupied all the seats by the first light of dawn. For those who came late, there were no seats. Few of the new students in the girls' dorm chose to go. When I entered my third year, the War of Resistance had ended in victory and Qian Mu returned to Chongqing. Listening to the boys talk about those grand events, I was envious. I never expected that thirty years later in Taiwan, I would have to call on Qian Mu on business for the National Translation and Compilation Center, and also have the honor of visiting him over the following twenty years, often seeking his advice and conversing with him.

Ma Yifu, a master of the Chinese classics, set up the Fuxing Academy across the Min River at a place called Wuyoushan that year. Xiong Shili stayed and lectured there; Qian Mu also lectured there. There were a hundred students. Late in life, Qian Mu wrote a piece titled "Talks We Both Benefited From" in which he recalled having lunch and dinner with Zhu Guangqian.

At the beginning of September 1945, I returned to Leshan and found the atmosphere of the university entirely changed, for that which had originally bound us together through our sufferings had now disappeared. The students brought together by the National Joint College Entrance Exams would be returning home to all parts of the country with high career hopes (in those days there were very few university graduates relative to the rest of the population), and politics had permeated all extracurricular activities. Wall newspapers, stage plays, and even literary works and journals were either left or right. Even purely scholarly lectures were attributed political positions based on the degree of "progressiveness." Twenty years later, the Chinese Communists would utilize this drawing of lines as the basis for struggle. The fragmentary information we received across the strait in Taiwan and the news from behind the iron curtain we read overseas all seemed familiar to me.

Starting in my third year at university, Zhu Guangqian stepped down as dean to devote himself to teaching and running the Department of Foreign Languages and Literatures. He invited those of us who were his advisees to his house for tea.

That was in the middle of autumn, so his courtyard was covered with a thick carpet of leaves that rustled as you walked. One of the male students took a broom from a small room by the door and said he would sweep up the fallen leaves for him. Professor Zhu stopped him immediately and said, "I've waited so long for such a thick layer of leaves. At night as I read, I can hear the patter of the rain and the blowing of the wind. This memory is more vivid and profound than reading many poems about autumn." As that was the same year we studied Shelley's "Ode to the West Wind," my memory of this courtyard is inextricably linked with the poem. After my father passed away, I read "To Autumn" by Keats, through which I deeply felt the beauty in the passing of time and recalled with gratitude how my father and my teacher awakened me to the savor of life.

Academic work in the Department of Foreign Languages and Literatures only really began in the third year, by Professor Zhu's standards. The faculty lineup had been great, but unfortunately, important and famous teachers such as Chen Xiying and Fang Chong, who taught the history of English literature, had already left the school for England in 1943. Professor Sun Jiaxiu, newly hired to teach our class, had just returned from England and was certainly qualified. After teaching for a short time, she placed instructional emphasis on the Middle English of Chaucer's *Canterbury Tales.*

She was a big woman who read medieval English in a vigorous voice, which she did for about two weeks, leaving us in awe. To use a contemporary Taiwanese phrase, it was like "a duck listening to thunder." It was difficult going for us with Langland's *Piers Plowman* and Malory's *Morte d'Arthur.* From the fifteenth century to Thomas More's *Utopia* in the sixteenth, we hurriedly looked over some early sonnets and breezed through Spenser, the poet of poets, and then winter break arrived. The following semester we were introduced to Marlowe's *Doctor Faustus,* read a few of Shakespeare's representative sonnets and the outlines of some of the famous plays, and looked at the relationship between Milton's *Paradise Lost* and the book of Genesis, and then at John Dryden. After a couple of classes, she took sick leave and we never resumed our class on the history of English literature. Later, we were all "demobilized" and went back downriver (the people of Sichuan call people from other provinces "people from downriver").

When I graduated, I had studied the history of English literature only up to 1700 and was completely ignorant of the subsequent two hundred fifty years after Dryden, which left me chagrined for many years. The second time I went to Indiana University for advanced study, I spent an entire year working very hard, taking four courses on the historical periods of English literature: the fifteenth century and before, the sixteenth and seventeenth centuries, the eighteenth century, and the nineteenth century. When I taught the history of English literature (it was a two-year course at National Taiwan University and was required in the second and third years), I arranged everything so that I would have enough time to get to the mid-twentieth century, so that my students wouldn't feel the same sense of chagrin that I had experienced.

Two other classes were a bit more stable, like the class on fiction taught by Professor Dai Liuling, who was a typical man of letters. He was a regular contributor to *Time and Tide*, and though he wasn't a great speaker, his classes were rich in content with a high level of analysis. In discussing *A Tale of Two Cities* by Dickens, he told us to pay close attention to how the English perceived the mobocracy during the French Revolution. To this day I can still recall the descriptions of the housewives sitting at the plaza of execution, knitting while counting the heads as they were lopped off by the guillotine. The scene of knitting the number into a warm sweater still sends shivers through me. Stammering, he asserted that having that English lawyer stand upon the guillotine out of love and still see a beautiful future was simply writing fiction that was not of this world (I thought that was the way love ought to be). He was the first teacher to teach us how to read fiction from different perspectives. The reading list he gave us was very helpful later.

The first time I met Professor Miao Langshan was in a class on modern literature. He was perhaps the most charismatic teacher, whose specialty was Russian literature. Almost all works of Russian literature were representative modern works.

The students liked his course, and with the cooperation of the Nationalists and Communists during the War of Resistance, it was far more useful than any sort of Communist propaganda. Professor Miao was a big man with a resonant voice. He was very learned on the subject of Russian literature, his lectures being a mine of information, and his teaching was more like a stage performance, as he moved briskly but never paced. His face was expressive and his talk humorous. One male student described him as "big and small pearls falling on a metal plate." He gave a fervent introduction to Gorky's *Mother*, Sholokhov's

The Silent Don, and Goncharov's *Oblamov*, which is a brilliant book about a lazy man. The lazy nobleman's servant is so lazy that his hands are described as being as dirty as the soles of his shoes. Professor Miao actually took off his beat-up shoe and held it next to his hand. We never encountered such an enthusiastic teacher, before or after.

PLAYING THE WRONG MUSIC

A huge change in my life at Leshan took place in my third year—someone came and "stood guard" over me at the dorm.

In my first and second years, the only extracurricular activities I participated in were the Nankai Alumni Association and the Christian Fellowship, a small circle in which everyone knew that there was someone in my heart, and in that serious period of "single-minded love," no one could ever get me to go out.

Shortly after victory and after I had returned to school from Chongqing, just before classes began, I received a letter containing a musical composition with my name on it. The composer was Mr. Huang, a recent graduate; in his letter he claimed to have adored me for more than a year, and seeing the disdainful attitude I had toward others, he hadn't had the courage to approach me. Not many people on campus recognized him anymore, so if I didn't object, he would quietly come to Leshan to see me before going to work, trying to build up a rapport between us.

In addition to several choirs at Wuhan University, there was one other musical group that had attained a quasi-professional level (or at least had received professional training). It was a small musical group of three to five members, who were much sought after and respected in that period without music. There were two violins and a male alto; Mr. Huang had played second violin. Onstage, he was tall and elegant, and many of the girls were crazy about him.

At the beginning of June 1944, in order to celebrate the graduation of our classmates, the Nankai Alumni Drama Troupe gave a public performance of *Everlasting and Unchanging*, a well-known spoken drama from the War of Resistance derived from *La Dame aux Camélias*. That they dared to perform the piece, creating a sensation on campus, was because Lu Qiaozhen and several other alums from Shapingba had successfully performed it in the past. As a student drama troupe totally lacking sound equipment, they had to rely upon people's assistance behind the curtain. When they performed Cao Yu's *Thunderstorm*, several male classmates stood on ladders behind the stage and poured basins of water onto the stage while one strapping fellow held a sheet of metal and another struck it with a hammer with all his might, creating the sound of thunder. Mr. Huang wasn't an alum, but he was quite amiable (the first violinist was not) and was asked to provide music from backstage. The student directing the play said to him, "I don't know the names of the pieces you violinists play, just have a lively piece and a sad piece, and when the time comes, I'll tell you which one to play." That night, all of us alums were put to work—Wang Shirui, a first-year student, and I went on stage and sat on swings for two minutes, representing pure bliss, after which we went backstage to help with prompting. I don't know if the director or the violinist got it wrong (backstage was narrow, dark, and dirty), but when the male and female leads were happily in love, someone told Mr. Huang to play the "sad one." With a good deal of emotion, he played Schumann's slow paced *Traumerei*, upon hearing which the actors could scarcely laugh.

The following day, the local paper said the Nankai Alumni Drama Troupe had performed some nonsense—the male lead had no idea what love was and the show was stolen by Lu Qiaozhen, the female lead. Although Mr. Huang did not express anger, the Nankai alums could all see that he was a little embarrassed and felt somewhat at fault.

Shortly after classes recommenced, he made the long trip from Chongqing to Leshan, especially to see me. That really made me feel glorious, and those who knew about it were moved; soon everyone in that small county town "knew" about it. Every afternoon he reported at Old Yao's and Old Yao, with that voice of authority no one would ever forget, shouted up to the third floor: "Someone to see Ms. Chi Pang-yuan!" Old Yao addressed all the girls in the second year and above as "Ms."

He said that all the girls who went to the university should have something special about them, but he seldom used that form of address in the dorm, probably because he saw how the girls really were in their daily lives.

It was in my third year that I sat alone with a boy on the rafts by the river for the first time. The mouth of the Min River at Leshan was the collection and dispersal place for timber, which was bound into rafts and pushed into rows, waiting for the river to swell to be floated down from the mountains to a port on the Yangtze River where it would be sold. After sunset, the students liked to clamber up on the rafts and sit, as it was an atmospheric place to sing and talk. National Day soon came, and he suddenly reappeared.

Mr. Huang displayed his adoration in this earnest manner, but at the worst time. . . .

Since June, my grief for Zhang Dafei had been too heavy and painful to talk about. I didn't know how I should refer to him—he wasn't my brother and he wasn't a lover. We had been in love for years but had never declared our feelings. When I thought about him, the sadness I felt went beyond the individual to encompass all who had died in the war, but I also still harbored complex feelings of grief and loss that I couldn't express. Anything frivolous said about him was blasphemy. My grief was like that Coleridge wrote about in "Dejection: An Ode":

> A grief without a pang, void, dark, and drear,
> A stifled, drowsy, unimpassioned grief,
> Which finds no natural outlet, no relief,
> In word, or sigh, or tear—

Under normal circumstances, any girl of my age and experience would have wanted an elegant young man writing songs for them or journeying three days upriver to see them, or would be moved to spill their heart for someone who had traveled five hundred *li* to see them. But perhaps everything had already been determined by heaven. When Mr. Huang provided the musical accompaniment to *Everlasting and*

Unchanging and mistakenly played a sad song during a happy scene, it had been an omen that we were not destined for each other.

In my last year at Leshan, at least in the first semester, everyone studied hard. Wuhan University maintained high standards. In the Department of Foreign Languages and Literatures, for example, Professor Zhu taught English poetry, modern literary criticism, and translation, and as head of the department he had developed a strong curriculum that had produced strong graduates over the last six years. Unfortunately, in the second semester, many of the faculty had new jobs and would start in a matter of months, so they left early. At the same time, a student movement appeared with protest marches both large and small.

THE STUDENT MOVEMENT

Victory for China in the War of Resistance came after eight years of persistent tears and bloody struggle, but the sudden arrival of the atomic bomb left the government unprepared. The expectations implied by the word "victory" could not be realized immediately. The difficult days experienced in the rear were gone, never to return. Starting in northern China, the Communists, using common ownership of land and the power of propaganda in the rural areas, expanded rapidly in the rear, and were extremely attractive and convincing to the intellectuals who were dissatisfied with the status quo and passionate about reform. On November 29, three months after victory, progressive students from National Southwestern Associated University in Kunming and Yunnan University initiated a student movement opposed to civil war and American interference in domestic politics. An extremist threw a grenade, injuring thirteen students and killing four. The teachers decided to go on strike, and several dozen published a letter in which they sympathized with the students who opposed civil war. Classes did not resume until January 17.

The student movement spread to universities all over China. From 1946 to 1948, university campuses were filled with political unrest and shouting. In the forty years after the Communists occupied the country, university education became a political tool and professional academic standards were eliminated.

In the student movement as I experienced it, Wen Yiduo (1899–1946), a professor at National Southwestern Associated University, was extremely influential. He was a famous poet, and the literary youth of the day could all recite his "Dead Water," a signature work with a sense of the times, and "Perhaps," his elegy on the death of his young daughter. To this very day, I can still remember the sixteen lines of the poem and continue to find them moving:

> Perhaps you have wept till you can weep no more.
> Perhaps, perhaps you want to go to sleep.
> Then tell the nightingale not to cough,
> the frog not to croak, and the bat not to fly.
>
> Do not let the sun stir your sight,
> nor the cool breeze brush your eyebrows.
> Let no one startle you.
> I'll hold a umbrella of shading pine to protect you as you sleep.
>
> Perhaps you hear the worm turn the soil,
> hear the grass roots absorb the water.
> Perhaps you hear the music,
> more beautiful than man's curses.
>
> First close your eyes tight,
> then I'll let you sleep, I'll let you sleep.
> I'll cover you gently with the yellow earth,
> have the spirit money slowly take flight.

Very early on, Wen Yiduo had a genius for literature; at thirteen he tested into Qinghua School, the precursor of Qinghua University, where he finished the middle school and university curricula and also laid a foundation of Western learning. He was very patriotic and took part in the May Fourth Movement, and while studying art in the United States, he and his classmates organized the Great River Association to promote nationalism in Chinese culture. After he returned to China, he taught art and actively participated in cultural activities, becoming famous for his poetry.

At the beginning of the War of Resistance, he trudged with students from Qinghua, Beiping University, and Nankai from Hunan to the newly established National Southwestern Associated University in Yunnan, where he taught in the Department of Literature, with noteworthy studies of the *Songs of the South*. Teachers had a difficult time in Kunming during the war, and Wen Yiduo had five children. He supplemented his income by carving seals. The Japanese bombings coupled with the difficult lives of the people and the active courting of intellectuals by the Communists encouraged Wen Yiduo to study the communist system after reading Edgar Snow's *Red Star Over China*. His friends in the party underground encouraged him to participate in the Chinese Democratic Alliance, as being more advantageous to the democracy movement. The book *Wen Yiduo*, by Wen Lipeng and Zhang Tongxia, his son and daughter-in-law, mentions that he adopted the spirit of "If I don't enter hell, who will?" to meet the demands of his new life of struggle. His old friend Luo Longji said, "Yiduo was very changeable, and changed quickly and suddenly."

Wen Yiduo began to write and lecture, sharply criticizing and attacking the government and all conservative traditions. For example, he called conservative Qian Mu stupid and stubborn. On the afternoon of July 15, 1946, after a ceremony memorializing the murdered Li Gongpu, Wen Yiduo was assassinated, leaving behind his five small children.

Wen Yiduo's death triggered the student movement across the country. For the Communists in Yan'an, it was more effective than thousands of troops and horses, and it had a far-reaching impact on the fate of the country. His impact on the attitude of intellectuals toward politics is worth studying by scholars of cultural history, but in the academic community on both sides of the strait, seldom does looking forward and back rise above the personal.

I recall my father saying that any intellectual under the age of twenty who is not enamored of Communism lacks passion, and anyone who becomes a Communist after the age of twenty is immature. I frequently wonder how Wen Yiduo could have believed that China could be saved by toppling the Nationalists and replacing them with the Communists after reading about the Communist system (not communism) when he was forty-five. Did those two years of sharp calls for regime change arise from the dispassionate judgment of a middle-aged scholar? And my generation, after eight years of suffering and with the cities still in shambles, responded to his passionate call by marching in protest, not going to class, not allowing for freedom of thought, and neglecting their studies, with most falling for all sorts of hateful movements, ending in the Cultural Revolution. Did he, who was an idol to the youth, ever think about the consequences of impulsive passions?

The book *Wen Yiduo* records that among his possessions was an unfinished seal carving that said, "His foolishness knows no limits." Regardless of how you explain it—as the juncture between life and death or the "darkest moment before the dawn"—this "badge of self-encouragement" explains his final decision to solemnly follow in the footsteps of Qu Yuan and Byron. Thoughts of regret and self-recrimination will come to most readers; after all, he did write many sensitive and wonderful poems, deeply studied the essence of Chinese characters, and was in the process of carving a stone seal with five characters, so he should have already been clear as to what he was about. Although in those two fanatical years he couldn't have foreseen that his death would not bring happiness to his beloved country and family.

If in 1945 the central government had been able to catch its breath, and the people regain their livelihood and rebuild China with an attitude of protecting the country, could China have risen up earlier, avoiding millions of deaths due to class struggle and a protracted period of suffering for several generations?

These have been among my greatest perplexities, laments, and resentments over the years as I have thought about the times I was forced to participate in protest marches in Sichuan and Wuhan.

THE END OF MY STAY AT LESHAN

In that chaotic November, when joy and anxiety ran together, Pastor Ji Zhiwen, the preacher, was invited to Leshan by the Inland Mission of the Methodist Church. He advised me to be baptized to calm myself for the longer road and to preserve the soberness of my soul. The congregation to which he preached was largely composed of faculty and students from Wuhan University; his knowledge and the spirit of his talk were of a high order and did not provoke political mockery from either the left or the right. Over those few days, he led the singing of hymns in his Zhejiang accent; one with which I was less familiar had the refrain: "Wash me, make me pull grass breathing." In those days, the church didn't have the common hymnal for congregations, When I was at Nankai, I grew accustomed to hearing standard Mandarin spoken with a Tianjin accent (they used to laugh at my northeastern accent). I figured that it was probably like when I sat by the river and could hear the pulse of nature and its harmonious breathing. Only later, after I arrived in Shanghai and someone gave me a copy of *Hymns of Universal Praise*, did I learn that the original was "I shall be whiter than snow," a metaphor meaning to be washed clean. However, that first impression of "pull grass breathing" was hard to forget.

On Christmas Eve that year, Pastor Han from the United States invited a number of the students who attended church to his house to celebrate the holiday. Entertainment was arranged for after dinner. In one instance, the boys and girls had to draw lots, and those with the same numbers formed a pair who had to answer questions that had been written down, competing to see who could answer the most questions correctly. When writing the answers, the pair was covered with a choir robe so they could consult in secret. After the answer had been written down, it would be taken from beneath the robe. Mr. Yu, a fourth-year electrical engineering student, and I ended up together. When he approached me holding the robe, I felt more nervous and excited than I ever had before.

I recall my first winter in Leshan just after I arrived, when I was ignorant of everything, watching from the dorm window of the room shared by Yu Xianyi, Zhai Yiwo, Feng Jialu, and Lu Qiaozhen as the male students in a torchlight procession walked down White Pagoda Street back to Dorm 6 of the Engineering School after a concert. Around a hundred people shouted and clamored happily. Halfway, a large group began singing songs from the evening's performance. My elder classmates all pointed at a tall, handsome young man: "Oh, look, that's Mr. Yu."

He was singing the "Drinking Song" from *La Traviata*. That confident tenor gradually rose above the other voices, passed under the window, and moved on its way. In the window I could clearly see the joy and adoration of my older female classmates. Two years later, his name resonated throughout the girls' dorm.

There I was, shoulder to shoulder with such a "stranger" under a choir robe, whispering in secret. It was so romantic, I could scarcely breathe! To make matters worse, I couldn't answer the first question asking the names of the three greatest Western classical composers and the second question asking for the identity of the three greatest conductors. In the dark, he wrote out six names. Following that were questions about Bible stories and names from mythology, none of which I knew. My only contribution was to provide the name of the male protagonist in *Jane Eyre*. Although my shame was concealed in the darkness under the robe, it was still one of the ten worst moments in my life. That evening we ended up with the most correct answers, all of which he provided. In addition to the excitement, this opportunity of "putting our heads together" allowed me to see that there was a world beyond my life of twenty years.

In those days, the musical education at Nankai Middle School was considered among the best, and our chorus was well known in the rear. Nearly half of the songs we performed were from the English *One Hundred and One Songs*; we sang in the original language, and songs of the War of Resistance were our forte. I never studied music history, either in class or on my own. The radios at Nankai and in the *Time and Tide* office broadcast only news of the war and political discussions; there were no systematic music programs. During the War of Resistance, Mr. Yu had been unwilling to receive a Japanese education, so he had transferred from Shanghai to the rear as a student from fallen areas. He was assigned to Wuhan University along with Yao Guanfu and Su Yuxi. When I graduated, Yao Guanfu sent me the complete works of Shakespeare from Shanghai as a gift. It's still on my shelf today. Su Yuxi also later became a friend of mine, but he died in the political struggles shortly after victory. They both had received good educations in Shanghai and had a rich knowledge of Western culture and art, and both became dear friends. Mr. Yu had received voice training from a famous teacher. His father had been the head of the Episcopal Church in Shanghai, but he had already passed away.

At dusk on New Year's Day, he suddenly showed up at the girls' dorm (it was said he'd never been there before). Old Yao's shouted announcement brought me downstairs. Mr. Yu gave me a copy of *Great Composers* in English and wished me a happy new year. He also asked if it would be okay to come and visit after exams. As I nodded, he strode out the main door (later he said that with so many eyes on him he had grown nervous).

During winter break, he invited me to walk around the grassy slope at the Baptist Church. For two twenty-year-olds, our lives couldn't have been more different. He talked about the changes in Shanghai after it fell to the Japanese; I told him about the patriotic education at Nankai and running for shelter during the air raids in Chongqing. He said he was going to Chengdu to see his older sister, who had come with him to Sichuan after graduating from college, was working for the American military advisors in Chengdu, and really liked literature.

At the end of February that year, just after classes recommenced, the students at Wuhan University, like those in the middle schools and universities throughout the country, began massive demonstrations to protest the "secret agreement at the Yalta Conference" and demanded that Russia withdraw from the northeast and commemorate the memory of Zhang Xinfu.

Zhang Xinfu was an engineer and a comrade of my father's in the anti-Japanese underground in the northeast. After victory, he was sent from Chongqing to Liaoning, where he was to take over the largest coal mine in the country at Fushun. On January 16 as he was passing through

Shenyang, he was bound and taken off the train by the Communists to a snowy place where he was killed, along with eight others. The Russian Communists quickly dismantled and moved the large factory machines in the northeast. Each time they left a place, they helped the Chinese Communists garrison it. This was the second nationwide student movement after the first demonstrations, which had been launched the previous November by National Southwestern Associated University and Yunnan University to oppose civil war and American interference in Chinese politics. Some of my classmates, whose political positions were clear, organized activities with stridently antagonistic slogans. The protesters squeezed into the damaged street that had been bombed in 1939 and still not repaired. The street was so narrow that the banners couldn't be lifted, and all that could be heard were slogans being chanted till people grew hoarse: "Down with . . . down with . . . Long live! Long live!" Soon afterward, the protest march commenced and the target of the "down with" changed. In addition to the commonly chanted slogan "Long live the Republic of China," others were frequently heard and changed.

I participated in the march commemorating Zhang Xinfu, because he was an anti-Japanese underground comrade of my father's of many years. I had grown up together with his kids during the war. However, I did not join in the planning before the demonstration or utter a sound during the march; I just kept up with everyone, expressing my sincere grief. But where White Pagoda Street met Jade Hall Street, I was pushed to the side of the street. Later I realized that since I didn't belong to any political camp and if I didn't actively participate, I would always be pushed to the side of the street. If I were to stand up at any gathering and say, "We should first study hard," I would have been immediately charged and trampled to death, so I instinctively chose a lesser accusation of "living a befuddled life."

Half a century later, from the opposite side of the Taiwan Strait, I looked back at that ancient city at the confluence of three rivers and the sight of those classmates of mine, who for so many years had received their shabby clothes and insufficient food from the government, hoarse and exhausted from shouting slogans. Their anger at China's weakness and many years of chaos exploded in those collective demonstrations and that unceasing student movement, ending with the toppling of the government of the War of Resistance and the welcoming of the "liberation" by the Communist Party. Their joy was, in fact, as transient as dew. Those classmates who went to China to visit relatives after the opening up said that few of the student leaders or political activists were satisfied and had ended up either dead or suffering degradation over the years from Liberation to the Cultural Revolution, owing to their strong idealism. My generation was one consumed by the times. Many people were forced to emigrate or wander by life's difficulties or disaster. Taking up a load and putting it on their back, a single person or a whole family would start off to open up uncultivated land, with the hope of setting up a household. But my generation, with our universal education, ended up scattered and set adrift or sunk because of different political ideologies. Fifty years later, I returned to Beiping and got together with old classmates and friends. More than eighty female classmates all had the same ideals back in those days, but after 1950, very few had advanced in their education or were somewhat successful professionally. Those who hadn't seen their families in ruins and scattered were fortunate. Almost an entire generation had been sacrificed to politics.

When I was pushed to the side of the street during the demonstration, the roommate with whom I had locked arms was carried away, and I looked like a deserter as I walked home with my back to the wall.

At that moment I saw Mr. Yu over the shouting protesters separated from me as he stood by the stone wall at the corner of Shuixi Gate, wearing a dark gray overcoat and looking at me with a sphinx-like expression.

After the demonstrators had passed, he crossed the street and said, "So you also joined the demonstration!" I replied, "Uncle Zhang Xinfu was a good friend of my parents and they worked together for years in the anti-Japanese underground, so I felt I should join in the march to show my true grief." He said that up until before his father died of a heart attack, it had been hoped that he would go to a free country for his education and not stay in Shanghai, which was occupied and ruled by the Japanese. He said here, however, neither the right nor the left had sought him for their political activities, probably thinking that the guy from Shanghai had nothing to offer but good English and a talent for singing.

When the demonstrations grew more frequent, we continued to set out every morning from the dorm for the Confucius Temple to watch. Sometimes the demonstrations were announced, sometimes not. Few people stood in the classrooms and hallways and sometimes a teacher would show up carrying a book, but there were not enough students to hold class; sometimes half the class would show up but the teacher wouldn't. So we seldom had class. The school was filled with a dispirited atmosphere.

We had looked forward to victory through years of life-and-death struggle, but we enjoyed less than six months of happiness.

BIRDS SING IN THE FOREST WITH THE MUSIC OF NATURE

At around nine in the morning, the three or four of us who memorized English poems together as we walked left the Confucius Temple and took the stone steps on the left side of the square to Dingdong Street. An old man who sold roasted potatoes always sat at the side of the stone steps. Buying an average-size potato would keep your hands warm along the way, and it was just right to eat once you were back at the dorm. On County Street, a small shop sold small homemade sesame cookies, which were fresh and crisp yet soft. Whenever we passed by the store, we had to buy a small bag. We chatted as we passed Shuixi Gate onto White Pagoda Street. Passing the gate to the Baptist Church, we saw Mr. Yu striding through the gate of Boys' Dorm 6. My companions hurriedly left me to face him alone as they scurried into the dorm.

On a cold spring morning like that without any wind, he would take me to the river to ride the flat-bottomed boat across the Dadu River or the Min River to the most beautiful embankment on the opposite side for a stroll, surrounded by the beauties of nature. To the right was the silhouette of Emei Mountain; to the left the Ginat Buddha Temple of Wuyou at Leshan and the slowly rolling foot of the mountain. That was my last March in that enchanting place, and the beautiful view offered more than flowers and birds that could be painted! It was the first time I had seen it up close, and then I never saw it again. Holding the already cold potato and the sesame cakes, I admired the way Mr. Yu talked about music and only then realized that music could be talked about. Walking along the embankment, we always went into a small rural teahouse with coarse wooden tables and bamboo chairs and hot *tuo* tea, which was heavenly. He would ask me how my kitten cookies were, and when I laughed at his Shanghai pronunciation of "sesame," I would feel a little self-confident.

From that time on, the student movement protests never ceased. Almost every other day I would "run into" him coming up White Pagoda Street, and I began to have certain expectations.

For two months, he took me to walk all along the riverbanks in the area. We went to my favorite cedar forest several times, sat for ages in the country teahouse the likes of which we had never seen before, and ate countless sesame cookies. In addition to music, we also talked about the Bible. I had just started Bible class at the Methodist church, hoping eagerly to better understand the doctrines prior to and after baptism. To this day I still remember him sitting on the embankment and talking about the differences among the four Gospels and why it was difficult to write music to accompany the psalms, and using tea to draw the levels of the seven seals in the book of Revelation. His clear explanations, straightforward drawings, and rapid analysis were naturally all quite different from Bible class. Everything he talked about was basic knowledge acquired growing up in a preacher's home, and I, who was eager to learn, made the perfect audience. Perhaps my being all ears for what he had to say also helped him to ease his homesickness.

Several days before Easter, the Christian Fellowship arranged a trip to the mountains to enjoy the outdoors. We had free time after lunch. He whispered, "I'll take you to the woods to listen to the birds sing." We walked a short distance and came to a clearing surrounded by trees, which was pretty quiet without many birds singing.

We sat down on a huge tree stump. He started to softly whistle and all the birds stopped singing. He continued to whistle when the birds in the surrounding trees suddenly sang together, as if questioning and answering each other in their different songs. It was as if on a stage suspended in midair, musical instruments for which I had no names were tuning but not performing together, as if millions of skylarks and nightingales in the blue sky of April were competing to tell of immortality and the friendship, love, suffering, and redemption that come with life. It was as if God were inspiring me to encounter the music of nature, for which I would willingly shout "long live" in that clearing in the forest.

In the hundred or so days from the beginning of winter to the end of spring, we visited every place we could reach and return from in half a day, the normal places the feet of young people would take them. A drizzle wouldn't stop us (in those days the best oilcloth raincoat weighed a ton), and we would remain full of enthusiasm under a coarse oilpaper umbrella. For both of us, our excursions were our first and last opportunity to see the beauties of Leshan. He had come for his final two years and would graduate and return to Shanghai during the summer break, and I would be going back to school in Wuhan to finish my senior year. We were both looking forward to going through the spectacular Three Gorges during our trip down the Yangtze River.

With all the trips we took, no one would believe—and I myself have never been able to explain it over the years—that we never talked about love. In any age, such "rationality" was so hard for people to accept, but I think the main reason for it was that my childish sincerity injured his strong sense of self-respect.

During our first trips, he would ask me about my Bible class homework. I just explained to him my greatest perplexities, such as that I didn't understand why God tested Job in such a cruel fashion, depriving him of children and property, covering his body with sores and making him sit in ashes, scraping his flesh with a piece of tile, unable to plead for life or obtain death. Mr. Yu's reply was the same as all those I have ever heard, that one must understand that the book of Job is, in its entirety, a story of tests, doubts, and maintaining faith. The main point comes after Job's debate with his friends, when Jehovah replies from a whirlwind: "Where were you when I laid the foundations of the earth? . . . Canst thou lift up thy voice to the clouds, that abundance of waters may cover thee?" Because Job was secure in his faith, he saw new sons and their sons over four generations and lived 140 years, and died satisfied. But this standard answer was not enough to convince me then and for many years after.

He asked me, "Why are you so resentful?" I told him that Zhang Dafei from fourteen to twenty-six had led a sad and short life, though a pious one, and never witnessed redemption before he died. (Or perhaps he had redeemed himself?) He then asked me why I had been baptized after his death. I said I had hoped through my own belief in Christian doctrines to understand the sadness and suffering I had seen since I was young, and that I had insisted upon studying philosophy because I was searching for the meaning of life. In my account, I was clearly longing for someone. Later he told me that he couldn't compete against a dead hero. He had never actually seen war, and because he knew that he didn't have such "soaring ambitions," he couldn't compare with the spirit of such a man. At that age I had violated the taboo of "not having intimate conversations with a slight acquaintance." I didn't know it, and at first I thought we were just friends. Since there was only one semester left at Leshan, after which everyone would go their separate ways, I didn't consider any repercussions.

Therefore, we talked about music, the Bible, novels, and movies, but not about personal feelings or love. He helped me up and down the embankment, took my hand when the wind blew and held it in his coat pocket, but never once spoke the word "love."

By May we were all busy with exams. He was in the graduating class, so exams came earlier for him. Electrical engineering and foreign languages had lots of class work, and exams were moved up for the entire school so that we could all be demobilized early. The office at the Confucius Temple was busy packing the memos, files, and student records for shipping.

By the beginning of June, the library was empty and the dorms half empty, and soon the Wuhan University students, teachers, and their families, who, though threatened with bombs, hunger, and the proximity of war, continued their schooling without interruption, would all vanish from Leshan. I also packed three years' worth of luggage into one small suitcase, the most precious thing being a small box Zhang Dafei had given me when he returned to Chongqing after finishing training in Colorado. It was a small blue leather box with a chain in which I put a small bottle of rouge, lipstick, and two embroidered handkerchiefs, things seldom seen during wartime. I kept it in my suitcase under the bed, and when no one was around I would take the things out, touch them and look at them, put them away again, and carefully close the lid. I gave away my quilt and pillow, and all that was left was the deep blue comforter cover I had asked my mother for when I left home, and which I've always kept. Several years later, in the National Taiwan University singles dorm on Wenzhou Road, I opened the small suitcase that contained all my "property" in the sunlight, only to discover that that beautiful silk and embroidered surface was streaked with white from the tears at the Wuhan University dorm in the winter of 1943 when I had covered my head and cried. Those streaks were made by the abundant tears I shed when so young, between waking and sleeping!

The same summer, Lu Qiaozhen graduated from the Department of Economics and took an earlier boat back to Chongqing to look for work and for interviews. My new roommate, Tang Jingyuan, also graduated and left. Qiaozhen stayed the night in my room before boarding the boat the following day. We talked the whole night through.

Over the past year we both had emotional debts. She, of course, had many admirers, among whom was Chen Xuzu, a Nankai alum, who was simple, honest, and well mannered, and one of the few from Leshan. People often used the Leshan dialect to get his goat. In our small circle, he referred to her as "Little Fish Sun" *(stack up "fish" and "sun" in Chinese and you get the last name Lu).* We found the way he silently watched her quite touching, but we couldn't do anything to help him. One time he came and invited Little Fish Sun and me to his house for lunch. It was the first time we had ever been to that ancestral home referred to as the "local place of evil power" by the progressive students. The house on the opposite bank of the Min River was even larger and more exquisite than the one we had seen in Yibin. The row of floor-to-ceiling windows had been added after the bombings in 1939, and the house was filled with calligraphy and cultural objects. His parents spoke with a heavy Jiading accent but were very elegant people. After lunch we stood by the railing in front of the courtyard and observed the imposing mountains and river, something we never saw from the dorm. Chen Xuzu told us that his parents had left Chongqing and returned home when the massive bombing began and soon discovered that the garden here was more elegant than any other. There were many ways to live, but they decided to stay and be at their ease. Qiaozhen and he were not fated for each other and they probably had no chance to meet after this, but occasionally in this noisy, mundane world I think of that enviable lifestyle. After the Chinese Communists came to power, they may not have been able to flee persecution. The poor Chinese people seldom have a choice of individual lifestyle.

FAREWELL TO PARADISE

After Qiaozhen left, Mr. Yu suddenly showed up at the dorm to visit me, accompanied by his sister.

She had just arrived from Chengdu and decided that before leaving Sichuan she wanted to take a trip to Emei Mountain. She was accompanied by Lieutenant Colonel M, who was in charge of the American Military Advisory Group stationed in Chengdu. She was a very friendly and beautiful girl, and when she saw me she said that her brother had been talking about me for more than six months. She invited me to go with them to Emei Mountain the following day and stay one night before returning to Leshan.

I had spent three years amid the region of mountains and rivers near Emei Mountain, but had never been to the mountain itself. Student groups often took three-day trips, traveling there in different ways, but I had never found the right traveling companion. In those last few days, I was actually afforded the opportunity to climb the mountain and admire it, so I accepted the invitation with pleasure. I spent the night in excited anticipation.

Early the next morning, Lieutenant Colonel M drove a jeep ninety *li* to quickly arrive at a small town at the foot of the mountain. We climbed to Baoguo Temple. That verdant and impressive temple had a courtyard of large stone slabs that seemed to go on and on without end. The huge bluish-gray and pearl-gray stone slabs seemed to surge like waves on the sea that swept over my feet and my body. We went through temple gate after temple gate, and inside the high thresholds, above the high roof ridges in an even deeper and darker boundlessness, echoed the sound of chanted sutras as they had been recited for a thousand years. I have seen many impressive temples since then, but none could produce the sigh of admiration from my heart at the first sight of Baoguo Temple.

After lunch, we again set off up the mountain. Shortly afterward, my chest began to hurt, as it often had when I was a child. My face went pale and I broke into a cold sweat, and sat down on a stone step beside the path. Mr. Yu and his sister naturally grew alarmed, but Lieutenant Colonel M, with the calm manner of a battlefield soldier, said that it was probably the initial stage of altitude sickness brought on by a lack of oxygen. He had medicine in his bag and took it out and had me take some. Soon I was feeling much better.

They insisted I ride in an uncovered sedan chair, the sort seen in Sichuan that consisted of two bamboo poles with a soft seat between and was carried by two men, one on each end. It was an extremely light sedan chair that allowed the bearers to tread steadily. So, at twenty-one, I ingloriously paid my respects to Emei Mountain. Mr. Yu walked in front of or behind us and frequently came to take my hand, saying that cold hands were the worst when ill. I said I had hardly ever been ill since high school and I had forgotten the pains in my chest. Now, having it occur as I was climbing Emei Mountain was embarrassing and discouraging.

Halfway up the mountain, we took shelter in an inn beside a mountain stream. After dinner, Mr. Yu and his sister (she was an alto) sang several pleasant songs together. The wind came from all sides of the small sitting room in the inn, providing accompaniment. The fire was warm and fragrant, the oil lamp flickered, and shadows danced on the simple four walls, which made me think of the golden sunlight glowing on the walls of the secret chamber where I had Professor Zhu Guangqian's English poetry class. When they sang "Die Lorelei," the stream flowing deep in the mountain below the inn provided accompaniment, and walking, sitting, or reclining, one could feel the flow.

The moon was visible that night in the mountains. Lieutenant Colonel M and Yu's sister crossed the small bridge over the stream to stroll in the open space on the other side, leaving us beneath the dripping eaves. Mr. Yu asked if I felt better. I said that if my classmates heard I had taken a sedan chair on Emei Mountain, I didn't know what they would say. In the three years at Leshan, I had never climbed Emei Mountain and was afraid of giving up halfway and being a burden to anyone. On account of this, I mentioned to Mr. Yu the thing I have detested most in my life—my stay at the sanatorium when I was ten years old. When I mentioned lime being scattered in Sister Zhang's sickroom and how Old Wang had boiled potatoes for me, Mr. Yu actually rolled up his sleeve and showed me his scarred left arm, which only the doctor and his family had seen. That two people could lower their outer guard and show their secret wounds left us with nothing to say, until his sister returned.

On a moonlit night in the mountains, two pure minds pouring out their souls is what I remember most strongly about him.

On the way back, Mr. Yu's sister invited me to Chengdu to take Lieutenant Colonel M's plane to Shanghai. I said that my father was then in Nanjing and that I ought to go back to Chongqing to stay with my mother until the end of July, and then return to Beiping with her. But she gradually convinced me, saying that I could stay with her in Shanghai, and from there it was easy to get to Nanjing or Beiping. Why bother taking the river steamer, boarding and disembarking at wharves, to get back to Shapingba?

Upon returning to Leshan, I immediately wrote a letter to my mother and enclosed the Yus' Shanghai address.

Before Sister Yu came to meet me at the appointed time, I had carried several bags down to Old Yao's office to say good-bye. With all my heart I sincerely wanted to bid farewell to him, because no one else knew as clearly as he did what I had been through those three years. The dorm was full of old books and waste paper, and nearly all the students had departed. When Qiaozhen and Yu Xianyi left, Old Yao told them that he would return to the countryside of Huangpo in Hunan. He really didn't have any family left, and if things didn't work out, he'd perhaps return to Leshan and find a small house in which to grow old, as Wuhan University was giving him severance pay.

While I was sitting in his office waiting for the car, Old Yao said, "When you first got here, you spent all your time waiting for letters from that flyer, right? He died more than a year ago. Later Mr. Huang wasted two trips here—it wasn't destined to be. Over the last three years, you've had your lot. Sister Yu is now coming to pick you up herself. It looks as if their family is sincere, which is a big relief."

I said, "Old Yao, they're not seeking a marriage. Besides, I have another year of school left."

Old Yao laughed and amiably waved good-bye to me.

When I left Leshan, I departed with Old Yao's blessing. In those three years, he was the only one to register my last light blue letter and the silence after the tide of letters subsided. Regarding the two men who had appeared in the last year, he used his omniscient powers of evaluation and commended me on my lot. But, what was my lot?

Without a second thought, I boarded the American military plane and was demobilized back to Shanghai. In a matter of a few hours, I again became a stranger in a strange land.

SHANGHAI: SEEING MYSELF IN A DIFFERENT MIRROR

It was already dark when I arrived at the Yus' home in Shanghai.

When Auntie Yu saw her son and daughter suddenly return home—in those days everything happened suddenly, because there was no long-distance phone service and there was no other form of contact between Shanghai and Sichuan—and with an oafish girl in tow, she was quite happy for a while. After settling me in Mr. Yu's younger sister's room, the whole family went to the living room to talk about everything that had happened since they had last seen one another.

Mr. Yu's younger sister was one year younger than I and played a key role in introducing me into Shanghai life. The following morning, I awoke in the bed facing hers and put on my nicer *qipao* and newer rubber-soled leather shoes. She seemed to look at me in surprise. Having grown up in the upper circles of Shanghai society, she didn't suffer materially during the eight years of Japanese occupation, even after her father died. A year after victory, Shanghai gradually had recovered a life of peace and prosperity befitting an international metropolis. She was the youngest of five siblings. By nature, she was kindhearted and direct, and if she had something to say, she said it, which shortened the time I needed to find my way around. When the family gathered for breakfast, she said she would take me shopping for clothes that afternoon, which she had not discussed with me beforehand. Later I gradually came to fully understand that being seen with me in my "Chongqing clothes" on the streets of Shanghai was embarrassing for her: in Shanghai in June, no one was seen wearing rubber-soled leather shoes or a *qipao* that wasn't tightly fitted, and speaking a language nobody understood. Everyone in the war zones was that way during the eight years of wartime hardship. My male classmates said, "There are a hundred ways to wear a blue *qipao*," but no one had ever considered me rustic.

Before leaving that afternoon, she practically forced me to change into a pair of her light beige summer shoes. I carried the white plastic handbag that Brother Dafei had brought back after training in the States and given to my mother. Such bags were never seen in the rear in those days, and my mother gave it to me when I started university, but I never took it out of my suitcase after arriving in Leshan. It disappeared during the "great theft" soon thereafter. Later everything was "discovered" under one of the girls' beds, and the bag returned to me. Fortunately, the bag was considered decent foreign goods, especially because inside were money for a boat ticket back to Chongqing, sufficient travel funds, and some "farewell funds." The first time I left for Wuhan University, my father cautioned me, saying, "If a boy invites you out to eat, you should try to return the favor. You don't want to take advantage of others." Therefore, I could cover all my expenses with confidence.

I remember looking in the mirror at the clothing shop and not recognizing myself, although I wore just a creamy, short-sleeved blouse and red skirt; it was the first time in my life that I had bought fashionable clothing. The scout uniform I wore in junior high had been handed out by the school; the long robe I wore from winter to summer in the high school, my mother had had made by a local tailor according to the specifications of the school. At the university, I had a couple of extra-long robes in different but solid colors. None of the female students wore bras, and all our underwear was hand-sewn. After we entered high school, several "princess lines" were sewed in our upper garments, making small curves. After changing clothes, I spent a number of days feeling very awkward. Mr. Yu's little sister greatly praised my "modernization" and went even further to say, "When my older sister came in with you yesterday, I didn't know what was wrong with Peter. Seeing you smile just now, I now understand why he likes you."

When he returned home to his family in Shanghai, Mr. Yu's name reverted to Peter. No one called him by his Chinese name except me. His mother addressed me as Miss Chi. He was the only person I relied on in those days; having arrived from far-off Sichuan, where we had shared our deepest hurts and secrets, we had developed a certain closeness. It was on account of him that I had a good first impression of Shanghai, that huge, strange, cold, and aloof city.

During the day, he took me walking everywhere, and I saw many streets planted with European sycamores, the schools he had attended, his voice teacher's house, and the Yangtze River from its mouth at the Bund to where it flowed into the sea. After dinner, we would sing and pray in the living room. He took me up to the attic, which was his father's library and also his room, and showed me a copy of Kipling's *The Light That Failed*, which had been left open at the page his father was reading the night he died. Then we sat on the sofa by the window, whispering about our feelings.

On my fourth day in Shanghai, a Monday, Mr. Yu took me to see my father after breakfast.

Anyone who has never encountered troubled times cannot understand my frame of mind in those days. And I, who had never really experienced the difficulties of the real world, suddenly found myself in a place like Shanghai, and only then did I realize how weak the links were holding my family and me together. All I knew was that since victory, my father spent half his time in Nanjing preparing for the government's "return to the capital"; returning once to Chongqing, he told my mother that when he went to Shanghai he would stay with the Dings and if anything came up, she could write to his old friend Wu Kaixian, who would forward the letter (his son also attended Nankai). Uncle Wu was the first to go home to Shanghai, where he served as director of the Bureau of Social Affairs and was responsible for recovering all the property stolen by the Japanese in the English and French concessions, resettling the people, and other things. I saw Uncle Wu and told him I wanted to see my father. Startled, he said, "You're a pretty capable young lady. The schools in the war zones just let out and the boats have been coming down the Yangtze one after another from Sichuan to Wuhan and then to Shanghai, but the students' turn hasn't yet come. How did you get to Shanghai? It's perfect. Your father should be arriving any day now from Nanjing. I'll have a huge surprise for him!" In a few days, my father showed up at the Yus' where he found his daughter. He thanked the Yu family for looking after me. Three days later, I accompanied him to Nanjing on the evening express train.

READING THE BOOK OF REVELATION AGAIN

Nanjing is the closest thing to a hometown for me, at least in my memories. I attended primary school there, but more importantly saw my parents reunited there. My mother had managed a comfortable and happy family, bearing my three little sisters, and the house was filled with laughter. The Chi family house on Ninghai Street had been a sanctuary for countless homesick northeast students of the Whampoa Military Academy, who had gone there on Sundays to eat a home-cooked meal and be cared for by my parents. Therefore, our flight in early winter of 1937, the tragedy of our country defeated and our home lost, and the massacre the Japanese carried out when they occupied Nanjing were not just a national tragedy but a personal one as well.

After arriving in Nanjing, we lived in a temporary government hostel. In those days, many organizations that squeezed into Shanghai and Nanjing added the word "temporary" to their name. My father went to the office in the morning and I would go out in the rain and walk around alone, seeking our old home and my primary school of eight years before.

After eight years of foreign occupation, the "temporary" attitude toward living of those returning after fleeing for their lives or those who were newly arrived made the capital, which was once at the forefront of a new life movement and filled with excitement, into a wasteland. Young as I was, this all made me hesitant. Only the Drum Tower was still recognizable. Coming down the grassy slope there and turning right, you gradually found yourself in an old, damaged avenue with ruined houses, which had once been the prosperous heart of the city. Xinjiekou had been a land of cultural inspiration—I had been taken there to buy books by my father's sullen servant Song Yichao, and went with my grandfather to see my first movie, *A Bible Story*. Continuing a little way, I suddenly saw a horizontal banner suspended on a church:

Commemorating the First Anniversary of Zhang Dafei
Giving His Life for the Country

Those words were like daggers that pierced my eyes and stabbed my heart. I stood dumbly on the street wondering if I should go inside, wondering if I had been led there by his departed soul. Less than ten days before, I had unexpectedly made the long journey across the country, returning from Sichuan to Nanjing, where we had first met. Had he led me at that moment to see the evidence of his life and death at God's holy church?

A person standing at the open door of the church watched me standing dumbly there in the rain for a while before walking over and asking if I was a friend of Zhang Dafei's. He invited me in to attend the ceremony and join them in remembering him.

As if in a dream, I followed him across the street and into the building, never even noticing the name of the church. Inside was a silk register to sign, which I hesitated to do before signing my brother's name, Chi Zhenyi. Today, sixty years later, I am still asking myself why I signed my brother's name and not my own. In the ten long months from the autumn of 1944, when he stopped writing letters to me, to May 1945, when he was shot down over Xinyang, Hunan, I never ceased trying to guess what sort of people were around him while he was alive, and who were now holding a memorial ceremony for him. Would they understand the significance of my name in his life?

At the end of the war, millions of bleeding hearts remained unhealed. At that very solemn ceremony, people recalled how he had maintained his calm and purity in the precarious life in the military and respected him for it. From the scriptures someone read a passage from the book of Revelation: "And I saw a new heaven and a new earth: for the first heaven and the first earth were passed away. . . . And God shall wipe away all tears from their eyes; and there shall be no more death, neither sorrow, nor crying, neither shall there be any more pain: for the former things are passed away." These words of scripture have helped me surmount many difficulties in life. I sat in the last row and left as soon as the ceremony ended.

I'll never be able to explain why I went to Xinjiekou that day and saw that memorial banner. Every person has some private miracles in their life that need not be explained. Since fleeing Nanjing at the end of 1937, I have only returned twice. The first time, I attended Zhang Dafei's memorial service; the second time was for three days in May 1999 when, with the assistance of my junior high school friend Zhang Fei, I found the Air Corps Martyrs Cemetery and ascended the steps to touch that black granite memorial on which was inscribed the year of Zhang Dafei's birth and the year of his death.

BEIPING, OUR TEMPORARY HOME

Three days later, my father took me back to Shanghai. He was actively preparing to revive *Time and Tide* in Shanghai, Beiping, and Shenyang, but he didn't foresee, amid the joy after victory when everyone left Chongqing and went their separate ways, and while cherishing the aspiration to publish nationwide, that the glory days of the magazine were over and would not return.

On the train I told him about how I had stumbled upon Zhang Dafei's memorial service. Face to face, we sighed continuously with grief.

My father said that since he had come south after the defeat of Guo Songling in 1945, his voice had fortunately been heard by the central government and he had been charged with organizing the anti-Japanese underground resistance work, ensuring that the people of the fallen Manchukuo would not forget China. Seeking students for Whampoa Military Academy at Sun Yat-sen Middle School had been done in order to foster a recovery of national strength. In fifteen years, many had come from the northeast to serve in the military—some, like Zhang Dafei, had sacrificed themselves for the country, and now their remains couldn't be returned home—and they now hoped that my father would return early and comfort their families. Russia only declared war on Japan a week before the Japanese surrendered. Thirteen days later, the Japanese Kwantung Army accepted the Potsdam Declaration of the Allies and surrendered to Russia in Harbin. Russia took Pu Yi, emperor of Manchukuo, prisoner, while capturing 590,400 Japanese soldiers and announcing the "liberation of Manchuria." A full year after victory, the industrial equipment that was seized in the northeast had been shipped to Russia, and all important areas, ports, and military equipment handed over to the Chinese Communists to assist them in their fight against the army of the central government. The situation in the northeast had become increasingly difficult, and the sacrifices made during the War of Resistance were not going to be exchanged for peace and happiness. When would the survivors of those who died for their country be looked after?

Our conversation on the train was the first time my father had treated me as an adult, and he talked with me for a long time. We had many long talks about life and the times that deserve to be remembered, up to the time he died in Taiwan.

Returning to Shanghai, I stayed with the Yus, which seemed to have been prearranged between us. I had only been gone three days, but my trip to Nanjing gave me a shock and made me reconsider my frame of mind in Shanghai, which had undergone significant changes over the past ten days. That deceptive show of prosperity made me uncomfortable, and I knew I was an outsider who would never fit in. Mr. Yu, who wished to show me Shanghai, was still the young man who had sung while carrying a torch down White Pagoda Street, and he had never stopped telling me stories on the riverbank about "the world outside." But he was gradually returning to his old circle of friends and to the city he had grown up in. On the prosperous streets, I often longed for Chongqing and Leshan at the confluence of three rivers.

About a week later, my father bought me a ticket on a military transport plane (during demobilization after the war, civil service employees and university students were allowed to take them) to go to Beiping to rejoin my mother and sisters, who had just arrived from Chongqing. The temporary military airfield on the outskirts of Shanghai was surrounded by nothing but reeds and consisted of a runway and a few small sheet-metal buildings. Mr. Yu saw me to the gate and watched as I walked onto the tarmac with the soldiers in full combat gear. As the prop plane taxied the runway just before taking off, I looked out the small window and saw him running through the reeds in his khaki pants, waving to the plane, until he vanished from sight.

Two rows of aluminum seats were arranged against the walls behind the flight cabin of the small transport plane. There were eight seats with canvas straps to hold the passengers in; the rear end was filled with cargo. After we took off, I seemed to daydream about the person running through the reeds; however, I was aware that the person sitting next to me was staring at me. Finally he spoke.

He said, "Miss, your seatbelt is not fastened tightly." I looked at the belt and saw that it was on the last hole, but still loose. All I could say somewhat apologetically was, "That's probably because I only weigh a little more than eighty pounds and don't meet the standards for military aircraft." He laughed loudly, and even the people in the pilot's cabin turned to look at me. He apologized and tried to comfort me. Before we crossed the Yellow River, he already knew my name and academic background. He also gave me the first name card I ever received in my life. His official title as stated on the card was: "Major & Staff Officer, Northeast Public Security Command." He said when he graduated from university he had heeded the call for "100,000 youth people for 100,000 troops" and joined the army. I said I was from the northeast. He immediately asked, "Is Chi Shiying your father?" Startled, I replied, "How did you know that?" He said, "Although I am from Guangdong, I was sent to the northeast with General Liang Huasheng. Shortly after victory, your father returned home as a representative of the central government to reassure the people. The newspaper said he had led anti-Japanese underground activities when it was Manchukuo. He is very famous, so of course I know who he is. Not many people have the surname Chi, and those who can get tickets on planes like this are even fewer."

When the plane landed at the Beiping Airport, he insisted on taking me to the Dayangyibin Hutong on the east side of the city in his jeep. When my mother saw me return home as if dropping out of the sky, and saw a handsome and armed young officer standing beside me saluting her, she must have nearly fainted (in the past, she had frequently fainted). She spent several days trying to figure out how someone would take her skinny daughter, who seemed reluctant to grow up, all the way from Sichuan to Shanghai and then, after arriving in Beiping by plane from Shanghai, insist upon driving her to her home.

Beiping never really felt like home to me. This was not simply due to having only spent two summers there but also because of its oppressive atmosphere. My mother took a civilian plane to Beiping directly from Chongqing for two reasons: she and my father wanted my grandmother (whose coffin was temporarily placed in a temple) properly buried as soon as possible; and she had to arrange how she was going to look after two aunts in the future.

The older aunt's husband was Shi Zhihong, who was one of the wealthy Shi family from Tieling County and a handsome intellectual. Husband and wife had both studied abroad in Japan, and on my father's account he had been involved in the anti-Japanese underground and had donated a lot of money. The husband of my second aunt was Zhang Niangtao, who was also in the underground. After the Marco Polo Bridge Incident, both had to leave Beiping. My older aunt was left behind to take care of five children and my second aunt to take care of two. They had a difficult time for eight years and had taken care of my grandmother until she died. Both uncles died shortly after arriving in Sichuan, and my father felt deeply responsible for his two younger sisters. Upon arriving in Beiping he rented a house large enough for three families and hired a housekeeper by the name of Mama Li, a doorman called Old Li, and his own driver, Li Xin. The day after I arrived in Beiping, I returned to wearing my Chongqing hemp *qipao*, more suited to the depressing tenor of the city and my own frame of mind.

In those days, Beiping and Shanghai were poles apart—to send a letter and receive a reply took ten days. After I left the south, Mr. Yu wrote daily and went on about how he missed me. When his older sister received my thank-you letter, she replied immediately and said that in the days after I left, her brother scarcely had energy to climb the stairs. He sent several books of fairy tales in English for my ten-year-old sister. My father returned to Beiping from Shanghai at the same time as my brother returned from Shenyang. We went and had our only family portrait taken. My youngest sister and I had our photo taken together as well, thinking I would send it to Mr. Yu. He soon wrote to say that he had obtained a job at the electric power plant in Shanghai and went to work every day on the outskirts of town. Gradually, he wrote about what happened at work, his friends, and parties, and began to live in a Shanghai with which I was entirely unfamiliar. And I was living in an unimaginably large family with little space of my own. At our big place in Beiping we followed the worsening situation in the northeast, and it soon became a place of refuge for relatives, friends, and underground comrades fleeing through Shanhaiguan. Wave after wave of people were mercilessly forced to flee, with countless harrowing stories. Leading different lives with different concerns and different expectations for the future, Mr. Yu and I gradually had less and less in common to talk about in our letters. We finally understood that the water of three rivers wasn't going to carry me to join his life in Shanghai. I couldn't just sever myself from my parents and their great concern for me.

In mid-September I went to Hankou, returned to Wuhan University, and registered for classes. I wrote fewer letters until I wrote none at all. Before leaving for Hankou, I wrapped up his letters and left them with Cheng Keyong, a good friend from Nankai who was studying at National Chiao Tung University. In November, I had her send them all back to Mr. Yu, and wrote a short note saying that our paths would henceforth be different, bid him farewell, and wished him the best.

I wasn't very focused in my fourth year. Too much had happened in the three months of summer break, almost to a degree unbearable for my youthful heart. In three months I had traveled the Yangtze River from beginning to end and had gone halfway back upriver. In the three great furnaces of China—Chongqing, Nanjing, and Wuhan—I had truly experienced the joys of meeting and sorrows of parting for the first time in my life. I often seemed to find myself in an illusory realm where nothing was real. The hero I worshiped when young was in heaven, and all that was left was a pure longing for him. And there was no place in the world of reality for Mr. Yu and I to coexist; he was a person who came on the wings of song. When I was young, I often thought of him, but it was like a song that gradually faded with time, leaving a reality without songs. In middle age, when I listened seriously to classical music I sometimes recalled the birds singing in the forest, but only far off in the recesses of my spirit.

LUOJIA MOUNTAIN: 1946

We were the first group of demobilized students to return to Wuhan University.

I was deeply disappointed the first time I set foot on the Wuhan University campus on Luojia Mountain. Not only did the place appear desolate, but it had been so ruined by the Japanese and the neighboring villagers that it was hardly fit to live in.

While we were in Sichuan the teachers were always saying how impressive and beautiful the palacelike buildings were and how they faced the vast and lovely East Lake. However, in September 1946 when I went to find the women's dorm, the workers were still putting glass in the windows and installing wooden doors. I was assigned to the very last room, along with my classmate Kuang Shufang, who was always nice to me in four years at school. Soon, school recommenced and Xie Wenjin arrived from Shanxi.

That year, the three of us had class together, and on weekends we often took the ferry from Wuchang over to Hankou, where we would buy surplus American military canned goods sold on the avenue along the river. Mostly we bought powdered ice cream, and when we returned to the dorm we would add hot water and drink it as a substitute for milk, which was comparatively more expensive. After evening dorm inspection in the winter, we would light a small coal fire to roast various things such as small potatoes and gingko nuts, which were really very tasty. Life was much better here than at Leshan. Two years previously, Xie Wenjin had married her childhood sweetheart, Meng Baoqin, and taken leave from school, and after she gave birth to a son, she returned. She was more settled then, and after studying she would write long letters to her husband. She was very diligent in doing her homework and had a stabilizing influence on us. Shufang and I admired that marriage of hers.

The motto of Wuhan University was "Intelligence, honesty, and a broad and strong mind." Like all university mottoes, it consisted of four Chinese characters that had a deeper significance, though I can't recall what it was. In any event, the pragmatic attitude of the place was everywhere apparent. Most people in China in 1947 seemed to be running all over and moving house like a bunch of ants with no apparent goal. Most of the faculty in the Department of Foreign Languages and Literatures had opportunities for better employment elsewhere. Professor Zhu Guangqian was already at the School of Literature at National Beiping

University making new plans. Before he departed, he hired Professor Wu Mi (styled Yu Ceng) to head the department at Wuhan University.

Professor Wu had not returned to Qinghua University when National Southwestern Associated University moved back to Beiping; instead he had gone to Wuhan University, probably out of his personal friendship with Professor Zhu. In my fourth year, I took two of his classes, one of which was called Literature and Life, which was open to the entire university, and was said to be a well-known class he had taught at Qinghua University upon his return from Harvard University. He offered the class again at Wuhan University and taught it for only two years. He was extremely well read and highly idealistic. His course outline and the content of his lectures covered everything, classical and modern, Chinese and foreign. If it had been an era of peace, order, and prosperity, he could have given an early boost to the study of comparative literature in China. Unfortunately, in 1947, most students were full of worries and it was difficult to find a settled young person, totally unlike the previous generation who had solely pursued the ideal of a "moralist of realism." He edited *Measure of Learning* magazine, and throughout his life he stressed that literature must have a serious purpose and rhetoric must be based on sincerity. But stories of his blind passions became the stuff of legends in those days.

The thing I remember most clearly about Professor Wu is that he offered a class called The Long Poem for third- and fourth-year students, which served as a continuation of Professor Zhu's English poetry class.

He started with the 152 lines of Milton's "L'Allegro" and the 176 lines of "Il Penseroso." The vocabulary and many allusions made them very difficult for us. The Italian titles were quite sonorous and have stayed with me to this day.

Having memorized poems for Professor Zhu's class, we had good memories and assumed we had to memorize these two long poems, so we set about intoning and memorizing them. I still remember large portions of them, which proved fairly useful when I later went on for advanced studies or taught English literary history.

We read only a few important parts and key lines from Milton's *Paradise Lost*, but it was only when he taught Coleridge's "The Rime of the

Ancient Mariner" that we found out we didn't have to memorize the long poems; however, for exams we were required to provide commentary from a much broader perspective and point of view. Later we read "Alastor" and "Adonis" by Shelley and "Endymion" by Keats, and he explained the conflict between the two poets' early Romanticism and reality.

After classes started again, Professor Wu announced that he would be directing the theses of those students who had been advised by Professor Zhu, including mine. Before leaving for Beiping, Professor Zhu told Professor Wu that I wanted to write a thesis about Shelley or Keats. It's quite possible that Professor Zhu also told him about the sadness from which I could not escape—teachers do talk about the private feelings of the students they are concerned about!

Professor Wu suggested that I write my thesis about Shelley's long poem "Epipsychidion" (Greek for "dedicated to a young soul"). I wrote to my father and asked him to have someone in Shanghai find the appropriate book for me, because the school library was not fully back in place yet. *Time and Tide* had started publishing again in Shanghai and the chief editor, Deng Lianxi, was himself a graduate of foreign languages and literatures. Later, when we met, he teased me and said, "So, you're researching Shelley's view on love now, because Professor Wu Mi is your advisor." Upon receiving the book, I flipped through it and decided that Shelley's view on love was different from my own "love-at-first-sight school" and really wanted to switch to a poem by Keats, but both time and my knowledge were insufficient.

Soon, Professor Wu summoned me and corrected about half of my huge draft outline. He used a writing brush to write a two-page outline in English and added one line in Chinese: "The Buddha said love is like a torch that attracts ten thousand others. Its fire always remains." He told me that I needed to consider transcendental love, because loving others, having compassion and sympathy, was a "love" that was not limited to two people.

I diligently read secondary works and wrote a childish first draft based on my teacher's outline, which I handed in by the middle of April, and then proceeded to revise half of it, laboriously writing it by hand (I had never seen a typewriter in those days) until I had my thesis.

Professor Yuan Changying taught Shakespeare to the fourth-year students. She fixed the year's rate of progress using her accustomed steady pace. From Shakespeare's thirty-seven dramas, the tragedies, comedies, and histories, she selected representative plays to introduce to us, but we had no book. All we had were excerpts read in class and the notes we took. Note-taking was my specialty and would come in handy if I ever had the chance to read the works. The topic of Shakespeare is vast and deep and would require a lifetime of study, something I never attempted.

Professor Yuan led us through the palace gate, the third-year class on drama. First she explained the readings and then we read several plays. Our textbook was Hatcher's *Modern Continental Dramas*, an anthology like *Palgrave's Golden Treasury*, which we'd read in English poetry class. I remember her expressions as she taught us Hauptman's *The Sunken Boat* and Edmond Rostand's *Cyrano de Bergerac*, which was translated by Wong Ruobi as *The Big-Nosed Sage of Love* and published by Yuanliu, Taipei in 1994, and how moving it was, inspiring us for a lifetime. Later I read a piece written by my classmate Sun Fali titled "The Shakespeare Bequeathed by an Outstanding Teacher," in which she remembers how Professor Yuan analyzed drama using the fifth dimension. The three quadrants of line, face, and body were the quadrants of space, with time as the fourth quadrant, and their interrelationship (the structure) was the fifth dimension. We were indeed fortunate to have such a fine beginning to our career in literature in that chaotic period of war.

BACKWARD AND "PROGRESSIVE" LITERATURE

Shortly after classes resumed, a notice was pasted up outside the classroom stating that Dr. Tian Dewang, who had recently returned from Italy, was offering an elective course on Dante's *Divina Commedia* for the third- and fourth-year students.

Seven or eight of us were very interested in the course and made it known that we would take it, but in the end only three of us signed up for it. A few days before class, one withdrew, leaving me and one other male classmate, who also decided to drop, not being in the mood to study such a profound classic. The program head summoned the three of us for a talk and told us that to be able to have a real scholar and professor of Italian literature who also satisfied the standards of the Ministry of Education at this place and time was something that ought to be treasured. He said it was up to the three of us to allow the program to open the class so as to retain a talented professor. When we came out, I pleaded with the others not to withdraw from the class. In a spirit of compromise, they said, they would wait until the time to add and drop had past and then withdraw due to a class conflict. In short, I ended up being the only student to face the teacher.

September in Wuhan was the middle of autumn. The classroom was small, and although the windows and door had just been installed, it was still cold and drafty.

Professor Tian wore a Western-style suit and was thin and elegant, with the bearing of a European man of letters. At first he stood behind the podium and wrote on the blackboard; later he sat in a chair and I sat alone below him, and all I could see of him was his shoulders and above. After two weeks of class, we both probably felt a little funny, so one day he said, "The distance from the girls' dorm to the classroom is about the same as to the faculty dorm. It would be better to have class at my house, and it's warmer. There's just my wife and me and the baby."

I went and asked Professor Wu Mi about it and he said, "Give it a try and see. We really don't have enough classrooms, and it would be safe at Professor Tian's place."

After that, I climbed halfway up the slope to Professor Tian's house and during class had a cup of hot tea. Professor Tian's wife was fairly young, unassuming, and warm. The male students said that Professor Tian had studied theology at the Vatican but was never ordained as a priest. Prior to the end of the War of Resistance, he had obtained a doctorate in literature and returned home and married. They also said that at Leshan, there was only one student in Professor Zhang Yi's (Zhenru) class on Hegel, and the two of them often dozed off facing each other.

They wondered if the same thing might transpire while I studied the *Divina Commedia* in Professor Tian's room.

I clearly remember the class that semester in which both teacher and student played their respective parts. Professor Tian diligently guided my reading of the most important parts of the *Commedia*. Of course, the focus of the class was not unlike other literature classes. More time was allocated to the *Inferno* than to the *Purgatorio* and the *Paradiso*, and special importance was attached to the beauty of the meter and rhyme and power of the imagery. In the second circle of hell, the story of the lovers Paolo and Francesca is heard amid the whirlwind. Dante writes: "I fainted with pity, as if I had been dying; and fell, as a dead body falls." I later came to understand that the frequent treatment of sin and love in Western art and literature came as a commentary on the *Commedia*. Professor Tian produced and showed me different editions and illustrations of the *Commedia* that he had brought back from Italy, something that never would have happened in a regular classroom. He was a fairly restrained speaker and during class never discussed anything beyond the text, doing his best to make the class as substantial as possible.

However, his dorm accommodations were not very big, and any noises from the neighboring room where his wife held the baby could be heard. And since I was a girl, we soon became familiar and when no one else was around, she would hand the baby to her husband. Embarrassed, Professor Tian would blush furiously, and I would stand up and take the baby, holding the seven- or eight-month-old boy for him as I listened to class. Later, his wife would hand me the baby at five o'clock, while she would go fan the fire in the kitchen and cook dinner. One time, a classmate came to get me for a class meeting. He returned and told the others how he saw me there holding the baby while the teacher's wife fanned the kitchen fire and the teacher lectured on the eighteenth or some other circle in the *Inferno*. Soon everyone was talking and laughing about it.

But that first reading of the *Commedia* provided a solid foundation and allowed me to avoid Professor Miao Langshan's class, Contemporary Russian Culture, which was, at the time, an extremely popular and full class (I had already taken the required one-year course on Russian literature). My insistence on taking a class on the *Commedia* was an act against the current of the times. I had decided upon a simple path when many others were misled by an unreasonable enthusiasm for political literature and by their own political zealotry and pessimism. In my last year at the university, I chose to take the deserted course on the *Divina Commedia* rather than Contemporary Russian Culture. I did so out of my ambition to study, and it had real meaning.

THE JUNE 1 MASSACRE

The activities of the leftist students were carried out more or less openly in the classroom, dorms, and cafeteria, and on the playing field. Reading groups and singing groups no longer had the spirit of the War of Resistance but were filled with an enthusiasm for Russian books and revolutionary songs such as "The East Is Red," among others. That year at Luojia Mountain, the reddest female classmate was Wang Yuncong, who was pretty, cool, and never engaged in "girl talk" in the dorm. One afternoon as I was crossing the playing field, I saw a volleyball match, which was surrounded by a sea of people. All eyes were on Wang Yuncong. Not only was she a skilled player, but also she was the acknowledged leader, not in the least like an ordinary university student. To this day I still clearly remember her fighting charisma.

Professor Miao Langshan exercised a great deal of influence, but it was negligible compared to that of Wen Yiduo, Li Gongpu, and Pan Guangdan at National Southwestern Associated University. At Southwestern Associated, their speeches criticizing the government and condemning the current situation, their fiery activities, and even the sacrifice of their lives led to a nationwide student movement and allowed the Communists to influence the intellectuals, and as such it was significantly different.

Since he had arrived at Wuhan University to teach midway through the War of Resistance, Professor Miao Langshan's classes, lectures, and forums had been very popular with the students. He used the rich content of Russian literary works to condemn the current situation in China and condemn the government. His talks were interspersed with lots of humorous remarks and mockery of others. They were hilarious, and the house was always full. He led many students who were dissatisfied with the current situation to be "progressive" and to throw themselves into the leftist camp. But he was not himself a Communist Party member.

At the beginning of February 1945, the garrison headquarters wanted to apprehend him, so he went to see University President Wang, who told him he couldn't protect him and suggested that he leave for his own safety. Student response was fierce. Some of the other professors felt he liked to talk too much and that talking so much about politics in class was inappropriate. Professor Zhu Guangqian, the program head, wanted him to stay, but for the school, no one could guarantee his background. The changes in the frontline situation, however, resulted in an official memo never being sent. When classes began again after winter break, Professor Miao Langshan's job was secured by the Allied victory in Europe and the Russian occupation of Berlin. As a result, I took his one-year class on Russian literature. From the autumn of 1945 to the summer of 1946, he still attended to course content and progress, holding to his role as a teacher of literature. But upon our return to Luojia Mountain, Professor Miao's classes became one-third literature, two-thirds politics. His political attacks accompanied by dramatic gestures became more forceful and inciting as the Communists began to go from taking land and cities behind enemy lines to coming out in the open and doing so. With a shortage of recently demobilized qualified professors, his stage expanded greatly to include the entire university. It was a current, a trend, and no one dared openly criticize his talks.

Professor Yuan Changying's husband, Professor Yang Duanliu, who had studied in England, was a specialist on currency theory and joined with Professor Liu Naicheng to make the economics department at Wuhan University into a key center for nurturing a generation of talented economists. Husband and wife had taught at Wuhan University for more than twenty years. During the difficult years of the War of Resistance, these scholars, who dedicated themselves to serving the country, maintained academic standards and the dignity of scholars. When their progressive daughter Yang Jingyuan attacked the current situation, her father offered her the following advice: "Although the present government has many faults, if you stop and consider, without it now, would we be able to be as well off as we are today? The Japanese would have destroyed the country long ago. Although the Nationalist government is not perfect, without it, we would not have been able to hang on until today. It is not fair to say that it has accomplished nothing. A great deal has been built since the Republic was founded; just compare it to the Qing dynasty and the progress will be clear." His daughter replied, "What's the point of a university education? What good is simply studying? It has nothing to do with reality." Her father said, "How can a person understand the world without studying? How can one tell the difference between what is right and what is wrong? A person is entirely reliant upon their mind for an understanding of an issue. Without study, how can a mind be trained?"

Opinions like Professor Yang's were mentioned by the president and teachers at every school meeting during my three years at Leshan. In those critical days when withdrawing the students to the Lei-Ma-Bing-E mountainous region was considered, a Ministry of Education directive also said, "Studies should go on uninterrupted." Even in the class on Russian literature, Professor Miao required us to read a number of important works in order to understand the depth of and changes in Russian culture. Perhaps he lacked a similar depth of perception regarding the changes in Chinese culture. He and other left-leaning professors, such as Wen Yiduo, incited students on campus to oppose the government, and the effect of such efforts outstripped those of the early military power of the Communists. If anyone on campus dared to refute their inciting words, they were first mocked and then condemned as a professional Nationalist student, and later the insults grew more real. After the June 1 Massacre in 1947, violent beatings occurred in the boys' dorm.

Starting in 1946, the civil war between the Nationalists and Communists was in full swing. In 1947, under the leadership of the Communists, the student movement with its stated opposition to civil war and famine, which had spread throughout the land, was getting out of control. In May, 6,000 students in Nanjing, Shanghai, Suzhou, and Hangzhou who took to the streets to demonstrate met with suppression. Following this, more than 1,700 students from Wuhan University set off another wave of demonstrations and petitions. The students stormed the provincial government, surprising the Wuhan authorities, leading to the garrison headquarters action of entering the Wuhan University campus to arrest Communist teachers and students on June 1.

That morning at around six, some classmates in the boys' dorm near the school gate had already got up to wash when they discovered that several military trucks were parked at the gate. Soldiers with guns and live ammunition were putting Professer Miao Langshan on one of the trucks. He shouted loudly for help and a number of students went to stop them; in the ensuing scuffle, the soldiers fired and three people fell to the ground dead, one of whom was still holding a washbasin, and several others were wounded.

Instantly more students gathered and rescued Professor Miao. Under orders, the military trucks sped away. The wounded were taken to the clinic and the dead were carried to the auditorium on wooden doors, their bodies covered with blankets. All had been shot in the head, so their chests and above were left uncovered.

The faculty and students all gathered in the auditorium. The president and teachers were in charge and the place was filled with the sound of crying. At that moment, a leader-type student ran up on stage and spoke loudly, saying that we all knew the school would handle the funeral matters, but that some student representatives had to participate. Several names were put forward and written on the blackboard on stage. Three or four from the girls' dorm were nominated, among whom was Wang Yuncong. Suddenly I heard my name clearly pronounced, but I couldn't see who said it amid a thousand heads. I just saw my name written on the blackboard.

After the meeting, those whose names had been written down were asked to stay and take part in the final arrangements. Before the meeting broke up, everyone walked in front of the dead to show their respect.

I recall one who had a huge wound from which the blood still flowed. I could also see his eyes were still open.

I had seen many dead people along the road when we took flight from Nanjing; I had also seen many charred corpses after the bombings in Wuhan and Chongqing. But I had never seen one so close. Being shaken that way is something I will never forget, and something tears cannot assuage.

Staying behind after the meeting, I wondered why I had been nominated, since I had taken no part in any school activities outside the Nankai Alumni Association and the Christian Fellowship. No simple matter, clearly it was a challenge that couldn't be avoided. I thought of my father's constant admonishment, "You must be able to stay composed!" I wasn't going to speak first, but wait and see. Sure enough, after the dozen or so students discussed the important matters, someone suggested that Chi Pang-yuan write the words for the memorial ceremony.

I stood up and said that I was afraid I wouldn't be able to write such an important piece in just two days. "Aren't you Zhu Guangqian's prize student? It should be a simple matter for you." Someone else with a softer voice said, "Doesn't the petit bourgeois *Divina Commedia* contain revolution and violence?"

After going two days with scarcely any sleep or food, I managed to produce the memorial text. As I wrote, I saw that bleeding wound flash before my eyes and I could hear Professor Zhu intoning the lines, "The ship has weather'd every rack, the prize we sought is won; / The port is near, the bells I hear" from the poem *O Captain! My Captain!*. I wrote that the three had not died at the hands of the invading enemy, but at the hands of their compatriots after victory. When would poor China be able to rise above the blood of suffering and hate and allow the safe pursuit of knowledge, and freedom of thought? If that were to happen, they would not have died in vain. . . .

I wrote that brief elegy in all sincerity. It was taken and written as a large poster and many copies mimeographed. The response was positive. I started with the human heart and finished with the freedom of knowledge and thought. I sincerely expressed what most people thought, as well as foretelling my own lifelong attitude. When I read it at the impassioned and fervent memorial ceremony, it seemed to possess an earnest solemnity. Perhaps the progressive students weren't entirely satisfied, but they could not condemn me for anything.

Professor Wu Mi, my advisor and the head of the Department of Foreign Languages and Literatures, assured the safety of Professor Miao and personally took him to the airport and put him on a plane to Hong Kong. The central government ordered Peng Shan, the Wuhan garrison commander, to resign, and seriously undertook to apprehend those who had fired their weapons. The June 1 Massacre became a big cultural weapon for the Communists in their struggle for power, but twenty years later, when countless students and teachers were killed in the Cultural Revolution, who was there to appeal to?

UNIVERSITY GRADUATION, FUTURE VAGUE

At noon on the day after participating in the student representative meeting, my roommate Kuang Shufang; Xie Wenjin and her husband, Meng Baoqin; a few Hong Kong classmates from the English Association; and I went to a small restaurant near the school gate to celebrate our graduation and to say good-bye.

Everyone was in pretty high spirits and we ordered a big bottle of sorghum liquor (it was probably all they had there). The restaurant owner brought some small teacups to serve as wine cups along with some small plates of peanuts and dried tofu. Even the patterns on the plates were the same as those in the small teahouse on the riverbank at Leshan (probably all the same Yangtze River culture).

In one year, the ancient city at the confluence of three rivers, the beautiful scenes of the various trees and bushes in flower in late spring in March, and the friends who had strolled hand in hand had become strangers. I found myself in such a complicated situation, as if it were another world. Everyone raised their glasses. I emptied mine, followed by five more, leaving everyone so startled they didn't know what to do.

Wenjin and Shufang carried me back to the dorm. It was quite a ways, and no one had a bicycle. I felt like I was walking on clouds, stepping on emptiness, but managed to get back. Entering the dorm room, I fell on the bed and passed out.

The following day I woke and wondered where I was going and what I was going to do.

I was graduating from university, but love and work were unknowns. Shufang left first for her home in Sichuan. Wenjin was anxious to get back to Shanxi and be reunited with her family. For as long as I could remember, I never had a home to which to return. My father was busy in Nanjing and Shanghai; my mother was living temporarily in Beiping; my brother was a war correspondent in the northeast, following the seesaw battle between the Nationalists and the Communists. There weren't many career options for women in those days, and I still thought about pursuing a master's degree. With Director Gui Zhiting's help, I applied to and was accepted at Mount Holyoke College in the United States through his Christian Fellowship connections. However, my father was opposed to my going abroad and felt that I should first consider marriage before pursuing advanced studies; otherwise, given the unpredictable nature of the situation in China, I might find myself cut off from my family for the rest of my life and end up as an "old spinster."

At noon, with a scorching hot sun directly overhead, I turned in my last final exam. Even the final goal of my struggle was missing. I was graduating and returned to the dorm, exhausted in mind and body. In the half-empty room, I cried for a while over my vague future and grieved for the uncertainty of my country. At my age, my father had wanted to save China with all his heart and mind, and now I, faced with greater troubles within and without, wondered where I was going and what I was going to do. A long time ago I had been childishly presumptuous enough to want to study philosophy and understand life; that day, my own spirit, which was minuscule and powerless, had no place to rest.

At least I still had my reason amid the confusion, and my parents were still around, and as long as they were alive and kicking, I had a home to which to return.

Finally, the day of my last trip down the Yangtze River arrived. In the latter part of June, Yu Linwei and some classmates from Hong Kong and I boarded ship in Hankou for Shanghai. The boat had cabins, but they were so hot and stuffy, it was impossible to get comfortable. Along the railing around one hundred young men (new soldiers) were bound together with coarse rope. They were on their way to the northeast to help in the war to eradicate the Communists—in those days it was not permitted to say "war between the Nationalists and the Communists."

After sailing for half a day and one night, the soldiers outside the cabin watched us drinking water. They looked so thirsty that we couldn't drink. Occasionally we would sneak a few of them some water to drink, and then others would ask us for some.

The officer on patrol heard and came over to look, and told us that the time to give them food and drink was fixed and that we shouldn't break military discipline. When the army was on the move, the greatest fear was that they would become too relaxed or desert.

Under that sun, the lips of some of the soldiers had become black and cracked. Only when we closed the door of the hot, stuffy cabin did we dare drink water, because every sip we took felt like a sin.

We went to bed that night totally exhausted. We were drifting off to sleep when someone outside the cabin shouted, "Man overboard!" The officer scanned the water with a large flashlight. How could anyone survive when the Yangtze was swollen and rolling along?

One of the soldiers started crying, which caused many more to cry. A man said in a coarse, heavy, and stern voice, "I'll shoot if anyone cries again!" The crying suddenly stopped and the darkness fell totally silent.

I'll never forget their sunburned faces and the thirst in their eyes for as long as I live. Sometimes when I'm watching a movie about a battle, even in the ancient West, I'll break into tears when I see the soldiers raise their shields and rush into the fray behind an awe-inspiring general. Ancient or modern, East or West, those soldiers rushing across the land so that one general can establish his reputation on thousands of dead make me sad, a concrete symbol of war that hurts my soul.

Back in Shanghai! Although it had only been a year, it seemed like ages, but I couldn't recall it without pain.

I had a home. My father had revived *Time and Tide* in Shanghai, moving it from northern Sichuan to a large building on Jessfield Road (renamed Fanwangdu Street after victory) in what had been the British concession. It was rented municipal property that was once the mayor's residence, about which there were many mysterious rumors from the Japanese period. Most of the rooms were occupied by the staff and families of *Time and Tide* and the employees and families of the Northeast China Association in Chongqing, leaving three rooms for my father. Gradually, quite a few comrades from the anti-Japanese underground in the old days showed up in Shanghai and stayed there. The place was packed with people. Coming and going every day, countless old friends who had lost touch for years would run into each other and talk endlessly about all the thrilling things that had happened since they parted.

I stayed in Shanghai for one week before going to Beiping to be reunited with my mother. My father hoped I would find work in Beiping and help look after the family. It seemed like the only reasonable route open to me at the time.

My return to Beiping after graduating was a great comfort to my mother. In her mind, I had grown up and could take care of myself and had become a daughter with whom she could now discuss her concerns.

She had been back in Beiping for one year, and all her dreams of returning home had seemed to vanish. The war in the northeast to exterminate the Communists was being fiercely fought. The two armies were fighting a bloody battle from street to street in Changchun. Those who had said nothing and become "subjects" of Manchukuo for fourteen years were now fleeing through Shanhaiguan. Our house in Dayangyibin Hutong in Beiping became the destination of friends and family seeking refuge. All the rooms were full and we had two tables for each meal, and sometimes two seatings. In all, there were the ten members of my two aunts' families, four in my family, three paternal cousins (Zhenyong, Zhenfei, Zhenlie), two maternal cousins, and some relatives recently arrived from the northeast. Inflation was on the rise in those days and we only had three or four large dishes at each meal, such as eggplant stewed with potatoes and cabbage stewed with tofu and some meat. The quantities were large, but they were in no way gourmet dishes. My aunts' kids and my sisters ranged from ten to fifteen or sixteen years of age, an age when they didn't yet understand life's difficulties.

The money my father sent home every month didn't keep up with the inflation, and my mother was finding her role more difficult to play. Taking advantage of my return, she accompanied my father when he made an official trip to the northeast and bravely returned to her parents' home at Xintaizi to spend a few days and visit the graves of my grandparents, and my three uncles. During that period I helped my aunts do the marketing and discovered how much it cost for daily necessities such as fuel, rice, oil, salt, vinegar, tea, and sauces. The money my father sent at a fixed time every month no longer sufficed to cover expenses.

Rumors abounded in Beiping. The Tainjin–Pukou Railroad was disrupted because it was often being worked on or due to fighting. My mother was extremely worried when she returned to Beiping. She had no jewelry left to sell—the jewelry that was part of her dowry and the several thousand silver coins she had saved had all been exchanged by the banks for paper currency at the end of the War of Resistance. Later it was worth enough to buy a bolt of indanthrene fabric. If the Tianjin–Pukou Railroad was cut, there would be no hope of buying a plane ticket either. My father was working in Nanjing and Shanghai, so how would she survive with two children to care for? And there were also the ten members of my two aunts' families. I slept in her room on a temporary bed. Hearing her tossing and turning all the time and sighing, I said, "Mom, don't sigh so much. I can't sleep."

ACROSS THE SEA, ALONE

Several days later, I went to the Red House of Beiping University to see Professor Zhu Guangqian.

He was very happy to see me and showed me his newly allocated housing, and said that his family would soon be joining him from the south. Those several temporary rooms were in an empty, newly built concrete one-story building. Actually, his new place wasn't as good as his old house at Leshan with the courtyard in which you could hear the falling rain and rustling leaves, but he seemed pleased and said that now after victory, he could pursue academic development. He asked me what my plans were, having graduated. I simply said that I wanted to continue my studies and my family wouldn't let me go abroad, but I didn't mention anything about being an assistant, lest Professor Zhu think I had come to see him for the sake of a job, or perhaps I simply hadn't made up my mind to stay in Beiping. Since childhood, my memory of old Beiping was just a gloomy old city gate, yellow dust blown down the winding *hutongs*, and off in the distance, desolate Western Mountain and the rooms scattered with lime.

That night, my mother asked me about my visit with my teacher at Beiping University. In all seriousness, she said, "Since you didn't ask your teacher for work, I hope you can find something in Nanjing or Shanghai. If Beiping were cut off from Nanjing and Shanghai, it would be hard enough for me with your two sisters, and who knows what your brother will be doing in the war-torn northeast. If you stay close to your father, it will be one less burden for me."

I returned to Shanghai. Through Sun Jinsan at *Time and Tide Literature and Art*, I applied for an assistant tutoring job at National Central University in Nanjing, but they kept only their own graduates. If I were to teach in Shanghai, I'd need to speak the Shanghai dialect, and my functional English was insufficient. I didn't want to think about it, so never applied. Besides, I didn't really like the false prosperity and the pomposity of Shanghai.

August went by, then half of September. I was in Shanghai and had no idea where I should go or what I should do.

One day I suddenly saw Uncle Ma Tingying among all the coming and going guests. At the start of the War of Resistance, he had quit a seventeen-year career in Japan as a geology scholar and come home to serve his country. He had served as principal of Northeast Middle School of Shenyang when it moved south. Starting in 1937, whenever he came to Nanjing or later to Chongqing, he would stay at our house. Since he was single, my mother would pay particular attention to his food and clothing. He was a big man with a resonant laugh, and we all liked him and felt close to him. He once gave me a small bag of clamshells, the first I ever saw. He told me about diving under the sea to see the coral reefs, which really opened my eyes. He didn't marry until he was forty and had a son and a daughter. His son's name was Ma Guoguang; later he became a writer in Taipei, under the pen name Liang Xuan.

When I saw him again in Shanghai, it was like old times. He saw me looking confused and hesitant at the edge of ten *li* of red dust of Shanghai. He said he had just arrived from Taipei and was looking for professors for the School of Science of Taiwan University, and had heard that the Department of Foreign Languages and Literatures was looking for teaching assistants. "They have no one, just a couple of Japanese professors waiting to be sent home! Why not go and be an assistant?"

My father and my uncles at *Time and Tide* all thought it impossible and didn't approve of a single girl crossing the strait to Taiwan, which had recently experienced the upheaval of the February 28 Incident. To my mind, going alone to the south meant personal exile, but at least I'd be able to break free from the deadlocked situation of wavering between one city in the north and one in the south. Moreover, the whole country was caught up in a political whirlpool in which if you weren't left, then you were right, and there was no place put your head in the sand like an ostrich. Everyone told me to go and see and experience a new place. Look around and then come back—everyone gave me an ample road for retreat. At the end of September 1947, I ventured across the sea to Taiwan with Uncle Ma, to see an unknown new world.

My father bought a round-trip ticket for me, but I knew I would be buried in Taiwan.

Father Chi Shiying (front row, center) and Fourth Aunt Chi Jinghuan (front row, right).

Mother Pei Yuzhen (center), with eldest son Chi Zhenyi (first from right) and eldest daughter Chi Pang-yuan (third from right).

Father Chi Shiying, 1923.

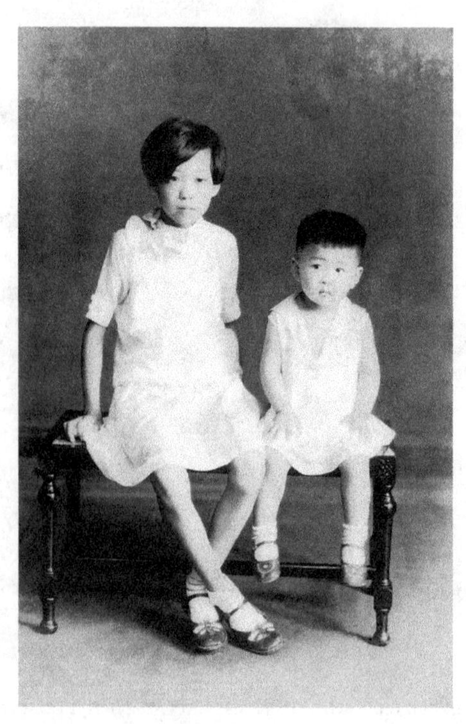

Chi Pang-yuan and her sister Ningyuan.

Chi Shiying (center) with friends Mei Gongren (right) and Huang Henghao, 1930s.

On the first anniversary of the founding of *Time and Tide*, 1939.

Chi Pang-yuan's notebooks from Professor Zhu Guangqian's poetry classes at Wuhan University.

Nankai alumni on the occasion of seeing off Wang Shirui (front row, second from left) to join the army.

The Chi family. Front row, from the left: mother Pei Yuzhen, father Chi Shiying, sister Xingyuan. Back row, from the left: sister Ningyuan, brother Zhenyi, Chi Pang-yuan.

Zhang Dafei.

Chi Pang-yuan at Wuhan University.

Chi Pang-yuan (right) just after graduating from college. Mother Pei Yuzhen (seated), sister Ningyuan, and sister Xingyuan, 1947.

Chi Pang-yuan, Luo Yuchang, and their three sons, 1969.

Chi Pang-yuan and her mother, 1950.

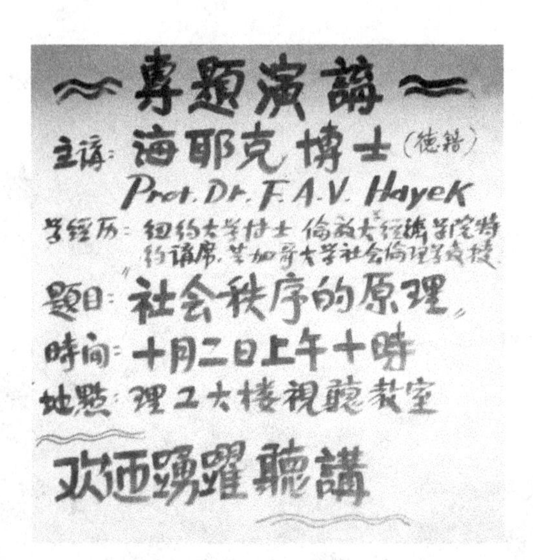

Announcement for a lecture by Professor Friedrich A. Hayek in Taichung in 1965.

Seminar on the teaching of English and American literature organized by Chi Pang-yuan at Chung-Hsing University in Taichung, 1971.

Professor Friedrich A. Hayek (right) with Tang Huisun, president of Chung-Hsing University (left), and Song Miannan, dean (left, rear), 1965.

PEN translators and friends. Front row, from the left: Ding Zhenyuan, Chi Pang-yuan, Linda Scott, Nancy Du, Michelle Wu; back row, from the left: Carlos G. Tee, Edward Vargo, John Deeney, Li Dasan, Yanwing Leung, Yuan Hexiang, Nicholas Koss, Tien-en Kao.

The idiot mountain climbers. From left to right:
Yang Junxian, Yu Yilie, Luo Yuchang, Chi Pang-yuan, 1983.

Chi Pang-yuan (right) and her sister Chi Ningyuan on Guanyin Mountain, Taipei, 1984.

Chi Shiying (left) at his home in Neihu and Luo Yuchang (right).

Chi Pang-yuan at the Memorial for the Aviator Martyrs of the War of Resistance against Japan, Nanjing, May 2000.

Chi Pang-yuan and David Der-wei Wang.

At the opening of the Chi Shiying Memorial Library, Sun Yat-sen Middle School, Shenyang. Chi Pang-yuan (front row, third from left), brother Zhenyi (second from left), sister Ningyuan (first from left) and sister Xingyuan (sixth from left).

6

TAIWAN

Trials and Hardships

IMPRESSIONS OF TAIPEI

My first trip across the Taiwan Strait by prop plane in October 1947 was very exciting, because the name of the body of water was from a geography book and I felt as though I were flying across a map, arriving quickly in a matter of a couple of hours.

The name Taipei was quite unfamiliar to me, and there wasn't much to the airport, which was probably just "temporary." Taiwan was said to be a small island, so I ought to have the immediate opportunity to see the "jidangao" (chicken egg cake), with which everyone was familiar (Jilong, Danshui, Gaoxiong, as we were taught in Wu Zhenzhi's geography class). At least one of the first things I could do was see real bananas and pineapples.

My first view of Taipei was not what I had expected—no beach with waving palm trees or small colorful buildings, just a small grayish city with a few two-story concrete buildings among a host of single-story Japanese-style wooden houses. There was little or no greenery to speak of, nor was there a public square. I stayed at the home of Uncle Ma Tingying.

Uncle Ma Tingying, styled Xuefeng, was born into a farming family in Jin County, Liaoning Province, in 1902. As a young man, he decided to serve the country through studying science. He tested and was admitted to the Tokyo Teachers College in Japan to study natural sciences, and upon graduating first in his class entered the geology department of Tohoku Imperial University in Xiantai, where he studied with the famous paleontologist Dr. Shikama Tokyo, specializing in the growth rates and changes in coral reefs and other related subjects, such as paleoecology, paleoclimatology, paleogeography, and plate tectonics. He published many outstanding papers and received two Ph.D. degrees, one from Berlin University in Germany and one from the Imperial Academy in Japan. In 1936, he overcame Japanese obstructions to use what he had learned to repay the nation, becoming a professor in the geology department at National Central University. The following year, after the Marco Polo Bridge Incident, the inland provinces lacked salt, so at the behest of the government, Uncle Ma traveled to survey the coastal and other salt-producing areas and directed the mining of well salt and rock salt, thus successfully facilitating the national administration of the people's livelihood during the War of Resistance.

At the start of the war, all the schools of Beiping and Shanghai moved to the southwest, behind the lines. After the Mukden Incident of September 18, 1931, my father was responsible for running the Northeast Association for anti-Japanese underground resistance and had cordially invited Uncle Ma to serve as the principal of the Northeast Middle School (the school was established in Shenyang, but moved from Manchukuo to Beiping with the teachers and students in tow, unlike the National Northeast Sun Yat-sen Middle School, which was later set up to accommodate those students who had fled). Uncle Ma led the teachers and students through Shanhaiguan to Beiping, then to Nanjing, up mountains and over rivers with great difficulties from Hubei through Hunan and Guizhou to Ziliujing in Sichuan, reestablishing the school at Jingning Temple. After leaving his job as principal, he went back to doing research and during the eight years of the War of Resistance, he conducted research on glaciers, the formation of peneplains, laterization, and the ancient ecology of coral reefs and their changes, completing seven major works.

After victory in the War of Resistance, he was sent to Taiwan as a special envoy by the Ministry of Education to take charge of the island's educational institutions, particularly Taipei Imperial University. Having lived in Japan for twenty years and gained a deep understanding of the Japanese mentality, and possessing the open-minded generosity of a Chinese intellectual, he did his utmost to preserve and safeguard the facilities, materials, and system of Taipei Imperial University. The Japanese had not yet been repatriated, and they deeply respected Professor Ma's academic standing and the way he handled things; however, he refused to accept any government position while setting up the Department of Geology and an oceanic research institute, mentoring students, devoting himself to research, and forming survey teams that visited Lanyu, the Spratly Islands, and the Diaoyutai Islands. His "On the Formation of Oil" had an immense impact on the opening up of Taiwan's resources. Later, he published a series of nearly twenty articles titled *Studies in Paleoclimatology and Continental Drift*, offering proof for the theory of plate tectonics, which was discussed and affirmed by international geological circles.

Uncle Ma's house was located on Qingtian Street, the old name for which was Number 6 Sanjyoudori, a narrow lane of Japanese-style houses with low walls and wooden gates. There was no need to knock, one had only to push open the gate and walk in. Inside was a small Japanese garden with a small artificial hill and pond, almost toylike, but the row of large trees along the wall was somewhat imposing. The door opened onto a vestibule, and the visitor would be met by a girl who was kneeling (she wasn't sitting or squatting, but kneeling) and in Japanese rattled off a long string of what were probably words of welcome. Her name was Kinchan, and to this day I can still clearly recall her face, because her serious respectfulness contained an element of craftiness, as did her spoken Japanese, which was something I had never encountered before. Everyone removed their shoes and put on the straw slippers that Kinchan handed to them, entered the room, and walked unsteadily across the tatami mats, which was like walking across someone's bed, stepping uneasily. She cooked authentic Japanese-style fish, fried or roasted, and miso soup, which was very tasty, for someone trying it for the first time.

In the hallway outside the kitchen sat an extremely thin, middle-aged rickshaw puller with a white towel at his waist. They called him

Hide-san. In the side yard was parked a rickshaw, which was supplied by National Taiwan University for Uncle Ma's use (at that time he was dean of the College of Sciences). Uncle Ma weighed 180 pounds and was about six feet tall; Hide-san weighed in at about 120 pounds and was about five feet tall. But that was of no matter. What mattered were the wooden pull handles on the rickshaw—the first time Uncle Ma took his seat, they broke. After they had been repaired, he took his seat and they broke again, but he once again took his seat though they couldn't be repaired. The rickshaw puller was a public employee who clocked in and out every day. After I got there and sought work in the Department of Foreign Languages, Uncle Ma had Hide-san take me to school and return me to Qingtian Street in the afternoon. In this way he was able to "fulfill his duties"; otherwise he would have been dismissed from his job, the salary from which went to support his family.

The first two times I rode in the rickshaw, Hide-san spoke in Japanese the whole way (he didn't understand Chinese), expressing his gratitude to me. After I was "employed," I turned over all my rice and coal coupons to him, which made a couple of teaching assistants living at Uncle Ma's place mock me for "showing off my wealth." The third time I rode in the director's rickshaw, as I was proceeding down Xinsheng South Road through the fields, I suddenly recalled what my father had told me about not riding in public cars when I was young. I immediately got out and walked.

A NEW WORLD: FRIENDSHIP

I arrived at National Taiwan University as a muddleheaded teaching assistant. Landing at Uncle Ma's house upon arrival, I got an overall picture of the university. Lu Zhihong, who was soon to take over as president of the university, and a number of other professors from those early days who lived in the other two nearby lanes, conversed with Uncle Ma about academic duties nearly every day as they came and went, and from time to time they inquired about the way things were going with the Japanese professors who were still residing on Qingtian Street, awaiting repatriation. Arriving at Uncle Ma's gate, they frequently heard his resonant laughter. They were all thinking about the big picture for the future, with the most important points initially being to maintain Taipei Imperial University's strong schools of Tropical Biology and Medicine, and to strengthen the teaching and service at the medical school. That year the foundation, which remains strong today, was laid.

After three months in Taiwan looking at those two rooms full of books in the Department of Foreign Languages and Literatures, I began organizing the piles, examining each book and roughly classifying them. It was actually a fortunate job that allowed me to forget myself. However, my mind was unsettled. After work, I would walk, following Liugong Irrigation Ditch toward Heping East Road and Qingtian Street, feeling empty, wondering if I should go home to Shanghai during the winter break. If I went home, should I come back? If I came back, was there anything more important for me to do than moving books around? In Taiwan there were probably only six people who even knew of my existence. All alone and filled with worries, I made my way at dusk along the ditch to a strange Japanese-style house with straw mats.

On Lunar New Year's Eve, I locked the department door and headed home. It was already dark, and when I got to the lane off Qiangtian Street, a light was already on in a house there. Looking over the low wall, I could see a family sitting around a table, already eating New Year's Eve dinner, a warm scene that made me think of my mother and sister in Beiping and my father in Shanghai, and as I considered my own inexplicable "independence," tears welled up in my eyes as I quickly made my way to Uncle Ma's house, where a number of older people who had come to Taiwan alone were sitting around the dinner table drinking warmed sake.

One afternoon after the New Year, my solitude was completely disrupted.

That day it rained without letting up. Bored to death, I put on my heavy raincoat and went to the intersection of Qingtian Street and Heping East Road, where I caught a bus to Rongding (now the area around Hengyang Road, Baoqing Road, and Bo'ai Road) to buy a few things. At that time there was only the number 3 bus in front of the police station (sixty years later, it is still there).

In the heavy rain, only one other woman was waiting for the bus. She was covered entirely in a raincoat and her rain hat was pulled low. We waited for ages and no bus came. I took a look at her and at that moment I thought I recognized a familiar face. She looked at me and we almost simultaneously asked, "Aren't you Yang Junxian from Wuhan University?" "Aren't you Chi Pang-yuan from Wuhan University?"

Unexpectedly, I had found a link with the past.

Yang Junxian had been an economics student two years ahead of me at the university. I had seen her in the girls' dorm, but we hadn't interacted. She had come to Taiwan with her sister and was working in the accounting department of the Taiwan Power Company. Yu Yilie, who was from the same class, was also in Taiwan, working in operations at the Taiwan Sugar Corporation. The two were engaged and living at her brother-in-law Ge Fujiang's (we all called him Ge-san) place in the Japanese-style dorm of the Department of Agriculture and Forestry, in what was probably Lane 9 on Qingtian Street, just three or four lanes away from Uncle Ma's place. Her older sister, Yang Xixian, taught home economics at the Normal University and had been program head for the previous three terms. Husband and wife were straightforward and welcoming. Their daughter, Ge Dingyu (baby name Ningning), was only four years old and possessed the good humor of her parents, and often sang the new songs she had learned in kindergarten, and even danced. The Ge family gradually became the most appealing of warm families for me. Many years later, when I taught the history of English literature, each time I read Bede's "The Conversion of King Edwin" and got to the part that describes the situation after he came to believe in Christianity as being like a sparrow flying into a great dining hall where there was food and a warm fire, and how upon flying out, it encountered the cold and a contrary wind, reminded me of those early days in Taiwan.

After the New Year, Junxian and Yilie invited me to join the Wuhan University Alumni Association in Taiwan. Most of the several dozen people were elder schoolmates from the schools of engineering and law who were either working in government offices or teaching. The head of the alumni association, Li Linxue (a chemistry graduate, highly placed in China Petroleum), did the most to help settle alums arriving in Taiwan. He lived to be very old. Heng Gaoshou you could say was the soul of the alumni association. Knowing that I was a recent graduate who hadn't been in Taiwan long, he asked me to report on activities at our alma mater over the last two years. I stood up and gave my report as I saw things. Among those present at the time was Luo Yuchang, an electrical engineering graduate now working for the Taiwan Railways Administration. Later he told me that he decided upon seeing me at the alumni association meeting that he would marry me.

Three or four days after the alumni association meeting, Luo Yuchang and Tan Zhongping (a mechanics graduate whom I had met at the Leshan Christian Fellowship) came to Uncle Ma's house to see me. We sat in the living room for a while, but I didn't give it much thought. They came again the following week and invited me to see Yang Junxian at her place, where we talked about the situation of alums recently arrived in Taiwan. The three of them were from the same class, the last class that graduated at Leshan, and were the earliest technocrats to arrive in Taiwan, so they had much in common to talk about. For a student of literature like myself who knew little of the world, they were a bit like an old horse that knows the way home. We have been together in Taiwan for fifty years, and their protective attitude toward me has never changed.

It was winter break, and ever since I had seen that warming scene of a family sitting down together for New Year's Eve dinner, my thoughts kept revolving around the idea of going home. I would go to Shanghai first, and perhaps my parents would finally return to Nanjing to reestablish our home there, and then I could settle down and find a job. I went to the airline office with my return ticket and reserved a seat for a flight a week later. When I returned to Qingtian Street, Uncle Ma said, "The university has hired you as a teaching assistant for one year. You've been here one semester, and now you want to leave. It will be difficult for the university to find a replacement. There are fewer than ten in the Department of Foreign Languages and Literatures, so you ought to at least wait till summer break to make things easier for everyone." Junxian also said, "It's too bad that you haven't seen any of Taiwan and now you want to leave." Two days later, Luo Yuchang and Tan Zhongping showed up at Uncle Ma's and tried to convince me to stay.

Just when I was feeling hesitant and indecisive, Professor Guo Tingyi (he taught history at the university and later transferred to Academia Sinica, where he established the Institute of Modern History) came to visit Uncle Ma. He was a friend of my father's and came to plead with me to stay and help the Department of Foreign Languages and Literatures organize those two rooms full of books, and told me that I could read in peace. He said, "The present situation in mainland China is chaotic, with the north being the most volatile. All the universities are in the process of getting reestablished, so you won't be able to do any studying when you go there." Uncle Guo was on the point of giving up a room in the singles dorm on Wenzhou Street to move to the dorm for families. He had asked the Office of General Affairs to allocate the room to me so that I could settle down with a short walk to work.

With so much friendly advice, I returned my ticket and prepared to move to the singles dorm.

At that time, the university, like so many government organizations, was still in the process of "accepting." The letter of temporary appointment written with a brush on fine paper would probably have some "documentary" value today. Personnel and School Property didn't have any rules in writing, so a teaching assistant such as myself could in fact formally succeed to a professor's apartment in the singles dorm. I had applied for a room in a military-style singles dorm that the university had recently built out of concrete beside the Liugong Ditch. Each section contained eight rooms, but they were already full. Hua Yan, an economics teaching assistant, and Pei Puyan and Liao Weiqing, both Chinese professors, all lived there.

The morning I moved to Wenzhou Street, Junxian came to help me. Actually, I didn't have all that much to move—a small leather suitcase, a quilt and pillow I had purchased a couple of days before at Rongding, the makeup case with a mirror and three drawers in which I could keep small items as if I were playing house, and which I had purchased shortly after arrival from a Japanese kneeling with goods spread out on the ground for sale under the arcade. Hide-san hauled everything over for me. When Uncle Guo lived there, I had never been over for a visit. The first time I saw the Japanese-style room with no tables, chairs, or bed (Uncle Ma had a bed and other furniture), I felt really sad.

Junxian arrived in the morning, accompanied by Luo Yuchang. Glancing at the room, he said a few words to Junxian and then left, saying he would be back soon. Before noon he returned with a thick and heavy tatami to serve as a mattress, a kettle, a thermos, two cups, and an enamel basin. In the small shared kitchen, he boiled a kettle of water and filled the thermos. I had never ever bought such things and never thought of them as basic to life.

At noon, the Ge family invited us to lunch. I went out and purchased a few necessities and returned to Uncle Ma's for dinner. Junxian and Yilie took me back to Wenzhou Street. After they left, I looked out of the floor-to-ceiling window at the garden and saw the artificial mountain in the deep shade of the big trees along the wall. The first time I slept on the tatami, I could hear the wind in the trees outside and didn't know what to do with myself throughout the long night. In those days, I experienced the same fear at the onset of night that I had felt in the sanitorium on West Mountain. I lived in the room farthest to the right, which was about forty-eight square feet with a hallway outside, and at a slight distance from the other rooms. I rarely saw anyone, even during the day. Two months later, husband and wife assistant professors moved into the room nearest mine. The sound of their baby crying became the sweet human tidings for which I waited every evening.

A few days later, Luo Yuchang and a couple of classmates came to see me. He brought a wooden radio he had built himself. They said he was well known among their circle of friends as one who could fix a radio. He said that the electrical engineering department at the university was divided into electric power and telecommunications, and he had majored in the latter. Before he had arrived in Taiwan he had passed the test to be a communications technician in the Ministry of Economics. He volunteered for the railroad because when he was in Sichuan, he had been teased by his classmates about never having seen a train. Then and there he decided to work in railway transportation and not go to work for the power company. At the time, it was much better to work for the power company than the railroad, as the railway transportation equipment was rather backward. In his free time, he built radios for fun and helped others fix their radios for free.

The one he gave me was probably one of the more successful ones, and could receive the programs from the Taipei Radio Station. It contributed a great deal to dispelling my feelings of solitude. Every night there were news broadcasts, music, and classical Japanese music and songs that the Japanese had left behind. One of the most unforgettable songs I listened to at night was "Night in the Ruins." While listening, I forgot that it was a Japanese song and I would sometimes recall the time we fled as refugees, listening to the wind blow and dogs howl on the deserted outskirts of town, and think about the hundreds of thousands of Japanese who had died on the battlefield after invading China. Although we detested the enemy, they did have families waiting through cold nights for them to return home. When I first arrived in Taiwan, I saw Japanese all over the place awaiting repatriation; shivering and timid, they knelt on the sidewalks selling their belongings. I didn't really feel sympathy for them, but I didn't feel that they should repay a blood debt either.

A NURTURER: MR. GE FUJIANG

For the few dozen students studying foreign languages and literatures at NTU, the most important classes were still being taught by two Japanese professors, who never came to the department office. As I moved books downstairs to the library room, I saw a number of middle-aged people coming and going, but no one introduced us or said hello. Soon only one Japanese was left, and he was repatriated the following year.

Every weekend I'd go back to Qingtian Street. Professors newly arrived from mainland China were frequently guests at Uncle Ma's; some of them were also friends of my father. They ate in the medical school cafeteria, where the chef had recently been brought in from the mainland; he was quite famous in Taipei. There were few places that served authentic mainland cuisine, so eating at the medical school cafeteria was always a pleasure.

Sometimes I'd visit the Ge family and have a home-cooked dinner. At that time, Yilie and Juanxian were just getting hooked on playing bridge (later they represented the Taiwan Sugar Corporation and the Taiwan Power Company, competing all over the island and frequently winning). I had learned to play in my senior year in college from some teaching assistants in the fellowship. Naturally, I wasn't a great player, but they patiently invited Luo Yuchang and me as a pair. Sometimes when Ge-san was free, he and some classmates would set up another table. With my studious concentration I joined in and read some books on the subject, and my interest increased until I moved to Taichung, where it came to an abrupt end.

One weekend in April of that year, I went to the Ges'. When I entered, Junxian told me to come and look at Yilie's room. I said, "Hasn't he already moved to the Taiwan Sugar dorm?"

Just then, Ge-san came out of another room and pulled open the *shoji* door. I was startled by what I saw: the eight-tatami-mat room was covered with chirping baby yellow chicks.

Ge-san, who had been secretly busy these days, had been expecting the first batch of incubated eggs to hatch. We were fortunate enough to be the first to witness this dramatic success. For the Chinese who had known hunger, these little chicks that were hatched in wooden crates under warm lights were as good as gold.

Two years later, Ge-san quit his job as a professor in the School of Veterinary Medicine at NTU and at the age of forty went to Taiwan Sugar and established the newest scientific pig farming business. Using the materials from the sugar production process, he produced animal feed and with American help, set up the Cyanamid Company for research on livestock products and yeast powder to prevent epidemics, the improvement of breeds for large-scale export to Japan and Hong Kong, and increasing the pork production in Taiwan. While mainland China was smelting iron in traditional ways and millions were dying of famine, Taiwan was implementing nine years of compulsory education, and the salaries of all middle school teachers for the entire province were paid for by taxes on pork.

Ge Fujiang (1913–1983) was from Hebei Province and a graduate of the School of Agriculture at Henan University, specializing in livestock products. In 1946, after coming to Taiwan, he joined the Department of Agriculture and Forestry and established the Animal Husbandry Research Institute and the Animal Husbandry Company. As the national representative to the United Nations in their plan for the development of animal husbandry on mountain slopes, and being a successful researcher in Taiwan with an international reputation, he became involved in international scientific exchange quite early. Subsequently, he established the Animal Husbandry Institute of Taiwan Sugar, the Institute for Scientific Pork Raising, and a cattle breeding station in Zhubei, to all of which he devoted thirty-six years of his life. Owing to the many years of hard work, he suffered from chronic asthma, which, if it acted up at night, would prevent him from sleeping. Despite this, he remained active during the day, running to Zhubei to check on his experiments, examining and evaluating the results.

After retiring in 1981, he lived in California, believing the climate there would be beneficial for his chronic asthma. Unexpectedly, he died two years later from coronary thrombosis at the age of seventy.

I was deeply saddened by the shocking news. Many years later, we returned to Zhubei and entered the Fujiang Building erected in his memory by the students (later demolished under new planning). We could almost see the big and robust Ge-san coming to greet visitors and hear his resonant laughter, the same as in 1970 at the founding of the research institute, when he explained his ideals to us, ideals that I shared in my life and the glorious fruition of which I witnessed.

MARRIAGE

The gatherings at the Ge house grew in size, because Xie Wenjin and Meng Baoqin arrived in Taiwan with their two-year-old son. Xie was a good friend of Junxian's and taught English at Jianguo Middle School in Taipei; Meng, her husband, worked in maintenance at the Railways Administration and lived in the singles dorm, where Luo Yuchang lived. The situation on the mainland was deteriorating and increasing numbers of people were arriving in Taiwan.

Luo Yuchang frequently came to visit me on Wenzhou Street, sometimes with friends, sometimes alone, and nearly every morning would phone me at NTU. In those days there were only two phones in the College of Liberal Arts—one in the head's office and one shared in common in the Office of General Services. Each time the call would come, Chen, the middle-aged secretary, would step out in the hall and shout: "Call for Miss Chi!" I felt very uncomfortable under everyone's watchful eyes and didn't know what to say. One day we arranged to meet in the Chaofeng Coffee Shop across from the Sun Yat-sen Hall (perhaps it was the only, or one of the few places that had classical music). In all frankness, I said that in the two years since victory I had been incapable of forming new emotional bonds and that I had come to Taiwan because I was dissatisfied with the political situation in mainland China. My parents lived apart, one in the north, one in the south, and I was on my own here and was clearly aware of the many inconveniences, but even though I felt self-exiled, I was happy in my solitude. I said that during the summer break I was thinking of returning to live with my parents, and that I could not accept his good intentions.

A few days later, he wrote a long letter in which he said he had cried while watching the movie *Madame Curie* and that he had admired her perseverance and unwavering strength. He wrote of his ideals and having a plan to realize them: how life ought to have a center and one should strive and conserve one's energy, including cutting back on meaningless conversation.

This attitude toward life was one that I had not encountered before, and his proclamation, accompanied as it was by strong words of love, was very different, even interesting, to the young bookish person I was in those days. Going through a lifetime of letters after sixty years together, I realized that at that time I didn't know anything about life. When we first became acquainted, Yuchang was already able to clearly articulate his attitude toward handling things in life; I, on the other hand, was very different with my sensitivity, curiosity, propensity to mull things over, and imaginativeness. But, having supped enough on the bitterness of my own sentimentality and finding myself in a difficult position, I did envy the strength and reason of others and was willing to accept their protection.

All my friends in Taiwan, including Junxian, Wenjin, and Cheng Keyong, who worked at the Jilong Port Authority, felt that Luo Yuchang was stable and reliable and urged me to have fewer illusions about life and settle down soon. As the summer break of 1948 was nearing, I wrote to my father to come to Taiwan to see for himself what sort of person Yuchang was.

In my letter, I wrote:

> Mr. Luo is twenty-eight years old and an electrical engineering graduate from Wuhan University and works for the Taiwan Railways Administration, where he is a section chief in the Communications and Signal Division. He lost his father when he was nine and the family lived in straitened circumstances. He has four sisters and one younger brother, and his mother lives at home in Zizhong County in Sichuan. He has worked hard to get ahead and is strong willed. . . .

On two occasions my father had planned to visit Taiwan, but ultimately had to cancel both times. With the arrival of summer break, I had to decide whether or not to stay at NTU the following semester. By then, my mother had finally left Beiping for Shanghai, and even my perennially optimistic father had to admit that the situation in China was not very hopeful and told me that there was no need to come home and look for work, and that I should take the NTU contract. My mother hoped that I would come home during break to discuss things and said that I couldn't get married on my own in Taiwan.

So I returned to Shanghai in August and, after receiving my parents' consent, I visited Pastor Ji Zhiwen at the New Tian'an Church in Shanghai to ask him to officiate at the wedding. Three days before we were married, Yuchang was baptized. By then many people had come to

Shanghai from the north, some of whom had been sent to the northeast by the government to take control of various things but had been unable to fulfill their duties (either because the Communists had already taken control or the battles were still seesawing). Not knowing where to go or what to do, most just lived in sorrow. Prices in Shanghai changed from morning to night, and the currency was so devalued that a whole bag of money couldn't buy anything to eat, so goods were being hoarded. Our wedding rings were 14 karat gold, because nothing finer could be had. The wedding guests filled the church (we passed on having a wedding reception in a restaurant, because a head count in double figures couldn't be fed and would have to be served in two batches, which would have been embarrassing). Among the guests were the last six of the "ten great heavenly kings" of the anti-Japanese underground resistance. After my parents passed away, I went through their belongings and found "The Noise of Drums and Gongs Fills the Air," written by Wang Feifan while he was in jail, with the following inscription:

> *Revered Tie, I love and respect you and fifteen years have been but like a day.*
>
> *In fifteen years I have not forgotten you in times of happiness or despair.*
>
> *Nor when hungry, cold, crying, smiling.*
>
> *Today from afar I wish you good health*
>
> *And hope you shine like the autumn moon in all your endeavors.*
>
> *Respectfully, Wang Feifan*
> *Beiping, in the enemy jail*
> *July 7, 1945*

This was written one month before victory, and I have treasured it to this day. These men risked their lives working for the national government in the anti-Japanese underground in Manchukuo. One in nine died; the remaining persevered until victory. The several dozen hot-blooded men arrived in Shanghai from the vast open spaces of the northeast, and my wedding reception was the last time they would be together as a group to talk loudly about the bad old days and beating the Japanese. From what they saw in Shanghai, it was probably clear that yet another nightmare was about to commence. Those men who raised their glasses to me that year were constantly on my father's mind late in life, making him shed a few tears each time he raised a wine cup.

Ten days after the wedding, we returned to Taiwan by ship. Without the least hesitation, I returned to work and set up my own household in what was now familiar Taipei. My parents no longer worried and my friends felt envious of me, leaving Shanghai and going "abroad." I no longer harbored any illusions about life.

Upon returning to Taipei, we first moved into the residence of Zheng Zhaobin, a section chief in the Communications and Signal Division of the Railways Administration. About one month later, we brought home the first furniture we ever purchased: a table, two chairs, a double bed, and a small chest. We moved into our first home, which was in a Taipei Power warehouse that had been divided into two residential dorm units using bagasse board. We resided in the temporary dorm unit closest to the street, while Li Zhihou, a new section chief, and his family lived in the other. They had six children who were all fine elementary and middle school students.

Taiwan Sugar produced cane sugar, the sale of which was one of the biggest sources of foreign currency. The extracted cane was a by-product used for feeding pigs and for making bagasse board, both of which contributed greatly to Taiwan's development. The bagasse board produced by Taiwan Sugar helped solve the housing problem for the countless new arrivals to the island. The only shortcoming was that when the kids next door played and pushed the bagasse board between us, our room grew smaller.

I remember our new house of three small rooms and an exterior of thick wooden boards, which sat on the busy intersection of Yanping North Road, to the left of the police station and across from the Railways Administration. There was a small street that ran behind the train station, half of which was filled with small stands, most selling fabric and some selling vegetables. After the morning vegetable sellers did their business, the fabric sellers arrived. They shouted in Taiwanese, "One *chi*, twenty *kuai*! One *chi*, twenty *kuai*! Really cheap!" which was followed by bolts of cloth being unrolled noisily on the stands. A dozen or so voices rose and fell in this fashion until around two in the afternoon, when the shouts of the rickshaw pullers filled my narrow and small room.

It was even more noisy and confused on weekends when people were off work. Often I just had to get out and take a walk, so I'd head down Yanping North Road to Dihua Street and look to where the Damshui River entered the sea off in the distance. The commercial streets of old Taipei that I became familiar with were quite different from those I had seen as a refugee in Hunan, Guizhou, and Sichuan. The storefronts in Taipei were smaller and the stores were closely packed together, and seldom were there gateways or signboards between. Fabric and gold shops came at the head of the streets, followed by dry goods shops. Sometimes we would walk halfway and then make a right to the traffic circle. We started to enjoy meat soup and fried rice noodles. These dishes were like dumplings for a northeasterner, but for someone from Sichuan, they didn't count for more than a snack. Each night, we had to cook rice and make a soup in that makeshift bamboo add-on kitchen, and then it would seem like home.

After dinner, Yuchang would go work on his tube radios while I read books that I had brought home from the university. Sometimes I would write in my diary. Every time I took up my pen, I would be filled with worry and grief. A few days later, I would look at what I had written and tear it up as not being up to snuff.

After about two months spent in this fashion, we suddenly received a letter from my father saying that my mother and sisters would be coming to Taiwan in the middle of the month for a visit, as life in Shanghai was becoming increasingly difficult.

A few days before Christmas, my mother arrived with my youngest sister by plane, while my younger sister arrived later on the *Taiping* steamer, accompanying Uncle Han Chunxuan and his family along with their luggage. Although living in our small house was far from comfortable, it was the first time I had been able to spend time with my mother, eating what we liked and experiencing a full range of emotions, since I had left Chongqing in 1944 for my second year of college at Leshan.

There was no hope of going back to mainland China. A friend of my father's in Taipei helped with the paperwork to enroll my two sisters in Taipei First Girls' Middle School partway through the term. After winter break, Ningyuan began her third year of middle school and Xingyuan her first. The situation in Nanjing and Shanghai was becoming more unstable and the government moved to Guangzhou to handle official business, but the decision to move to Taiwan had already been made. My father boarded the last plane to Taiwan.

1948: DAYS OF MEETING SHIPS

Starting from about the end of 1948, I became very busily engaged in a "life of meeting ships."

Almost every time the *Chung Hsing* or *Taiping* arrived from Shanghai, Yuchang would take a truck from the Taipei Communications and Signal Division to Jilong Harbor and come back carrying a load of luggage. At the height, more the a hundred pieces of luggage were piled in another warehouse. Among the new arrivals were those from the older generation who had attended my wedding banquet, those who worked at *Time and Tide*, and those who after victory had returned home, some of whom were elected to the Legislative Yuan while others served as members of the National Assembly. Some came to teach or to work at newspapers and magazines. Almost all of our old acquaintances came to Taiwan. My father ordered us to do everything we could to help. The provincial government also ordered military transport units to assist, so when Yuchang requisitioned a truck from the Railways Administration, that too fell within its purview.

Our house, which was only three hundred yards from the train station, became the most convenient place of contact. That small twenty-four-square-foot living room was always full of those waiting for others or for the truck carrying their luggage. At first, Mother always had people stay and eat; later we couldn't cope with it, but we always had hot tea ready and waiting for any new arrival. Countless contact addresses for inns in all cities and government offices were pinned on the bagasse board walls. It was very similar to when we had fled to Hankou ten years earlier, except there were no air-raid sirens or bombs falling on Taipei.

From the joy of victory to the present state of affairs, few ever thought they would spend the rest of their lives on the island. The fortunate ones brought their parents, wives, and children, while others came alone to first have a look-see, after which they remained forever, separated from their loved ones, their homes amounting to a few pieces of luggage in the Communications and Signal warehouse.

The last time I went to Jilong to meet a ship was Lunar New Year's Eve in 1949. We went to meet Uncle Deng Lianxi, the chief editor of *Time and Tide* (Aunt Deng had arrived earlier to give birth and had brought their other children), together with my father's best revolutionary comrade, Xu Zhen (born Xu Shida; he served as chairman of Liaoning Province after the war) and the six members of his family. Early in the morning, we took the train to wait for the nine o'clock arrival but never saw a steamship enter the harbor. We asked at the shipping office, but they hemmed and hawed and said that two ships had collided the night before, all communications had been cut, and they had probably sunk. The *Taiping* tragedy was difficult for Pacific Steamship; today, sixty years later, the two of us standing on the wharf at Jilong feeling shocked and sad seems just like yesterday.

This stage of our "life waiting for ships" made newly married life very special. In the beginning, the two of us, who were so very different, had come to this island for our own reasons and had met, but we still had not gotten to really know each other or begin to live a normal family life. Then we were swept up in the tide of my father's final "revolutionary act." The revolution against Japan he had helped organize and mobilize after the Marco Polo Bridge Incident in 1931 had come to naught. Some of his comrades said that under his leadership they had gone to Taiwan to rise again. My father viewed his son-in-law's efforts to do everything to help those coming to Taiwan as no different from my mother's efforts to look after the Whampoa students on weekends or to help care for the defeated and wounded volunteers. At the time, I watched as Yuchang ran back and forth between Jilong and Songshan Airport as the pile of luggage in the warehouse reached the ceiling, moved in and out by the workers; how he directed and arranged everything, without ever once complaining to me; and how he got along with my mother and sisters. This was not the situation I had foreseen when we married, and it laid the foundation for our "comradeship," which I termed the first deposit in our "stabilization fund."

My father finally arrived in Taipei that year, and my elder brother followed the Central News Agency to Guangzhou and also arrived in Taiwan with his new wife, Wang Xufen. After they ended up in our small house for a while, they pooled their resources, and with more than ten taels of gold got a Japanese-style house in a lane off Jianguo North Road. It was slightly larger than my dorm room and sectioned off with bagasse board. Two generations lived together until the Legislative Yuan allocated a concrete bungalow in the new Ziqiang Development in Banqiao to my father. The house on Jianguo Road was let out and the proceeds were used to resume publication of *Time and Tide* in Taiwan. My father still optimistically believed that there was a future in the struggle.

Several months later, we were allocated an apartment in the concrete dorms that the Railways Administration had built behind the train station. We joyfully moved in and lived there three days or so, only to find out that each time a locomotive was changed, black coal smoke would flood the apartment and before it had time to dissipate, the next engine was there filling the place with smoke again. My cough returned, so we couldn't stay and had to flee back to our bagasse house, but could not reapply for staff housing.

Living there for the time being wasn't a long-term plan. I was growing weaker by the day. At that time a famous doctor from mainland China by the name of Han Qifeng was in Taipei. During the War of Resistance, he had contributed an airplane to defend the country and had opened a clinic in front of the train station. My father didn't think Chinese medicine was scientific enough, so my mother had to drag me to see him. He easily read my pulse and said, "Things were insufficient previously and later you suffered imbalance." My mother nodded and said, "Right, right, she was premature and often sick as a child." He had me take his famous black-bone chicken white phoenix pills and said I would grow more robust. I went home but wasn't serious about taking them, and soon I only weighed about ninety pounds. Just before the New Year I discovered I was pregnant and needed a fixed place to stay.

A YOUNG COUPLE UNABLE TO RETURN HOME

Mainland China fell in 1949, and Mao Zedong announced the founding of the People's Republic of China, with its capital in Beijing (it had been named Beiping with the success of the Northern Expedition in 1928), and announced the intention of "liberating" Taiwan. Taipei became the capital of rumor; at the height of our "life meeting ships" (actually, sixty years later, it is clear that this was the nadir for the Republic of China) a number of Central News reporters, who were friends of my brother's, came and went from our bagasse living room. They graduated in the year of victory against Japan and had a very optimistic outlook about the future of the country. Everyone believed that after fighting the War of Resistance for eight years, the Communist Party coming out of Yan'an wasn't a big issue. These young reporters were looking forward to having opportunities like those of the famous Central News reporter Lu Hongqi, whom they so admired. At the beginning of the War of Resistance, he had braved shelling by Japanese ships on the Yangtze River and a hail of bullets, following the defending troops through gunpowder smoke and ruins, through Qiaokou, which soon was on the point of destruction, to pen his famous "A Temporary Farewell to Wuhan," in which he encouraged the people: "We vow to defeat the Japanese though the War of Resistance might last a long time." The piece was carried by practically every newspaper in the country, becoming a best-seller in an instant.

Chen Jiaji and my brother were among a generation of reporters embedded with the troops in another war, a civil war. They saw famous generals such as Du Yuming, Guan Linzheng, Sun Liren, Zheng Dongguo, and Liao Yaoxiang lead the troops into battle and witnessed the sufferings of and sacrifices made by tens of thousands in harsh winter conditions. Yang Kongxin, who was a great friend of the family, had left home on his own during the Chongqing days and gone to behind the lines to study. He was a classmate of my brother's in the Foreign Relations Department of National Zhengzhi University and a frequent guest in our house at Shapingba, one my mother worried about, afraid that he might be hungry or cold. Later he was dispatched as a special envoy to Paris and London; when he returned to Taipei on official business, his visit to our home was like a homecoming. Zheng Dong was another person everyone in the family liked. After the war, he was sent to the embassy in Greece as second secretary to Ambassador Wen Yuanning, the famous literary translator, where he acquired a sound foundation in speech and diplomacy. Unfortunately, his fate followed that of the nation, and he lacked ample opportunity to develop. He didn't return to Taiwan and worked and drifted around abroad, unable to extend his career.

Chen Jiaji, who went to the northeast with my brother as an embedded reporter, was a straightforward guy from Hebei, but his Mandarin didn't meet the standard of Beijing, and he was a bit slow in doing things as well. He liked to delve deeply into things and loved nothing more than a debate. His debating style was unique and unforgettable. He would argue without resting and if he lost, he'd be back the following day for another exuberant go at it, but he never hurt anyone or was unkind. After arriving in Taiwan, he was unable to forget what he had seen in the northeast as a war reporter. He wrote *Elegy for White Mountains and Black Waters*, *Dethroned Emperor with a Hero's Tears*, and *Warning Signals in the Northeast*, among other books. In 2000 he published *A Record of Changes in the Northeast* at his own expense, in which he organized the historical facts he had witnessed and reported into a detailed, accurate, and objective historical account. In the preface he wrote,

> I've been retired for many years, and in the blink of an eye I find that I'm now eighty. Every time I close my eyes and daydream, it is

> usually about past events in the northeast. While writing *A Record of Changes in the Northeast*, I would lay aside my pen and sigh, thinking about how the northeast had changed when it shouldn't have. The first mistake was the Soviet Union breaking its word, the second was the mediation by the United States, and the third was the generals being at loggerheads . . . which led to 300,000 troops rapidly collapsing in western Liaoning.

The scope and treachery of what he saw in those three years formed the unforgettable history of blood and tears for another thirty years.

Of course these Central News reporters had a tumult of stories, some of which could be printed and others that couldn't: unconfirmed reports were that the Communists had said when they liberated Taiwan, they would force those who refused to surrender into the sea at Danshui in the north, at Xinzhu in the central area, and at Oluanpi in the south. Peng Tingde, a friend of mine from the Christian fellowship at Wuhan University, had been unable to find suitable employment in Taiwan and planned to return to Shanghai. Yuchang and I saw him to his ship at the wharf at Jilong. The shipped was so packed with people that some had tied themselves to the stern, hanging half overboard, to keep from falling, just to get back to Shanghai so that they could at least face what was coming with their families. We had stable jobs and had already decided to stay in Taiwan, so we gave him six silver dollars, which was all the money we had, for his traveling expenses, never thinking that we would never see each other again.

After losing everything and coming to Taiwan, these friends were not yet thirty and couldn't know that they would never be able to write anything glorious. My brother's wife gave birth to a girl when Taiwan was at its most chaotic. To deal with the change, he rented a small wooden building on Nanchang Street in Taipei to open a rice-husking mill (while fleeing from the southwest, my brother saw that despite the changes, rice-husking mills could provide a livelihood). There was also a relatively low second floor to the building, so a number of his good friends and we would visit them after dinner. Their debates would be as lively as a chess match. Reporters had access to many materials and were full of opinions about the past and present, and they spoke sharply. The lofty sentiments of those young people overflowed the small room. Sometimes as a visitor was descending the wooden stairs, the debate would continue as they turned their heads back. Around dusk the following day, they would return and find temporary relief from their grief, indignation, and anxiety. A half century later, looking back on those days actually brings warm memories. Later, everyone set up their own households and we all went our separate ways, never again to experience those gatherings of talented persons.

TAICHUNG: THE AGE OF TRAINS BELCHING SMOKE

My workload at NTU grew heavier. More teachers arrived from mainland China, and Shen Gangbo took over as head of the College of Liberal Arts (Qian Gechuan returned to mainland China and later went to the United States), and Ying Qianli became the head of the Department of Foreign Languages and Literatures. Ying, who came from Furen University in Beiping, was alone in Taiwan and at first didn't keep regular hours. Every morning I would open the door and every evening I would lock up. All department memos and teaching materials went through my hands, as I was responsible for typing and distributing them. The newly arrived teaching assistants Hou Jian and Dai Chaosheng worked downstairs in the research office.

NTU had taken over a number of small Japanese houses for faculty housing down a lane off Zhoushan Road and Roosevelt Road. Teaching assistants with "seniority" could apply. Hua Yan in the Department of Economics received one and told me to apply quickly. I was the only senior teaching assistant in the Department of Foreign Languages and Literatures, so I was eligible for one. The full-length windows of that small room with tatami mats opened out onto a nicely planted garden. I was very happy to give Yuchang the good news, hoping to also make him happy, but he unexpectedly grew silent when he heard the details.

The following day he spoke to me in a serious manner, saying that a newly married husband such as himself could not become dependent on his wife. The two of us, a teacher and a civil servant, could have only one lodging supplied by the government. If he went and lived in NTU housing, he would subsequently be ineligible to apply for Railways Administration housing. More importantly, he worked all year round and had to keep the railroads open and unimpeded, and couldn't be expected to take two buses and get to work on time. He would have to rely on a bicycle to get around (my dowry included a Feilipu bicycle, a lovely thing that would be the equivalent of a new car today), but if emergency work had to be done, it would take half an hour for him to ride from Jingmei to the Taipei Station, and he would hold up official business. The over one hundred miles of rails in the Taipei area was a great responsibility, so he was not in favor of moving to the NTU housing. My father was in complete agreement with him, and after leaving Shanghai to return to Taiwan wrote repeatedly, saying, "You cannot delay your husband from his work and you must respect his dignity."

Shortly thereafter, the post of head of the Taichung Communications and Signal Division of the Railways Administration became vacant. Yuchang wanted to transfer to Taichung, so he discussed it with me. He felt the division chief's housing there would be very good with a large yard, which would make it a good place to raise children; in Taipei the workload was heavy, with a lot of duties only aggravated by the many personal matters at work and outside. In addition, Taiwan was facing a political situation that was worrisome. By moving to Taichung, we could have some peace and live our own life, calmly read, and think about the future. If Taiwan were to stabilize and pursue development, the central part of the island, not Taipei, would be the pivotal point for railway operations, and perhaps the Communications and Signal Division would be in charge of more than just maintaining the power poles and communications along the railways.

When he asked to be transferred to Taichung, everyone in the Railways Administration said, "Old Luo is a strange guy. He's done a good job in charge of Taipei, the biggest division, but now he volunteers to be transferred to a lesser division!" When I handed in my resignation at NTU, Wang Guohua, the previous head of the Department of Foreign Languages and Literatures, said, "Miss Chi, no one resigns from NTU." Throughout my life, my work has followed that of my husband, and so I followed him to Taichung, where we stayed for seventeen years.

On June 5, 1950, when I first entered the front yard at No. 25 Fuxing Road in Taichung, the tree outside the vestibule was in full bloom, as if it were festooned with lanterns to welcome us. The approximately 120-square-foot tatami-floored house was divided into two small rooms. Beyond the portico was a spacious garden, at one end of which was a large banyan tree with air roots that descended to the ground. I fell in love with the new house at once.

I was six months pregnant at the time. I bore my first son on September 9 at Zhang Yaodong's gynecology and obstetrics clinic. Owing to the protracted labor, which lasted into a second night, I fell into a coma. My mother, who was by my side, cried in fright and called my name, just as my uncle had done for her at Hankou. She snatched my life back from the hands of death. The doctor used obstetric forceps to deliver the eight-pound baby. I couldn't walk for about twenty days.

When my baby was about three months old, my mother had to return to Taipei, because my brother's wife had had her second child at the end of December.

One evening, several days after my mother left, Yuchang still had not come home. The house was dark and cold. I dared not stay inside, probably because of debility, so I took the baby and sat on a stool outside the door. The house faced the street—Fuxing Road was large, and there were many pedestrians and people on bicycles passing by.

Thirty Railways Administration houses stretched from the switching yard to the sugar factory. I sat by the door until nine o'clock, when Liao Chunqin, a colleague of my husband's in Communications and Signal, passed by. He had no idea that I was sitting outside because I was afraid, and told me, "Today the division chief took us to the Fazi River, which was swollen, to make some emergency repairs on the electric line. Half of the bridge foundation had been washed away, so the division chief tied the electrical wire to his waist and took several of us crawling out over the ties hanging in the air to prop up more wires. One by one, inch by inch, we climbed, and got out with our lives!"

Shortly thereafter, Yuchang's tall, thin frame appeared out of the darkness beneath the first streetlight. I wept with joy, and the hungry baby also cried. He trotted across the street and with a hug pulled us inside. He too was crying and said, "I'm back. That's all that matters. Quick, prepare some formula for the baby."

My married life was filled with all sorts of railway disasters until 1985, when Yuchang retired. In nearly forty years, with all the typhoons, mountain torrents, and earthquakes, he had to rush to disaster scenes and direct emergency repairs. Midnight phone calls still quicken my heartbeat. I often had to shake him awake and watch as he put on his heavy raincoat and rushed out into the stormy weather. Then I would be worried all through the night until he called to say he was okay.

Actually, before Yuchang retired, he was rarely at home after a natural disaster or a railroad accident. The railroads that served all of the ten major development projects were his responsibility. In his office were clean clothes and a travel bag so that if a call came in, he could rush off to Kaohsiung or Hualien. How long would he be away? No one knew. When the Su-hua Line was being expanded, he sat on a bench in the engineer's car so he could see the work on the railroad bed. If a tunnel collapsed, it had to be excavated, so he wouldn't be home for days at a time. During holidays, he was even busier and couldn't rest. Chen Denian, our neighbor on Lishui Street in Taipei, was also an electrical engineer and in the five years he served as director, he was never once home for the New Year. On New Year's Eve, he would take a slow train along the line to express his sympathy and solicitude for the railway workers who couldn't be at home for the holiday. Just before his wife fell ill and passed away, a key juncture in the electrification of the railroad occurred and he had to be on site to bolster morale instead of by his wife's sickbed. I am filled with sympathy and respect for all engineers in the world.

MY FOREVER WANDERING FATHER

Twenty days after we moved to Taichung, dramatic changes suddenly occurred in the world outside: the Korean War exploded. U.S. President Truman announced that the Seventh Fleet was being dispatched to help defend Taiwan, to check any potential attack on the island and maintain its neutrality. Following this, the U.S. Navy, Air Force, and land forces joined the war (Seoul had already fallen) to keep North Korean troops from crossing the 38th parallel and attacking South Korea. At the end of July, General Douglas MacArthur, commander of the Asian Allied Forces, visited Taiwan and received an enthusiastic welcome. A year later, he was dismissed and returned to the United States, where the great American hero was welcomed by seven million people in New York. President Chiang, after retreating in defeat to Taiwan and several difficult years, once again rose to a partnership in the nations allied against communism; not only was security safeguarded but also counterattacking the Communists was being considered. Taiwan at that time had a population of about 10 million (in 1946, statistics from the Department of Civil Affairs put it at 6,330,000); the population of mainland China in 1954 was *656,630,000*. How was there to be a counterattack?

On August 4 of the same year, Chen Lifu, who had been in charge of Kuomintang (KMT) Party affairs since Nanjing was named the capital after the Northern Expedition, was ordered to attend the annual World Conference for Moral Rearmament in Switzerland in 1950. After the conference, he went into self-exile in America, where he raised chickens on a farm in New Jersey (until 1970, when he retired to Taiwan). At the meeting of the Central Reform Committee of the KMT government, convened two days after he left, the cadres unanimously expelled the brothers Chen Guofu and Chen Lifu, replacing them with people from the Political Study Clique or the China Youth Corps and choosing Chen Cheng to serve as premier in the Executive Yuan. Chiang Ching-kuo appeared officially responsible for the discipline and training of cadres and other loyalty and intelligence work. In the process of reviewing and discussing the military defeat, it was determined that the main reasons were betrayal by the military and dissatisfaction among the people incited by the Communists, and that a rigorous anti-Communist and antiespionage network had to be developed to consolidate President Chiang's power as leader.

In the early days on Taiwan, the biggest organization of Legislative Yuan members was the Reform Club, with around 170 members (more than thirty members of the Legislative Yuan came from the northeast), convened by Chen Lifu, Xiao Zheng, Zhang Daofan, Cheng Tianfang, Gu Zhengding, Shao Hua, and Chi Shiying for the promotion of democracy, rule of law, human rights, and freedom in the hope that the KMT might take the path of democracy. After Chen Lifu went into exile and lived abroad, some people entered Chen Cheng's cabinet and became full-time members of the Reform Club of the Legislative Yuan, occasionally criticizing the administration of the martial law system.

In the Legislative Yuan, Chi Shiying openly opposed increasing the price of electricity in order to increase military expenditures at the end of 1954. President Chiang was furious and had him stripped of party membership. This was a huge story at the time and the Taiwan media naturally had misgivings, but the Hong Kong *World News*, which had more of an international impact, printed a story with the headline "Chi Shiying Expelled from the KMT?" that held that since the KMT could not tolerate a legislator who had served loyally for twenty years, it was no more than an ignorant dictatorship. Furthermore, if Chiang Kai-shek couldn't tolerate Chi Shiying, it was not solely due to his opposition in the Legislative Yuan but because, as editor of *Time and Tide*, he had more of an international perspective and his words were infused with free thought and respect for the individual, and he had no respect for martial law as a way of ensuring Taiwan's security.

On New Year's Day 1955, the Taiwan Power Company, as directed by the Legislative Yuan, raised the price of electricity by 32 percent. Naturally, the Legislative Yuan would approve the increase, and the political life of Chi Shiying, who had opposed it, was like the head of a revolutionary in the old days—it was chopped off and hung on the city wall!

At home, my fifty-five-year-old father read and entertained visitors unperturbed, and when the visitors became fewer, he read more. When he had to attend a meeting, he would energetically catch the bus for the office. Laughing at himself, he'd say that the smaller his house became, the bigger the buses grew. For more than ten years, the people who kept him under surveillance were regularly outside the door, never giving thieves a chance to break in. My father never used his position to do business or buy an estate. Fortunately, he still had his salary from the Legislative Yuan, so didn't have to worry about household expenses. My mother stuck with him through all the ups and downs, living a simple life. She never owned a single piece of jewelry.

Leaving the KMT in this way was a kind of liberation for him. At the age of twenty-eight, he had entered the party because of common interest and purpose, and he had devoted all his energies to it throughout his best years. At that time, he had expanded his love of home to encompass the country and the people, fighting the Japanese to save the nation. Who could have foreseen that in three short years after victory he would lose everything? How could the Zhejiang politicians at the side of Chiang Kai-shek understand the unique pain of the northeast? How could Chi Shiying's lifetime of ideals exist amid the honor, wealth, and position of this little capital?

However, in a case of ruptured relations, a gentleman never uses abusive language. My father respected Chairman Chiang's leadership during the War of Resistance and would support him to the end, and to the end of his days always referred to him as Mr. Chiang. In discussing politics in *Time and Tide*, he always focused on the issue, not the people. He still valued friendship, justice, and good manners in the political arena. Many of his students from Tongzhe Middle School in Shenyang, Whampoa Military Academy, the Political Academy, and the Police Academy, and quite a few students from the Northeast Sun Yat-sen Middle School came to Taiwan and worked in education, the party, politics, and the military. My father, along with Lei Zhen, Xia Taosheng, Li Wanju, Wu Sanlian, Xu Shixian, Guo Yuxin, and Gao Yushu, got together and planned to establish a new political party. In 1960, after Lei Zhen was imprisoned for the "Free China" case, several dozen senior members of the Reform Club of the Legislative Yuan publicly stated, "Please inform the authorities that if Chi Shiying is implicated, we will not keep silent." This perhaps had the effect of keeping my father out of jail. Liang Surong, who was only thirty-four at the time, in an article titled "Chi Shiying During His Time in the Legislative Yuan" (in *Interviews with Chi Shiying*) stated that this action "expressed the close comradeship among early political figures, something that will never be forgotten."

Liang Surong (1920–2004) secretly joined the KMT in Shenyang at the age of twenty-four and, under the cover of being a lawyer, engaged in underground anti-Japanese work. Jailed by the Japanese, he was released two years later after victory, and the following year he was elected to the Legislative Yuan as representative of the northern region of Liaoning Province. Soon thereafter, the northeast fell and he took the seven members of his family, including his aged mother and young children, to Taiwan. He and my father were very close, and he was deeply involved in politics. However, he was a man with a passion for justice and ideals and served as defense attorney in the Lei Zhen treason case, which put him in the spotlight at home and abroad. Although Lei Zhen was sentenced to ten years in prison, Liang had defended him with great composure on the principles of freedom and human rights before a hundred people, including Chinese and foreign reporters, in the courtroom, and wrote a new page in the history of Taiwan's legal system. Later he served as defense attorney for Professor Peng Mingmin, who was not a party member, and assisted him in leaving Taiwan for the United States. He stood up for human rights in the legal system with courage, wisdom, and nobleness, displaying the incorruptible fortitude of an intellectual. Unfortunately, Peng Mingmin returned to Taiwan after the founding of the Democratic Progressive Party and denied that Liang Surong had provided him with any assistance, on account of Liang's position of attempting to reform the KMT from within. After the start of the debate on reunification or independence, Liang became their enemy.

When Liang finished his term as speaker of the Legislative Yuan and retired and established the Council for Cross-Strait Peaceful

Reunification under his own name, he was already seventy-five and had no thought of personal gain or loss. He was loyal to a lifetime of political beliefs to which he and his friends had dedicated themselves. There was no way he would believe the Communists, and he called for peace across the strait, even in illness, hoping to assist in establishing a peaceful world of democracy, freedom, and widespread enjoyment of human rights. This was also the great affection that evolved from a half century of longing for his homeland in the northeast. Whether it was his tall and robust body or his resonant voice, he always made me think of a heroic man riding his horse over thousands of miles of the open spaces of his homeland: "blue the sky, vast the land, the grass blown low by the wind and there to see the sheep and cattle."

It takes more than one cold day to form three inches of ice. My father's dissatisfaction with Chiang Kai-shek began with the crisis in the northeast after victory. The history and ethnic background of the length and breadth of the northeast is inextricably linked with China's two-thousand-year history of vicissitudes. Around the time of the fall of the Qing dynasty in the early twentieth century, Russia with a shared border of a thousand miles and neighboring Japan across the sea thought to take the land. Prior to launching the Marco Polo Bridge Incident of 1931, the Japanese knew that they had to kill Zhang Zuolin and his top generals if they were to invade and occupy the northeast, because Zhang's power was based on the "wisdom" best understood by the feelings of the people and had preserved peace in the area for twenty years. Authority was concentrated in his person, and as long as he lived, the Japanese had no hopes of taking Shenyang, much less the entire northeast!

Victory over Japan came too quickly, and perhaps Chiang Kai-shek did not have enough time to think much about it before sending Xiong Shihui to be the head of the field quarters to handle the huge task of the handover of the northeast. In addition to being totally inexperienced in such matters, Xiong also lacked political style—even in the military, he was not a learned general—with his highest office having been chairman of Jiangxi Province, where he had helped Chiang Ching-kuo attack the Communists in the south of Jiangxi and thereby had earned the trust of the Chiang family. He had probably only seen the vast borderland of the northeast on a map, so because he had no knowledge about or feeling for the place, this hasty or selfish move planted the seeds of tragedy.

For those who knew the northeast, Chiang's attitude toward disposing of the situation there at such a critical moment only spelled disaster.

When Xiong first started, he kept his distance from members of the anti-Japanese underground, who had been under the command of the Northeast Association of the Central Party Headquarters, to avoid any misunderstandings with the Russians who had arrived first to take possession from the Japanese. In the spring of 1946, Chiang Ching-kuo, in the position of special diplomatic envoy to the northeast, sent a telegram to Chiang Kai-shek privately from Changchun and reported that Northeast Party Headquarters could not be restrained in their anti-Communism, and that this was affecting Chinese-Russian foreign relations (signed "your son, Ching-kuo"). Chiang Kai-shek in a telegram ordered Command Headquarters to arrest all those who could not be controlled and send them to Chongqing. Command Headquarters turned the matter over to my father to deal with. The members of the underground who had for the past twenty years held to the Three Principles of the People and fought the Japanese to restore the country were entirely confused upon receiving these orders in their widely scattered and distant revolutionary bases. They didn't understand why, after the bitterly awaited victory, they had to stand by and watch as the Russians took control of their homeland, even raping, killing, and taking prisoners. After the Russians left, the troops sent to the northeast by the central government had no sympathy for the long-suffering people.

In "An Interview with Chi Shiying," the start of handover going sour is discussed in the following words:

> I could see that Xiong Shihui was a petty bureaucrat and not a statesman, clever and tricky, with absolutely no understanding of the northeast. The troops sent to the northeast by the central government were all, with the exception of those of Sun Liren, cocksure and cruel. Xiong was entirely incompetent and incapable of cooperating with Du Yuming and Sun Liren. The civil and military officials sent to the northeast by the central government were all corrupt and, seeing how

rich the northeast was, twisted the law to obtain bribes, distorted facts to serve their own ends, and even treated the local people as if they were colonial subjects, till discontent was widespread. . . . The biggest political shortcoming was being unable to take in the Manchukuo army, leaving them to pursue their own goals and giving the Communists the upper hand. Lin Biao was able to utilize the material and human resources of the northeast along with the Japanese and Manchukuo weapons captured by the Soviet military to form the Fourth Field Army, which fought all the way from the northeast to Guangzhou and Hainan Island. It is said that to this day (1968) many of the local officials in Hunan, Hubei, Guangdong, and Guangxi were in the Fourth Field Army from the northeast. We don't use our own people but let others use them, which is kind of distressing. Our party affairs in the northeast in those days (mostly focused on anti-Japanese underground activities) were conducted admirably. I think if people such as those could have been summoned to serve locally, the Communists never would have arisen in the northeast. In the past, the organizational strength of the Communists in the northeast was trifling. Even as early as the days of the Zhangs, father and son, the Communists were never treated with leniency. In Beiping, Zhang Zuolin had raided the Russian embassy and killed Li Dazhao. Even the Japanese when they invaded China were against the Communists, and Manchukuo carried out Japanese orders. . . . Up until we recovered the northeast, the Communists had no strength there and only gained the upper hand with the support of Russia. The main reason for the fall of the northeast was no doubt the support of Russia. It must also be admitted that the government didn't use the right people and adopted the wrong means. Especially after victory, all the people of the northeast, regardless of gender or age, all leaned toward the central government. If the central government had shown more warmth and utilized the locals, they would have been more than happy to work for the nation.

"Warmth" in the heart is very important to the people of the northeast; it is a place of severe cold where the people are extremely warmhearted. It is also a place where people will fight with their lives and be bathed in blood for the sake of justice. After Zhang Xueliang and the Xi'an Incident of 1936, Chiang Kai-shek did not trust people from the northeast and relied upon Xiong Shihui from Jiangxi to handle the return of the region. The government, lacking foresight in administering the northeast, ensured that the military might of the Communist army far surpassed that of the Nationalist Army. One of the three greatest decisive battles between them in the northeast was the Battle of Western Liaoning (also known as the Battle of Liaoning and Shenyang). In fifty-two days from September until November 1949, the fighting cost the Northeast Field Army of the Communist People's Liberation Army fewer than 70,000 casualties to annihilate and reorganize more than 470,000 Nationalist troops, as well as to occupy the northeast. Winter came during the course of the battle, so was it any wonder that troops from Yunnan, Guangdong, Guangxi, and Hunan should suffer? Wasn't the one condition left after victory to save your skin and hightail it home? Had the soldiers who garrisoned many places in the vast, sparsely populated lands of the northeast, which grew colder by the day, ever dreamed of such a day? Not one soldier's grave was to be seen in the boundless land of white snow and black soil, because they became "enemies" of the usurper.

The northeast fell in November 1948. My father sent a telegram to his comrades in the anti-Japanese underground telling them to get out and not stay in a Communist-controlled area, as there was no future there. However, most of his comrades were unable to get out, first of all because they had no place to go, and second, because many had fled their homes after the Marco Polo Bridge Incident and had been away for fourteen years. Having tasted the bitterness of exile combined with the difficulty in returning home, they were not willing to undergo the same thing a second time. Formerly, when someone from the northeast crossed the Yellow River, they already felt too far from home, and if they crossed the Yangtze, they felt as if they would never get home. Third, there were no planes flying south from their remote areas, so even if they were willing to leave, there just wasn't the means. What happened to those who remained in their homeland? After all communications were cut, someone wrote a letter and said: "We have spent half our lives dying to recover our country. In those days you encouraged us by saying that with us there would be China, but having abandoned us despite the consequences, do you have peace of mind?"

My father followed the central government to Guangzhou and then went to Chongqing to attend a meeting of the Legislative Yuan. On November 28, 1949, a meeting of the standing members of the Party Central Committee was convened. Two tables of food were prepared for afterward. A somber mood prevailed as everyone ate because it felt as if they were disbanding. The following day, my father took the last plane to Taiwan. Just after arriving, he spent some time in the hospital due to lung problems. After surgery, he awoke from a nightmare in which a bloody head hanging on the city wall opened its mouth and asked him, "Who is going to take care of my wife and children?"

After twenty years of struggle, my father was now in his fifties. Disillusionment in his ideals filled him with sadness, but like a man, he refused to weep. After he settled peacefully in Taiwan, I could finally be certain that he would be around and there was nothing to keep me apart from my parents. Two years before he passed away, I was hospitalized due to a traffic accident and he came to see me, and actually cried when he saw me, injured like a wounded soldier. After that, his tear banks collapsed. I then understood the weight of his tears, the tremendous remorse and deep suffering in a man's tears.

SWEAT AND TEARS SHED ON TAIWAN

The situation in Taiwan gradually stabilized in the 1950s, and the government in its early stages was able to improve life on the island (although the slogan for retaking the mainland was shouted for many years, few actually held such illusory expectations), and modernization of railway transportation was extremely important. During the Japanese occupation, all midlevel workers and above were Japanese. Before they were repatriated after the war, they told the 17,000 Taiwanese workers that Taiwan's railroads would come to a standstill within six months. In those days, when a train arrived at or departed from a station, flagmen brandishing red and green flags had to be relied upon; between stations, the conductor's skill and dexterity had to be relied upon in proper order. They were the heroes in the minds of all children. Electrical research and scientific technology aimed at replacing human labor were to be developed under the administration (in those days even traffic signals on city streets were not very common), but no one knew where to start. Chen Shuxi, a graduate of National Chiao Tung University and head of the transportation section, was a proud character whose most common expression to his subordinates was, "Do you understand?" He mentioned the central traffic control (CTC) system used by some Western railways, but no one had ever seen it. The meeting ended and everyone dispersed in silence.

The matter was perpetually on Yuchang's mind after he returned to Taichung. CTC was a new concept in telecommunications engineering, and the only materials were available in the United States. I knew that Yang Junxian's elder brother was teaching in the United States; perhaps he could help us acquire some materials. Few people had friends or relatives in the States in those days, something hard to imagine now.

I wrote a letter to Junxian in Taipei to ask if her brother could help us. Two or three months later a large, heavy parcel arrived at our door at 25 Fuxing Road. It brought the future employment prospects for Yuchang.

Junxian's parcel contained the manual *American Railway Signal Principles and Practices* in more than ten volumes, published by the America Railroads Association. The fourth section included a detailed explanation of central traffic control, with charts and diagrams in 177 pages. Inscribed on the flyleaf was: "To Yuchang and Pang-yuan and our Nephew Siji on his third birthday. From Yilie and Junxian. August 14, 1953."

The book was difficult to acquire. The new technology had been developed during World War II and was not available in Taiwan. Older Brother Yang had managed to purchase a copy for the purpose of academic research.

Overjoyed, Yuchang glanced through the first part. Excited, he jotted down some notes, and in order to further pursue research, he decided to translate the manual into Chinese so as to understand it more conclusively and comprehensively in its entirety. He believed that I would surely help him, so he gave me the introduction, the sections on the purpose of the new equipment, and the necessary conditions for the work to translate into Chinese; he took responsibility for the technological explanations, electrical circuits, and important diagrams relating to operations. Every day after work, we'd take care of household matters, get the children to bed (our second son, Sixian, was fifteen months old), and then discuss the translation for at least an hour. In approximately six months, we translated the book, including the more than 100 charts and diagrams, into 166 pages of Chinese.

Yuchang attended a meeting at the bureau and learned that they had already purchased the set of books about CTC from the American Railroads Association. However, it had not been determined who was to do the research, nor had a plan been drawn up. Of the twenty or thirty people in charge of the Communications and Signal Division, not one had been educated in fully automatic signaling. No one had heard of it before. It was said that after the war, the Japanese National Railway had installed a semiautomatic system with the assistance of the American occupation forces. After the start of the Korean War, Taiwan was paid to supply provisions, and the shipment of material goods from inland to the coast increased dramatically. The importance of the Railroads Administration also increased greatly, with a pressing need for modernized equipment.

The administration first sent Yuchang and others to Japan, which was followed by a fact-finding trip to the United States, led by Chen Denian, for observation and further study. After 1954, plans were drawn up to install a CTC system based on the actual situation of Taiwan's railroads, the first phase being the single-track line from Changhua to Tainan, a stretch of 142 miles, for the switches and signals at 27 stations, as detailed by Yuchang. The control section invited international bids. Ericsson of Sweden won, and the installation work commenced in 1957, starting in Changhua. One year before the start of work, the administration sent a number of those in the Communications and Signal Division to Sweden for training. *Central Traffic Control*, translated by Yuchang (published in 1959), was originally prepared for his own research interest and printed as a simple manual; it became required reading for all engineers. He went to Sweden to pick up the equipment to be installed. Those in charge at Ericsson found that Mr. Loh [Luo] had a thorough understanding of the system, was "able to carry on dialogue," and was confident about the start of work on Taiwan's railroads. Both sides were happy working together.

However, for the Swedish, Taiwan in 1956 was probably a mysterious as well as backward and undeveloped place, a jungle in Asia. They sent an engineer to Taiwan by the name of Mr. Jocobsson. While he was saying good-bye to his family at the airport before flying from Stockholm to Hong Kong and then to Taiwan, his mother cried as if she would never see him again. After having been in Taichung several months, he felt he could make a go of it and then sent for his wife. He said he could travel the world with only four hundred words of English. His wife knew more English than he did, and when she arrived in Taichung and found that I knew even more and could help them with everything, she was greatly relieved.

In those days, no one in Taichung (or all Taiwan, for that matter) used coal gas (or gas), but still used coal cakes with a diameter of seven or eight inches, in the tops of which many holes were drilled and which were placed in an earthen burner over which food was cooked. More well-to-do people cooked and heated water on charcoal stoves. Staffers at the Railroad Administration rented a small, newly built concrete Western-style house for the Jocobssons and hired an "English-speaking" maid, and bought the necessary furniture for them. They were taken to their new house in one of the pedicabs that had just recently replaced the rickshaws. I pointed out the pedicab stand at the entrance to the lane and even wrote my address on a slip of paper so that they could come to my home if they needed anything (that was in the days before phones were installed in the city).

That very evening Mr. Jocobsson took a pedicab and came to knock on our door. He asked how could he ever sleep with so many mosquitoes?

The maid said they could not drink from the tap, but the big kettle of boiled water was too hot to drink and several bottles were needed to hold cold water. I gave him the mosquito nets from the guest rooms, along with several clean, empty rice wine bottles.

A few days later, it was Mrs. Jocobsson's turn to take a pedicab and come to visit me. Shortly after sitting down, she started to cry. She said that every morning her husband set off for Changhua to work and didn't get back till very late, and that she was terribly homesick. I found a lovely kitten and gave it to her, thinking the very cute little thing might be able to dispel her homesickness. I often went to take her for a walk, but the differences in culture and climate between Taiwan and Sweden were just too immense. For her it was a case of not having a single relative or friend around. She returned to Sweden after about six months.

Changhua station was the construction site for the railway to install the CTC and was about a twenty-minute drive from Taichung. In those days the civil servants and engineers used the earliest model jeeps with a canvas top produced by Yulong Company. Every morning Yuchang would go with Mr. Jocobsson and Assistant Section Chief Chen Ximing and would return in the evening. After the work started, the Chens moved to the railroad dormitory in Changhua. Work never ceased, not even on Sundays. Our three boys and I would ride in the canvas-topped jeep to the Chens' place. We liked going to the empty carriages lying idle in the Changhua switching yard most of all. My children grew up with the Chens' two boys and two girls. Mrs. Chen, nee Zhang Qiongxia, became the best of friends, and over fifty years, we shared in the births of our children and in raising them, worried our young heads over our husbands, and saw the results of their work upon which they concentrated so much thought and to which they dedicated so much energy. She took us to see her ancestral home in Taichung, her sister's place in Xiluo, and the homes of many of colleagues in the Communications and Signal Division to share in eating food offerings for deities in religious festivals, and in this way we really came to understand the local customs and practices of Taiwan.

I, who to this day have never understood the difference between the positive and negative poles of a magnetic field, feel honored to have seen a group of CTC engineers, who accepted the technical challenge night or day, properly arranging the maze of electric circuits, climbing mountains, wading waters . . . to set up the earliest communications network for the modernization of Taiwan's railways, sharing in their failures and successes, large and small. It was like going back to the days of the War of Resistance when everyone helped out with everything they had.

In 1959, the work entered its most difficult stage. The steel bridge over the Dadu River between Changhua and Taichung was knocked down by a typhoon, the city of Changhua was flooded, and the CTC primary machine room was threatened. Fortunately Yuchang had stayed behind in Changhua to push ahead with some work that evening. The August 7 flood was one of the worst typhoon disasters in the history of Taiwan, with the Dadu River basin awash in a vast expanse of water. Only three days later in the morning did the banks of the river reappear, and groups of engineers who raced against time making repairs could be seen coming and going on small wooden rafts.

Yuchang called me and said that the situation at the primary machine room was serious, and asked me to go get Mr. Jocobsson and another Swede by the name of Andersson, who was a circuitry expert, at their homes and bring them to the riverside, where a colleague from the Taichung Communications and Signal Division would ferry them to Changhua in a small boat. Also, I was to buy some bottled water and crackers and bring a flashlight and a change of clothes, because they would stay in Changhua until the water receded. I had to take care of this, because I had to explain to them in English the situation they were facing and I was the only one who knew where to go and whom to meet.

That morning I rode in the Yulong canvas-top jeep with the two very uneasy-looking Swedes to a point on the Dadu River that had recently been underwater, stepped onto a still loose embankment that had recently been constructed, and handed them over to the person there to meet them. I watched as the two engineers set off in that small wooden boat as it danced in the turbulent, turbid flood; they attempted to cut across the surging current, finally arriving at a dry place on the opposite bank, where they disembarked. The first thing I wanted to do was tell their weeping wives that they had safely made it across the river.

July 25 of the following year (1960) was a memorable day in the history of Taiwan's railroads. Following a grand launching ceremony, the provincial chairman, the premier, or an official of that stature turned a knob and a train set off from Changhua Station to Huatan Station, four miles away, becoming the first train to travel under fully automated traffic control in all of Asia. The train pulled into Huatan Station, which had been decorated for celebration. Returning home, Yuchang said, the engineers who stood on the railroad tracks (the platform being too small) behind the ranks of officials had shed tears of joy. That evening they all got drunk celebrating.

However, the happy times didn't last more than a day. The next morning, the dispatcher and the engineer in the central control room shouted at each other and everyone's hearts seemed pressed under the fingers of the dispatcher. One false turn would set off a disaster, and the control board, which was lit up like the Milky Way, was more complicated than they had dreamed. They seemed to run along with the train each mile it traveled. They scarcely returned home at that time, and if they did, the phone would ring immediately. I frequently heard Yuchang shouting into the phone on the wall for railroad business: "How can he be so stupid! Tell him not to push any buttons. I'll be right there!" Then he'd grab his raincoat, rush to the jeep, and speed on his way to Changhua. The only cars on the road in those days were his and those of the Highways Administration. Often the Highways Administration driver would stick his head out the window and ask if my husband had a death wish.

I took care of our three boys, the oldest nine, the youngest five. I had to teach during the day, prepare the class lessons at night, and correct homework. I lived like a spinning top, and if there was time to pray, I'd pray there'd be no accidents, because the cars and trains always seemed to be speeding on the verge of a disaster.

As expected, shortly after the large-scale launch, traffic control had reached Ershui Station, and a typhoon again destroyed the banks of the Dadu River that had been ruined during the flood of the previous year. Changhua was again inundated by a vast expanse of water, and the railroad was washed out in many places, the CTC equipment was dead, and all the passenger and freight trains were behind schedule. One military train was forced to stop at Shiliu Station in Douliu City (thirty miles from Changhua). It was a small station used specifically for loading gravel and had been washed away by the flood. Stranded in such a desolate place, the passengers suffered under the scorching sun for half a day without potable water. Impossible demands to get under way came via the phone on the train, and one officer said if they didn't start, they'd use artillery and blow up the dispatcher's office. But safety came first, and only at dusk did the passengers arrive at their nearby destination of Tanzi Station.

Amid the large-scale destruction caused by the storm, the dispatchers and the engineers worked anxiously night and day, gradually developing friendships cemented in adversity, supporting one another, taking turns working over twenty-four hours, doing everything they could to solve the problems. Despite the hardships, they were honored to participate in this epoch-making and innovative work. However, four months after the flooding, when everything was back on track, a man-made catastrophe occurred: one freight train hit another from behind on the Zhuoshui River Bridge. The engine of the second train was hanging over the side of the bridge, and the pulling and hanging made it extremely difficult to get things fixed, so the times for all trains the following day had already been changed and a new schedule published. According to the dispatcher Cai Renhui in his memoir *Digressions on Fifty Years of Taiwan Railways,* "All those associated with the CTC found themselves in a nightmare. The abnormal train operations reached the nadir and the 'faults' of the workers were really hard to imagine. One could say that it was unprecedented (and 'should never happen again')."

In the age when the railroads were the sole means for large-scale shipping, the goods were piled high in the stations and freight and passenger trains were of equal importance. After the flooding and the total rescheduling of the trains, when the central CTC equipment was down, old-style manual signaling had to be used and freight trains often spent more time sitting and waiting in halfway stations than running on the tracks. There were twenty-four stations monitored at the central dispatcher's room in Changhua, with fifty-eight telephone loudspeakers for station relay offices. During these times, engineers and repairmen, station workers, and those on the trains all vied vocally with one another. By the end of a four-hour shift the dispatchers were hoarse, and they were never without their throat lozenges. When they went home, they would end up shouting in their sleep, frightening everyone in the family. They didn't have any family life to speak of. Those in the administration initially opposed to reforms believed that those in the Communications and Signal Division had overestimated themselves and embarrassed everyone. The newspapers (fortunately there was no TV) assigned blame every day, with freezing irony and burning satire. One cartoon depicted a passenger getting off a train, opening his umbrella and walking, and still arriving at the next station before the train.

RAILWAY WORKERS TOGETHER THROUGH THICK AND THIN

Those were times of trials and tribulations! Yet it was a key period in which our lives took root. A young Sichuan middle school student, called "Geometry Luo" by his classmates on account of his dream of speeding trains joined the Taiwan Railways Administration. During those desolate days in a marginalized Taichung, he sought to give his life and work focus, concentrating on his research, starting the work of a lifetime, actually leading his own troops to modernize Taiwan's railroads. The most difficult stretch of CTC construction was from Changhua to Tainan. From a halting start to steadiness and after successful dispatch operations, the second coastal CTC line from Changhua to Zhunan was installed in 1964 by the original players. In 1969, the CTC mountain line was finished at a total of two hundred miles.

This group of companions who went through thick and thin, braving the elements without rest, worked together until they retired. Chen Ximing, Yuchang's first assistant section chief, was born in Tianzhong, Changhua County, in 1928. He graduated from the Electrical Engineering Department at National Taiwan University in 1950, joined the electrical section of the Railways Administration, and was sent abroad seven times to Europe, America, and Japan to examine railroad signaling and electrical technology. He served for a total of forty-two years in the Railways Administration, working his way up through the ranks as an engineer, from section chief to assistant department head to department head, chief engineer, and deputy director, retiring only in 1993. For over thirty years they labored together, becoming lifelong friends (each admiring the intelligence of the other). In our two families there were a total of seven children who grew up together, from diapers to youth. Today they are all middle-aged, and when we get together from different places far and wide, what they like most is reminiscing about the happy times pushing the empty carriages on the deserted railway tracks in the Changhua switching yard.

From 1950 to 1960 was a time of struggle and of laughter and tears—it was a golden decade for us all. From the rafters of that small Japanese-style house on Fuxing Road in Taichung, we suspended a cradle for three babies. At six months, they were moved to a small wooden bed built by a carpenter based on a picture in Dr. Spock's *Baby Care* book. The bed was covered with screen on all four sides and on top. Our friends and relatives referred to it as the screened closet, which was no safer than most baby beds made of wood. "Growing a little each night," they grew up in the blink of an eye. One by one they soon graduated from National Taichung Primary School (Taichung in the school's name doesn't mean it was the earliest primary school in the city, but the name is significant). Lin Haifeng was a student there and after becoming famous, winning the Honinbo Go title, he returned to his alma mater, and we all felt extremely honored.

During that decade, I watched countless dodgeball games on that large playground; it was a new ball game for me, and to this day it seems to make a mockery of life. I had attended so many elementary schools and never once seen it played. The game seemed to involve little skill, victory being determined by how many opponents a player could hit, a very passive sport, as if one could exist in a crowed spot only by eliminating enough other people. I've always been repelled by the dodgeball view of life, sadly watching all those children on the dusty playground doing their best to dodge a ball so as not to be removed from the game.

I wish all children throughout the world could grow up in peace and stability and not have to develop strong and vigorous bodies just to flee from disaster.

I envied the children their serene environment: that screened baby bed, the yard full of generations of cats of all colors, large and small, along with the huge banyan tree in the back, which together constituted the three sights of the Luo house in Taichung. The air roots of the banyan tree were long and abundant. There was also a hole in the trunk, and every time guests they particularly liked arrived, my three boys would hide the visitor's shoes in that hole and then would come in and announce: " "You can't leave now!" The guests would feign surprise. The boys never tired of these games, until they entered middle school. In those seventeen years, the five of us all grew. Taichung is the homeland of childhood memories for my children and me. My own childhood memories do not contain such a beautiful place.

SILENT WAVES

In 1966, the Railways Administration transferred Yuchang to the General Administrative Division in Taipei to take part in the railroad electrical planning of the Ten Major National Construction Projects. The following year we left our home of seventeen years in Taichung and moved to Taipei. Our two older sons, who were in senior high school, had to sit for a test in order to transfer schools, and our youngest son, who had just graduated from primary school, was facing the fiercely competitive junior middle school exams in Taipei.

From that point until 1979, Yuchang focused his energies entirely on electrification engineering. The comprehensive modernization of the railroads meant that trains that didn't burn coal and emit smoke were about to travel on electrified railway tracks! The project was supervised by the government and watched with great interest by the populace. The progress was reported nearly every day on television, a recent addition to most households. As the engineer responsible, Yuchang frequently had to be on the scene to explain things; his life and his family's were not easy during those years. His official title went from head of the Communications and Signal Division to chief engineer to deputy director, all just names suitable for his work. The Railways Administration honors an old tradition of the *yamen*, with a rigid hierarchy in which those with insufficient rank are not allowed to speak (to me it was a very cold place). However, Yuchang was of a tranquil disposition and indifferent to wealth and fame. Carrying out this project was an affirmation of his abilities. He concentrated his mental faculties on each stage of the line, each diagram, and the system, watching as construction from one station to the next became a reality. Seeing a train travel over new track was deeply satisfying and his greatest reward. It could be said that the period of time from the installation of central traffic control in 1950 to the electrification of the railroads constituted the glory days for an engineer.

But unexpectedly during that busiest of times, the "Two Road Case" of the intelligence agencies actually delayed things.

My own understanding is that the Two Road Case was an investigation of a number of high-ranking technicians at the Railways Administration and Highways Administration conducted by the Bureau of Investigation from 1970 to 1980. No contact was allowed across the Taiwan Strait, and the investigation was mounted as a result of a number of engineering personnel from the Taiwan Veterans Engineering Department Office, when repairing highways in Thailand and Indonesia, writing to family members in mainland China, which resulted in propaganda from mainland transportation circles being directed at the Taiwan engineers, calling upon them to return to serve the motherland. Thenthe relevant agencies had doubts about their "degree of loyalty" to the nation. Those who were detained, interrogated, and convicted were all from among the more than forty people in the 1946 class of transportation specialists who arrived in Taiwan on the same ship as Yuchang. The construction of the electrification project was being highly publicized, and Dong Ping, who had succeeded to the post of director of the Railways Administration, strenuously guaranteed to the Garrison Office that Yuchang was in no way involved, and insisted that the

the administration could not lose the person responsible for carrying out the present stage of the project. The Bureau of Investigation agreed to allow Yuchang to write and submit a detailed account of his activities, his work, and his family life since arriving in Taiwan before anything else would be done.

During that period, I recall him dragging himself home, exhausted and eyes wide open, to sit down at the dinner table in the evening and write until midnight. After the first fourteen-page account was submitted, he received orders that more information had to be supplied. The tympanitis Yuchang had suffered from in his youth flared up as a result of overwork and lack of sleep. During the day he would go to the Railroad Hospital and get an anti-inflammatory injection, but there was no time for further treatment. In 1979, the electrical modernization of the railroads came to a glorious conclusion and the launch ceremony announced the success of the Ten Major National Construction Projects. Yuchang was awarded a level five Order of the Brilliant Star and inducted as a researcher into the Council for National Construction. But he had lost half his hearing. His remaining efforts went into finishing the extension project for the north–south railroad, and he saw the opening of the direct rail line between Taipei and Hualien, but he was already deaf to the delightful sound of the waves striking the shore. By the time of his retirement in 1985, only 10 or 20 percent of his hearing remained. When we had something to discuss, we often relied on writing. It was difficult for him to have dealings with others after he retired, and his tranquility deepened in silence.

7

SPIRITUAL DESCENDANTS

TAICHUNG FIRST HIGH SCHOOL

After the Lunar New Year of 1953, Shen Zengwen, the Nankai classmate I had become reacquainted with, arranged for me to fill in for her in her high school English classes at Taichung First High School, because she was going to the United States for six months for training in the teaching of English. She was the recipient of an American postwar fellowship for cultural exchange, known later in the 1960s as the Fulbright Exchange Program, which has had a long and profound impact on international cultural exchange.

I was very interested in teaching. The most memorable teachers, aside from my parents, were my Nankai Middle School teachers. Meng Zhisun, my favorite among others, was an excellent model of learning and classroom performance. Later, when I attended Wuhan University, my teacher Zhu Guangqian not only possessed high standards but also was able to provide me with guidance at a confusing period in my life, ensuring that I had a fixed goal. For three years, I had been at the "stay-at-home university" (as my mother laughingly referred to it), and the substitute teaching work would have a critical impact on my life.

The first time I walked through the front gate of Taichung First High School on Yucai Street, I saw the plaque commemorating the founding of the school, and each time I reread it over the next five years, I was deeply moved. On the front was carved:

> At first, we Taiwanese had no middle school until this school was started. Since then, in everything that has been established and in the public schools under township administration, the emphasis has been on language. Due to the ever improving environment, some, not shunning difficulties, went to the mainland across the sea. Leaving home in childhood, dwelling far away from home, and being short on funds to study gave rise to countless doubts and anxieties. The educated were deeply troubled and found it imperative to set up a middle school. In 1915, the committee members Lin Lietang, Lin Xiantang, Gu Xianrong, Lin Xiongzheng, and Cai Lianfang rose up and took charge.

Donations amounting to twenty-four million *yuan* were collected, the Lin family donated ninety thousand square feet of land, and the school was constructed in 1915. It was the most important school for the Taiwanese during the fifty years of the Japanese occupation. Even so, to keep the name of the school required years of struggle.

This justifiable pride at establishing a school elicited my respect. I taught there for five years and proudly became a small part of that admirable tradition. Taichung First High School made me frequently think of the Nankai spirit of my own education and the Northeast Sun Yat-sen Middle School established by my father's generation, not only for the sake of "childhood education away from home" for the children of my homeland in the northeast but also to guide them at a time when the nation was destroyed and families were shattered and nurture them when they suffered deprivations and hardships as refugees. But the Sun Yat-sen Middle School, upon returning to the place where it began after the war, actually had less support, with the school's name and history being buried for forty-six years, until in 1995, through the efforts of some early alums in Shenyang, the school recovered its name and history. Taichung First High School hung on to its founding ideals, educating first-rate talent and steadily developing for a hundred years despite many hardships, with its alums forming the backbone of Taiwan society.

Schools founded upon such a spirit of survival all have a driving atmosphere of self-confidence. At that time, the Japanese colonizers had been gone for less than a decade and most of the educators were from mainland China and had experienced the chaos of war before coming to Taiwan. Most had graduated from good schools and, generally speaking, were enthusiastic teachers with high standards. For them, Taichung First High School was a place of physical and spiritual stability.

I felt fortunate at being able to "steal" a few hours from the market, the coal stove, baby bottles, and diapers and once again talk about knowledge, precious knowledge, including fine lyrical, descriptive, or expository prose. A classroom of forty or so responsive faces looking up and listening to me lecture gave me a sense of being understood.

One year was a long time, and even with winter and summer vacations a lot could still be discussed in nine months. By effectively making use of a fifty-minute class period and keeping the students' attention focused, a teacher could be like a pilot navigating rivers and seas, with each lesson being like a voyage, allowing the students to see a different world.

Teaching is indeed a delightful thing. Upon entering the classroom you hear "stand and bow" and see a roomful of uniformed students stand in unison, their minds immediately focused, their spirits cleansed, all outside concerns expunged, ready to challenge and be challenged.

It seemed to be clearly stipulated for high school English classes in those days that two-thirds of the class time would be devoted to lecture and one-third to discussing grammar, which was probably the ratio devoted to those subjects on the National College Entrance Exams in those days. Difficulties arose at the mere mention of grammar. My first challenge was to teach it in a clear and interesting way, blending it with the textbook lesson. Parts of speech, tense, and rules of grammar all formed the trunk and branches of the tree of language, while words and sentences formed the leaves and literary feelings the flowers and fruit. I didn't translate each word and sentence into Chinese, but rather encouraged the students to freely use their own imaginations to make a deeper impression on them and increase their vocabulary. The wind could "whisper," "sob," "groan," "roar," and "howl," and the flow of water went from "rippling" to "rapid currents" and "overpowering flood" to "violent torrents." The comparative degree of adjectives was not just a matter of adding -er or -est. The Chinese like to say so-and-so is the greatest, but in English it is usually "one of the greatest," because there is always someone greater. I taught using the method used when I was studying English myself to explain the lessons, effectively expanding the students' perception of words. In a lifetime of teaching, I have used this method at all levels and found it much welcomed by the students. The students at Taichung First High School were all at a good level, eager to learn, self-confident, and unafraid of difficulties. It was a good start for my teaching.

Shen Zengwen returned from America during summer vacation and my period of substitute teaching came to an end. Principal Jin Shurong asked me in all sincerity to stay on as a high school English teacher. Fate seemingly had provided me with a greater challenge, but I had to take stock of my own real difficulties: first my husband had to agree, and then I needed the support of my parents. In those years, my mother ran back and forth between Taipei and Taichung. When I was pregnant or ill or Yuchang went abroad for work, my mother always arrived to help out in a timely manner. During that same period of time, my father began to find himself in a difficult position politically. My parents were concerned that my less than robust health would not allow me to handle the twin responsibilities of home and work. However, being young and self-assured, I soon regained the Nankai spirit while substituting. Ultimately, I accepted the offer from Taichung First High School and from that moment entered the world of education, which I had admired from a very young age. I had another secret reason for taking the job: in three years' time, I wanted to take the test for a Fulbright exchange. If my middle school and college classmate (Xie Wenjin, who was a year ahead of me) could pass, then I probably could too. In those days, one could only apply for a passport if one had such funding. This was to be the first stop for my future.

In addition to the uniformly high-level curriculum at Taichung First High, the senior class strived toward the goal of passing the National College Entrance Exams with every breath they took. Not only did they want to get into college, but they also wanted to get into specific schools and departments. I was unfazed by this because I had once lived and breathed the same way. It was said that students were assigned to the four sections of the senior class based on student ID numbers. Math and English were the focus of the striving, and the teachers of those classes, in order to enhance the performance of their own students, secretly offered extracurricular competitive exercises.

It was in this environment that I met my lifetime friend Xu Huifang. She was ten years older than I and a graduate of the English department of Hujiang University. Her father was a famous book collector from Wuyi in Jiangsu Province. Her brother, Xu Zhongnian, studied abroad in France and returned to serve as a professor in the Department of Foreign Languages and Literatures at National Central University during our days at Shapingba in Chongqing. He was also a famous writer and critic, and I read a number of his books at the Time and Tide Bookstore.

The teachers' lounge at Taichung First High was quite big, with several rows of long tables that my colleagues from the various departments used as their own space. Soon after I started, I met Yang Jinzhong, who once taught at Taichung First High, through a letter of introduction written from America by Lin Tonggeng, a lecturer at National Taiwan University. Yang would soon accompany her husband, Hu Xuguang, when he took up his post as an envoy at the embassy in the United States. Her friends, Li Yunxian of the Chinese department, Meng Wenkan of the history department, and Lu Hanfen and Xu Huifang of the English department, all of whom were senior faculty, looked after me. Xu Huifang taught the second section of the senior class and I taught the third. She lived on Lide Street, only two hundred yards from my house. Sometimes we returned together after class, and eventually we arranged to go together in the morning, taking the same pedicab. The first thing we would talk about was that endless topic of class work, and then our households. She had come with her husband, Jiang Daoyu, and family to Taiwan, where three generations lived under one roof as a large family for several decades.

In the last month of the final term of the senior year, all classes ended and we began providing guidance for the advancing students. Based on their individual specialties, the teachers of each department would rotate, teaching the four sections. We had to prepare our own teaching materials, focusing on the potential questions on the National College Entrance Exams, sharpening the students' minds and ability to answer precisely. Xu Huifang and I were assigned to the fields of translation and changes in the parts of speech and other grammatical issues. Each of us also had to provide several short pieces that could be read aloud for practice and to enhance reading ability.

We did our utmost to collect materials. At the time, I started going to the library at the United States Information Service in Taichung, and my brother and his old classmate Yang Kongxin, who worked at Central News, sent me some English texts, mostly articles on literature and culture. After sufficient discussion, and after the children had been put to bed in the evening, Xu would come over to my place and, sitting at my desk, would write the teacher handouts or practice questions for the entire class, and I would cut the stencils for them to be printed at the office the following day. The stenciled handouts were quite successful and several years later were "stolen" for a number of commercially produced guides for scholastic advancement. Naturally, none of us in those days had any notion of copyright. My handwriting is blockish and not very elegant, but ideally suited for making stencils. Not yet thirty years old, I was very happy at being involved in such "important" matters.

The first thing that comes to mind about the seventeen years we lived in Taichung, besides life at home, is my small desk, often placed at the end of the hall. I hung a red carpet to separate the space from the bedroom. In the circle of light created by the low shade of a small desk lamp, we wrote and stenciled. It was both romantic and bitter. Actually, it wasn't all that romantic; most of the time we were just a couple of housewives who didn't enter that space to face the mental challenges until everyone else had gone to bed. English has a most accurate word for this: necessity. We and our families knew that once we started, we had to finish. Working at that small desk of mine in our small living space (it was only in 1972, when we moved to the faculty dorm on Lishui Road, that I had a study of my own) required the understanding of my husband. He "consented" to our work because he worked seven days a week and was frequently away on business, something about which I never complained.

That small desk laid the foundation for our lifetime friendship, until Xu Huifang passed away at a ripe old age in 2007. None of life's changes came between us in fifty years. My three sons warmly remember her as Mama Jiang. That shared spirit hunched over the small desk writing and stenciling has remained with me throughout my life in Taiwan, from when I first started teaching at Taichung First High.

At around 10 p.m., I'd walk her back to the intersection of Lide Street via Fuxing Road. We never ran out of things to talk about in all the times we saw each other home. We remained close, even years later after I had left Taichung First High. In addition to schoolwork, we discussed life and our families. Her dignity, wisdom, and magnanimity had a tremendous influence on me.

In those five years, looking at the roster of successful entrance exam candidates each summer was another big thing for me. Like a new coach watching a ball game, I constantly told the students not to think about winning or losing, but inside I was anxious for them and was upset that I couldn't get the first newspaper off the press. I'd circle the names of my students in red on that densely packed list. It is no different today than it was fifty years ago: first I'd look for the names of those on the rosters for National Taiwan University Medical School and the School of Engineering, especially those in electrical engineering, because they had the highest scores. I cannot claim to have been above such "vanity," and the success rate of the students advancing under my tutelage filled my young mind. During those few days, the only thing missing was the setting off of firecrackers at my door. The students who had passed and made it onto the roster came in a steady stream to thank their teachers. Overall, the students did quite well; however, for some the results were less than ideal and they failed to make the rosters for the public universities. Several days later, they would show up at my door. Some came in and wept. I not only tried to comfort them but also encouraged them to retake the exam the following year. Most were satisfied.

Sharing their successes and failures resulted in me developing a long-term "comradeship" with many of the eighteen- and nineteen-year-old boys. As they grew older, some would write, and some would come see me when they came home to Taichung to visit, especially during the summer they completed their military service. I heard many interesting anecdotes about training new soldiers. A constant stream of students rang at my door, and every Sunday I'd prepare sweet-sour plum infusion and steam plenty of tasty *baozi*. Even after many years, I still remembered many of them. The most unforgettable story I heard about soldiering was told to me by Shi Jiaxing. He asked me for a number of small passages in English, which he then recited while on sentry duty, leaving me with a feeling of great respect. While he was studying biology at National Taiwan University, he met regularly with a number of classmates to discuss issues of literature and culture. He fell in love with Jian Chuhui (who later became the famous writer Jian Wan) and even brought her along to visit. After graduating, he taught for several years. When he obtained his Ph.D. from Cornell University, he invited me to take a walk around Hu Shi's campus, where I saw the place he had lived and pursued his advanced studies. That evening he invited several classmates and his wife's younger sister, Jian Jinghui, to chat about all the happy events of those years. In fifty years I saw him go from a young person to a scholar of international caliber. In 2008 he was awarded the World Poultry Science Association prize for research, an awarded bestowed every four years, and I was really able to share in their feelings of accomplishment.

Traditionally at Taichung First High, fewer students went on to study the humanities at the university level. Those who frequently stayed in touch over the decades included Luo Zhiyuan, the outstanding diplomat; Zhao Shoubo, the political commentator who ran the Broadcasting Corporation of China; and Professor Liao Yinan of the National Taiwan University School of Law. Those who graduated from the Department of Foreign Languages and Literatures include Lin Borong, Zhang Heyong, Zhang Pingnan, and Chen Da'an. Lin Borong was in the first class of students I taught. He had spoken to me of his ideal of doing something for Taichung before he established Liren High School and eventually ran for mayor of the city. I had left Taichung by the time he served as mayor, but it was obvious from the literary style of the written election announcements that he had received an education in literature, even though he was clearly aware that the world of politics he had entered was something completely different. When Zhang Heyong, who was in the same class, was working at Tatung Company, he translated a number of classic works of the humanities for the Hsieh-chih Industrial Library. Zhang Pingnan was the student of whom Xu Huifang was most proud. His Chinese and English were both excellent, and he was also widely read in works of literature. When I was working at the National Bureau of Translation and Compilation, I asked him to translate Erich Auerbach's (1892–1957) *Mimesis: The Representation of Reality in Western Literature*, a book that was required reading in literature courses, into Chinese. Youth Cultural Enterprise Company published this very significant work in 1980.

Chen Da'an, who was in the last class I taught, studied in the Department of Foreign Languages and Literatures at National Taiwan University. He was a student who really loved literature and had deeply original ideas about the literary works he read. When he was at university, he frequently asked me what books he should read outside of class. In five or six years he wrote a good deal of new poetry that was both profound and creative, and I was always his first reader. Later, he too went to the United States to engage in cultural work. At the beginning of 1990, I watched on TV as Muse Cordero Chen Advertising Company, which he and a friend had co-founded, won the silver medal awarded by the Association of National Advertisers. In 1994 they won the Effie Gold Award given by the American Marketing Association. To win such a competitive national prize clearly indicates that someone possesses a firm foundation if literature and art and is creative in such a way as to touch the hearts of others.

Taichung First High also produced some outstanding members of the engineering and medical professions, which was traditionally the main strength of the school. Medicine was the ambition of all of those with the best grades. There was always one grinning student who would say to me, "Teacher, I'll look after you when I become a doctor." Being young at the time, I never thought I might one day need a doctor to look after me. Years later, I read how they had become famous physicians and even saw their names on their clinics, but I never sought them out on account of an illness. In one instance, a former student, Liu Maosong, who was deputy director of the Ren'ai Hospital, came to visit and chat about old times. My stomach was bothering me at the time, so he arranged a gastroscopy exam for me. In the middle of waiting my turn, I fled and felt so bad about it that I never went back. Several years ago, I gave a final lecture at the Hexin Hospital entitled "Pain and Literature." Cai Zhexiong, an old Taichung First High alum, had come back to Taiwan after practicing medicine in the United States to serve as deputy director of that famous oncology hospital. Thinking about the old days, he came and visited and asked me to give that boundary-crossing lecture. I described how at the key juncture when I had suffered from an illness, I had memorized poems to help relieve the unendurable pain. And, as was my usual practice in the classroom, I copied a number of English poems for the audience to memorize and recite.

In the summer of 2006, Academia Sinica member Liao Yijiu, who was in the first class I taught at Taichung First High and who later made contributions in the field of hydroponics, along with Wang Zhenxiu, an expert on lightning who had returned to Taiwan for the first time in forty years, and Zhang Heyong paid me a visit. When we met again after fifty years, I was retired and my hair all white, and they were all in their seventies. We talked about professional accomplishments and the vicissitudes of life with no small sense of wonderment. They mailed me a group photo of that visit, and I keep it on my desk even today.

Over the decades, I have met Taichung First High students from all walks of life, in Taiwan and abroad. Meeting them always brings back warm memories. What many people remember about my class was the concentration and how they all felt enriched in class and outside. Fang Dongmei once said, "Students are our spiritual descendants." For me, teaching has always been more than just a job; it is more a form of transmission, of sharing with others what I have read and thought. It is something more profound than just holding class. My students are all my spiritual descendants.

THE START OF CULTURAL EXCHANGE

By the start of the summer of 1956, I had taught for three full years at Taichung First High, passed the U.S. State Department Fulbright Exchange Teachers' Program exam to receive funding, and was set to go to the United States to study English teaching for one semester. The trip was for six months, and it had been nine years since I graduated from the university.

The Fulbright Cultural Exchange Program is America's most successful postwar program for the promotion of world peace. It was proposed by Senator William Fulbright, of the Senate Foreign Relations Committee, in 1946 for the selection and mutual exchange of American cultural figures and educators with cultural representatives from other nations, and intended through cultural exchange to console people who had suffered from war, as well as to further world peace. In fifty years, there have been more than ten thousand exchanges between Taiwan and the United States, with more than ten times that number from the rest of the world. It has had the most profound and far-reaching influence of any American program for cultural diplomacy. In this, my lifetime of literary exchange had such a fine beginning.

In Taiwan, the selection process was run by the U.S. Information Service (USIS), and, much like a student exam, the seventy-two qualified applicant teachers sat at a number of long wooden tables and wrote in English their replies to a series of questions. Those who passed the first round also had to do an interview with a five-person committee. I was asked one question that I never expected. A Miss Whipple of the USIS asked me, "With three such young children at home, will your husband allow you to leave?" In addition to saying that my mother would be there to look after them, I added with quick wit at the spur of the moment, "My husband encourages me to go. He is a domesticated man." They all burst into laughter, and this no doubt contributed in no small part to my score. In the 1950s, the feminist movement had barely begun, and the idea of a "househusband" was just a dream. Once in *Time* magazine—the only English magazine in the Taichung First High library—I read an article on the concept of the "domesticated man," which had left a deep impression on me. It was also one of the most interesting examples I had of how English words change. However, if the same question had been asked two years later, I wouldn't have answered in the same way, because once my husband started work on CTC engineering, until he retired more than twenty years later, he was rarely at home.

Catching our breath after the war during the early years of the Republic of China on Taiwan, life was pretty hard. Many children didn't have shoes to wear to school, and electric fans during the summer were a luxury. America, on the other side of the Pacific, was the home of heroes of World War II such as Douglas MacArthur and Claire Chennault, a distant and beautiful dreamland, and tourism was just a word in the dictionary. After I had obtained the program funding, my dreams were becoming a reality: I could apply for a passport and a visa, which were unavailable to the average person, and the best arrangements were made for me to further my studies for the future advancement of my career. The evening I arrived in Washington and stood looking out a window on the eighteenth floor, I was stirred by feelings of disbelief.

The group of exchange teachers (both university and high school teachers) of which I was part came from more than twenty countries, mostly from Europe and South America, with four each from Iran and Japan (perhaps they were in greatest need of peace exchanges). Also on the list was Go Ok-nam, a lecturer from Ewha Womans University in Korea, and myself from Taiwan. In Washington we received ten days of basic training, directed by Mr. Shamblin from the State Department. He made many incisive and humorous comparisons of American attitudes and lifestyle with those of our countries. I admired the attitude of this intellectual who worked in the service of his country.

We were then sent to the University of Michigan, Ann Arbor, for two and a half solid months of English training. Fortunately, we made it in time to attend the last class with Dr. Fries, the founder, before he retired, and were able to hear his observations about ways of improving English grammar. The more than thirty of us were together day and night, so we had plenty of time to learn about the culture of each of our countries on a fairly deep level. Living with a host family that had been arranged for us, we were able to experience the American lifestyle for ourselves at first hand. I lived with Dr. Albert Wheeler, a biology professor at the University of Michigan, and his family. It was my first encounter with a highly educated black American family. His nickname at the university was Dr. Sunshine. In 1960, I read in *Time* magazine that he had been nominated for the Nobel Prize in biology. During my stay with them, they treated me very well and discussed issues between blacks and whites as well as answering my many cultural questions. Martin Luther King, Jr., was a family friend, and Dr. Wheeler was also one of the earliest and founding members of the Michigan chapter of the NAACP. During the 1970s he was mayor of Ann Arbor, and one of the city parks was later named after him. On language-teaching weekends, we visited automobile plants and Midwestern farms, watched several basketball games, and even learned to chant for the UM team.

I left the freezing state of Michigan that winter, having chosen to go to freezing Evanston High School in Minnesota for practice teaching, using the new grammar of Dr. Fries. Everyone was surprised by my choice, which I made because it was a little closer to Utah, where my youngest sister was studying, and I wanted to experience the same severe cold as northeast China, the home to which I had never returned. I was warmly received by the people of Minnesota, who rarely saw a young woman from China. Several ranchers took me to see their huge spreads. One older gentleman said it was getting crowded because someone had moved to a new ranch about fifty miles away. For three months, the temperature was ten below and colder, but the comforts of their homes, their normal life, even their cheerfulness fully demonstrated the American spirit, which sometimes reminded me of my father's half-a-lifetime struggle for his homeland. One day the temperature dropped to forty below zero, and I got out of the car to experience the beauty of ice and snow for as far as the eye could see. Within five minutes I was picked up by a police car and taken home so as "to avoid a fool's death."

Our stays at an end, the more than thirty of us met once again in Washington, where we described our individual experiences and thoughts. It was really hard to say good-bye when the time came. I took the famous tourist train, the California Zephyr, from the east all the way across the country to San Francisco on the West Coast. Along the way I was able to observe the majesty of the country's mountains and rivers and the scenery of the different states. It was really an eye-opening trip.

My coursework for the Fulbright Exchange was completed in the spring of 1957, and I flew back to Taiwan. On the plane back, I sat next to an older American gentleman who asked me all sorts of questions about Taiwan, which I did my best to answer. Before getting off the plane, he handed me his card: Dr. Anderson, the president of the American University in Washington. Once back in Taiwan, I returned to Taichung and resumed teaching at Taichung First High. At the time, Zhang Qiyun was head of the Ministry of Education. On one occasion he came to Taichung and informed Song Xinmin, the principal of Taichung First High, that he wanted to see Chi Pang-yuan. In those days only people of a certain status rode in pedicabs. Excited, the principal took me in the pedicab, which the government provided for him in his position, to visit the Minister of Education.

Minister Zhang said to me, "In several of his speeches, President Anderson mentioned you, praising you highly and saying that Taiwan has extremely high-caliber high school teachers. The ministry hopes that you can come and work in the Department of International Culture and Education." Returning home, I discussed the matter with my husband and my father and, as I expected, they were against the idea. Later the minister wrote a letter stating that if I was willing, he could also make arrangements to have my husband transferred to Taipei, but my husband was not one to accept such offers. I wrote back saying that I was committed to teaching and learning, and I thanked him for his kind intentions.

"I HAVE A DREAM"

In the autumn of 1958, after I had taught at Taichung First High for two years following my return from America as an exchange teacher, I transferred to the Taiwan Provincial College of Agriculture to teach first-year English. This was the actual start of my academic life.

In 1961, the Taiwan Provincial College of Agriculture became Taiwan Provincial Chung-Hsing University; it later became National Taiwan Chung-Hsing University. English was a required course for all students along with Chinese, history, the Three Principles of the People, and physical education. All sorts of conversations took place in the faculty lounge for teachers of required courses; therefore I decided to push for a Department of Foreign Languages and Literatures and to have a discussion and study group for those interested in literature.

Around 1960, the school started two classes of second-year English, which I was requested to teach. I also had to decide on the teaching materials.

That year, John F. Kennedy was elected president, and I acquired a copy of his inaugural address along with copies of Hu Shi's last lecture (he died in 1961) and Martin Luther King's famous "I Have a Dream" speech from the USIS. I had probably read every literary work the service had on hand. In those days the Taichung City Library and the university library had pitifully few English materials.

To these materials, I added a number of good essays that I had read as a student, along with poems by Emily Dickinson and Robert Frost. In class, I also compared the differences between Eastern and Western culture, and the students found what I said quite novel. This was especially so in the international climate after Kennedy and King were assassinated, because by then the tide of students going abroad to study in the United States was just beginning, so any articles about American culture and recent articles of any depth were most welcome.

The class was an elective course with seventy or eighty students enrolled, but about one hundred students actually crammed into the classroom. The seventy or eighty seats were insufficient, so chairs had to be brought in from the neighboring classrooms, frequently resulting in disputes.

The school president in those days was Lin Zhiping, and later Tang Huisun. In the days when Liu Daoyuan was president, I began to request that he establish a Department of Foreign Languages and Literatures. He often asked me to be present at important events.

In 1965 Professor Friedrich A. Hayek, winner of the 1974 Nobel Prize in Economics, gave lectures at a number of schools in Taichung. I was asked to interpret. He said, "In a moment, I'll speak a passage, and then you interpret that passage for me." I was somewhat apprehensive, because even though I had studied the basics of economics, I hadn't really understood much. At the venue, I saw that he was accompanied by a number of people from Taipei, among whom were famous professors from National Taiwan University including Shi Jiansheng and Hua Yan. The place was packed, which really alarmed me.

Professor Hayek didn't give me a copy of his lecture and he spoke English with a German accent, making him difficult to understand. He usually spoke for five or six minutes before letting me interpret, which was a tremendous challenge. Fortunately, he occasionally wrote on the blackboard. That was the first time I had heard the terms "open society" and "closed society." My interpretations of the two terms caught on, which gave me a lot of encouragement.

Later Professor Shi Jiansheng of the National Taiwan University School of Law said to me, "In all the places I have taken him, you have been the best interpreter." He also made the same comment to others.

Later, many important people visited Taichung. I interpreted for the Baptist bishop, which I was equal to. In the 1960s, President Chiang Kai-shek invited the chief editor of *Reader's Digest* to Taiwan, because he had written an article about Taiwan being a new jeweled island. I was asked to interpret for him when he arrived in Taichung. Such experiences greatly encouraged me. Of course it was impossible not to be nervous: each time I stood on stage, I felt like a soldier in armor on the battlefield, and survival was my main concern. The translation of literature requires an even higher level of ability. Later I would promote several plans for the translation of Chinese books into foreign languages, an even greater challenge.

THE PALACE MUSEUM IN BEIGOU

It wasn't something I had expected to do, but while teaching at Chung-Hsing University, I also ended up moonlighting for six years at the Palace

Museum, which was then located in Beigou in Wufeng Township, Taichung County.

The phone rang shortly after the Lunar New Year, 1959. It was Li Ziyu, who was ahead of me at Wuhan University, and now in charge of the Palace Museum. The museum was in desperate need of a secretary and, flipping through the alumni directory, they found that I was a foreign-language graduate living in Taichung and that I had just returned from advanced studies in the Fulbright Program, so I seemed to be the best choice.

In those days, in addition to teaching, I had three children in primary school and kindergarten, so how could I go and work at Beigou? Li Ziyu said all I had to do was translate Chinese and English (in both directions) and that official documents would be delivered to my house and picked up when I was finished, so there was no need for me to go to Beigou. The tone of his voice sounded more like a command than a discussion, and the way the work was to be handled had been settled, so there was no reason for me to refuse.

The job was eye-opening. In order to translate each document, I had to ask experts such as Zhuang Yan, Tan Danjiong, and Na Zhiliang, among others, my art-related questions. I researched pertinent writings, took notes, asked them all sorts of questions, and without expecting to, learned all sorts of things. To have a better grasp of the materials, I remember as if it were yesterday holding my youngest while memorizing the names of famous kilns and their distinguishing qualities.

In addition to translating materials, I sometimes had to serve as interpreter when heads of state visited the museum. The two most memorable occasions were when Foreign Minister George Kung-chao Yeh accompanied the Shah of Iran and the King of Thailand. Meeting them in person left an indelible impression.

Mr. Yeh was of the generation of my teachers. Without turning to look at me directly, he would ask as if testing me, "What is that called in English?" Given his personality, I didn't dare delay and would answer him immediately. There was also Kong Decheng, but I learned the most from Zhuang Yan, the most senior of them all.

The Shah of Iran, Mohammad Reza Pahlavi, was tall and handsome, and his imperial majesty was combined with the elegance of a modern gentleman. He was nothing short of the king on a white horse in fairy tales.

I looked upon him with something akin to adoration and took notice of any stories about him in the news. I'd like to look at a few books to see how he is judged by history. I feel deeply honored when I think of how I served to explain things to him at the Palace Museum. I still remember that day and how he closely examined the bronzes and porcelain. As he proceeded, he noticed that everyone there was a man and was afraid I would be ignored, so he made a point of frequently speaking to me. While looking at the porcelain, he commented to me, "In my palace there are a number of pieces of porcelain like these, but not as good." He also asked me, "Are there many young ladies like you in Taiwan who work?" I replied, "Probably quite a few." Actually, I had no idea, but I thought my answer sounded better. Iran is an Islamic country, so he probably had some difficulty imaging a working woman.

Mohammad Pahlavi was a wise ruler, not a tyrant. When I was studying in the United States in 1968, I read a headline that said: "He Did Not Want to Be the King of Beggars," under which was a photo of him in his crown. He had waited more than ten years before being officially crowned, because he wanted to wait until Iran became a country without beggars; therefore, it happened only after the success of the economic reforms. The news made a deep impression on me. Never did I expect that the years of nation building would actually end in a coup, with the shah being forced to flee to France, where shortly thereafter he sadly died, an exile from his homeland.

That evening, returning to my ordinary home, putting on the clothes I wore there, and cooking dinner on a large coal cake, I could still see the shah's majestic and elegant figure in the smoke. I suddenly thought of the story of Cinderella and wondered if the old car that had taken me home had become a pumpkin.

In a short period of time, the Palace Museum received a number of important guests. Later the King and Queen of Thailand arrived. King Hussein of Jordan, a number of presidents and vice presidents, but even more importantly, a host of art historians from the major museums and universities of Europe arrived at Beigou. All that glory and splendor along with the country road from Wufeng to Beigou often made me think of the palace in Beijing and the vastness of China's rivers and mountains.

Hu Shi frequently came to the Palace Museum, and would stay in the guest house a few nights to escape the busy world and do a little work in peace and quiet. The year before he died, the museum held a banquet for him and I too was invited, probably because of my father.

That evening they talked about collecting antiquarian books. Hu Shi also talked to me a little about modern literature. I remember he said, "A woman writer recently sent me a book and asked for my opinion. I also received Jiang Gui's *Whirlwind*. There is no comparison, the woman writer's book can't hold a candle to Jiang Gui's; she just can't write on the same epic scale." His words had some impact on me, for in 1968 when I was studying in the United States, I took two courses on epic literature, to understand precisely what it is. He also said his own work fell somewhere between literary and historical research, and that he used literary techniques to express himself. He said, "But don't feelings consist of only joy, anger, sorrow, and delight? Also there is depth, which is a difficult thing to talk about, but you know it when you see it. If you have it, you have it; if you don't, then you don't; but it can be cultivated." His words were enlightening. Hu Shi understood my father's situation and respected him and so sometimes had something to say. Later, when I taught or lectured, I felt that style, emotional appeal, and depth were all essential to literature, but impossible to expound.

While working at the Palace Museum, there was a spell when I thought I'd like to study art history with these scholars and learn another academic discipline. Considering it later, I knew I had insufficient background and that I liked nothing more than talking about literature, so I went back to teaching and planning for advanced study.

In 1965, the Palace Museum moved to Shuangxi outside of Taipei. I would visit on occasion because I still knew quite a few people, until they passed away, one by one.

BROADENING AND DEVELOPING MY TEACHING

In 1967, Yuchang was notified that he was being transferred to headquarters and that he would be in charge of research on railroad electrification in preparation for implementation, so as a result the whole family moved to Taipei.

At the beginning of the year, I received a letter from the prestigious American Council of Learned Societies via the USIS, which said that they were just starting to offer two large scholarships for advanced study to people in the humanities from Taiwan. Among the requirements was that the scholarships were only open to those under forty-five years of age. I would be forty-four that year and had entered middle age. When it came to advanced studies, I had missed out on ten years without even being aware of it! For many years my father had told me on more than one occasion that it was unfortunate that I would spend my entire life as a mere teacher. He seemed to have forgotten that after I graduated, he had been opposed to me going abroad to study during wartime, despite the fact that I had been accepted by Mount Holyoke College. He was afraid that we would lose contact, and even more fearful that I'd become an eccentric bookworm and delay getting married. In that ten-year period, the school had received a number of notifications about international exchanges, but my husband was busy and exhausted and we had three small children, and so I never dared look at them, much less consider them. But now I realized that forty-five was the age limit for such funding. Since we were moving to Taipei, we could move someplace close to my parents to make it easy for my mother to help out. If I wanted to continue teaching at the university level and not be left out, then this was my last chance.

My application made it through the first round, but I had to be in New York prior to August 30 for an interview before a final decision could be made. I also applied to the Fulbright Program for travel funds and money for books, which meant yet another interview by committee. One of the Fulbright committee members was C. T. Hsia, who had just come from Columbia University to visit Taiwan. He asked me my opinion of T. S. Eliot's dramas. By coincidence, the previous summer I had read his three dramas *Murder in the Cathedral*, *The Family Reunion*, and *The Cocktail Party*, so I did have something to say. That summer our two older boys were preparing for the first and second year of high school, and the youngest tested into his first choice of Da'an Junior High School. (I thought everything had been settled, but looking back now, I see how naïve I was.) Chung-Hsing University arranged for me to receive sabbatical pay for one year so that I would be eligible for the scholarship. However, upon completion of my course of study, I had to return to the school and teach for three years. That summer, the Ministry of Education authorized my promotion to regular professor. Twenty years after arriving in Taiwan, I was still struggling to obtain a degree to establish myself in academia!

That July was unforgettably hot. Our family of five had to give up our cats, but kept one dog when we moved from our spacious Japanese-style house with a big yard to a tiny apartment on Jinhua Street rented by the Taiwan Railways Administration. It felt as if we had been squeezed into a steam pipe (there was no air conditioning in those days). The three boys lost their space to spread out and grew constantly annoyed and impatient. And right after getting settled, I was immediately going to set off across the sea for an "academic ideal," something they didn't understand then and perhaps still cannot understand and forgive even today! Many years later, all I can remember is the unease of that ordeal and being unable to see the stars on that awful summer night.

SAINT MARY OF THE WOODS

Per the ticket with which I was provided, I boarded a Northwest Airlines flight on August 30 and more than twenty hours later arrived in New York via Anchorage and Seattle. A friend in the USIS in Taipei had reserved a hotel room for me in New York and had reassured me that the cabs there were among the safest and most reliable in the world. The following morning (the last day for the interviews) I headed over to the Council of Learned Societies for my interview. Later they sent me a letter at my sister's house informing me that they couldn't support my plan for obtaining an advanced degree. Thereupon I decided to go to Saint Mary-of-the-Woods College in Terre Haute, Indiana, west of Indianapolis.

The world works in mysterious ways. That year I had gone to teach at Providence University, where I met the English teacher, Sister Mary Gregory, and Jeanne Knoe, a Fulbright Exchange Scholar. Sister Mary Gregory knew of my plans to go abroad and had encouraged me to study at Indiana University, where she had obtained her Ph.D. three years earlier. At that time, the Department of Comparative Literature at IU was the first and strongest in the United States. Masters of comparative literature theory of German descent, Ramak, Nina Weinstein, Horst Frenze, and Newton P. Stalknecht, all taught brilliant classes that, chances permitting, were not to be missed. She also loaned me several books on the topic. She was the first to do a Ph.D. in English on *Dream of the Red Chamber.* At the end of April 1967, she knew that I had not yet decided on where to teach for my Fulbright, so she invited me to Saint Mary in-the-Woods College, the school that had founded Providence University, to teach a course on Chinese literature and another on a specific topic of my choosing. The school was only seventy miles from Indiana University, so while teaching, I could prepare to register to take classes at IU and study both English and comparative literature. For me, this unexpected invitation was a compassionate arrangement made by the Good Lord.

Saint Mary of-the-Woods was a Catholic order in the United States, with the convent situated on three thousand acres of forested land in Indiana. The female college was founded in 1940 and was a famous and prestigious school in the area.

Ten years earlier, I had learned about America, a vast land rich in resources; this time, in a small school, I felt the actual strength of the land even more. That endless green forest was nothing less than a Shangri-la! To the right was a pear orchard, to the left an apple orchard. The apples ripened starting in October, but they seemed to go unpicked, and so they fell into the grass, making it look as if it were covered with red flowers. The first time we saw this, we cried aloud, bent over, and pick up the biggest red apple we could find. Later we learned this was just a drop in the bucket. The people who picked the fruit drove small trucks, their tires rolling over the fresh red of millions of apples. Each year when the longan tree in my small garden in Taichung bore fruit, the neighborhood kids would get a long bamboo pole, cut a fork in the end, and then reach over the wall to pick the fruit. My sons would rush out shouting and scatter the children. Everyone was very excited, and it became an annual autumn ritual. When I saw the tires soaked with apple juice, I wondered what the kids would have thought had they seen the apple orchard.

One evening shortly after arriving, I noticed that the forest beyond the cafeteria window was edged with maple red and that the light mist rising from the forest was illumined by the setting sun. It was like some marvelous world captured in a traditional Chinese landscape painting. I left the cafeteria with Han Yunmei, a student from Providence University in Taiwan, hoping to get a closer look at the maples. As we were admiring the scene, a police car pulled up and took us back to the dorm. I asked them how they could not pause and enjoy such a beautiful scene. Frowning, the head of the campus police replied that the forest was huge and it was their responsibility to protect the girls and see that they did not wander off and get lost.

Even more memorable things occurred when you went from the enchanting forest into the college. One of the most amazing things to me was the status of my friend Sister Mary Gregory.

I've always been somewhat obtuse when it comes to official positions. In Taichung, when she invited me to come to her school and teach, she held an umbrella while Sister Frances, who was in charge of Providence University, vigorously offered her support. I thought it had to do with her authority and the way she did things. What she said carried weight. But Sister Mary Gregory was a friend with whom I discussed literature, merely the person who extended the invitation. In September, I flew from New York to Indianapolis and then took a Greyhound bus to Terre Haute. She had dispatched Miss Hu Hongrui, who worked in the library, to meet me at the bus station. Seeing me worn out from traveling and carrying a suitcase, she rushed over, gave me a welcoming hug, put my suitcase in the car, and then drove the thirty minutes or so to the woods. The campus was not big, but the large red brick buildings were imposing. A short distance away was a small courtyard and the small, pale green building of the teachers' quarters where I would live comfortably for a year. She carried my suitcase and led me into a cozy suite. She suggested that I rest a bit and she would have Miss Hu (Janet) take me to the dining hall at six.

The dining hall, which was situated deep among some trees, was high-ceilinged and spacious, capable of seating the nearly one thousand students and teachers. The area in front of an altar to Saint Mary holding the sacred child was reserved for the faculty, and also served as the site for administrative meetings. Here I was able to get a good picture of the changes in a Catholic religious order in the 1960s, the debates in the process as well as the conflicts and pain.

Upon entering the dining hall, we sat in the second row of long tables. Dinner was quite formal. An elderly nun, after leading everyone in a prayer of thanks, said to all assembled, "The school president shall now introduce a new teacher."

At that moment, I witnessed my friend Sister Mary Gregory rise from the center seat and motion me to come forward, where she introduced me to everyone. I'm sure I was confused and tongue-tied, not knowing what best to say, because I had no idea that after she left Taichung, she returned to the United States to serve as school president (the former president had signed my letter of appointment). No one had informed me of this before arriving at the dining hall, nor had she mentioned anything in our talks and communications. Inviting me to teach a course on Chinese literature was part of her "new administration."

I thoroughly discussed the course content and materials with her, making sure they were of the appropriate level, so as to avoid any difficulties for either one of us. About twenty students signed up for the course, which was considered a good number. Shortly after I started teaching, an Asian cultural exhibition was held, which added more depth to the literature class. As for my daily life, Sister Mary Gregory looked after all the details. Miss Hu Hongrui was a fine Chinese cook and the new school president, a Korean student by the name of Chong Yeong-hye (later I learned she was the daughter of Chong Il-kwon, the Korean prime minister) along with two Chinese nuns (one of whom, Cai Yingyun, has worked at Providence since returning home) were often our honored guests. She also located several Indiana University teachers who drove regularly to the Bloomington campus and could take me with them, but arranging times wasn't particularly easy. There was no regular bus service between Terre Haute and Bloomington. For Americans, driving seventy miles is nothing, but for me it was seemingly an insurmountable obstacle. When I visited Professor Horst Frenz, chair of the comparative literature program, I mentioned my difficulties. I returned to the woods with a course listing, accepting my fate and deciding to focus on teaching and see about taking classes the following semester.

Those four months were the beginning of a lifetime of systematic reading. Saint Mary of-the-Woods College took a professional attitude toward scholastics and was not focused on just producing refined young ladies. Although the library was not large, it was of high quality with a substantial collection. For my course, I read all the books in the library on Chinese literature and looked over their holdings in modern Chinese literature, which included a few volumes by Lu Xun, *Spring Silkworms* by Mao Dun, *Family* by Ba Jin, *Camel Xiangzi* and *City of the Cats* by Lao She, as well as Communist works such as *The Golden Road*, but nothing from Taiwan. Of course in those days, nothing from Taiwan had been translated into English—this also planted a seed in me that would become my later avowed aspiration to see Taiwan literature translated into English. I also unexpectedly witnessed the process of "modernization" of the form and content of the Catholic nuns' system.

After lunch, three days after my arrival in the woods, the nuns cast a historic vote in which they decided to get rid of the habit. After the vote, there was a debate full of sound and fury, and the group of young nuns who had advocated getting rid of the habit was victorious, with some even whooping for joy, while the older conservative faction was visibly saddened and angry. A few days later, it was decided to raise the hemlines to three inches below the knee. Soon nuns in the new habits were seen walking briskly around the campus, their unchanging faces even more serious looking. Additionally, the rules governing their lives in the convent were relaxed quite a bit. The following summer, many young nuns left the order and returned to secular life. Western culture and religion are closely related, and I was fortunate to witness the shift in form and content up close; as someone from an ancient culture, I found it emotionally exciting. I also made a number of lifelong friends from a Catholic order with whom I can share knowledge and ideas, as well as real life. A year later, I would return to the woods from Indiana University to teach another semester, feeling much like I was returning home.

BLOOMINGTON

Since there was no way to overcome the transportation issue of that difficult seventy miles, I quit my teaching job at the beginning of January 1968 and went to Indiana University in Bloomington, where I registered for classes and concentrated on my studies. When I was in Taipei to apply for my visa before going abroad, I ran into Guo Zhichao, a student of mine who was teaching translation at Tunghai University. Coincidently, he too was going to Indiana University to study, so he knew I was first going to Saint Mary of-the-Woods College to teach. Later, he helped arrange dorm housing for me in the married student quarters, owing to my age and status as a scholar. When I moved in during that cold month of January, I saw a note in Chinese tacked to my door that read: "Teacher Chi, we are friends of Guo Zhichao's. He is away today, so we will come see you at eleven o'clock. From Xu Xiaohua and Cai Zhongxiong." Once inside, I looked out the large window and saw two young Chinese men in their twenties carrying a large basket, trudging over the snow-covered hill toward my place. These two young men, who became lifelong friends, were carrying a basket filled with pots and pans, bowls, cups, a teakettle, cans, and jars, as well as curtains—everything a person could possibly need.

My single dorm room had a large window. A lawn extended from my window to the foot of the hill. There were always a number of birds with red breasts about the size of pigeons that walked there. I was told they were robins, but from my readings of English literature I thought robins were small, intelligent birds. Perhaps the grain in the American Midwest had caused them to grow so large, making it difficult for them to fly.

1968 was the most exhausting year of my life, but also the most enriching. From January 8 onward, anyone coming across that grassy slope would see me sitting at the window, hunched over a book or typing. I knew better than anyone that each day was stolen from my dual occupations of wife and mother! In one semester and during the summer session, I took six classes: Comparative Literature and Theory and Background and Development of Western Literature were required courses, while Literature and Modern Philosophy, Literature and Culture, Western Literature Before the Seventeenth Century, and American Literature: The Age of Emerson were my elective courses.

Professor Mueller taught Literature and Culture and spent half the time in class asking "Why?" in order to push the students into pondering the deeper significance of a book. For example, what cultural changes are evident through Thomas Mann's *The Magic Mountain*, which rewrites the theme of Goethe's *Faust*? His method substantially influenced my own teaching. In American Literature it was through Emerson's "self-reliance" that contact was made with everything of a higher existence, which propelled American literature to a higher realm. He spoke fully, accurately, and movingly. I was always prepared for class and took in every word. That was a precious time of seeking knowledge; the only other time I had experienced it was at Leshan during the war, but now I was mature and calm; I knew what I wanted and strived for it each and every day. The literature classes at Indiana were among the best in the United States, so I was extremely attentive in class, taking copious notes, and always felt that a fifty-minute class was too short.

There were more than twenty students speaking more than five languages in Western Literature Before the Seventeenth Century. Under that sort of competitive pressure, we were mutually consoling. One big-bearded Russian classmate, who was an expert in French, German, and Latin, was envied and referred to as "the monster" by students and teachers alike. One time, he asked Professor Gross Louis, who had recently received his Ph.D. from Harvard, who King Alfred was. This was as embarrassing as a Chinese person asking who Qin Shihuang was. The classmates from other countries sitting next to him nearly pushed him off his seat and onto the floor.

Not only were the class discussions invaluable, so were the lists of reference works, some just a few pages, others as long as eighty pages. After I returned to Taiwan these lists were invaluable teaching resources. This was especially true in the case of The Background and Development of Western Literature. The teacher was a big-name professor from the English department. He had a white beard and made everyone feel secure. His class, which was full, was held in a large lecture hall. In three months' time he provided a framework, a structure for the comprehensive development of my somewhat random knowledge and thoughts. From then on, my studies were more systematic. He also awakened in me my lifelong love of studying epic poetry and utopian literature. Go to the fountainhead first, and then proceed.

Before the semester ended on May 20, I spent day and night at the typewriter, churning out three reports. After an exam, I went home and fell into bed and slept soundly until around midnight. When I awoke, a bright moon hung in the sky, which made me think of a scene in *Dream of the Red Chamber* when Bao Yu awakens to see the same sort of moon. I, a modern woman, feeling guilty about leaving my family, living in a small room on campus in a foreign land, could not really feel at ease with myself. I got up and in tears wrote a letter to my parents, telling them of my sadness (my parents were nearly seventy, and I don't know why I had to burden them even more!). The next day, I walked down the hill and dropped the letter in the mailbox and started back, but about halfway up the hill, I couldn't take another step. I sat down on the grass, my head lowered, and cried for some time. At the time, the poem "A Moonlit Night on a Spring River" was swirling in my mind: "Last night he dreamed that falling flowers would not stay, Alas! He can't go home, although half of spring is gone." At that very moment, my young friend

Cai Zhongxiong and Mr. and Mrs. Xing Ji drove by. They picked me up and drove to behind Ballantine Hall. The road was lined with Chinese mahogany trees in full bloom, with red and white flowering trees alternating, growing densely but uncrowded, with each limb spread beautifully in quiet elegance. It was a poetic dreamland.

A few days later, I went to the department office to pick up my report card. I received an A in four classes and an A- in one class, for a 4.0 GPA. I asked my other young friend Xu Xiaohua, who had just received his Ph.D. in physics, what the 4.0 meant. He replied straight A's, to the honor of the Chinese! I replied that it was a rather tardy honor, and that just having begun their lives, they couldn't understand how much it had cost for me to study a little so late in life. During the summer session, famous teachers from all over arrived. As usual, I took three difficult courses. Bearing the guilt of leaving home and having such a precious opportunity, I didn't want to waste a day.

During that period of hard study, my world was limited to the sight of the ever-changing clouds in the sky outside my window. News from Taiwan arrived in letters from home and the *Central Daily News* a week late. That humble room in Bloomington was the closest thing to heaven in my life.

My social circle at that time was limited to a few Chinese students and their families. There were about three hundred Chinese students at IU at the time, 90 percent from Taiwan and the other 10 percent from Hong Kong and Southeast Asia. There were no students from mainland China, as the nightmare of the Cultural Revolution had just started. The political situation in Taiwan had not yet devolved into the division between the Taiwanese and outsiders from other provinces, and everyone was a little simpler and looked after one another. Those leaving would place usable household goods into cardboard boxes, which would be given to new students at the beginning of the next semester. Outside of Bloomington were a number of small lakes surrounded by trees, and I was often invited to go along by those driving there. One time, in order to make a match between Yang Qiaoxia and Zeng Ye, who had once lived with me, six carloads of us went out to one of the lakes to "view the moon" and sing Chinese songs. It was very late and we were dispersed by the police. On a number of occasions, I went by car with Xu Xiaohua, Cai Zhongxiong, Hu Yaoheng, and others to Chicago, Ohio, and Iowa. On those trips, I came to experience the vast breadbasket of the American Midwest, which made me yearn for the endless expanse of fertile land that was the homeland of my forefathers.

Indiana University's famous library and the bookstore were two places I frequented. At the Asian Library, I met Professor Teng Ssu-yu (1906–1988), a respected expert on the modern history of China. His works in English, including *Historiography of the Taiping Rebellion*; *New Light on the History of the Taiping Rebellion*; and *Hung Jen-kan, Prime Minister of the Taiping Kingdom and His Modernization Plans*, were all published by Harvard University and were required reading for all Western sinologists. Professor Teng was from Hunan, and although he had come to America years earlier and had a family and career there, he was deeply concerned about China's difficulties, about which we had a lot of conversation. When he retired, the university held a large banquet for him and he invited me to sit at his table. During the event, a letter from John King Fairbank was read in which he stated that when he had just arrived at Harvard for graduate study, Professor Teng had offered him all sorts of guidance and that he would be eternally grateful to such a model Chinese scholar.

My simple, pleasant life of study came to an end during the winter break of 1968. When I had applied for my Fulbright, one of the requirements had been that I had to teach and that the valid period was for one year; I could not extend my stay to obtain a degree. I had applied for a six-month extension, so I had to first return to Saint Mary in-the-Woods College and teach another semester. In that semester I matriculated at Terre Haute State University, where I took Sixteenth- and Seventeenth-Century English Literature taught by Professor Mullen, an expert on Spenser. Another very enriching class for my future research was Literary Criticism. Indiana University accepted the six credits and I returned to Bloomington for my M.A. qualifying exam, which I passed. All I needed was six units of French and I would have my M.A., but I never had the opportunity to go back and finish the degree.

When my exchange scholar visa ran out, I was still vacillating as to whether I should apply for another six-month extension. Then I received a letter from my father in which he said that Yuchang's heavy workload was taking a toll and that my family badly needed me. The legal limit for my stay was at an end, and promises had to be kept.

In Genesis, Jacob dreams of a stairway to heaven. At Indiana University in Bloomington from spring flowers to winter snow, I too had dreamed of my academic stairway, with angels ascending and descending. But just as I placed my foot on the first step, the stairway was withdrawn, which provided me with regrets for many years; I was only able to accept my fate after many a realization and wisdom acquired that the world is not necessarily without an academic stairway or angels. Although I was summoned back by reality, by no means did I fall from the stairway. I finally understood that throughout my life, beginning with my sickly childhood, I had been building a stone stairway, book by book, climbing upward with every word and sentence I read, and that I would never stop.

THE DREAM I BUILT BECOMES A REALITY

A myriad flowers fell and the stairway disappeared. I returned to Chung-Hsing University in Taichung to resume the three years of teaching required by my contract. My husband and sons were in Taipei, so every Tuesday I would take the 7 a.m. train to Taichung, and every Friday I'd take the 6 p.m. train to Taipei. On Saturdays, I'd teach advanced English at the graduate school of National Taiwan University. Two days a week I'd vigorously play the role of housewife with the help of a female servant. We lived across from my parents, so everything was just a call away. But my parents were already in their seventies and my three sons were already young men. I'd get up at 5 a.m. every Tuesday and prepare breakfast for the family and then rush off to catch my train, my mind full of anxieties. Sometimes the waning moon would still be hanging in the sky when I left the house. I'd look back three times every step of the way—at first just to keep my promise, but gradually, I'd return to Taipei filled with anxieties about my responsibilities at work in Taichung.

The establishment of the Department of Foreign Languages and Literatures at Chung-Hsing University was the fulfillment of a dream of many years. With all the power I could muster as one teacher, I had pushed for this under three school presidents—Lin Zhiping, Tang Huisun, and Liu Daoyuan. Because Chung-Hsing was the sole national university in the central part of the island, a school of liberal arts was essential. Once the school was established, the departments of Chinese and history were the first to be set up. Finding highly qualified faculty was the biggest problem for a department of foreign languages and literatures. There were few such qualified teachers in Taiwan at that time, and Ph.D.s in English and American literature were worth their weight in gold. Gradually, a few who had completed their studies began to return, but they were immediately snapped up by National Taiwan University, the Normal University, Zhengzhi University, Danjiang University, and Fu Jen University, all located in Taipei. The degree holders were unwilling to go to other cities. In Taichung, Providence and Tunghai universities had faculty available to them through their religious orders, while national universities had stricter standards. This problem was precisely where ideal and reality most diverged. In all those years of talking about the importance of liberal arts education, I had never anticipated this problem.

When I returned to Chung-Hsing University at the start of the spring semester in 1969, I discovered that I had been presented as the new chairperson of the Department of Foreign Languages and Literatures. Not only that, but the first class of forty-five students had been admitted and had already completed one semester. The administrative work for the department had been handled by the dean in addition to his other duties. The curriculum had been established as required by the Ministry of Education, with nearly all common core courses, with combined elective courses being offered by all departments. Courses in logic and literature were not offered until the second semester. The first time I entered the school president's office after returning from abroad,

I understood that the two letters I had written from the States in which I had truthfully informed them that I had not obtained a degree, that I didn't know anything about running a department and was not ready to do so, and that I was only suited to be a literature teacher were understood by the school president and the dean (there was no dean of the school of liberal arts at that time) as mere politeness on my part. I had been promoted to regular professor and was certified as such by the Ministry of Education, and had been lobbying vigorously for a department of foreign languages and literatures for years. The message was, now that the department "has been established for you" and the teachers (six teachers teaching first-year English, French, and German, half of whom were over sixty) have been waiting for you for six months, who is going to run the department if you don't?

As I was coming out of the president's office, Dean Wang Tianming, seeing the look of trepidation on my face, said, "I believe you are capable. Feel free to come and discuss any issues of official business with me. We have conservative expectations for the department chairs, so in the future please don't wear such flowery dresses." Short skirts were in fashion in those days, but I had neither long nor short skirts. I always wore a loose-fitting *qipao*.

In that way I went from being a hardworking bookworm to department chair, who faced nothing but real problems. Luckily, the students who came to us via the National College Entrance Exams were all pretty good. This was in the days before National Sun Yat-sen University and National Chung Cheng University, and only four of the national universities had departments of foreign languages and literatures. Moreover, acceptable scores for departments of foreign languages had to be higher, so the quality of the students was on the whole quite good, and later in life they performed above the average.

In the three and a half years that I served as department chair, the biggest torment was faculty appointments. New hires Shi Zhaoxi, Xu Jingtian, and the young Zhang Hanliang, all confirmed by my "discerning eye," were all well liked by the students. Those who had been teaching in the department, including Ding Zhenwan, Yao Chongkun, Sun Zhixuan, Tang Zhenxun, and Xiao Kunfeng, all worked together strenuously.

The department possessed a harmonious centripetal force: anyone arriving at the two rooms of our small office on the second floor would inevitably hear the sound of laughter. The door to my office was always open, and teachers and students came and went with smiles on their faces.

The first class of students was divided equally between young women and men. Shortly after I took charge, the young women held a welcoming ceremony for me in the dorm, with several plates of crispy cookies and soft drinks. They had planned no entertainment such as singing, but simply surrounded me and asked lots of questions. They said they were happy to have tested and been admitted to the department, but after one semester, they still weren't sure what they were going to be studying. They felt the courses had been much like those in high school, including Chinese, English, and modern history, the only difference being that the teachers were a bit older. This meeting established our way of direct communication. I accompanied those forty students every step of the way from their initial confusion through the pressures of their workload over the next three years. I had a moral duty of one who was building a dream of taking that department from nothing and making something out of it. I possessed a loving motherly concern for those nineteen- and twenty-year-olds, who were in search of their dreams.

My greatest moral duty for the new department was to establish its academic standards. In the first year, the Taichung USIS donated our first books, largely because of my relationship with them, having borrowed books for years as well as having been a Fulbright scholar twice. Ding Zhenwan also borrowed several paintings by her husband, Chen Qimao, and suddenly our empty office was transformed into something with culture.

USIS advised me that the U.S. State Department's Embassy School in Taichung had a number of students with M.A. degrees in English and that the wives of some of the Americans stationed at the Qingquangang Air Base at Shuinan in Taichung were qualified teachers. That was during the Vietnam War and there were quite a number of civilian medical and communications personnel, many of whom might have spouses who were qualified to teach at a public university. Having these two sources, the following year I divided the second-year class into four sections and offered English conversation classes as required by the Ministry of Education. I was able to get four students from the Embassy School to teach two hours each week, and in the following two years I had six or seven of them. They fit in well both in class and in extracurricular activities. Our students were simple and sincere and invited their teachers on extracurricular field trips outside of town; some even invited their teachers to their homes for a meal, allowing them to gain a deeper understanding of the lives of the Taiwanese. I was also able to get the wife of a doctor to teach Shakespeare and a communications officer to teach a class on fiction. Not only were they qualified, but they also had experience, and the class content was of the hoped-for quality; thus I was able to get through those early difficulties. I taught the history of English literature, and in the second year I was able to get Professor Peter Shay from Tunghai University to come and teach English poetry. He was from England and taught the best class on English poetry at Tunghai. Our students were inspired by his natural depth and charm, which was different from the other faculty members.

In the early days of the department, our basic faculty consisted of the teachers who taught the common courses in English, French, and German. Miss Tilford and Mary Sampson, who taught first-year English, had been with us since the days of the Agricultural College. They were both conservative Southern Baptist missionaries, their church being located behind a row of flame trees outside the school gate. We had been on extremely friendly terms for years, but they did not approve of the "radical" course content of some of the younger teachers. The first-year English textbook that I edited was used instead of the one published by Young Lion Company, for which I was censured by some of the really "old" professors. However, having just returned from studying abroad, I had done a good deal of research on basic teaching materials for English and American literature, had collected numerous examples, and knew that the students couldn't go on using the same old standard selections, requiring instead new pieces from all cultural fields of the postwar period. Fortunately I received lots of support, including from the students. The first-year curriculum included the course An Outline of Western Literature, taught by William Burke of our department. He was a Presbyterian missionary with fairly progressive ideas who was widely supported by the students. That year we coedited a textbook to fill the void we had been facing. Gu Baohu and Wang Yongqing (principal of the Weidao Middle School), who taught French, were both Catholic priests; both had high scholastic attainments in French and were hard-working teachers. The first-year Chinese teacher was Chen Guimiao, and the first composition topic he gave the students was "Clusters of Sunshine for You." The students who had just graduated from high school and taken the National College Entrance Exams had never encountered the like! Thirty years later he was still a great talker. I had him teach first-year Chinese until he went to Taipei and became involved in politics, running for the Legislative Yuan, with many students as his enthusiastic supporters. Another memorable teacher was Zeng Xiang-duo, who taught A General History of China. His open-minded and critical perspective on contemporary history was quite inspiring. Later, during politically troubled times, he ended up in jail and after being released, he hosted a political talk show. I ran into him in Taipei and I didn't know what to say or how to begin.

In the fall of 1970 after the start of classes, I made plans for convening the first Symposium on Teaching English and American Literature at Chung-Hsing University. Such conferences were very rare at the time; in fact, there were few academic conferences at all in those days, and even fewer in Taichung. I sincerely hoped to have the opportunity to increase educational exchanges among schools, to help out the schools other than National Taiwan University. In all of Taiwan only four universities had departments of foreign languages and literatures, but that major was the first choice among humanities students. However, there were not enough teachers, and teaching materials badly needed updating in response to the times. About thirty people who taught literature courses came from all over the province, with Zhu Limin and Yan Yuanshu from National Taiwan University being the stars of the conference. With a limited number of participants, everyone talked to their heart's content. That small new department of mine was busy for some time, and the happy enthusiasm of that early event was something rarely encountered in future conferences.

Inside and outside of class, we were busy all the way until the summer of 1972, when the first class of students from Chung-Hsing University's Department of Foreign Languages and Literatures graduated. What came as a surprise to the whole school was that I quit. As required by my contract, I had taught three full years. I was far from willing to abandon the department that I had promoted, effected, set up, and headed; it seemed that every little thing bespoke the sadness of parting. After arriving in Taichung, I lived there for twenty years (the whole family lived there for seventeen, while I commuted back and forth for three years), and my most settled years were spent there. But there I was, seeing that promising tree finally beginning to bear fruit, and I had to leave! At the farewell dinner, all the students held candles and circled me, everyone in tears. No one knew that I, who had always been so active and so full of vitality, was feeling helpless and confused in the face of an entirely unknown future.

The students of that class, all of whom were about twenty-two years old, were just beginning their lives. For four years each one had been like my own child; I had looked after them and guided them to reach the appropriate level in their studies and become self-confident and clear-minded in character. Many of them later became hardworking teachers. Most of the young men entered professions such as trade and became successful. And today, twenty years later, we often see each other or write. The members of the whole class are like siblings to one another, and they still look upon me with the same affection as all those years ago.

Riding around campus on my bicycle those last few months, I was reluctant to part with everything I saw, for everywhere I looked bore the traces of my youth. In bidding farewell to Chung-Hsing University, I also bade farewell to the first half of my life, a life that had been simple those seventeen years in Taichung, and also filled with human warmth. With my own eyes I had seen the name plaque of the agricultural college at the gate replaced with that of National Chung-Hsing University. I had also watched as buildings sprang up over the largely empty campus. When the Department of Foreign Languages and Literatures was first set up, all the classrooms had to be borrowed from other departments. The "base" for first-year classes consisted of two brick buildings with a small courtyard and a large tree, the earliest use for which was as classrooms for training people in a government aid program for agriculture in Africa. The second-year classrooms were borrowed from the Department of Animal Husbandry, which stood right next to the pasture. One day, as I was talking about *Beowulf* in the class on the history of English literature, a lovely calf wandered into the classroom. It was as startled as we were; fortunately, no one shouted. Finally, with some difficulty, it managed to turn around and leave through the door by which it had entered. Later, the head of the Animal Husbandry Department told me that it was an Angus calf that had recently been imported to upgrade Taiwan's agricultural output and that since I had taught it about literature, both of us should be deeply honored.

Actually, from the time of the agricultural college, all the departments treated me well, mainly because after I offered second-year English, my classes were always full. In the 1960s, academic research on agriculture was already quite modernized, being one of the vanguards of Taiwan's development, so the departments all encouraged the students to go abroad and study. The Graduate School of Agricultural Economics, which was very impressive, was headed by Li Qinglin, who was a member of the Legislative Yuan. He sent all his grad students to take my class and, with the tone of a father's friend, he ordered me to give them more composition assignments so as to further correct their English. He probably wanted most of them to go to the States for professional degrees, so that upon returning they could make real contributions.

In the 1960s, many graduates set up modern farms in the central part of the island and on the Jianan Plains, and often sought "guidance" from their teachers. Professor Liu Zuoyan, the wife of Song Miannan, the college president, and I were English-teaching colleagues. We were often invited along. At the time, a number of foreign exchange professors were living in the dorms on campus, and they too often went along to visit the countryside. During those years, we went to many out-of-the-way places deep in the mountains, and from the mountains to the sea. We really got to know Taiwan and saw how higher education on the island took root and prospered during that period of collective and concerted effort. One frequent destination where we took our foreign friends was a rose nursery in Yuanlin. The wife of Zhang Zhun, the nursery owner, was later elected Rose Queen. Upon first seeing such a large operation using scientific breeding methods, hearing the names of their new hybrids and about their hopes for large-scale export, no one would ask a superficial question like "Do you love Taiwan?"

I'll never forget the beginning of winter 1966, just after midterm exams. I suddenly heard the news that Tang Huisun, the president of the college, had died while climbing a mountain on an inspection trip of the experimental forest run by the forestry department of Ren'ai Township in Nantou County. While climbing, he had a heart attack and died on the forest floor, supported by Director Song. Forty years later, each time I hear of Huisun Forest being a tourist destination, I can't help but think about him and Director Song and those other warm, scholarly, and refined early pioneers. I also think of Yu Yuxian, the first director of Taiwan's Agricultural Commission. When I first started teaching, he was a lecturer in the Department of Agricultural Economics, and he married Ji Chunyu, one of my first students. When they were fighting for Taiwan agriculture, they would talk to me about their idea of an army of one hundred thousand farmers, and about the names of their improved fruit cultivars such as Sweet Miss Star Fruit, Yang Guifei Lichee, and Immortal Grapes, as well as share the joys of their foundational work with me. When I see a lovely tree-lined street, I also think about how he died at fifty-eight, after a three-year bout with cancer, his last wish being to be able to see the trees outside his window.

At Christmas in 1968, while I was in America pursuing advanced study, I received a Greyhound Bus ticket from A. B. Lewis, a visiting professor at Providence College of Agriculture, and his wife. Mrs. Lewis's father had been a missionary in China at the end of the Qing dynasty, and she had been born in Tianjin. In Taichung, she had always looked upon me as another northerner and frequently shared her pleasures of reading with me. She invited me to take a real American Greyhound Bus trip from Indiana to Connecticut, a trip of two days and one night. They then took me on a road trip of New England to see their village. Wearing high snow boots, we trudged through deep snow to see the woods of the poet Robert Frost and to pursue a hare through the snow. Early one morning as we drove, they said, "We're going to take you to see someone." We drove six or seven hours along the narrow country roads, which were bordered by dense shrubs or corn stalks, giving an air of mystery. Just after noon, a hillside bright with sunlight suddenly appeared before us, on which sat a solitary small farm. A Chinese woman wearing a *qipao* and with her hair done up came out of the house to welcome us. The normally reticent Professor Lewis introduced us: "This is Mrs. Buck." Appearing at the door was John Buck, the former husband of Pearl S. Buck, the Nobel Prize-winning author of *The Good Earth*. Pearl Buck had accompanied her missionary father, A. Sydenstrieker, and once lived near our house on Ninghai Road in Nanjing. In 1921, after marrying, she and her husband went to Fengyang in Anhui Province and took part in improving village life in the early days of the Joint Commission on Rural Reconstruction, during which time she collected the materials for her novel *The Good Earth*. The novel made her famous overnight. Later she divorced and married her publisher. Mr. Buck took a young Chinese woman in marriage. After coming to America, she insisted upon entertaining guests in a *qipao*, as a way of remembering her homeland. Sitting in front of the farmhouse fireplace, we talked about suffering China, where he had once worked and where I was born. Working with him had been Yan Yangchu and Qu Junong (whose daughter's name was Ningshu), who were fathers of my Nankai classmates.

These people and events formed fated and unforgettable moments in my life.

After my family moved to Taipei in 1967, I had been constantly busy with my work and academic career, and half the time I was not at home. In the three years I had been back since returning from America, I had spent more time in Taipei, but rain or shine, I did take that 7 a.m. train on Tuesday for Taichung and the 6 p.m. train on Friday back to Taipei. When I was not in Taichung, department matters were all handled by Ding Zhenwan in collaboration with Huang Chunzhi. She wrote dozens of "love notes on putting out fires" for me. Saturday mornings I would go to National Taiwan University and teach advanced English for the graduate schools of history and Chinese. Most afternoons, I'd go to Cave's Books on Zhongshan North Road to look at the latest pirated books, to see if anything could be used as teaching materials. I was exhausted in those days but said nothing. Living across from my parents, we had help, but I was burdening my mother too much. Yuchang's work on railroad electrification was peaking, and my unease gradually became an ordeal. In those years, the only place I could have the peace of mind to think or read was during the three hours on the train between Taipei and Taichung. I was thankful to have those hours to myself. Now that the first class had graduated, my request to quit was finally accepted by the president, Liu Daoyuan.

Where was I going after leaving Chung-Hsing University? I had no time to make plans, and no one in any department in Taipei would believe that I would leave such a fine new department. I didn't really feel like providing fodder for speculation by looking for a job. Perhaps it would be best just to stay at home for a year before looking for work.

Perhaps once again it was fate that reached out. Dean Wang Tianming was invited by Luo Yunping, the new minister of education, to come to Taipei to serve as director of the National Institute for Compilation and Translation. Wang Tianming (1911–1983) was a revolutionary comrade of my father's and a graduate of the history department at Peking Normal University. In the northeast, he had thousands of acres of cropland and had contributed harvests for the sake of the country. When Manchuria became Manchukuo, he went to the Northeast Sun Yat-sen Middle School, which had been established in Beiping, to teach history. From Beiping he went to Nanjing, Hunan, and Sichuan, and watched me grow up on that road of exile. When Sun Yat-sen Middle School moved back to Shenyang from Sichuan after victory over Japan, he served as principal. He initially thought he could return home and work in education, but in 1948, when the Communists entered the city, he and ten family members fled to Taiwan. His students said that his history classes, from the ancient to the modern, covered the rise and fall of dynasties in rich and voluminous detail. At the beginning of the 1970s, the Institute for Compilation and Translation played an important role in university, middle school, and primary school education. He knew that I had left my job, so he invited me to come and run the section on humanities and society, with the idea of doing some intellectual work for the good of the country. He especially hoped that I could implement a plan for the translation of Chinese writing, first with a number of collections of Taiwan literature in English, so that the island might have a voice abroad. He said to me, "You have spent your whole life teaching and never worked as a civil servant. You can start at the Institute of Compilation and Translation and help me. If it doesn't work out, we can give it some more thought." In this way I once again set off on a totally undreamed of road.

8

UNIVERSITY TEACHING, TAIWAN, AND LITERATURE

ADVANCING UPON THE WORLD LITERARY ARENA: ANTHOLOGY OF MODERN CHINESE LITERATURE IN ENGLISH TRANSLATION

Facing an entirely new life situation, the only thing I could do was to settle down and begin to understand my new job.

The first thing to be done was to draft a plan for the English translation of an anthology of modern Chinese literature, but first I had to find people with whom to work. Fortunately I was able to recruit the famous poet and translator Yu Kwang-chung, Professor Wu Xizhen of National Taiwan Normal University, Professor He Xin of Zhengzhi University, and Professor John Deeney of the Department of Foreign Languages and Literatures at National Taiwan University. Together we formed a small editorial committee of five. Professors Wu and He were both important editors at *Time and Tide* during the Chongqing days. Professor Deeney was one of the first American professors to study comparative literature and had a deep understanding of Chinese literature; he taught the history of English literature at National Taiwan University. They were all interested in the plans for the English-language anthology and more than happy to participate.

Starting in February 1973, the five of us met twice a week. We first settled on the three genres of poetry, prose, and fiction, and then chose the pieces to be translated and selected the translators. The process of reviewing and discussing the translations through countless critical readings took two years before we were able to finalize the contents. Every word of every translation had to be weighed and considered before a decision was made. After countless afternoons of diligent and cooperative discussion, the manuscript of the first edition of *An Anthology of Contemporary Chinese Literature: Taiwan 1949–1974* was final. The book was released in 1975 under the auspices of the University of Washington Press in Seattle. This was the first comprehensive anthology in English introducing contemporary Chinese literature to European and American sinologists. Beyond the iron curtain of mainland China, Taiwan's writers, since 1949, had been able to continue the Chinese literary tradition and produce widely read works, opening a new era.

The anthology covers the period from 1949 to 1974 and includes works of contemporary poetry, prose, and fiction in three volumes. In the preface, I offered a brief description of the past twenty-five years of literature:

> Amid the vicissitudes that have beset the entire world since the end of World War II, Taiwan has been steadily pushing its way forward toward greater modernization and cultural self-identification. This process of transition, adaptation, and innovation has affected the traditional life-pattern of the fifteen million Chinese living here. Their struggles, triumphs, setbacks, and sufferings have naturally found an echo in literature.

I believe there are numerous reasons literature flourished in Taiwan; foremost among them was the widespread rise in the level of education, which produced a strong sense of cultural mission. Owing to the twin forces of politics and economics, the vision of the island's writers broadened, their stylistic mastery deepened, and a more reasonable balance between literary ideals and real life was achieved. Another important motivating force was the competition among literary supplements of the newspapers and literary magazines. They demanded not only a large number of literary works but also works of a constantly higher quality, resulting in some very positive results in thirty years. In addition to the annual prizes awarded by the government, the Wu Sanlian prize and the *United Daily News* and *China Times* awards were set up in an eight-year period. This led to increased contributions, open judging, and greater authoritativeness, which had a far-reaching impact on writing. During the diplomatic setbacks after 1970, Taiwan relied upon itself and fought to produce its economic miracle, which provided a sense of pride internationally. But internationally in the cultural arena, we were practically mute! Some ridiculed Taiwan as a cultural desert, and we were unable to counter such claims! Actually, literature on the Chinese mainland over the last thirty years had been all but silent, with the exception of some protest literature and the Misty poetry; whereas in Taiwan, literature had matured naturally owing to a diversity of subject matter and style; whether realism or art-for-art's sake writing, it reflected real human life without taking a back seat to politics.

Since the three volumes of the anthology were edited with the global literary arena in mind, the criteria for selecting the works to be included were different than if they had been edited for a domestic readership. It was deemed best to select works with themes and vocabulary exhibiting less Western influence in order to provide a picture of what the people of Taiwan were thinking. Overly pessimistic and decadent works were avoided because they were not what the many years of struggle in Taiwan had been about. Space was limited, so repetition in terms of theme and style was avoided. The works were arranged by author age, from oldest to youngest, an arrangement that naturally delineated the various stages of creative development, with very few exceptions.

Of the three genres, modern poetry showed steady and firm development with the clearest successes. The poets of the early period organized important poetry societies including Modern Poetry, the Blue Stars, the Epoch Society, the Bamboo Hat, Dragon Race, Great Earth, and Mainstream. With extraordinary talent, the poets wrote new poetry rich in imagery, attuned to the times, and concerned with the fate of the country. They wrote and responded to each other, debated, competed, and were mutually encouraging, together creating a vibrant new Chinese poetry. Theme and technique fell between the schools of Western poetry and traditional Chinese poetry, exercising an enormous influence to this very day.

From my perspective as chief editor of the anthology, fiction required the most effort, whereas poetry required genius, and the prose essay, the mainstream of Taiwan's creative writing, required inspiration. During the editing process, Lin Yutang had just come from abroad to live in Taiwan and Liang Shiqiu's *Sketches of a Cottager* had elevated him to a lofty status, respected for his artistic mastery and learning. Both were active in literary circles, and their works were included because of their fame, but also because they really were actively writing in our midst. The elegant writing of each generation from Lin Yutang, Liang Shiqiu, and Qi Jun to the middle-aged generation of Yang Mu and Xiao Feng to the youngest such as Hei Ye displayed a refined use of language and apt content with regard to life and thought. Perhaps because this was the first substantial anthology of Taiwan literature in English, the University of Washington Press sent us sixteen reviews after publication, all of which were positive in their praise. The most gratifying was that by A. R. Crouch in the summer 1976 issue of *China Notes*, one passage of which says: "The English of the translations is superb. All the writers are from the Republic of China, which some may find a limitation, but none of them has written propaganda under political pressure. With the exception of two or three poems that deal with the 1911 Revolution or the Vietnam War, few of the works express a political position, which was a welcome relief from the standard propaganda fare from mainland China." This review was a special delight for those of us who were translating into English and not into our mother tongue.

In those days before computers, I was very fortunate to have a reliable assistant in my secretary Zhuang Wanling. When I decided to go to the institute, I chose her from among the students of the first graduating class at Chung-Hsing University, because she wrote well, had a warm disposition, and was steady and pleasant. In her position as secretary, she helped me to establish a good working relationship with others at the institute. I relied on her quite heavily in matters both of spirit and work. At the time the *China Times* was running a cartoon titled

"Security Is . . ." One day there appeared a cartoon with the following caption: "Security is when I say something, you do it." When I showed it to her, we looked at each other and laughed. She was a great comfort in a precarious place. After the anthology was completed, she married and moved with her husband to the States. Two years later, I too left. I was never able to replace her and continue to cherish the memory of our days working together.

The first year spent working on the anthology was the happiest time of the five years I spent at the institute. With the help and support of Director Wang, I was able to handle all the business of the Department of Humanities and Social Sciences; able to devote all my energies to all the issues, large and small, pertaining to the anthology; and was especially happy to work directly with the writers, translators, and editors. All aspects of the anthology were considered by the five of us, and I found that the whole process enhanced my ability to evaluate literary works. Today, thirty years later, when I look through the anthology over which we slaved, I feel a modicum of pride. If I hadn't been exiled in those years, I might never have realized my long-cherished ambition of working in academia.

SOWING THE SEEDS OF LITERATURE: NATIONAL TEXTBOOK REFORM

In life, no happy time lasts forever. In my second year at the institute, the days I felt like singing and when my fingers flew over the keys of my typewriter came to an abrupt end.

Huang Fa'ce, who had been in charge of the textbook group, resigned on account of illness, but the work couldn't stop for a day. The textbook group was not simply in charge of compiling, writing, printing, and publishing of all the middle school textbooks, they also had a sword of political correctness hanging over their heads. Director Wang put me in charge to make sure things kept running as usual—this in addition to my other duties—while he looked for a suitable replacement. In order to help him out in a difficult situation, I took charge of the operations of the textbook group.

At the time, there was only one set of authorized textbooks in Taiwan. In 1968, President Chiang Kai-shek implemented nine-year compulsory education, with interim textbooks to be compiled by the institute and fully authorized editions to be printed in 1972. That was the year I followed Director Wang in through the gate on Zhoushan Road.

Every middle school in the country had to implement nine-year compulsory education; therefore, the Ministry of Education wisely decided that there would be a three-year transition period in which interim textbooks would be used, during which time actual recommendations from teachers and the concrete response from public debate would serve as the most helpful basis upon which the institute would go on to compile the authorized textbooks. When we first took charge, the institute was the biggest target for public opinion. Nothing was right, especially with textbooks—the compiling, writing, printing, and publication all had problems. Every column in the magazines and newspapers, large or small, took delight in execrating the national textbooks and their production, saying everything from "stultifying and misleading the people" to "vacillating on the national textbooks." At the institute someone was in charge of collecting all of these, any putative comment up to and including questions from the Legislative Yuan. There were enough clippings to fill a notebook each week.

Our greatest difficulties came with the first set of authorized Chinese textbooks, which seemed to have been everyone's focus. In three years, public opinion was highly critical of the six volumes of interim textbooks for the three years of junior middle school. Apparently, the selected texts were inappropriate and the levels of difficulty were all wrong. However, and more frankly, it was claimed that the students simply weren't interested in the textbooks. Which lessons, in fact, were inappropriate or wrong? Why weren't the students interested? No one offered any concrete suggestions; they just beat around the bush and kept making appeals: Save the children! Let them know the joys of reading! Develop in them a free and lively character! In all the criticism, no one came right out and said that the interim texts contained too many party, government, and military pieces. Even if someone dared to write as much, no periodical or newspaper would dare print it.

Before arriving at the National Institute for Compilation and Translation, I did some research on the work I was going to be doing. In Taichung I had quite a few teacher friends, which placed them truly among the people. The various editorial advisory boards had been newly formed, and experts and scholars in tune with the times could be considered and recruited, not just the big names from the past. In this regard, Director Wang and I had both spent years on campus, so we ought to have had sufficient insight and decision-making ability. One of my jobs was to handle the plans for compilation and writing for the various areas of the humanities. I had to work simultaneously running the textbook group and planning, including the formation of various editorial advisory boards, as well as decide on the content of textbooks. In 1972 that was a job of not only academic decision making but also political decision making.

The first thing I did was to carefully read and analyze the contents of the temporary textbooks. I wondered what group of "scholars" had edited the books and with what sort of "correct politics." I realized what an enormous challenge I was facing, but it was too late to turn back. I could only move forward.

The first thing I had to do was form a new editorial committee, and to hire a scholar with seniority and prestige, and backbone, to be in charge. He would have to not only produce textbooks of quality but also be able to ward off any attacks from the old guard. I had Professor Qu Wanli (1907–1979), head of the Chinese department at NTU, in mind. He was a first-rate scholar and a serious and dignified presence on campus.

Fate works in mysterious ways. At the time, the twenty-seven-year-old Ke Qingming was Professor Qu's teaching assistant. Sincere and enthusiastic, he was also the chief editor of *Modern Literature*, the literary journal founded by Bai Xianyong and others in the Department of Foreign Languages at NTU. He had a profound knowledge of Taiwan literature and was an enthusiastic proponent.

Ke Qingming was very interested in what the institute hoped to accomplish, understood its importance, and, as editor of *Modern*

Literature, provided a great deal of assistance, including compiling a list of works and making selections. Through his assistance we were able to set up channels of contact with the writers. Aware of the importance of universal education, he also agreed to speak to Professor Qu and help convince him to take on the important task of editing the textbooks. Eventually, Professor Qu agreed to see me at his office.

We had a lengthy conversation about the shortcomings of the old textbooks as well as public opinions and hopes. It our responsibility to edit the books, but also to inspire a younger generation for the sake of the future of the culture of the nation, and we had to move beyond politics to do so. I clearly recall Professor Qu sitting in his old office, taking a deep drag on his cigarette, and then sighing and saying, "Okay! I'm in. I'll join you in this difficult enterprise and board your rebel ship."

Professor Qu took charge of the new committee that was composed of professors from NTU, the Normal University, and Zhengzhi University as well as middle school teachers. To have the first two volumes ready in a year, the manuscripts had to be finalized by the coming August. The meeting rooms at the institute were therefore occupied every day, and sometimes even into the night.

As a result of all this work, several generations of students since 1973 have had real Chinese textbooks and not political propaganda materials. Professor Qu devoted substantial time and energy to this valuable task, but unfortunately, when he passed away, few obituaries mentioned his contributions in this regard.

Society was just starting to open up in those days, and a heavy political atmosphere permeated cultural circles. The Ministry of Education's Chinese and history textbooks were often the focus of public scrutiny. By chance I found myself in the maelstrom and had to observe the turmoil around culture from different angles, and even at times the danger. After setting up the committee, I began to become aware of some of the hazards. Zhang Jieren, a senior official at the institute who at one time worked for the Northeast China Association, knew me as a sickly child given to tears. Learning that I had joined the institute, he asked me, "What brings you to this sort of place?" I later surprised him by no longer being prone to crying, because before coming to this sort of place, I had experienced a good many difficulties.

My first experience in not crying came shortly after the proposed contents of the first two Chinese textbooks had been submitted for committee review. The director of the institute gave me a memo from the Ministry of Education demanding that I reply to Lin Yi, a member of the review committee. He was troubled by the direction our editing had taken, criticized us for losing sight of the national consciousness, for selecting juvenile modern poetry and translated reports, and for a lack of refined taste. The director had me first pay Professor Lin a visit and explain things in person. At the appointed time, I arrived at his residence. Entering the living room, I was not asked to take a seat, nor did we exchange pleasantries; instead, I was severely reprimanded for the contents because they went counter to educational policy. For example, Yang Huan's new poem "Night" compared the newly risen moon to a coin, which went beyond reasonable limits, because it taught children to think of money when they saw the moon; the passage selected from *Journey to the West* was bad because it was the one that showed the monkey stealing the divine peaches; and what literary value did Shen Fu's writing about the joys of his childhood have? I was just starting to explain when he seemed to become even angrier, and said, "The way I see it, even the mainland textbooks are better than the ones put together by you new people and your new administration." As he was speaking, he went to the other room and came back with a junior high textbook from Communist China to show me. In a fit of inspiration, I replied, "Well, may I ask you to loan this book to me so that the committee can use it for reference? I will let them know it was your idea." He suddenly must have realized that this woman from a foreign languages program who dared to take on this job was not all that simple. And now his praise for the textbooks of the "Communist bandits" might just prove troublesome for him, for if I persisted, then perhaps he would be hauled in to face an "inquisition." So he asked me to sit down, and in the gentle tone of a modern policeman asked me where I was from, with whom I had come to Taiwan, whether I was married, what my husband did, and what schools my three sons were attending. Finally, he asked quite respectfully who my father was. I told him my father's name and what he did. Much to my surprise, he said, "Why didn't you say so earlier? Committee member Chi and I are like brothers!" Then he shouted to the other room, "Bring some tea, good tea."

For the more than thirty years that we lived on Lishui Road, I kept the six volumes of the Chinese textbooks as well as the two thick volumes of *An Anthology of Contemporary Chinese Literature* in the place of honor on my desk so that I could see them at all times. They were graced with the calligraphy of Tai Jingnong, which I had requested. The textbooks were finally delivered to my office on the National Taiwan University campus by Teacher Tai. I don't even recall how I thanked him. I do recall that he encouraged me by saying, "It takes guts to compile textbooks the way you have done." Such a show of support was worth more than a thousand accolades.

RED LEAVES, STONE STEPS: REMEMBERING QIAN MU

There are often marvelous turns in the course of events. As a student at Wuhan University, I never had the chance to listen to Professor Qian Mu lecture. Unexpectedly, after I went to work for the institute, I had the opportunity to meet him on account of the "Martial Sage Yue Fei Incident."

Before I arrived at the institute, they had received a manuscript for the University Series from Lin Ruihan, a history professor at National Taiwan University. The book was still under consideration and publication was still up in the air. However, a newspaper reported:

> Professor Lin Ruihan's *A General History of China*, which is a required text for all NTU freshmen, actually maligns Yue Fei, saying he defied authority and that as a general, when he was far away from court he was unwilling to obey the emperor's orders unless he received the

> urgent delivery of twelve gold tablets a day. That Gao Zong, the Song emperor, had him executed was not such a simple matter. Finding that such disrespectful language is actually found in teaching materials at NTU, and, to make matters worse, that the Institute of Compilation and Translation will soon publish Professor Lin's *A Synopsis of Song History* has shaken the principles of the nation.

A certain Li, who referred to himself as a fellow townsman of Yue Fei, wrote a series of pieces in which he said, "Insulting the Military Sage as you have done makes you ingrates!" A legislator by the name of Wu Yanhuan was even more strident in his abuse. Under the pen name "Shihuan" (Return Oath), he made constant attacks in a column for the *Central Daily News*, and brought it formally before the Legislative Yuan, demanding a response from the institute. The newspapers continued to publish abusive articles, with one going so far as to print: "It was learned that the person in charge of this matter is a woman and a high school graduate with no background in literature and history." Director Wang, who had been a history professor himself, knew that there wasn't a single scholar in any university who was willing to bear the scrutiny and who could stem this politically motivated tide. He told me to pay a visit Qian Mu, who had just relocated in Taiwan from Hong Kong, and ask him to act as an arbitrator and offer a few words of guidance on the institute's position.

I was hesitant to do so, and Director Wang, who had always been so polite to me, said, "It can't be helped, you'll just have to go, regardless of the inconvenience."

In Taiwan, Qian Mu's residence was called Sushulou and was located on a hillside behind Dongwu University at Waishuangxi, Shilin, that was reached via a pathway of stone steps built into the hillside. Just as I was wondering how I had wound up in such a position, the car arrived at Waishuangxi, then we took the Dongwu University road to the end, where I rang the bell at the gate. From there, I went up the stone steps with some trepidation. When Qian Mu came out and before I had taken a seat, he said, "I already said on the phone that I won't serve as reviewer." Embarrassed, I stammered, "I only arrived at the institute three months ago from the university. This manuscript was left by the previous person, and up until now, there has been unremitting unfavorable public opinion. Would you please have a look so that we can break the impasse?" Probably out of sympathy on his part, Qian Mu took the manuscript and placed it on a small table. After thanking him, I left hastily and practically ran down the stone steps, figuring I probably wouldn't ever need to come back.

Unexpectedly, three days later, I received a call from Qian Mu asking Professor Lin Ruihan to come over for a talk. A few days later, Professor Lin himself visited the institute with a twenty-two-page manuscript in his small, neat hand that incorporated six new sources of information provided by Qian Mu during their talk, to supplement the section on Yue Fei. The material was substantial and reliable, which provoked a lot of discussion.

And so began eighteen years in which I was destined to climb these stone steps to visit him. After that spectacular Yue Fei Incident came the compilation of the middle school Chinese textbooks, followed by a new edition of the high school *History of Chinese Culture*, each project in the media spotlight. At that time, I served as head of both the Humanities and the Textbook sections, and at any time could be hauled in to face an inquisition. Fortunately, with my family background and having gone through such tempestuous times, my father and brother often made light of my situation, saying that with such a minor position but with troubles daily in the papers, I must keep in mind President Chiang's directives and always "Respect the homeland and strengthen the self" and "Respond to change without fear." My father had told me, "You are such a timid girl; you are always afraid of change." I never thought that in the seventies, the institute would become my research institute for courage.

Actually, public opinion is not one-sided. Lots of people are idealistic innovators who hope for academic neutrality. At that time, such hopes were alive with members of the older generation such as Tao Baichuan, Huang Jilu, Chen Lifu, and Wang Shijie, who all praised junior and senior high textbooks based on literary sentiment rather than the propagation of political ideas. At least Luo Pingyun, Minister of

Education at the time, was supportive. When I finally got up the courage to speak about the ideals behind editing the books, it was to Qian Mu and not the "Master of the Studies of Ancient Chinese Civilization" of great reputation. His face was gentle, and when he listened to someone speak, he was calm and thoughtful, which was also encouraging.

From the start, I diligently carried out official business, climbing those stone steps to deliver books and manuscripts, and to ask for advice; later, after he learned that I was Zhu Guangqian's student, he talked about how he had lectured at Wuhan University in Leshan, Sichuan. I told him that I had heard from the upperclassmen how they went to the auditorium by torchlight for his class. After that, he often talked with me about those days. When there was no official business, I'd pay him a visit on New Year's Day and his birthday, until he was forced to leave Sushulou. In eighteen years, I walked up and down those stone steps, on either side of which grew tall maple trees, hundreds of times. In 1985 when I was hospitalized after my accident, his wife came to visit me and told me that he had been worried about not seeing me. A year later, I went to see him and slowly climbed those stone steps and saw that the ditch was filled with red maple leaves, something rarely seen in Taiwan.

Of course he had to face the various crises that arose around the time of Chiang Kai-shek's death in 1975. He recalled the turbulence during the War of Resistance and, with the mind-set of a historian, sigh with emotion that his hope for a stable China was lost. He had completed his *A General History of China* when Kunming and Chongqing were being bombed by the Japanese and the bloody fighting had yet to end. In the preface to that work, he wrote: "That we can speak of a war of resistance and establishing a country despite the unworthiness of the people and the backwardness of the culture is because our traditional culture still exists." Reading his essay, I understood why he left Hong Kong and came to Taiwan at the invitation of Chiang Kai-shek, because he thought he could live out his final years in peace. Like so many other Chinese people in those days, he believed the nation would be saved after eight years of war and that after 1950 Taiwan was still the bastion of Chinese culture.

Although I'm not a historian, I am interested in culture, especially the influence of intellectuals in times of political crisis. In my university days, *A General History of China* was one of my textbooks, and I have reread it at many stages in my life. I recently learned that the book is now once again required reading in mainland China. If that is the case, then after half a century of turbulence and human cruelty, it should have an even greater influence in terms of kindness and self-esteem.

I recall twenty years ago sitting at the table, sometimes just the two of us, sometimes with his wife present, listening to Qian Mu speak, analyzing Chinese culture in different ways during different crises. When he spoke, sometimes he was calm, sometimes passionate, and sometimes indignant. In his Wuxi accent, he frequently spoke of Chinese culture but was never hard to understand.

I recall speaking to him once about how cruelly teachers and people of culture were being treated by the Red Guards and wondered where they would lead China when they grew up and ruled the country. I was deeply concerned. Qian Mu said that when the Cultural Revolution came to an end and the people in their fifties, who still preserved some of the national legacy, could regain their voice, there would be renewed hope for the continuation of Chinese culture.

THE INSPIRATION OF THE GOLDENRAIN TREE

In the summer of 1977, John Deeney, who taught English literary history in the Department of Foreign Languages and Literatures at National Taiwan University, left to teach in Hong Kong, upon which Hou Jian asked me to return to NTU full time and teach the course. For me, this was a lifelong ambition.

In my time at the National Institute of Compilation and Translation, I worked diligently day and night and courageously made many reforms to complete many cultural and literary plans, including the translation of contemporary works of Chinese literature for the global literary arena; the compilation of new Chinese textbooks from a literary perspective rather than from a political point of view; and the compilation of a series of Western classics and a “Modernization Collection.” Many people expected me to continue in this line of work, but what I wanted more than anything else was to return to the classroom. For this reason, I left the institute with no attachments.

The morning I left the National Institute for Compilation and Translation, I stood alone in front of the desk I had occupied for five years, looking at the lovely goldenrain tree outside. Amid the daily routine and frustrations, I had often looked up from my electric typewriter to watch the magic of the changing light of day, with Joyce Kilmer's poem "Trees" coming to mind: "A tree that looks at God all day, / And lifts her leafy arms to pray."

Ah! That tree made me think of all the difficult junctures I had passed through in my life, coming up with so many solutions, consulting so many scholars and experts, struggling and engaging in discussions to arrive at the sound conclusion of an international publisher. The learned investigations and opinions of these people, in that age before Xerox machines or computers, amount to page after page of treasured tracts. The names of these scholars are a veritable who's who in Taiwan's cultural history from 1960 to 1980. Their voices and smiles and the goldenrain tree outside my window are so vivid to me.

By the summer of 1977, Director Wang had retired and I had left the institute, body and mind, and returned to that quiet building at NTU that houses the College of Arts and Sciences, to those bright halls.

DEPARTMENT OF FOREIGN LANGUAGES AND LITERATURES, PAST AND PRESENT

Descending those steps and walking down Zhoushan Road, which no longer exists, you entered the NTU campus through the old wall. Passing the campus security office, the school store, and then following a walkway between the administration building and the Department of Agricultural Chemistry, you came out in front of the College of Arts and Sciences. Then down a broad walkway planted with azaleas and palm trees, past the school clock in memory of school president Fu

Ssu-nien, you'd pass through a wide and imposing gate to enter the corridor, which for me possessed a sort of ceremonial feeling. That old bright and spacious corridor with its arched ceiling was situated at the heart of the old Taiwan Imperial University campus (built in the third year of the Showa reign, 1928). Small gates stood at either end and it surrounded a central courtyard, which was completely unchanged since I had first seen it thirty years earlier. During the long Taiwan summer, it possessed a faint whispering coolness.

At variance with my memory was the fact that the Department of Foreign Languages and Literatures had moved downstairs and was now a very busy place. At the right upon entering the college door was a row of large rooms, the door of only one of which was always open. There you found yourself facing a wooden cabinet on top of which was placed one of the large aluminum teakettles that were a standard fixture in offices those days. The day you no longer had the strength to take it down off the cabinet was the day you retired. Tea was kept in a small white hempen bag, which was supplied to each department office by the general affairs office. To this day, I remember the taste of the astringent, coffee-colored tea, which was always too hot to drink between classes, and so a large cup was always eventually consumed cold. The cabinet had several dozen pigeonholes that served as faculty mailboxes, behind which were several desks and chairs side by side where five teaching assistants sat along with an office clerk, who handled a never-ending stream of people and tasks. Even by the time I retired, the Department of Foreign Languages and Literatures never had a formal faculty break room, and all faculty contact between classes was conducted in the hallways. I still remember how we'd come out of Classroom 24 and lean with a good deal of fatigue against the wooden windowsills to wait for the bell for the next class. You might see an old friend whom you had not seen in ages and then there would be a hurried exchange of phone numbers, after which you'd both run off to class.

In those days, the department had about eighty regular faculty members as well as quite a few adjunct faculty. That first group of old faculty, including Ying Qianli, Wang Guohua, Huang Qiongjiu, Su Weixiong, Li Benti, Xia Ji'an, Li Liewen, Zhou Xuepu, Cao Qinyuan, and Zeng

Yuenong had all left. Of the department after 1970, someone once dramatically remarked, "The carved railings and jade steps ought to be there still, but the vermillion (Zhu) color (Yan) is changed." In the old and mottled, though spacious corridors, many of the students were there because they had such high college entrance exam scores, so there was no doubt a sense of traditional prestige. But there had been, in fact, enormous changes to "modernize" the curriculum, and the biggest movers and shakers for change were surnamed Zhu and Yan. Zhu Limin and Yan Yuanshu had returned from the United States with Ph.D. degrees, and on the NTU campus they were described as "worth their weight in gold." Shortly thereafter, Hu Yaoheng also came back to NTU with a Ph.D. He taught Western drama with the latest pedagogical methods and through a comparative literature approach guided his students in a loving concern for the development of Chinese drama.

The reform with the greatest impact was compiling a new textbook for freshman English to increase the level of English proficiency of all students and to broaden their knowledge of the humanities and science. For department freshmen, a course titled Reading Literary Texts was opened, and Literary History of China was made a required course. The latter was taught at one time or another by Tai Jingnong, Ye Qingbing, Lin Wenyue, and Ke Qingming from the Chinese department. This not only helped to increase the students' knowledge of the Chinese literary tradition and its development but also strengthened the collegiality among the faculty of the Chinese and foreign languages departments, which had a broadening and deepening effect on student development.

The History of English Literature became a two-year course for twelve units: the first year covered the Middle Ages to the eighteenth century; the second year covered the Romantic period to the twentieth century. For our textbook, we used *The Norton Anthology of English Literature* of about five thousand pages, which was the international standard then and included important works along with discussions of background, trends, and developments.

At NTU, I taught the second-year courses, except for one year when Yan Yuanshu went abroad and I taught the first-year courses in his stead. I had taught the same courses at Chung-Hsing University for four years, so I was well prepared. In the course of the week, you always had to make some adjustments; for example, I had to teach the Old English epic poem *Beowulf* in the second year, and this meant playing some recordings of the text being read. The following day, I had to teach the "The Mental Traveler" by the profound English Romantic poet William Blake. The poem describes two opposing cycles of human life and nature, and the entire class time was required to thoroughly explain the profundities of the text. In middle school I had read an article by an Englishman that asserted that the brain had different compartments for storing different types of knowledge. I kept the important works of each period of English literature separate in my brain, each with its own dazzling brilliance, so that I never confused them or made some anachronistic error.

ADVANCED ENGLISH

Another cornerstone of my teaching after returning to NTU was the course Advanced English, which I had offered to the graduate students in Chinese and history since 1978. It was my greatest and most steadfast challenge, but it was also the challenge I most relished.

In those days, most grad students in the College of Arts and Sciences had plans for advanced study. Unlike the graduate students in foreign languages and literatures, those in Chinese and history often lacked the foreign language ability necessary for conducting cultural research, and for this reason the range, depth, and speed of their reading had to be enhanced. In 1970, when I first taught the class, I mimeographed some articles in English on cultural issues to measure their grasp of English. After they had read the pieces, I would ask them questions. I was startled to discover that few first-year grad students had read articles on Western cultural concepts or had ever had the experience of struggling through books written in English, volume after volume. I believe that to reach an advanced level in any language, one must read entire books for a more complete understanding, rather than just reading selections. It was my hope to read two books in the first semester, and three or four in the second semester. When I mentioned my plan, I heard some faint gasps: "What? Read five or six books in the original?" But I knew that NTU grad students would never admit to something being "difficult."

My biggest difficulty then was how to talk with people from diverse fields at the same time. I had a great deal of respect for people in the fields of Chinese and history, but they studied different curriculums and had different goals when it came to advanced study and career. How was I to get them interested and help them reach an advanced level of English competence? The only way was to appeal to a common interest in the spirit of literature.

That was at the height of the Cold War, when the world was polarized between the United States and the USSR. Taiwan, after twenty years of anti-Communism, had a lengthy list of proscribed books. Most teaching materials came from the United States, but only a few of the latest books were available near NTU, such as the simply bound, authorized with copyright editions of books on culture, psychology, and philosophy from bookstores like Ouya and Shuangye. Fortunately, *Time* magazine, which was readily available, had a list of the top ten fiction and nonfiction best-sellers in each issue. Photocopied editions of many of these books were often available in bookstores on Zhongshan North Road, such as Cave's Books, which I frequented. The moment the list was published, pirated copies would be available. I still remember carrying those Western books down the sidewalk on Zhongshan North Road to my home, where I would devour them that very night. The books I used in class had to have weight and be of interest to the young people. They had to be well written, but not be too political to the left or right, not too thick and not too thin, and copies pirated in Taiwan had to be available so that the students could afford them.

Although I cannot remember all the books we read year by year, I'm sure that the teaching materials would reflect twenty years of Western cultural concerns and changes. Pirated and read in Taiwan, they had a great impact.

The first book I taught was Aldous Huxley's *Brave New World*, which was not widely read in Taiwan in those days. For most of my students, the book had to be read in the original in a few weeks' time, probably making it a "Vexing New World" for them. After *Brave New World* came *Nineteen Eighty-Four* by George Orwell. Both books were about two hundred pages long, but very different in terms of story and style, and both were extremely successful literary works against totalitarianism or communism.

Brave New World and *Nineteen Eighty-Four* were always on my reading list, and sometimes I'd have the students read them on their own. However, in 1983, I once again taught the two books, because the year 1984 was upon us. After writing this famous prophetic work in 1948, the author died, and a distance of thirty years separated us from that frightening world he foresaw, but time passes and in the years just before and after 1984, everyone compared, weighed, and examined the world Orwell prophesized and the real world. A tremendous number of articles were written and it was a momentous time, culturally speaking.

In the eighteen years that I taught Advanced English, I forced the students to read and study books in the original language and made them answer my innumerable "whys." To reply in English was only possible after having done the readings, there was no getting around that. In the course of one year, I probably asked around a hundred questions. In eighteen years, I did everything I could to make the course truly advanced. The more than four hundred students who went through it are probably all in their fifties now and the core of society. The members of that generation serve in academia, education, and the world of culture, and have achieved notable success in the fields of literature and history.

After leaving my classroom, the students would enter real life, and among those young people, there were always a few who became understanding friends. In middle age after a life of joys and sorrows, they still remembered some lines and ideas, like a sound heard in some other forest of falling leaves.

SEEKING A DEFINITION FOR TAIWAN LITERATURE

What is Taiwan literature? The term has always elicited much debate, with political objectives often having dictated the discussions and arguments. Sometimes full of sound and fury and at other times silenced, the nature of the debate depended upon the situation at the time. But what people didn't know was that literature is like roses: by whatever name it is called, it does not change its essence. Taiwan literature is a natural happening, its existence unchanged by its name. Since there have been written records, Taiwan literature has included works usually written in Taiwan about the Taiwanese and events there, and even about its myths and legends. Generations of writers residing in Taiwan have naturally written Taiwan literature. During periods of upheaval in Chinese history, adherents to the former dynasty and immigrants have come to Taiwan, so works of homesickness are also part of Taiwan literature.

The so-called first patriarch of written culture who came from over the sea to the east was Shen Guangwen (1612–1688). With the fall of the Ming dynasty, he drifted on the ocean, "taking a small boat to the south, endlessly buffeted about by the waves." Meeting with a gale, he was pushed to Taiwan, where he remained the rest of his life. He experienced Dutch rule and rule by three generations of Zheng Chenggong's family before the island was unified under the Qing dynasty. In 1685 (the twenty-fourth year of the Kangxi reign) he and a number of officials who had been sent to Taiwan organized the first poetry society, the Eastern Song Society, which can be called the origin of Taiwan literature. A full three hundred years after Shen Guangwen, approximately two million people—soldiers, civil servants, educators, and their dependents—arrived in Taiwan with the Nationalist government. They came from all over China, each with his or her own sad story of separation, a huge homesick contingent!

On Retrocession Day, 1946, the Nationalist government drafted its language policy: all newspapers and publications had to be in Chinese. The literary careers of most of the local writers who wrote in Japanese during the half-century occupation (1895–1945) came to an end. Works written in Japanese by important writers such as Lai He, Long Yingzong, and Lu Heruo, among others have been translated into Chinese and now form part of the Taiwan literary canon. Most of those who began writing in Chinese in those first ten years after retrocession, whether they were from mainland China or local writers, had the feeling that they were making their way through the fog, perhaps with the exception of modern poets, who seemed to have the most confidence. "Bridge," the literary supplement of the *New Life News*, was edited by Gelei (Shi Ximu) for twenty months. A sincere promoter of literature, he encouraged all kinds of writing without any sort of regional favoritism. Although the many works of homesick literature were often crude and repetitive, still, a sense of warmth was provided for those who had just arrived from mainland China after such great misfortune. Narrative maturity came gradually, and the literary works provided supplementary reading beyond textbooks for a younger generation of writers.

In 1973, when I first began compiling and translating *An Anthology of Contemporary Chinese Literature*, Taiwan literature was fully formed. The desire to translate Taiwan literature was latent during my two Fulbright visits to the United States. In various activities in those days, I was frequently invited to "say something about Taiwan." From 1957 to 1969, many people would ask things such as: "Are you in Africa?" "Are you from Thailand, that place with the gold Buddha temple?" ("Taiwan" sounds a lot like "Thailand.") After this, whenever I found myself in a public gathering, I'd do my best to wear a low-collared, loose-fitting *qipao*, slit to just below the knee, so as not to restrict my walking. I never wore a hat and hoped at the very least not to be mistaken for a Japanese. In the earliest exchange programs, the United States seemed even a bigger proponent of "returning good for evil" than Chiang Kai-shek. In my first question-and-answer session, there were actually four Japanese, while I was the only representative from the Republic of China, so I had to uphold the honor of my country—I could lose for myself, but not for my country.

"Say something about Taiwan," a seemingly easy topic was, in fact, difficult. Go Ok-nam, a teacher from South Korea, and I were frequently in the same group. In introducing herself, all she had to say was "I am from Korea," and everyone understood who she was, because the United States had just finished fighting the Korean War and everyone in the States knew that Korea was an "ally." But the Republic of China, which I represented, was not on the Chinese mainland; my family was from the northeast; and our government was on Taiwan, across the Taiwan Strait from the mainland and more than six hundred miles from Shanghai. Things didn't seem to get better with time, so I had to say with a good deal of self-confidence, "On Taiwan, we are a free and democratic nation, preserving a high degree of Chinese culture, while pursuing peace and prosperity." In those days, such words were not merely slogans or propaganda but were the fervent hopes of all the people. On this thirty-six thousand square-mile island with a population close to ten million, approximately one-third of the people lived with this belief. Before 1949, the ragged and exhausted "quilted soldiers" and their surviving family members were still living in the temporary military compounds, longing for home and the old days while educating their children and getting on with life. After ten, twenty, and thirty years had passed, the government was done with shouting anti-Communist slogans and had wholeheartedly embraced development for Taiwan. Compulsory education was extended from six to nine years. This was probably President Chiang Kai-shek's last written order, and the one with the greatest long-term influence. Gradually, clear and resonant voices emerged in Taiwan's literary arena, which helped me when abroad to answer questions such as: "What is Taiwan like?" "How do the people live?" "What are people thinking there?" "Where will it be in the future?"

Another reason I had the confidence to serve as chief editor of *An Anthology of Contemporary Chinese Literature* was also a result of my two trips to the States. When I looked through the stacks at the large libraries at the University of Michigan and Indiana University, I was unable to find a single work of real literature from mainland China since 1949. Both universities had outstanding history departments, and although some scholars had positive things to say about China's "liberation," when it came to literature written since the founding of the PRC, most would point to shelves of propaganda works such as *Learn from Lei Feng*, Hao Ran's *The Golden Road*, Ding Ling's *The Sun Shines on the Sanggan River*, and Lao She's *Dragon Beard Ditch*, among others, and say, "Although Red China is closed behind the iron curtain, their ruthless political struggles and the sufferings of the people are known to all. But can we purvey this sort of propaganda in the classroom? How can we explain this nonsense to American students?" Then they would change the topic and ask me, "Does Taiwan have literature?"

Looking at the empty shelves set aside for modern Chinese writing, I thought to myself, *Perhaps after I return to Taiwan, I'll have the opportunity to say something concrete for Taiwan literature.* With this long-standing idea, I undertook the task of seeing that Taiwan literature was translated into English.

That age saw a common search for identity, a time when we all seemed to be making our way through the fog, trying to define what was ours. The young writers and readers did not have a strong sense of provincial identity or separateness, and everyone grew up together reading the same textbooks. Memory of the Japanese occupation gradually faded; connections to mainland China and the sense of loss were laid aside, and people were able to calmly discuss the word "exile." While editing *An Anthology of Contemporary Chinese Literature*, I believed we had found common ground. Since the anthology was being published by the National Institute of Compilation and Translation, the selections had to be representative of all the people and the selection process had to be fair, with no discrimination. Of the five members in our small group, He Xin and Yu Kwang-chung had been among the earliest to take part in literary activities in Taiwan and had extensive materials upon which to draw, and since returning to Taipei, I had read extensively of the most important works. After I started teaching Advanced English, I made frequent trips to the bookstores, where I acquired the newest titles and was able to keep up to date on the latest research on important writers, the way I had done when I was studying in the States. Beginning then, my small study gradually filled with works of Taiwan literature. For example, my copy of Huang Chunming's *Gong* with an inscription from the author sat next to my copy of *Beowulf*. My first-edition copies of

Sima Zhongyuan's *Wasteland* and *Dawn Train*, Zhu Xining's *Daybreak*, and Bai Xiangyong's *Taipei People* sat on the shelves with the copies of Shelley and Keats that I had brought from Shanghai. I particularly enjoyed the work of the young writer Xiao Sa, whose fiction I felt could stand with the work of American writers like Sherwood Anderson and Bernard Malamud. Moving back and forth between two languages was a great joy for me and helped me in terms of vision and arrangement when it came to writing literary criticism.

LITERATURE FROM BOTH SIDES OF THE STRAIT: THE SHOCK OF THE FIRST ENCOUNTER

Jeffrey Kinkley invited me to participate in a seminar on modern Chinese literature at St. John's University in New York. It was my first encounter with writers from mainland China, and of their three or four representatives, I knew of Professor Le Daiyun of Beijing University and the well-known writer Wang Meng.

Since editing the anthology, I had attended a number of large literary conferences around the world, but it was at this impressive gathering at St. John's University that I first saw how political snobbery was transferred to literary snobbery. It was also the first time I saw the devastating effects of the Cultural Revolution, which compelled me to consider the position and the name of "Taiwan literature" from a macro perspective.

It really was a grand meeting! Everyone was very excited and filled with curiosity; all eyes and ears were fixed on the writers from behind the iron curtain in this, their first appearance in the West. At lunch, I was assigned to the same table with them in what was probably a symbol of cross-strait exchange. And I seemed to be the least possessed of a combative spirit. Upon first meeting the people from the other side of the strait, I didn't really know how to proceed. Knowing that I was from northeast China, they said, "Come back to the motherland for a look!" Everyone laughed foolishly. C. T. Hsia, who was in high spirits, said, "In America, you should see as much as you can!"

After lunch we resumed the meeting. While we were listening to a Chinese writer give a report on the current literary scene in China, there was a huge commotion at the door and in ran a tall and handsome young Chinese man. He ran directly at the Chinese writer, shouting: "How can you come and speak for that tyrannical government here?" Following that, he took control of the podium and shouted about the cruelty of the Cultural Revolution. It was with great difficulty that the organizing teachers and students were able to remove him. Even at the door, he continued to swear before being dragged away. Only after everyone had calmed down did we learn that the young man was none other than Liang Heng, the author of the Western best-seller *Son of the Revolution*, which exposed the tragedy of the Cultural Revolution. He had married the writer Judith Shapiro and had been given political asylum in the United States, where he wrote his book in English and had it published. *Son of the Revolution* narrates the atrocities of the Cultural Revolution, showing the West how China had become a living hell. Readers shuddered at the cold-blooded cruelty of the Red Guards. When reading it, I asked myself with sadness and indignity: *Is this the motherland I can never forget?*

By the time the disrupter left, the atmosphere of the meeting had entirely changed, the pure excitement and curiosity at the beginning had been ruined. The various positions in the talks and the superficially calm responses had disappeared. Regardless of efforts to maintain order on the podium, most of the members of the audience were whispering about the young man who had disrupted the proceedings and his complaints. Everyone's curiosity about the mainland representative who now looked embarrassed became more complicated. At the time, nearly all of the new postwar generation of sinologists, who studied modern Chinese literature, were present. What were they thinking? But I, who was seeing writers from behind the iron curtain for the first time since I left mainland China thirty years earlier, felt agitated, as if I were watching history unfold and not reality mediated through film or fiction. It was sad indeed.

I remained in New York for several days after the meeting. One evening Lin Xinqin, who had been a student of mine at NTU and now worked as a reporter for *The China Times*, invited me to dinner. There were six guests, including the author of *Son of the Revolution* and his wife. After dinner, they invited me to their small apartment, where we talked late into the night. They became increasingly more excited as they spoke, describing things that were not found in books about the unspeakable betrayal and cruelty of some people toward their fellow human beings, which was more than shocking to hear. What was it that had turned this twenty-something Red Guard away from the tide of blood and cruelty and toward a more human shore to criticize the very violence he had participated in? How had several generations of young people—from the student movement to the Cultural Revolution—been hoodwinked into believing that a new China could only be built from turmoil and destruction? If their hearts were not made of wood, then they must be deeply scarred. How could they ever hope to return to a normal life? When they grew up and ruled China, what kind of country would it be?

Walking on the streets of New York on a summer night was like being in a different world! I could clearly remember when I was in my twenties, lying in my garret dorm room at Wuhan University looking up at the star-filled sky, listening to the flowing water at the confluence of three rivers, and crying because Elder Sister Hou had said I had no soul, simply because I did not want to go to attend the reading group with her and read those Russian books about class conflict and sing those juvenile songs: "The East Is Red," "The East Has Produced a Mao Zedong." . . . I remembered the narrow streets of Leshan and the troop of student demonstrators, their faces twisted, shouting for revenge. If I had not gone to Taiwan in 1947 and instead stayed in mainland China, what might have become of me?

In the West in those days, two other books that gave a shocking picture of the Cultural Revolution were *Chinese Shadows* by Simon Leys and *From the Center of the Earth* by Richard Bernstein. It wasn't until many years later that "scar literature" from mainland China was published in Taiwan.

REENCOUNTERING THE LITERATURE OF GREATER CHINA

Later I ran into Wang Meng five more times at international conferences and had a number of discussions with him. Although the literary arena in China is as vast as the land, Wang Meng was a prominent and representative writer. He not only possessed natural talent but also was perceptive and intelligent, which allowed him to survive such turmoil.

The second time I met him was in Berlin in 1985, but I was able to talk with him only many years later when we both served as fiction judges for the World Young Chinese Writers Award at the Chinese University in Hong Kong. He was invited to Taiwan in 1993 when the *United Daily News* hosted a conference titled "Chinese Literature: The Last Forty Years," which was organized by David Der-wei Wang, William Tay, and me. He led a group of mainland writers for a first visit to Taiwan; another sixty people were invited from abroad, along with more than a hundred people from Taiwan. David Wang and I edited the conference proceedings, which were later translated into English and published as *Chinese Literature in the Second Half of a Modern Century: A Critical Survey* to provide a comprehensive commentary on Chinese fiction in the second half of the twentieth century. Indiana University published a third edition of C. T. Hsia's *History of Modern Chinese Fiction* in 1993 and acquired our book as well, printing them simultaneously.

While in Taipei, Wang Meng invited a number of Taiwan writers to go to mainland China. In 1995, the Chinese Writers Association and the *United Daily News* Cultural Foundation arranged for fourteen writers whom I invited to attend a conference in Shandong organized by Wang Meng titled "Man and Nature." It was an unprecedented conference in terms of size. Among the participants from Taiwan were Liu Kexiang, Hu Taili, Wang Wenxing, Li Fengmao, Chen Xinyuan, Li Mingde, Walis Nogan, Jin Hengbiao, and Yang Nanjun, all of whom are nature writers. Their papers were solid and of an international caliber, of which I was quite proud.

There were more than fifty mainland writers, the work of many of whom I had read. While changing planes in Beijing for Yantai, Wang Meng introduced me to some important writers, including the highly respected Zhang Xianliang, who, as uncontrollably as the fan of a singer, said, "Oh, I found your *Greening Tree* so moving!" I remember several of the other writers had surprised smiles on their faces. Only later did I gradually come to realize that the writers on either side of the strait had quite different ideas about works dealing with the sufferings of the Cultural Revolution, such as *Greening Tree*. Even though everyone in Taiwan knew about Ah Cheng, the author of the stories "King of Chess," "King of Trees," and "King of Children," he was not necessarily held in the same high esteem by his peers. Whenever politics is involved, the distance between people grows.

At events like the opening ceremony and the many panels, we had hopes of sincerely sharing our views on literature. During the painful day we spent together at the Sino-Japanese War Memorial, Zhang Xianliang and I, as well as several other writers, had some deep discussions about the lot of the Chinese people over the last one hundred years. We took a small motorboat and made a slow trip around Bohai Bay where the huge Qing fleet had been defeated by the Japanese. The water was smooth and deep blue, and white clouds floated in the sky. Weihaiwei, which was once a national shame, had been changed to Weihai City and had been chosen as the cleanest city in China. It was a forward-looking, prosperous place with many plans for the future. We had several clear days and nights in a row, and those of us from Taiwan strolled by the sea every evening. Walking by the wave-lapped shore, we could see the skeletons of sunken ships from a hundred years ago. The beauty of the ocean was enough to make a person sigh and regret not being able to pack up the moon and take it home. A hundred years earlier, that moon had witnessed Taiwan being ceded to Japan.

A hundred years later, I found myself, an insignificant human being, standing by Bohai Bay looking north toward Dalian on the Liaodong Peninsula. If I crossed by steamship and took a train, I could be in Tieling, my old home, in a few hours. But all I could do was stand there foolishly for a moment and "gazing sadly, a thousand years, shedding a few tears," for I'd be on the plane home via Hong Kong the following day. I had been in Taiwan for fifty years, married, had children, and had a career, but I was still a "mainlander," and like the "Flying Dutchman," I could never go home. I could just stand by the waves looking toward a land to which I could not return.

In Taipei in the late 1980s, publishing houses such as Xindi, Hongfan, and Yuanliu published the works of many mainland authors such as Ah Cheng, Wang Anyi, Mo Yan, Yu Hua, Su Tong, and Zhang Xianliang, among others. All of these authors attended conferences, large and small, in Taiwan. And although we made friends with whom we could converse, we were clearly aware that "our" road and "theirs" were different. Truly, the wounds could not be entirely forgotten, as E. M. Forster wrote at the end of *Passage to India*, "No, not yet. . . . No, not there."

BERLIN *KULTUR*

"Going to Berlin" was something I must have longed for in a previous life.

When I was born, my father was studying in Berlin. In the ice-cold month of February at home, Berlin must have seemed like a place of dreams on the other side of the world. I spent nearly all of spring 1985 walking around the new Berlin, and I often thought of my mother's old dream of sixty years before as having been revived and how today that weak daughter of hers, who had not seen her father, was now in the city as a guest professor.

Six months earlier, I had received a call from Director Hua Yan of the Ministry of Science and Technology. He said that the Free University in Berlin was searching for a professor to teach Taiwan literature and that he wanted to recommend me, and asked if that was okay. Holding the phone, what could I say? I could scarcely believe my ears, an invitation relayed from so far away to go to Berlin, where my father had been a lifetime before.

I arrived in Berlin in early April. All the trees were still leafless, but occasionally a clump of yellow flowers welcoming spring was seen. Guo Hengyu, who met me at the airport, took me to the university dorm and showed me how to get from there to the university by bus. I lived on Thielallee, which has a delightful sound, so I never got lost. The following day, I took the U-Bahn to the university and met the students in the department.

Humboldt University of Berlin was situated in East Berlin and was forced to follow the Soviet line. Three years later, most of the students and teachers met in West Berlin and decided to set up a new academic institution, and so in 1948 in the American sector, with the assistance of the Americans, the Free University was established. On the sixtieth anniversary of the founding in 2008, it had become the ninth of Germany's premier universities, with more than thirty-one thousand students.

Two individuals were critical in establishing a regular course on Taiwan literature at the school. One was Dr. Dieter Heckelmann, who, in the 1970s, was a visiting professor of law at NTU for two years. He came with his wife and daughter and lived in faculty housing. A number of outstanding NTU professors had also gone to Berlin as visiting faculty. While in Berlin, I was frequently his guest; he often returned to Taiwan and got together with his old friends there, and he often went hiking in places outside Taipei such as Dadu Mountain. After German reunification, he served as head of domestic affairs for Berlin. The other was Professor Guo Hengyu, who was in charge of the China Research Institute. He was from Shandong and had come to Berlin from Tokyo University in 1960. He earned a Ph.D. in history from the Free University and stayed on to teach afterward. In 1990, he came to NTU as a visiting professor and taught German history for one year.

The China Research Institute of the Free University is housed in a famous five-floor mansion, which is bright and spacious and over a hundred years old. Bravely I set off from the spring flowers on Thielallee for the U-Bahn stop and from there to 42 Podbielskillee, where I stepped through a plain-looking gate and entered a different world.

Professor Guo Hengyu introduced me in German as a professor from Taiwan. I heard the term *kultur* mentioned frequently. Wasn't just thinking about the last hundred years of Taiwan or even Chinese culture a sad thing? I was asked to introduce myself and talk about my class. I had been under the impression that I would be meeting only with those students taking my class, but I had to address the more than one hundred students in the department. I started by telling them about when I was born and how my young father had just transferred from Berlin to Heidelburg University to study philosophy, committed to understanding history and life so as to strengthen China through education. Everyone knew the situation of Taiwan, and those at the Free University in West Berlin could certainly understand what we represented and our cultural significance. The students I taught at NTU were like them in that they were young intellectuals pursuing freedom of thought. I hoped that I could really understand Germany and that they could really understand Taiwan. Later Professor Guo said that my talk had been well received and was a good start. Before leaving, I had shipped over three hundred volumes of Taiwan literature to Germany, which I was donating to the China Research Institute at the Free University. In each book, the library stamped: "Donated by Professor Chi Pang-yuan, 1985."

My class focused on fiction, including Lai Ho's "The Steelyard," Wu Zhouliu's "The Doctor's Mother" and *Asia's Orphan*, and Bai Xianyong's *Taipei People*. In addition to works included in the anthology I had edited, I also included English translations of Yuan Qiongqiong's "A Sky of One's Own" and Xiao Sa's *My Son Hansheng*. The school required that an outline be handed out at each week's class. I taught the class in English, but had to supply the Chinese as well. The department asked Chen Huiwen to help out with interpreting into German when necessary. In our discussions we used German, English, and Chinese. Chen Huiwen had studied English twenty years earlier at Soochow University and had married Erik von Groeling, a young German studying Chinese at National Taiwan Normal University. She relocated to Cologne with her young husband, but he died unexpectedly during surgery. She went to Berlin and was living on a pension, taking care of a four-year-old and a one-year-old child. I felt sympathy and admiration for her. While I was in Berlin she looked after me both in class and outside, so we became good friends. She was also my guide in Berlin and made sure that I knew the real city.

After two weeks of class, I decided I wanted a place of my own, so Huiwen took me to see a number of advertised rooms, which is the best way to get to know a city. I was hoping for a desk and a garden window. I assumed that in Berlin, the old cultural capital, everybody read and studied, but what was surprising was that of the six or seven places we visited, not one had a desk. I was on the point of giving up when we visited a small shaded street and saw a little place set in a garden. The downstairs had two large rooms, with a kitchen and a dining table. Entering the first room, I saw a very large desk, and outside the window was a real garden. The rent was higher than for the other places, but this was what I really had in mind for Berlin. In the four months I was there, I watched as the various flowers in the flower beds went from bud to full bloom, and I came and went in the shade of trees. In all my life I never had such a restful environment, and on weekends I could hear the church bells near and far. I recall receiving a book from Lin Haiyin and writing back to her and saying that on Sunday the city was filled with the sound of bells. In her usual fashion, she replied immediately and said she wished she could go to Berlin.

On May 8, Professor Guo informed me that all the students in Berlin had to go see a documentary film titled *The Fall of Berlin*. I went to the Kurfürstendam downtown and saw that the street and bus stop in front of the KaDeWe Department Store I frequented were filled with protestors quietly holding up various placards, and down around the Kaiser Wilhelm Memorial Church were a number of ardently impassioned speakers. The documentary film was exceptionally comprehensive and clear—covering from the time Hitler started inciting people to the start of the war—and contained important scenes from the war and the lives of the people. But most of the film was about the last days of the Nazis, their defeat on the battlefields of Europe, as well as the systematic bombing of Berlin, including the warnings issued before the bombings that if surrender wasn't forthcoming, certain streets would be bombed. The film showed areas on the map with photos from before and after the bombings. It rained bombs, and street after street was reduced to rubble by the Allied planes. Ultimately about 60 percent of this once powerful capital was reduced to ruins. When the Allied forces entered the city on May 2, the survivors hid in basements. The Russian soldiers who first entered the city bayoneted and raped, the English who followed picked up the kids and fed them, while the Americans stood guard . . . the film was clear and detailed and one had to watch it, willing or not. It was a documentary the Germans had made for their descendants to watch.

I didn't return to where I was staying until after dark. The whole place was dark because the landlady had had an asthma attack and been hospitalized. That night I sat alone recalling the scenes of death and destruction in the film, and I couldn't help remembering those years when Chongqing was being bombed by the Japanese and the helplessness we felt. From seeing the map of the areas of Berlin that had been bombed, I realized that a new city had been built over the ruins! Were the bones of the last generation perhaps buried under my desk or bed? I was so scared, I couldn't sleep for nights.

The cover story in *Time* magazine that week was about the fortieth anniversary of Berlin's surrender. According to the editorial titled "There Is No Comparative Disaster," the Russians buried two hundred thousand alive along the Elbe River, while two atomic bombs were dropped on Hiroshima and Nagasaki before Japan surrendered. Both countries believed they had suffered the greatest disaster. But hadn't the Jews suffered the most, with millions of deaths? In fact, disasters cannot be compared, because for each victim, his is the greatest.

Over the past half century innumerable books have been written about the suffering of the Jews, while there have been almost no detailed accounts of how the Chinese suffered during the eight years of war against Japan. After the Communists occupied the mainland in 1949, the Nationalists, who had borne the brunt of the fight against Japan, had to renounce their past if they were to manage to survive. The people and the soldiers who had been dying for their country had to face a second death and were forgotten after the regime change. And why hadn't I, someone who had grown up during the war and had spent twenty years attending international literary exchange to promote "our Taiwan literature," written an account of those years?

From then on, my question-and-answer exchanges with the students at the Free University took on deeper implications. When reading Wang Zhenhe's "Little Lin Comes to Taipei," they said that a person had to visit Berlin in order to deeply understand Germany's recent history and that the wall, which was a tourist attraction, was nothing more than a symbol. I told them of my joy at first hearing the church bells of Berlin. Someone said that churches of many sects had been built on disaster sites, not just for the sake of the lost souls but also for atonement and as places to pray for peace. Look! There are so many churches in Berlin! After that, when I heard the church bells I no longer felt a sense of joy.

After the war, Berlin was reborn from the ruins. Trees were planted and death was covered over by a prosperous life. Real democracy was implemented in West Berlin, which was controlled by the United States and Britain, and there was political stability and economic prosperity. Germany's one great hope was to recover as a great cultured nation, so many international cultural events were held there. Shortly after I arrived in Berlin, I saw ads on the street for the Horizon World Literature Conference and learned that a large delegation would be coming from mainland China. Before the conference, I received a message from Bai Xianyong saying that he, Chen Ruoxi, Chung Ling, Lee Ou-fan, and William Tay had all received invitations to represent Taiwan and the overseas Chinese. After they arrived in Berlin, Profeesor Guo, Chen Huiwen, and I wholeheartedly received them; however, the organizers removed the talks and readings to be given by the five from the program. The names of the mainlanders were listed in the main hall, but not those from Taiwan, which angered us. Although the Free University first held a forum on Taiwan literature, circumstances dictated that the dozen or so mainland authors received all the attention. Berlin was like San Francisco in that everyone was curious about these writers fresh from behind the iron curtain.

After the 1990s, European research on Taiwan literature gradually shifted to research on the *kultur* of mainland China.

THE BRIDGE: INTRODUCING TAIWAN LITERATURE THROUGH TRANSLATION: THE CHINESE PEN

Even though I'd been involved in academic exchange, I had to first stabilize the footing of Taiwan literature. After my experience in Berlin in 1985, I began considering the present and future development of Taiwan literature from the perspective of a greater Europe. I was really shaken by something that happened at the annual PEN meeting of 1986 in Hamburg. The West German writer Günter Grass reproachfully roared at an East German writer who supported Russian Communist power: "Where is the conscience of literature there?" The 1992 meeting in Barcelona was used as something of a forum on the independence of the city from Spain. Half the documents that we received were in Catalan to signify that their ancient language was still alive. One of the most inspiring PEN meetings I attended took place in Czechoslovakia, where the theme of the meeting, which was presided over by the Czech President Havel, was "Nation, Ethnicity, Religious Tolerance, and Literature." There was one panel discussion titled "Small Languages, Great Literatures" and another titled "How Much Do We Know About Ourselves?" This was the first time I had heard a distinction made between major and minor languages. It was also the first time since the collapse of the Soviet Union that I heard writers—fifty of them—from countries that had regained their independence, and which, by resuming the use of their small languages instead of using Russian, had encountered new problems. Based upon their remarks, I authored a piece titled "Only the Cold Wind Hears My Voice," but I didn't explicitly state my concerns that the world of sinology had already started to shift its focus to mainland China, that important writers in Taiwan had stopped writing, that the tide of nativism was growing, and that the enthusiasm for writing in Chinese was missing. Would the day come when we would also find ourselves facing the unfavorable situation of a small language and a small literature? From then on, my concern for Taiwan literature was no longer simply a matter of encouraging and introducing it, but working to secure its future and position. In 1992, I formally took over the chief editorship of *The Chinese PEN*. For about ten years, I grappled with this problem of deepening the cultivation of Taiwan literature.

Since this English language quarterly was established in 1972, I had been a substantial consultant and, after editing the anthology, I had maintained a clear understanding of the development of Taiwan literature by continued reading. With the NTU Philosophy Department Incident (1973) and Zhao Tianyi being sent to the National Institute of Compilation and Translation, along with Ke Qingming taking over the editorship of *Modern Literature*, I developed a deeper understanding of nativist writers. At the time, poetry societies were popping up like bamboo shoots after a rain, and I was always a subscriber to their publications. Later, when making selections for the English quarterly, I maintained a fair attitude, holding no political position.

In a free world, writers didn't need an association. Writing is an individual struggle and the literary arena is no arena, but just writers from time to time getting together to discuss things. The International PEN (now PEN International) was founded in London in 1921 by England and some European writers. PEN is an acronym for Poets, Essayists, Novelists. In 1924, the Chinese PEN was founded in Shanghai and became part of the larger organization. Those who started it included Lin Yutang, Hu Shi, Xu Zhimo, and others, and the first president was Cai Yuanpei. They started doing all sorts of cultural exchange, translation, author visits, and other groundbreaking work. Since very young I was a voracious reader and often read unforgettable things; for example, about how they invited the Indian poet Tagore to visit China, which fired my imagination.

During World War II, PEN member nations faced off against each other and cultural exchange came to a halt until 1946, when they resumed once again in neutral Sweden. The Chinese PEN resumed in Taiwan in 1953; the first president was Zhang Daofan and the second was Luo Jialun. In 1959, it rejoined the international association and members attended every annual conference. In 1970, Lin Yutang was elected president and the third Asian Writers Conference was convened in Taipei, with writers from Korea, Thailand, the Philippines, and other nations being invited, and a hundred or so writers from Taiwan attending. Wang

Lan, Peng Ge, and Nancy Ing organized a vivid and dramatic event at the newly built Yuanshan Hotel, enhancing Taiwan's prestige. Lin Yutang suggested that they have a journal for publishing English translations in order to build a bridge between East and West.

In the autumn of 1972, the first issue of *The Chinese PEN* was published. Nancy Ing, whose native language was English, served as chief editor, with Wang Lan and Peng Ge as editorial consultants. Nancy served as chief editor for twenty years, from 1972 to 1992. I followed for nine years, after which came Perng Ching-hsi, Zhang Huijuan, Kao Tian'en, and Yanwing Leung, all of whom were my younger colleagues at NTU. One other person served as assistant editor and secretary—for the first fifteen years it was Norma Liu Hsiao, followed by Sarah Jen-hui Hsiang. When the issues of the quarterly were mailed out, a work-study student was hired. Such "loneliness" would be inconceivable for a large publisher. For years, like clockwork, the quarterly has been published without missing an issue, making it the longest running periodical produced by any of the national PEN associations. Taiwan therefore has quite a reputation among the more than one hundred member nations.

Nancy Ing was among the first to translate Taiwan literature. In 1961, the Heritage Press published translations of fiction and new poetry. Nancy Ing was the editor of *New Voices*, a collection that included Bai Xianyong, Qiong Hong, Wang Wenxing, Chen Ruoxi, and Ye Shan (who later changed his pen name to Yang Mu), among others. She therefore had several years of experience before she edited the quarterly.

Nancy Ing's name was synonymous with the quarterly: she made the selections, initially translated the poetry for every issue, sought out highly qualified translators, read the translation manuscripts, did the proofreading, and sent the edited proofs to the printer. In the third year of publication, she began using the artwork of Taiwan artists on the covers and also introduced them in the magazine, which proved another challenge for her. Wang Lan was a big help in this regard. After I took over, I had the help of friends like Lin Wenyue and Ding Zhenwan.

Nancy Ing's beautiful blond, blue-eyed mother married her classmate Zhang Chengyou, and moved from Virginia to Hubei in 1917 (after arriving in Taiwan, he served as Minister of the Audit). Nancy graduated from the Department of Foreign Languages and Literatures at West China University in Chengdu in 1949 and came to Taiwan with her husband, Glyn T. H. Ing, who founded Continental Engineering Corporation. Abroad for meetings she always used her married name, but at home she was known by everybody simply as Nancy. She loved literature and occasionally wrote poetry of her own, publishing a collection of verse titled *One Leaf Falls* in 1971.

In 1972, I moved to Taipei from Taichung. By coincidence we lived in neighboring lanes and often bumped into each other on the street when she was walking her dog. She edited the quarterly and I was editing the anthology, so we had plenty to talk about. Basic topics of conversation included what works to translate, good English translators, the translation of specific words and phrases, layout, final product, and reader response, all topics of which we never tired.

Warm and optimistic, Nancy was always friendly even when busy. Every year before the annual PEN meeting, she would make sure that papers, speeches, and discussion topics were ready. She also prepared gifts and at the conference venue would shake so many hands outstretched in friendship. After the Cultural Revolution, the China PEN of mainland China joined and on many occasions tried to have us expelled, but Nancy would take to the stage, her naturally warm smile having disappeared, and indignantly protect the rights of the free people of Taiwan to be represented. After Tiananmen in 1989, China stopped attending the annual meetings. With today's political situation, national position will be broached, but the international friendship established by Nancy Ing and the other representatives, the longtime stability of the quarterly, and the organization's professionalism all make the position of the Taiwan Chinese PEN unassailable. After the United States and the Republic of China broke off relations, Nancy was invited to do a TV program titled *Talk About Taiwan* in ten U.S. locations. With structured analysis and clear language, she was able to demonstrate the progress of Taiwan culturally, economically, and socially. The quarterly only helped to increase understanding. During those years, Nancy spoke a great deal for Taiwan in the Western world, but Taiwan was not a well-known place. Such contributions as well as her editorship of the quarterly were wholeheartedly supported by her husband. The income of the quarterly came from the few hundred overseas gift subscriptions provided by the Ministry of Foreign Affairs and the Government Information Office, as no more than a hundred copies ever sold in the local bookstores. Most of the expenses for translating, printing, distribution, and salaries received the financial assistance of Glyn T. H. Ing. Originally the PEN office was housed in the Continental Engineering Corporation building, but after Glyn passed away, space was rented on Wenzhou Street. Just when things were becoming difficult, the Hao Ran Foundation stepped in and began providing financial support, keeping the quarterly going to this day.

THE "US" OF LITERATURE

Publishing a quarterly is something that presses on you by the day and the month. In twenty years, the hotline between Nancy and me, as consultant, was always ringing. If something couldn't be resolved over the phone, we'd meet; for example: the order of the texts, meeting with a new translator, sharing the discovery of a new piece of writing, and the joys of finding the right word. At the end of 1978, when Lin Wenyue and I made an academic visit to Korea, we became fast friends. After we returned to Taipei, she often joined Nancy and me, and we were all soon frequently joined by Lin Haiyin. Every month or every other month for a period of ten years, we would get together and talk excitedly about what we had written or translated recently. These were happy occasions for all of us.

Lin Wenyue and I were colleagues at NTU. She was in the Chinese department and I was in the Department of Foreign Languages and Literatures. Books brought us together as close friends. The first thing I read was her *One Year in Kyoto*, which left a deep impression as the sort of travel book an educated woman should write. One day I was teaching in Room 16 at the College of Arts and Sciences building when a woman in high black boots walked down the hall outside. The students later told me that she was Lin Wenyue, the author of *One Year in Kyoto.* When the Association for Comparative Literature was founded, she along with Zheng Qian and Ye Qingbing were among the founding members from the Chinese program. We often sat together in the board meetings, and when we attended conferences and meetings we were often the only two women, so we roomed together. On our first day in Korea, we were taken to a hotel outside of Seoul, next to which was a farmhouse where cabbages and radishes for preparing pickles were piled, which reminded me of my old home in the northeast and the hired hands storing the cabbages in the cellar for the winter. That night I told Wenyue about my mother, and we talked long into night the despite being tired. After the trip to Korea, we also traveled to Japan for almost two weeks, where we shared our joys and sorrows and had many thoughts and views to discuss.

Starting in 1972, Wenyue spent the next six years absorbed in the translation of *The Tale of Genji*, which was eventually published in five volumes. I found her translation, the first scholarly translation into Chinese, admirable. Writers like to talk about fame, but this profession is one that really does provide fame. Among the four of us, Wenyue was seldom excitable or impassioned and was more often a good listener. In expressing her opinions, she was always calm and her speech measured, perhaps because she was ten years younger than I. Her translation of *The Tale of Genji* was followed by translations of *Tales of Ise* and *The Pillow Book of Sei Shonagon.* One time when the four of us were having dinner, Haiyin said that she wanted to publish Wenyue's latest translation of *The Diary of Izumi Shikibu*. The following month when we got together, the proofs were ready and Haiyin asked her if she could go over them in the next week. I interjected, "She'll probably have it done in three days." As expected, this refined volume with Gou Yulun's exquisite cover was published in a matter of two months as Chunwenxue's final commemorative book.

Shortly thereafter, Nancy fell ill and began to lose her memory. Before Wenyue relocated in the States with her husband, we frequently met at a coffeehouse between our homes on the corner of Hoping East Road and Xinsheng South Road. We never ran out of things to talk about, and she even helped me with the quarterly covers and other things. We sat by the window and watched the people coming and going. One day someone stopped at the window and looked in, following which he came into the coffeehouse. It was the poet Mei Xin, the editor of the literary supplement of the *Central Daily News*. He came over to our table and said, "You know, we often wonder what the two of you are talking about." That day we happened to be engaged in working on the cover of the commemorative hundredth issue. Wenyue had cut a number of laurel leaves and was assembling a crown, in the middle of which was written "Chinese PEN 100." Shortly thereafter, Mei Xin passed away, and we both had the impression that he had come to bid us farewell.

To date, Wenyue has published more than twenty volumes of essays and literary jottings, mostly about what she was reading, conversations, life, travel, and visits with old friends, always moving and sincere. In 1999 she published *Diet Diary*, in which through various menus, she recalled gatherings with family, friends, and teachers. The book created a fad of literature on food and drink, and described the pleasures of life in a time of peace and prosperity. Actually, her real intent by describing the gatherings was to recapture the sense of sadness that came when they ended.

After Wenyue left Taipei, Haiyin became bedridden and the living room lamp was extinguished.

Taiwan literature written in Chinese, which can be traced back over three hundred years, began with the Eastern Song Society established by Shen Guangwen in 1685. The Japanese occupied the island and vigorously promoted Japanese, and literature written in Japanese by Taiwan writers is still available today, much of it having been translated into Chinese as well as being the subject of research. The place of writers such as Lai Ho, Wu Zhuoliu, Long Yingzong, Yang Kui, and Lu Heruo are honored and established. The writers who came to Taiwan after 1949 and wrote about homeland and homesickness have been swallowed by time, but their writings are part of Taiwan. The writers who matured after the war grew up reading the works of these writers in the literary supplements and magazines, and never really made much of a distinction as to where a writer was from. Zhong Zhaozheng, Ye Shitao,

Ji Xian, Lin Hengtai, Yu Kwang-chung, Zhou Mengdie, Lo Fu, Ya Hsien, Yang Mu, Wu Sheng, Qi Jun, Lin Haiyin, Huang Chunming, Bai Xian-yong, Li Qiao, Zheng Qingwen, Zhang Xiaofeng, and Xi Murong all sit and laugh and talk together. For readers who have been torn apart by political discourse, it is undeniable that these older and middle-aged writers have cultivated a Taiwan literature of substance and beauty that is well received internationally. For literature there is no "them," no "you," just "us."

TAKING OVER THE EDITORSHIP OF PEN

One morning in May 1992, Nancy Ing called me and asked if I could come over to her house immediately. Upon entering her study, I found her with her arms around her typewriter, her head down on the machine, crying. She looked up and said, "Pang-yuan, I can't translate a poem for the next issue of the quarterly. What am I going to do?" It was Bai Ling's short poem "Kite." Over the last twenty years, the quarterly had published translations of about two hundred modern poems, approximately half of which Nancy had quite happily translated, but now she was facing the loss of her memory. Helplessly, like someone who was entrusted with something precious by a friend, I took over the editing duties at the quarterly.

I knew that Nancy had received regular financial support from her husband, and even after I took over, he still took the initiative to send another fifty thousand *yuan* (New Taiwan Dollars) to the quarterly, though he was ill. The Government Information Office and the Ministry of Foreign Affairs purchased several hundred copies to give away, which became our sole source of revenue. A sympathetic soul at the Council for Cultural Planning privately suggested that we apply for money under a plan of theirs called "Special Columns on Cultural Inheritance." I therefore asked Yan Junying and Chen Fangmei, former art history students in my NTU Advanced English class, to take turns writing an English essay for each issue. Yan Junying had received a degree from Harvard and was then a researcher at Academia Sinica, and she started off with a piece on Tang dynasty Buddhist art; Chen Fangmei had received a degree from London University and was then working for the Palace Museum, and she began with a piece on Zhou bronzes. They wrote for ten years, helping the quarterly to receive money from the council to cover printing costs.

At the time of greatest need, Wenyue was instrumental in applying for and receiving funds to help us from her father's Lin Bozou Foundation. On two occasions, monthly salaries could not be paid, but private contributions got us through those difficult times. PEN has a magnificent board of directors that only meets at fixed times, so for all my real difficulties all they could say was: "She who is capable will have to work more!" After a working meal, they could all return to their comfortable occupations, but being seventy, I was feeling pretty tired and asked the board to find a replacement. They laughed and said, "You're doing fine; life begins at seventy," and so the meeting ended.

Happily, while I was at the quarterly I did put together a stable team of translators, the first of whom was Nicholas Koss, who had come to teach at Fu Jen Catholic University in 1991. He was introduced to Nancy and me by Pierre E. Demers, who was teaching at NTU. Nicholas was a Benedictine brother and had a Ph.D. in comparative literature from Indiana University. After I took over, he was one of my most reliable translators and polishers. He also read over my "Editor's Note" for each issue.

In the early 1990s, Daniel J. Bauer joined the team. He taught English at Fu Jen University and for many years had written a column for the *China Post*, Taiwan's oldest English language newspaper. He was particularly fond of poetic writing and is still a good companion of ours.

Edward Vargo, who ran the College of Foreign Languages at Fu Jen University, also joined our team. He and Nicholas were anxious to promote a graduate school of translation at Fu Jen, and Nancy and I helped make a case for the proposal by speaking with Chen Qing at the Ministry of Education about the importance of training translators. Ultimately, the proposal was approved. Members of the first two graduating classes at Fu Jen included Michelle Wu, May Tang, Carlos Tee, and Nancy Du, all of whom have translated fiction, prose, and art criticism for the quarterly. I was thus able to actually see the program bear fruit, which was gratifying. Michelle Wu was a student of mine at NTU, and both she and Nancy Du had parents in the foreign service, so they received complete educations in both English and Chinese at home and abroad.

The late 1980s saw a golden age in comparative literature at NTU, when a younger generation of scholars that included Song Meihwa, Chang Hanliang, Perng Ching-hsi, and Kao Tian'en were all invited to join PEN and were soon helping out will all sorts of duties, ultimately editing the quarterly. An even younger generation includes Zheng Xiuxia, Karen Chung, and Yanwing Leung, who is the quarterly's current editor. Thus a group of people sharing the belief in the importance of Taiwan literature coalesced. In the process of recruiting talent, we were befriended by a number of expert translators from at home and abroad, including Howard Goldblatt, John Minford, Göran Malmqvist, Michelle Yeh, and John Balcom, who began translating poetry for the quarterly when he was in his twenties.

When I first took over the editorship, I frequently looked at the shelves of the quarterly beside my desk. Unlike in other magazines, there were no advertisements or adornments, with each issue looking much like a book. I wanted to give each issue the content, spirit, and permanence of a book, and for the quarterly to be more than just a place for periodic literary exchanges among friends. I wanted to give each issue a theme and a perspective so that it could stand alone.

The first theme that came to mind was literature of the armed forces, which was sometimes referred to as the literature of homesickness. Actually, most of the mainlanders who came to Taiwan around 1949 had something to do with the military. The military of China had a tradition of the soldier-scholar, and after arriving in Taiwan, some of these people left the military and went into magazine and newspaper publishing, and some taught. Among the more accomplished poets were Ji Xian, Qin Zihao, Lo Fu, Shang Qin, and Ya Hsien.

A second generation of writers grew up in the housing for military dependents and received fine educations. They were of broad vision and had the talent to absorb techniques from world literature. By then

Taiwan was prospering economically, and major newspapers established literary awards to encourage writers from the younger generation, including Ai Ya, Sun Weimang, Zhu Tianwen, Zhu Tianxin, Zhang Dachun, Xiao Sa, Su Weizhen, Yuan Qiongqiong, and Zhang Qijiang, to name a few.

I fought nine years for the quarterly, which, along with the previous twenty of Nancy, as well as the years since, have seen the publication of hundreds of short stories, essays, poetry, and art criticism. In those years, no representative writer has been missed. PEN International publishes two issues of its magazine a year, and almost every issue has included something reprinted from Taiwan. Someday when someone writes a history of cultural exchange, I wonder if they will mention the steadfastness of the quarterly.

In all those years, I knew that the one thing missing was the translation of novels, which would make a hugely persuasive case for Taiwan literature. In 1990, Guo Weifan, head of the Council for Cultural Planning, convened a fact-finding committee for a plan to translate Chinese books into English. Happily I attended the meeting to contribute my ideas. Lists of books to translate, translators, and examiners were drawn up. Director Guo personally ran the dozen or so meetings, listening seriously and discussing ways to proceed. The council actually came up with a budget. Suddenly, however, Director Guo was transferred to head the Ministry of Education. The next five years saw three different directors, each of whom wanted to convene the same fact-finding meetings, but in each case, the meetings were run by an assistant. The notes from the previous meetings were reviewed, a few comments added, and some changes made, after which the meeting was then ended with a few bureaucratic comments and thanks for our ideas. The third time such a meeting was held, I asked, "Why must we again discuss something that has already been settled?" The assistant director replied, "When directors change, the rules of the game must also change." I replied, "I am very busy and do not have time to play games." Upon which, I stood up and left. Since then, I have never set aside any time for such meetings, nor have I had any confidence in official cultural policy.

Since the founding of the quarterly, I had become an effective year-round consultant, but I was very busy and had never asked for an actual job description. I shouldered the task for nearly ten years! How would I describe the successes and failures of those years? I had been waiting, keeping a lookout for someone to take my place, but it was a strange job without financing, without a staff, without a salary, and without applause. Those who were younger than I and who were competent would briefly consider the sacrifices and, not knowing whom they were fighting for, would simply say they were too busy and refuse the job. Actually, I should have realized earlier that handling the quarterly was super lonely and hard work. All real writers work alone. Originally PEN was an organization of friends who met for the sake of literature, but after Nancy retired, the friendships she established with early members of the English and French associations gradually went cold.

My feelings for the PEN quarterly deepened with each passing year, but we parted just prior to the millennium. Not that I didn't want to stay, but time waits for no one, and parting is parting. I had put my shoulder to the yoke and moved ahead, and what I had accomplished was the fulfillment of my quixotic role.

AN UNEXPECTED PLEASANT SURPRISE: MODERN CHINESE LITERATURE FROM TAIWAN IN ENGLISH TRANSLATION

In 1996, David Wang invited me to participate in the planning of the Modern Chinese Literature from Taiwan in English translation series for Columbia University Press. The editorial board was composed of David Wang, Göran Malmqvist, and myself, with funding provided by the Chiang Ching-kuo Foundation for Scholarly Exchange. This was the last unexpected and pleasant surprise in my life, and a great opportunity to fulfill a cherished desire. Beyond the cultural significance of this cooperation, there was also an element of destiny.

David Wang graduated from NTU's Department of Foreign Languages and Literatures in 1976 and went to the United States, where he obtained a Ph.D. in comparative literature from the University of Wisconsin. In 1987 he was teaching at Harvard, and Nancy and I invited him to serve as an editorial consultant for the PEN quarterly. He frequently returned to Taiwan to see family and attend conferences, and his writing on Taiwan literature was as broad as it was deep and influential. In 1990 he went to teach at Columbia University and was taken on as an advisor for the Press, entrusted with carrying out the Chiang Ching-kuo Foundation plan for translating Taiwan literature into English. From the time our cooperation began until now, over thirty volumes have been published in the series.

In 1989, David Wang returned to Taiwan for his father's funeral. Shortly after the ceremony, Liang Surong, a family friend, asked me, "Do you know that he is Mr. Wang Jingren's son?" Hearing this, I was dumbfounded and overcome with a mixture of feelings. My own father had just passed away two years earlier and the events of his life were still fresh in my memory. My father arrived in Taiwan with nothing, but he did have staunch friends who wanted to help keep *Time and Tide* going, for which I was grateful.

When the Japanese occupied the northeast, Wang Jingren served as the director of the Bureau of Education in Changling County, Jilin, and secretly took part in anti-Japanese underground work, assisting in the revolutionary activities of which my father was in charge. He was a patriot filled with a sense of justice. Who could have foreseen that after victory in the war against Japan, international and national policy mistakes would allow the northeast to fall into the hands of the Communists? Making the arduous journey, he arrived alone in Taiwan, his home and country lost. Early on, he was recommended by Shi Jian, a revolutionary comrade, and joined *Time and Tide* as an editor when it resumed publication in Taiwan. Later he was in charge of the business office. From the end of the 1950s to the 1970s, he helped my father keep the weekly magazine going, sometimes without pay and even risking being jailed wrongly by the political powers. *Time and Tide* had the most weight of any publication with international political commentary in Chongqing during the eight years of the war. On the verge of bankruptcy, it shut down several times, but always resumed. In the last run, 153 issues were published, and they received 152 warnings from the authorities before they finally stopped publication. In those ten years in Taipei, they moved from Xuchang Street to Jinxi Street, where they rented a small room and, ignoring the precarious situation outside, shared in the difficult-to-realize ideals and aspirations of men of letters, which took a great deal of courage. I admired Uncle Jingren's sense of morality and justice and his strength of character. If the two old brothers get together again in heaven, it will be comforting to them to see that destiny brought David Wang and me together to continue their life and work in letters.

For a decade David and I communicated by letter, and when faxes came along, the first letter I sent to him by fax was on New Year's Eve 1998: "The cold comes in wave after wave, and there are far fewer firecrackers outside than last year. It's said there's a recession and everything is depressed. . . ." Actually, I wrote that letter about the English translation of Li Qiao's *Wintry Night*. One of Columbia's outside readers for the manuscript felt that *Wintry Night* had value in terms of the study of world literature, but that most English readers would not be interested in it. I said, "If the book has value, then it should be published in the series. Naturally, from the perspective of *Rose, Rose, I Love You* or *The Butcher's Wife*, books like *Wintry Night* or *Orphan of Asia* would be of little interest. But Arundhati Roy's *The God of Small Things* and Charles Frazier's *Cold Mountain*, two award-winning books in America and England, would be much the same type. Taiwan books such as *Wintry Night*, *The Three-Legged Horse*, and *A Thousand Moons on a Thousand Rivers* are dear to us, but the world contains many different us's."

Rereading this letter ten years later, I think of how David Wang and I struggled in various ways while selecting books to be translated, having them translated, and getting them published. I can say that it was a revolutionary feeling. Yunzhong Chongzhong, David Wang's mother, joined the Ethical Society in Shenyang and spent her life dedicated to female literacy classes, craft classes, kindergartens, and other social services. The Ethical Society in those days had a heart of religion but without the trappings of a religion, nor was it involved in any political activities; instead, it used the simplest methods to get close to the people. In the homeland to the north, which had been closed off, they helped countless women escape the sad fate of ignorance. It was the same when they came to Taiwan. David Wang was born in Taipei in 1954, and from a boy who liked to find a quiet corner in which to read he grew into a true scholar, one who enjoys helping others, regardless of whether they are family or not. We share a common attitude toward Taiwan literature: we wanted to contribute something out of our feelings for the place, even before "Do you love Taiwan or not?" became a political slogan. Fortunately, as long as Columbia University exists, the press will continue to operate and our series of books will continue to exist. When our descendants abroad read these books, they will have a truer understanding of the place of their origins. So, our efforts, David's and mine, ought to have some everlasting value.

9

CONFIRMATION OF THIS LIFE

From the Great Flowing River to the Sea of Silence

MOTHER'S PASSING

August falls in that season of intense summer heat in the seventh lunar month, but it was unusually hot in 1983. Mother grew noticeably weaker, so we took her to see a cardiologist for a check-up at the Tri-Service General Hospital.

She left the hospital three days later, a little after six in the morning. I received a call from her home in Neihu informing me that she had passed away. The suddenness of her departure left me inexpressibly frightened. I hurried home with my sister Ningyuan to see my eighty-four-year-old mother lying peacefully in bed. That morning she had gotten up and washed by herself, gone to the balcony to water the flowers, returned to her room, sat down on the edge of her bed and asked the maid to prepare lunch for her aged husband, and then clearly said, "Oh God! You call for me, so I go." Sitting there, she passed away. Father was sitting in a chair by the door and heard everything clearly. Her leaving the world with such religious conviction was our greatest consolation.

Mother had converted to Christianity at the beginning of 1950, just after I had moved from that bagasse-board room to Jianguo North Road. It was also at that time that the Chinese Language Church on Nanjing East Road started holding services in an old wooden house. Wu Yong, the pastor, preached in strong terms of heaven and hell in order to make comparisons between good and evil vivid and to explain the joys and sorrows of the world. My mother suffered sadly for half of her life: after a hard wait of ten years, she went to Nanjing to be with my father, and then spent another twenty years drifting and wandering, without ever having a house of her own. Then she crossed the sea to Taiwan, a place with which she was entirely unfamiliar, to live with the family of her son and daughter-in-law in a thirty-tatami room in a Japanese-style house. Cut off from the past, she didn't know what the future would bring. Pondering deeply, she couldn't understand what the suffering meant. Although she didn't believe in heaven and hell, those extreme forms of reward and punishment, she did begin diligently to read the Bible. Over thirty-five years she read my large Bible, which had been a wedding gift (a gift from my father's friend Uncle Dong Qizheng, who inscribed on the flyleaf: "Do unto others as you would have them do unto you") countless times, marking in red those passages she memorized, and passages that had provided answers to some of her perplexities were most certainly also marked. Perhaps this was her true form of worship, the only spiritual realm of her own, beyond having devoted her whole life to her husband and her children.

I was probably the only one who really understood her, and for the longest time! Following in her footsteps, I accompanied her through all the lonely days. Although we were of different times and had different educational opportunities, we lovingly and easily surmounted all "gaps" for sixty years. Those times when I was most in need of help, she was always there, arms outstretched, to help me overcome my troubles and move forward. During the seventeen years I lived in Taichung, each time I met her at the train station and saw her off, it was at a turning point in my life. In the years I was abroad studying, my three boys never lacked a mother because she was there. When she stayed with us on Wulang Lane in Taichung, many old friends from our refugee days would get together and talk about old times, which created a festive mood. Father supplied me with a profound idealism; Mother gave me my feelings for literature and attitude about the treatment of others. When I was growing up, suffering deprivations and hardships on the road and taking shelter in the woods during bombings, my mother told me stories of the wilds of our homeland and the family history. My children and grandchildren all know her stories and the need to get ahead through education: "You can't be a wolf hunter!" On no account can you fall behind because of idleness and laziness, to be the food of wolves. The homeland of her youth in the northeast a hundred years ago was a plain where packs of wolves were sometimes seen. The frigid wind of the first lunar month, the threat of tigers and wolves, the joy at the renewal of the pasturage in spring and summer in her stories, all inspired my imagination for a lifetime.

Before Mother passed away, we knew our parents were aging, but the thought of them dying never crossed our minds, much less did we ever talk about making final arrangements. Hastily, my younger sister Ningyuan accompanied a representative from the Legislative Yuan to Danshui and found a plot on a mountain slope in Sanzhi Township. It was an open spot overlooking the Pacific Ocean and resting on the slope of Mount Miantian. And so the Chi family had a foothold on Taiwan. Mother was buried there after cremation, and my father, in his last years, would often go there and sit before her grave, watching as the ships passed far out at sea. He said that from the grave you looked northeast and that the ocean flowed home toward Bohai Bay and Dalian: "We can't go home, so it's a good place to be buried." Four years later, Father was also buried there. Yuchang and I purchased a plot directly adjoining theirs from below. In the future, I will forever rest at the knees of my parents, together in death as in life, never again to wander. As of today, there are four generations of us on Taiwan, a place where falling leaves can return to their roots!

UNEXPECTED MISFORTUNE

In 1985 on my way back to Taiwan from Berlin, I stopped in London to attend an international cultural conference held at Cambridge University, where I was to present a paper on which I had taken great pains, titled "The Mellowing of Modern Chinese Poetry in Taiwan." When I returned to our empty nest in Taipei, I started preparing for classes that would soon begin.

On the Sunday morning before the start of classes, I had arranged for Yuchang and me to meet our good friends Yilie and Junxian and my sister Ningyuan to climb Mount Datun, because it had been ten years since we last climbed it. Yilie called us the "Idiot Mountain Climbers." The five of us used our brains in real life (Yilie was the assistant general manager at Taiwan Sugar; Junxian was the assistant chief of accounting at Taiwan Power; Yuchang was the chief engineer at Taiwan Railways Administration; Ningyuan was the assistant general manager of ZTE Ticket Co.; and I taught at National Taiwan University). Over ten years, regardless of the weather, we went to the seldom-visited scenic spots and climbed all the mountains in the Taipei area. Yuchang was a reliable driver and fancied himself a semiprofessional mountaineer! In the mountains, we leaped and shouted in a return to nature, our minds emptied, like idiots.

That Sunday morning, our reliable driver had to attend a meeting, so I went to the sidewalk in front of the Normal University across from Lishui Street to wait for a cab and then go on to pick up the other three. It was very early, so there were not many people or cars about. Absorbed in looking left for an empty cab, I did not see when a motorcycle suddenly flew through the intersection against the light and was struck broadside by a taxi, hurling it into the air toward the tree under which I was standing, as shiny fragments rained down all around. The next thing I was conscious of was that my head was resting on a beat-up tennis shoe, my left foot was nowhere in sight, and I couldn't move my right arm. I managed to prop myself up with difficulty using my left arm and saw my left foot in a new shoe, looking like the leg of a folding chair that had been broken off, pressed under my left leg. My right arm was broken and my sleeve felt empty. I just felt numb, for the pain had not yet set in. Three or four pedestrians looked at me to see if I was still alive; one of them asked me my name. I asked them to call my husband at once. A car stopped and out stepped a large man. When he saw the quantity of blood I had lost, he picked me up and put me in the back seat of his car. One of the pedestrians said, "You can't move her; you have to wait for the police." He shouted angrily, "If we wait for the police, she'll die from loss of blood." As he drove, he asked me which hospital I wanted to go to. I said "Tri-Service General! (For thirty years I always found the places I felt safest.) But first stop at Jianguo South Road. There are people waiting there for me." Under the bridge, I could see Yilie standing there anxiously looking around. My mind was still clear, and I told him to get my sister and meet at Tri-Service General Hospital. Upon arriving at the hospital, I remember that I grabbed the sleeve of the man who had brought me and asked him his name. He refused to say, but did reluctantly leave his address. My family was never able to locate him, but I will never forget him for as long as I live.

All of this occurred within a matter of fifteen minutes. The young man who ran the red light had just recently been discharged from the army. The rider, his two legs broken, and his smashed motorcycle flew through the air and landed under the tree where I was standing, and I was struck by a number of pieces. The doctor said the piece that struck my right arm missed my carotid artery by an inch. When I fell to the ground, my head landed on the beat-up shoe of the motorcyclist, which protected my head from the impact with the rocky ground.

For years now I have wondered how someone like me, a person who has remained aloof from the world, could meet with such unexpected misfortune. Was it God's wish that I experience for myself this level of human suffering? Was it punishment for my excessive happiness at traveling to Europe and visiting the historical and scenic spots to my heart's content, not knowing how to avoid the danger lurking on the dusty city street?

In more than a month spent in the surgery ward of Tri-Service General Hospital, I did indeed walk through the "valley of the shadow of death." After the numbness following the crash wore off, my whole body was in excruciating pain for which the painkillers, shouting, and cursing were useless, but I was able to maintain a degree of quiet self-respect. Over time, the bone-piercing pain spread, following sunrise and moonset, throughout my body. My left leg was shattered and could not be joined, so an eight-inch steel pin had to be inserted below the knee to provide stability, and my right arm was reaffixed through surgery and would heal naturally. Dr. Lin Liuchi, who performed the surgery, was a happy and self-confident young physician, in charge of my case. In addition to performing the surgery, he visited me every day and always said, "Today we have to conduct . . ." His smile brought me back to the world of the living, which I'll never forget.

How did I get through that hot beginning of autumn and those long nights? All I remember is freeing myself from the eighteenth circle of Dante's Inferno and clambering up to the most peaceful of Wordsworth's "Lucy" poems: "A slumber did my spirit seal, I have no human fears." I had to stand up and stride once again with happiness. I could not rely on painkillers forever and had to master the tyrannical pain with my own mind. A year later, under the guidance of the rehab physician at National Taiwan University, and supported by that steel pin in my leg, I returned to school to teach.

Thank God my mother had already passed away so that she didn't have to weep for me.

FATHER IN A SEA OF SILENCE (YAKOU SEA)

However, it was unexpectedly my father's turn to weep for me.

Mother had been gone for two years, and Father had never known such loneliness. Normally when he was at home, he would eat when meals were ready, and wear what was laid out for him. Mother had taken care of everything for decades, and the morning she passed away, she was still asking the maid to prepare a meal. He was left alone, and I had to resort to all sorts of stratagems, pleading with him, encouraging him, even duping him, to try to get him to move in with us, but he refused to leave the house in Neihu. My sister Ningyuan and I would take turns going to see him there on alternate days, after class or work, but he would be out on the balcony facing the street at nine in the morning watching for us.

After my accident, he hadn't seen me in days and kept asking my sister where I was, and she would reply, "She had to attend a conference overseas." He'd reply, "Didn't she just get back from Germany?" This went on for nearly two weeks, so my sister finally told him, "She slipped and fell and can't walk." He said, "Then I'll go see her." This went on for another month, when suddenly his stomach acted up and he was sent to the surgery ward at Tri-Service General, on the floor below me. By that point, my upper-body cast had been removed, but the one on my left leg was still in place. I was worried about my father's illness and a few days later, having received permission from the doctor, I went in a wheelchair to see him. The lower half of my body was covered with a blanket and I no longer looked like a mummy, as before. Entering his room, I called out to him, and his eyes filling with tears, he said, "What happened? How could you have taken such a fall?"

The floodgates of his tears, which he had kept shut for forty years, thus broke open, never to close again. Referred to as "Old Steel," he was never seen to shed a tear in adversity, but from that day forward in the last years of his life, he would weep incessantly each time he saw his daughter who had nearly lost her life. Sometimes he would say, "In the years I was involved in the revolution, your mother took care of you and suffered no less than I did. For all these years I never realized how much she suffered for this family."

In his final lonely years, recollections of past events filled his thoughts. Sometimes he'd say to me, "The mind is like a mighty charging force," and would lament the extreme fate of China. The Cultural Revolution was winding down and there was a lot of news about people and events coming from various quarters, which allowed him to understand those days more comprehensively. For example, in 1981 while he was in Disabled Veterans General Hospital, Zhang Xueliang suddenly came to visit him in his sickroom. Since they had parted on bad terms in Wuhan in 1935, this was the first time they had seen each other in half a century, which left my father greatly disturbed. The two dashing young men of those days were both eighty-two years old, and living thousands of miles from home with a lifetime of frustrations behind them; they had so much to talk about, but no need to say anything. Frequently my father would ask himself: *If we had been able to cooperate in those days, what would the northeast be like today? What would China be like?* In point of fact, even if time could flow backward, cooperation wouldn't necessarily be an easy matter. At twenty, Zhang Xueliang assumed control of the Fengtian clique and the territory it controlled, and without any decisive preparation and knowing only power, he rashly precipitated the Xi'an Incident with its grave repercussions, putting hundreds of thousands of soldiers from the northeast into China proper, losing the power to address the fate of the northeast. How could he cooperate with Chi Shiying, who respected human dignity and was an idealist for democratic reform? The day the two of them met, the only thing they had in common was their fond regard for General Guo Songling. Zhang Xueliang thought about General Guo assisting him in power; my father thought that if General Guo had been victorious at the battle of the Great Flowing River, the situation in the northeast would have been entirely transformed; the Japanese would not have been allowed to enter and establish the puppet state of Manchukuo, and even with war between China and Japan and Japan's subsequent defeat, the fate of the vast northeast would not have been decided by the Russians and those southerners like Chiang Kai-shek, Mao Zedong, Tu Yuming, and Lin Biao. Although these humiliations were no more, they continued to torment him for the rest of his life.

At dinnertime, my sister and I would pour him a glass of wine, and each time he lifted the glass, tears would flow as he recounted the events of those days: clearly the war should not have been lost, but it was, and the vast northeast was lost as a result. "All my comrades of those years who fought single-mindedly behind enemy lines for over a decade died in vain, and their hope that a victorious central government would look after their orphans and widows came to naught. Those who remained behind faced a difficult time living in the hands of the Communists. Patriotic intellectuals one and all, if they hadn't become involved in the revolution, they could have survived and raised their children. I harmed them all, for which I am profoundly sorry!" He repeated such words, tormenting himself to the end of his days.

After Mother passed away, he spoke less, becoming almost silent, as if he had gone from the surge of the Great Flowing River to the Sea of Silence. At the southernmost tip of Taiwan, to the left of Oluanpi

Lighthouse, there is a small bay called the Yakou Sea, or Mute Sea. The waves from the Pacific roll into this bay and seem to vanish without leaving a trace, without making a sound. It is just like the famous line from Shakespeare: "full of sound and fury, signifying nothing." Going all day without speaking, he'd sit alone on his balcony watching for our arrival. As the days of autumn gradually grew shorter, I'd sit with him and recite "To Autumn," the poem by Keats he so loved:

> Where are the songs of spring, Ay, where are they?
> Think not of them, thou hast thy music too.

And he asked, what of those foolish bees? We are those foolish bees, and as long as flowers bloom, summer will last forever. The poet remembers that autumn: "And gathering swallows twitter in the skies." Father said that the time spent in our homeland was all too brief, and I still remember all the swallow nests under the eaves of the house and how we always looked forward to their return in the spring.

On the afternoon of Father's Day 1987, he forced himself to get up and sit in a rattan chair beside the bed, where he suddenly passed away, quietly laying aside the ideals of a lifetime as well as the struggles and the sufferings of loss. We buried his ashes next to Mother's, facing the bowed rim of the Pacific. On this island where he lived peacefully for forty years, it doesn't snow in the winter, it's hot and humid in the summer, and the sun shines down fiercely on their gravestones.

Going through the things my parents left behind was a simple matter. In her entire life, my mother never possessed any jewelry, or anything of value. In her closet was a small beat-up leather suitcase that contained old photographs from Nanjing to Chongqing, from Beijing after demobilization, and from Taiwan, which she was reluctant to discard (there was not one photo of me as a child). On the top level of the closet were eight quilts. I know that after moving to Neihu, she'd often go to a quilt shop on Changsha Street in Taipei and have quilts of varying thicknesses made to order. She said, "We have our own house now and can take care of our guests when they come." Actually, the people she had taken care of were no longer around: revolutionaries, anti-Japanese volunteers, defenders of Shanhaiguan, those who fought in the battle of Taierzhuang, and those who gave their all on the Burma Road, refugees from home, young people wandering destitute . . . they were all gone. I kept two of her quilts and used them for more than a decade on Lishui Street. Even that age of traditional handmade quilts is gone.

Arranging my father's possessions was even easier. After leaving the KMT in 1954, he was always being watched. By the time Uncle Lei Zhen was arrested in 1960, my father had burned almost all his letters and papers to avoid possibly implicating others. For years afterward, he kept no letters. In a drawer in his desk, I did find a few letters from Zhang Qun, which discussed severing relations with Japan. One letter was from Yoshida Ayumi, the daughter of Prime Minister Yoshida Shigeru, who wrote thanking my father for going to Japan and for his condolences. There was also a small wooden box containing a red wrapping cloth on which was inscribed four lines of Chinese verse, presented as a gift at the funeral ceremony. In addition, there were also a number of birthday cards depicting little cats and dogs from his grandchildren. In his bedroom, I found his diary; a twenty-volume set of *Collected Philosophy* (1920, hardbound edition), which he purchased in Germany; and a complete set of the *Twenty-Four Histories* he bought in Shanghai, which always sat on his bookshelf. After my mother died, we didn't know if we should air his books, because they were damaged beyond repair by termites, with only half the pages and the covers remaining; the wooden box crumbled at the touch and was fit only to be burned.

After the passing of my parents, amid the complex feelings of loss, all I could do was struggle, unable to free myself from the sadness of a drifting existence he experienced, and which I had inherited. I retired early from teaching at NTU the following year—returning to the podium after the accident, I found it extremely difficult to stand for two hours and then carry my books, exam papers, and other materials after class and walk from the College of Arts to the main gate in the cold or the heat, then walk home if I was unable to get a cab on Xinsheng South Road. It was the time for me to sit down and to think and write.

CONVERSATIONS WITH CHI SHIYING

August 1990 was the third anniversary of Father's passing. My brother and sisters authorized me to prepare a book titled *Interviews with Chi Shiying* and the Institute of Modern History at Academia Sinica to publish it. The book was part of the oral history project drawn up in 1959 by Professor Guo Ting Yi, the first director of the institute. In 1969, with the support of Shen Yunlong, my father was interviewed a total of nineteen times by Lin Quan and Lin Zhongsheng. Lin Zhongsheng transcribed the tapes and prepared the final manuscript. Although the manuscript completely preserved the original meaning of the oral narrative, sedulously avoiding embellishment, through his smooth style, Lin is able to plumb the depths of the interviewee's complicated experience. Before and after the interviews, Lin developed a genuine interest in and sympathy for my father's generation and ideals. He assiduously checked and verified the facts and continuously discussed and checked the names of people, places, and events with my father, resulting in a book with very few errors. After it was finished, not only did the whole academic community recognize its value but also general readers enjoyed Lin Zhongsheng's sprightly, clear, and spot-on prose, and found the rich content of great interest.

Mr. Lin Zhongsheng was born in Yilan and graduated from the History Department of National Taiwan Normal University. He was only twenty-eight when he conducted the interviews with my father and displayed a genuine bent for historical research. Later he operated a large-scale cram school, which was tremendously successful. He founded the Lamp of Wisdom Advanced Middle School for the education of the children of his hometown. With his own funds and energy, he continued his interview work and set up the Taiwan Oral History Research Chamber in the United States, publishing *Memoirs of Chen Yisong*, *Memoirs of Zhu Zhaoyang*, *Memoirs of Yang Jiquan*, *Memoirs of Liu Shenglie*, *Memoirs of Liao Qinfu*, and *Memoirs of Gao Yushu*. Over a period of ten years, Lin Zhongsheng made the selections and wrote while his dear wife Wu Junying made the recordings, leaving a valuable history of local

Taiwanese personages that is both admirable and of profound cultural significance.

In the preface to the book, Lin Zhongsheng recalls his impression of my father at the time of the interviews: "Distinguished and dignified, gentle and polite in manner and elegant and refined in speech, he had about him the air of a high-ranking minister of old. . . . Regrettably, life has its vicissitudes: I left the Institute of Modern History nearly twenty years ago, and now the interviews with him are soon going to be published so I am again proofreading the manuscript. Both Mr. Chi Shiying and Mr. Shen Yunlong have passed away. These wise men recede farther into the past, but the events of their day remain clear; these paragons of the older generation remain imprinted on my heart. I deeply believe that his witness contains the element of the truth in this otherwise tumultuous and contentious age." In the preface he also succinctly mentions how when the mainland fell and the government came to Taiwan, Mr. Chi not only brought his work in the northeast to a close, but "was even forced out of the government's party to which he was prepared to give his life, no doubt affecting him profoundly. Only his poise and magnanimity allowed him to remain cool and composed." Unfortunately, at the time of the interviews, the Chinese Democratic Party my father and Lei Zhan, Li Wanju, Xia Taosheng, and Gao Yushu had planned to organize, which adhered to his ideals and held fast to his principles, with a sincere faith in the concepts of freedom, democracy, and the rule of law, had not come to fruition. The freedom and democracy that my father, Guo Yuxin, Wu Sanlian, and Xu Shixian spent their whole lives trying to sow were not mentioned at the time of the interviews.

These various misgivings and regrets were probably the reason the interviews were not published during my father's lifetime. He made sacrifices and contributions his entire life; most of the time he was unable to return home. Neither was he one to care at all about glory and rank, and he never acted out of concern for the comfort of his wife or children. Before he passed away, he felt his life had been deficient or a loss, all he had worked for having been swept away, and so there was no point in leaving any traces. There was no need for Academia Sinica to publish the interviews; it was better to forget and be forgotten by the world.

Not one word is devoted to the political situation in Taiwan in the section about his life after leaving the mainland and on relations with Japan, titled "Tearfully I Flew to Taiwan"; it ends with his attendance of the funeral ceremony for Yoshida Shigeru in 1967. Fortunately, Liang Surong wrote a piece entitled "Chi Shiying in the Legislative Yuan" for the book. Not only does he recall the friendship among revolutionary comrades but also he describes in detail my father's relationship with the KMT, and even the situation in the Legislative Yuan just after they arrived in Taiwan. "He was a man of upright character, who made contributions to the party and the nation. An extreme idealist . . . in the bitter struggle, he was unyielding and uncompromising. I understood him most deeply and learned from him the longest."

When the publication of the book was nearing, I was teaching advanced English at NTU. History graduates Li Xiaoti and Chen Qiukun, who had graduated with Ph.D.s in history from Harvard and Stanford respectively, were both researchers in the Institute of Modern History at Academia Sinica. They helped me to proofread the book and made some suggestions. Xiaoti accompanied me to interview Kang Ningxiang, who was running the *Capital Daily News*. In 1972, he was among the first group of Taiwanese elected to the Legislative Yuan, and he became a good friend of my father's despite the difference in age—at the time he was in his thirties and my father was seventy-three. For a period of more than seven years, he came to the house in Neihu two weekends a month to eat my mother's home-cooked dishes and to talk contentedly over drinks. When I visited him, he started off by saying, "I've always wanted to go on record about my relationship with your father, his relationship with the older generation in Taiwan politics, and his concern for democratic government." That day Xiaoti made an excellent recording for what was to be titled "In Memory of Chi Shiying, a Sower of Democracy."

My father didn't talk about what he did for democracy, freedom, and the rule of law after arriving in Taiwan, so I added a few obituaries written from different points of view from newspapers and magazines as an appendix. In this way the reader can get an objective view of his experiences in the second half of his life after coming to Taiwan, which was not only a simple extension of the idealism of the first half of his life, but rather also the fulfillment of his character. Fu Zheng, one of the founders of the Democratic Progressive Party, wrote a piece for *The Journalist* titled "The Last Man of Iron Will from the Northeast." Political commentator Yu Heng wrote "In Memory of Chi Shiying: The Man and His Relationship with Modern Chinese History," and Tian Yushi wrote "On Sealing Chi Shiying's Coffin." Tian Yushi had been secretary general of the Society of Four Ethical Principles established by Zhang Xueliang, which competed with the Northeast Association in which my father oversaw anti-Japanese activities in the northeast. But after the Xi'an Incident, and working in the government, Zhang developed a better understanding of my father. Very early, members of the Chi family moved from Shanxi to the northeast, and they had patience and calm, traditionally part of the Shanxi character. Tian Yushi's piece states:

> He carried on the pioneering spirit of the first people who moved from China proper to the northeast, and was influenced by the Germanic people while studying in Germany. The combination of the two qualities made him a resolute and daring soul and gave him a realistic approach in all that he did. He was enthusiastic and loyal and cool and thoughtful in all matters. Possessed of a strong will, he dedicated himself to the revolution and was untiring in struggle. . . . From middle age onward, he delved deeply into China's problems with a broad-minded perspective. From beginning to end, he always traveled a rough road that grew increasingly frustrating. . . . But he had an attitude that "gaining fame and fortune through disloyalty is to me like floating clouds."

The piece was not just an obituary for Chi Shiying but also a historical document about the people from the northeast who came to China proper in those days.

Another piece that was included consisted of passages selected from Ihira Naomichi's *An Appraisal of Yoshida Shigeru* (Tokyo: Yomuri

Shimbun, 1978) translated by Professor Lin Shuifu, under the title "Yoshida Shigeru and Chi Shiying." It provides a detailed account of Guo Songling's opposition to Zhang Zuolin, how he and my father met, and how they felt a strong rapport. Yoshida Shigeru was deeply disposed toward Chi Shiying's candidness. Both men worked for their countries during the war, but in the eyes of the Japanese, Chi Shiying was a respectable enemy.

When the book was finished, I penned the acknowledgments, titled "Voice of Twenty Years," in which I clearly state my personal views of a lifetime with my father:

> At the age of twenty-seven, Father joined the newly formed KMT; at fifty-five he was stripped of party membership for going against the powers that were; the golden years of his life were spent between idealism and disillusionment. Personal gain and loss were relatively unimportant in terms of worldly affairs. However, in 1948 the northeast was engulfed in that great suffering of being lost to the enemy. Late in life, that suffering was deep in his thoughts. Guo Songling was defeated and died because the times were not ready, but why was the northeast, and all of China for that matter, so quickly abandoned? What was the main reason? The formation of the new party had nothing to do with a sense of loss, but rather came out of hope for the future.

In the acknowledgments I also look back upon *Time and Tide,* which resumed publication in Taiwan utilizing Song Wenming's editorial "Learning from Adenauer's Memoirs" written in July 1966, when the memoirs of Konrad Adenauer were being translated and serialized. This old man, who rebuilt West Germany after defeat and destruction, had experienced Germany's defeat in two world wars and came to the painful conclusion when considering his country's past and future: "Democratic politics is a way of thinking that has its source in acknowledging the dignity and value and inalienable rights of the individual." Song Wenming wrote: "Although this sounds very plain and simple, within the actual context of German politics, each word and each sentence represent the blood of millions, the tears of tens of millions, and the sufferings and hardships of hundreds of millions." This basic but utterly constant political ideal was the heartfelt aspiration of my father from his student days until the day he was buried in Taiwan.

When he was alive he often said that since coming to Taiwan a lot of people were still hotly pursuing unimportant things like power and influence. He had extricated himself from that framework to seek and obtain freedom. Even though the novelty of revolution had worn off, he still scrupulously did his duty as a scholar, and with his cohorts in the Reform Club of the Legislative Yuan, promoted bills to strengthen the democratic rule of law, such as the publishing law, freedom of speech, an independent judiciary, a system of judicial scheduling, defense lawyer as an established profession, and guaranteeing human rights, all of which were considered in terms of their benefit to the people. Other things, such as establishing the National Library, the printing of the bulletins and records of the Legislative Yuan, the archiving of records for the reference of the people . . . all had immense significance in the political history of China but were not the result of his labors alone. In the first half of his life, he experienced violent storms. He respected Chiang Kai-shek's Northern Expedition and his achievements in the War of Resistance against Japan and didn't have to say anything about the current situation in the "little Chang'an."

On October 4, 1999, my father's childhood friend Chen Hongzheng initiated and Liang Surong organized an offering ceremony to commemorate the 100th anniversary of the birth of Chi Shiying at the Alumni Building at NTU. Chen Hongzheng was a successful businessman and had always been concerned about democracy, human rights, and culture. He understood my father and warmly proposed this idea for a ceremony. On the chosen day, in addition to the teachers and students and old friends, there were many politicians of divergent views present. The venue was packed. Chen Lifu, one of my father's old friends from the revolution, insisted on being there despite being close to 100 years old, because he had "a few words to say." When he arrived, the place was so packed there was no room to walk and he almost had to be carried to the front row, where he stood and spoke, saying that the revolutionary feeling of fifty years before and Chi Shiying's uprightness and straightforwardness, along with the strength of his character in politics, were admirable. He understood the depths of my father's feelings for the northeast and the sorrow at the loss of his homeland.

Gao Yushu also spoke and talked about attending the planning for a Chinese Democratic Party (in those days people would say "new party" or "outside the party"). Liang Surong, Kang Ningxiang, Du Zhengsheng, Liu Shaotang, and Guo Guanying also spoke, saying that if the new party had been established, the political factionalism in Taiwan today might have been avoided and not be so abrupt and bitter. Hu Fo and Zhang Yufa took the historical point of view that the people of the northeast and Taiwan had similar frustrations and hopes with regard to their fates because both had been colonies of Japan.

Over the last twenty years I have sat before the graves of my parents countless times, gazing at the waves on the vast Pacific, thinking of his life and feeling extremely fortunate that this life of mine was bound to two such parents.

SAYING GOOD-BYE TO MEET AGAIN

In November 1987, mainland China opened up and restrictions were relaxed so that people from Taiwan could visit their relatives, but I didn't return until six years after that. In those intervening years, most "people from other provinces" had been back for a visit. The intensely emotional homecoming literature gradually cooled and narratives of disillusionment even began to appear. Separated by the Taiwan Strait, people wondered and thought constantly about China and the friends and relatives they had left behind there, even though the parents in their minds had not aged in forty years. But what they saw upon return were the bones of a once lovely dream. Those who returned to their homeland were advanced in years and no less heartbroken, so I balked at returning, not just because I had no relatives to visit but out of fear, and lest disillusionment ruin my treasured memories. I lacked the courage to go home.

When I read in the May 1993 *Luojia*, the Wuhan University Alumni newsletter, that Lu Qiaozhen had lung cancer and that it had advanced to the final stage, the news came like a bolt out of the blue. I decided there and then to go to Shanghai to see her one last time. Qiaozhen was the first good friend to write after postal relations were opened with mainland China. Our friendship was one of the most beautiful memories of my youth at the confluence of three rivers in Leshan, deep in Sichuan Province. How could I have been so heartless as not to visit her earlier, now that it was almost too late to see her again?

I settled on a date to go to Shanghai, and then first called her husband Xu Xinguang, who had been an upperclassman at Leshan, and set a time. From our phone conversation, I learned that Mr. Yu, who had always lived in Shanghai, had died from a heart attack the previous year. If I had married him back then, I, with my background as one of the five evil types, would certainly have become bad luck for him. My old Leshan friends Yao Guanfu, Su Yuxi, and Peng Yande had all passed away. The only person left for me to see in Shanghai was Qiaozhen, and she was on the verge of death.

The Shanghai airport was pretty chaotic in those days, and I never found the Wuhan classmate who came to meet me. I'm afraid that after fifty years we wouldn't have recognized each other even face to face. Guided by a young woman, I almost got into an unlicensed cab, but fortunately felt something was amiss and returned to the main hall to find a policeman and take a licensed cab. At the Hilton, where I had a reservation, I left my luggage and went down to the lobby to wait for Xu to come and take me to the Post Office Hospital. Qiaozhen, who was helped to sit up, her eyes as clear and limpid as ever, said,

"I knew you were coming. I've been waiting."

She took a sheet of paper from beneath her pillow, and solemnly, as if welcoming a guest, read Du Fu's poem "Presented to Wei Ba, Gentleman in Retirement": "Life is not made for meetings; / like stars at opposite ends of the sky we move. / What night is it, then, tonight, / when we can share the light of this lamp? / Youth—how long did it last? / The two of us gray-headed now, / we ask about old friends—half are ghosts; / cries of disbelief stab the heart. . . ." Breathing weakly, she continued to read to the end: "Tomorrow hills and ranges will part us, / the wide world coming between us again." I leaned over the edge of her bed, unable to stop from crying. Gasping for breath, she continued speaking about things that had happened in the last fifty years and how reality had destroyed her youthful dreams. "All these years in Taiwan, you could really study and teach—I'm so envious." She urged me to cherish everything I had, and to live. Dazed, I left the hospital, knowing that meeting once again was also a farewell. After returning to Taiwan, I received the news that she had passed away. She was sixty-nine that year.

I was not favorably impressed by Shanghai and was in no mood to stay. Coming out of the hospital and taking a cab through what was once the most fashionable part of the city, I recalled how, a half century before, dressed in my wartime clothes, I didn't fit in. I wasn't sure if I should laugh or cry. The people and events of the past had all vanished. By that time, I had seen a good many of the world's major cities, their glories and splendors, but more important, I had read many important books that ought to be read and had done a number of important things that had to be done. I had not lived my life in vain. If I had been seduced by Shanghai's pomposity in those days and stayed, I would have long before been declared one of the five evil types and been done to death in struggle, and if I had managed to survive, I certainly would have wasted my entire life in denying myself.

HOMELAND OF STONE AND HERBACEOUS PEONIES

From Shanghai I flew to Beiping (now called Beijing), and with the help of my nephew, Gan Dawei, bought a train ticket for Tieling in Liaoning to see the land of my birth. I was on a daytime express train that left at 8 a.m. and arrived at 10 p.m., so, just like on that train sixty years earlier, I could see every inch of the land, and those places I had heard about all my life. The train passed through Xingcheng, Huludao City, Jinzhou, Goubangzi, Xinmin . . . I was in a constant state of excitement the whole way, and though I was physically tired, I didn't want to close my eyes even for a few minutes. In the winter of 1925, my father accompanied General Guo Songlin when he led thousands of troops and occupied this stretch of territory. When the train crossed the steel bridge over the Great Flowing River, it was already dark; the bridge was long and I couldn't see a thing. I had a return ticket and hoped that on the way back I'd cross the bridge during the day so I could see everything. Who could have foreseen that I would return by plane? I was unable to see the eastern bank of the Juliu River from that long bridge and thought with affection about my young father, with his lofty aspirations and great ideals, alongside General Guo, spurring his horse into battle, firmly believing they would enter Shenyang the following day, never imaging that one night later they'd be fleeing for their lives, and as they fled, traversing the bridge inch by inch.

On my journey home, I was so excited I couldn't close my eyes, but there were even more surprises to come. With my Taiwan ID I bought a first-class soft sleeper seat in a compartment for four people, the other occupants being two Russians, along with their interpreter. They were engineers contracted from Vladivostok, Russia, to work in Anhui Province, while I was a female professor of English literature from Taiwan. They looked at me as if I were from Mars, and looking at them, I thought of the great slogan of "Fight Communism and Resist Russia" of thirty years earlier, and how I was now going to spend fourteen hours with the enemy in the same compartment of this slow-moving express train! Restless, we sat facing each other, like people from different planets meeting in outer space. Their range of interest in Taiwan surpassed the scope of their interpreter's vocabulary, so we used the occasional English word. Spreading out the world map they carried with them, they never stopped asking me questions about Taiwan's geography, history, education, family life, the position of women in society, clothing, food, housing, and work. . . . I, in turn, asked them about Russia, from Tolstoy to Stalin. . . . It was a very enriching exchange.

When we arrived at Shenyang Station, there was a flurry of activity as some passengers got off the train and others boarded. An hour later, at 10:30 p.m., the train pulled into Tieling Station, which was pitch black except for the station sign; you couldn't see your hands in front of you. Over the train intercom we were told that work was being done on the electrical equipment at the station. Perhaps the platform was outside, but all that could be seen was a station attendant approaching with a lantern in hand, seeming to appear out of a black abyss, and there was no way to tell if there were other people outside or not. Picking up my suitcase, I stepped off the train, but the two Russians from outer space said, "Too black, don't go." I replied that someone was there to meet me, and they said, "But you can't see anyone." Unexpectedly, they jumped off the train and gestured for me to go with them to Harbin, saying that their interpreter could take me back to Tieling the following morning. Clearly they were uneasy and were in all sincerity deeply concerned about me. They were as simple and honest as peasants in a Tolstoy novel. Hesitating, I shouted out my cousin's name in the dark: "Zhenlie! Zhenlie!" From off in the distance I heard someone shout: "Third Sister! Third Sister!" (reflecting the numerical order in our family), which was followed by a flurry of footsteps as Zhenlie ran up, leading his entire family. Although everyone had aged, we still recognized one another. The Russians returned to their carriage, and as the train set off, they reached out and waved for all they were worth, and in the light in the compartment I could see that they were much relieved.

Years later, I still think of what a strange and symbolic trip home that was. We who had gone to Taiwan had spent half our lives hating and fighting the Communists and resisting the Russians, and in the pitch black of the station in my homeland, it was two Russians who had jumped off the train to protect me! And the impressions of Taiwan that they took home with them (a minute speck of a country on the map when compared with Russia) was of a modern and democratic place with an abundance of freedom, so that a woman on her own could take up her luggage and travel thousands of miles through Shanhaiguan in search of the homeland she had left behind sixty years before. That I was able to locate Chi Zhenlie and find my way home was no doubt the will of heaven.

In 1987, when Taiwan began allowing people to go back to mainland China to visit relatives, my father had already passed away. The Neihu house was empty, and gradually the neglect had to be put in order. The flower beds in the garden were overgrown with weeds, and my sister and I could no longer take care of a house in which no one lived; all we could do was return occasionally and look at the desolation. Before the New Year arrived, I went to the house and found a letter with a return address from Tieling, Liaoning, in the mailbox full of dead leaves.

Zhenlie and I have the same great-grandparents. After victory in the War of Resistance, my mother lived in Beiping for two years, and he and one of his brothers moved in so that they could attend school there—Fourth Elder Brother Zhenfei studied at Furen University, while Sixth Younger Brother Zhenlie attended middle school. He recalled two summers when I came home on vacation when I would always force him to study and strictly tutored him in English. I recall that the two brothers were handsome and very spirited. In 1947 when I went to Taiwan on my own, the people and events in my homeland were much the same as that pitch-black darkness in the train station that night. We had to shout our names of half a century earlier before we could find the road home. After mainland China was "liberated" by the Communists, Elder Brother Zhenfei passed through many places before arriving at Zhenjiang in Jiangsu Province. On account of his educational background or his work as an interpreter in the American Marshall Plan to mediate in the war between the Nationalists and the Communists, he was able to find employment at the Jiangsu College of Science and Engineering. He married a virtuous and dutiful wife who bore him three daughters, who, with their husbands, were all filial, making him one of the few truly happy people. After graduating from middle school, Zhenlie tested into the air force and was already at the stage of learning to fly when, owing to the numerous political movements, he was forced to halt because of his landlord family background and was ordered back to his home to farm; he planted crops on Little Western Hill for more than a decade before finally being "rehabilitated" and going to work at the Tieling Municipal Oil Company. His wife was a nurse at the Public Health Center. The family was warmly dressed and well fed. However, "falling from the sky to the land" (in the northeast, crop fields are referred to as land) was hugely traumatic to him and left him bitter about life. Before

I departed, his wife urged me to get him to take off his leather flight jacket, which he had worn for so long that it had turned white, but he was unwilling to throw it away because it constituted the most glorious memory of his entire life.

Chi Zhenwu, another cousin, farmed and was simple and honest by nature. In 1950, the Korean War (also known as the War to Aid Korea) broke out and mainland China called for citizens to "Resist America, Aid Korea" (a Chinese volunteer army took part in the Korean War). When my cousin attended the large village meeting, it was winter and everyone was sitting on the warm kangs. The cadres who had come to draft able-bodied men asked for those willing to join the volunteer army to stand up. At the same time they asked that the kangs be stoked so that they were too hot to sit on, and as the men stood up, they were applauded and welcomed into the volunteer army! With no explanation they were loaded onto a freight train, and by morning the following day, the train had already crossed the Yalu River and arrived at the Siniuju Station in Korea. From then on it was a life with a total absence of justice, an unending bloody fight, always shifting. People became gun-wielding machines, the enemy uncertain, and naturally, there was no way to contact home. In July 1953, the Korean War at an end, the survivors had free choice to be demobilized or return home. A total of fourteen thousand soldiers were unwilling to return to mainland China and ended up in Taiwan, resulting in 123 Freedom Day, which became the focus of world attention. These freedom seekers increased Chiang Kai-shek's prestige in the fight against communism.

Reporters from all over the world arrived at the camp for these freedom seekers. In looking at the name list, a reporter from Taipei discovered a Chi Zhenwu from Tieling, Liaoning. When he got back to the city, he asked my brother, "Is he perhaps a member of your family?" My brother went to check for himself, but before leaving asked our father how he would recognize him. Father said to ask him his father's childhood name, adding that it was "Old Lump." My father went to check himself and found that he was indeed the son of his cousin several times removed. We called him Fifth Elder Brother. After leaving the military, he got a job as a warehouse security guard. In 1970 he died of a cerebral hemorrhage. My brother and Mao Zhongying, the son of my husband's sister, who preached in Gaoxiong, buried him in the Christian cemetery in Yanchao Village, Gaoxiong.

Thirty years later, Chi Zhenwu's nephew Chi Changkai somehow saw my name in a PEN publication, called the Taipei PEN office from Shenyang looking for me, and was able to established contact. He said that since the end of the war to resist America and aid Korea, no one knew what had become of his uncle, and that he had been trying to locate him for years and had just learned of his death and that he was buried in Taiwan. On the phone, he began to cry and asked, "How did he die? How could this happen?" I asked Zhongying to have someone take a snapshot of his grave and mail it to Changkai. The sight of the white gravestone seemed to comfort the family.

How could this happen? When I returned to Little Western Hill, I too asked, How could this happen?

I took the day train from Beijing to Tieling on my own so as to see every inch of land. My cousin Zhenlie took me from Tieling to Little Western Hill, and I returned to our old place in the village; when asked, no one had ever heard of the "Hill of Weeping Ghosts and Howling Wolves." Only then did I realize that when my mother spoke of it, that was just a reflection of her mood.

Since my father had worked for the Nationalist government, the big old ancestral house had been demolished and the ancestral graves plowed under, and the village had been combined with the neighboring village of Cizilin. Half of Little Western Hill, on which I had run wild to pick ginseng, had been flattened as a quarry; the milky white stone in various sizes shone with a cold and hard light. The stone was said to be of a high quality, and that was why the train station five *li* away was known as Luanshi Mountain Train Station. The ancestral graves of the Chi family had been plowed under and the herbaceous peony blossoms I picked as a child were no longer to be found. I was no Rip van Winkle, who went to sleep in the mountains and woke up twenty years later, white-haired, to return to his village and stand at an intersection shouting "Does anyone know me?" I left when I was six years old, so it was unlikely that there would be anyone I knew. On this trip home over thousands of miles, all I saw was some windbreaks and fertile fields stretching toward the blue dome of the sky. I no longer had a footing in my ancestral homeland of stone and herbaceous peonies.

Over the years, I have looked for herbaceous peonies in many places but have rarely seen them; they are even less frequently seen in Taiwan, no doubt owing to the climate. Nearly everyone lives in high-rise apartment buildings without yards and has no leisure to grow such demanding flowers. I remember accompanying my weeping mother to the ancestral graves, which were surrounded by large pine trees, in the shade of which the herbaceous peonies bloomed, protected from the wind and snow. I recall that my grandmother placed a bunch of peonies that I had picked in a vase, which she put on the large dinner table, and how the whole room seemed to light up. The pines and the cypresses around the ancestral graves went the way of the old house, and those herbaceous peonies with their sparkling petals will always be the flower of my homeland.

THE DISTANT SPRING BREEZE OF 1943

I lived in mainland China for twenty-three years; a half century later I returned, and the only people who really recognized me were a few close friends from school. During the eight years of the War of Resistance, Chongqing was my home, and after coming to Taiwan, I recalled Shapingba most frequently. The three *li* between school and home, the countless paddy fields, and the simple road that ran to the Xiaolongkan Highway were all part of my growing up, as witnessed by the students in the class of 1943 at my unforgettable alma mater Nankai Middle School, for which I am most grateful. After mainland China opened for people to visit their relatives, the first to do so were my classmates living in America, some of whom produced mimeographed handwritten accounts. The first letter I received—just a simple postcard—was from Pan Yingmao in Canada, on which she wrote a couple of lines about her recent activities and current address. Yingmao was a good friend in my senior year of high school; she always sat in the neighboring seat and our dorm beds were usually very close. Her mother was French, so she was bilingual and often came across as a dreamer who seemed to waver outside of both cultures. When the lights went out and it was my turn to tell a story from a new book or movie, she was always my most faithful (I like to talk and you like to laugh) listener. I remember her crying without stopping through my telling of the first love of Lamartine's Graziella and her death for love. Lamartine was a French Romantic poet and Graziella, the heroine of the tale, is sixteen—the same age as we were at the time.

After victory, Yingmao and I lost touch, and when her postcard reached Taiwan, we were already seventy years old. I had originally intended to attend a conference in Europe, following which on my return flight I would stop in New York to meet Jennifer Crewe, the senior editor at Columbia University Press, and from there proceed to Canada to see Yingmao. My trip to the States happened to coincide with Thanksgiving, and the person organizing my itinerary said, "Everyone is on the road home to be with their family," as a result of which I didn't go to the States or Canada, figuring I'd go the following year to attend a conference. Unforeseeably, the following year I received a letter from Lu Wenjing in Beijing informing me that Yingmao had passed away after an illness. Not getting together with her was one of my biggest regrets. Feeling ashamed, I wrote a long letter that could never be delivered.

To Yingmao,

I'm sorry to be so long in returning your letter. Upon receiving it, I was quite excited for some time and all the beautiful, perplexing, and regrettable memories of those years came flooding back. Do you still remember? The summer of the year we graduated, we were all awaiting the results of the university entrance exam. We went to Chongqing to see you, and the five of us walked hand in hand to the train station. Suddenly a jeep came straight at us, scattering us, and after recovering from the fright, you

> *said in that calm voice of yours: "I'm afraid we won't see each other again. My mother's French superstition holds that when people holding hands are forced apart, it is just an omen for separation." Over the years I have sometimes thought about that farewell. That omen was quite accurate—we really did separate, all going our separate ways, never able to inquire after one another. . . .*

The long letter is an offering to our youth among the flames of war, snuggled close together for warmth, unable to check our happiness and sadness. I also mailed the letter to friends in mainland China from the class of 1943 who had been urging me to come back for a reunion. Soon thereafter, the *43 Newsletter* printed my letter, on account of which I received even more news and more urgings to return.

I was impelled to go to Beijing in 1999 and attend the annual reunion of the class of '43 on account of the news of the death of Lai Shuying, another good friend. We were classmates through primary and middle school. Her father was from Jiangxi and became acquainted with my grandfather during the Zhi–Feng wars. He was the oldest among my classmates' fathers.

As I recall, her family lived on the slopes of Zengjiayan in Chongqing, where my father took me to visit with a great deal of respect. Shuying wasn't among my sworn confederates of inveterate daydreamers, but she was a frequent guest at our house in Shapingba and closer than most to my parents. After family visits were allowed across the Strait, she immediately wrote to me and asked me to help find out the whereabouts of her brother Lai Guangda, who had gone to Taiwan with the Nationalist government. Before I had made any inquiries, I received word from another classmate that Shuying had died suddenly from an illness. I knew she had married a well-known Beijing physician surnamed Wu who gained the trust of high-ranking Communists after "liberation," and therefore she probably had not been tormented. But how could she have died at just seventy years of age? If I didn't return for a reunion soon, how many of my old classmates would there be left to see?

I arrived in Beijing at night during the third month, late in spring according to the lunar calendar, so it was still fairly cold in the north of the country. Xing Wenwei, who was responsible for keeping in contact with me, was already waiting for me at the hotel. Entering the lobby, among all the people coming and going, I saw a woman standing at the reception desk; her look of expectation was different from most. She walked over to greet me—it was Xing Wenwei! She was the true blossom of Nankai Middle School, and was the focal point of the girls' section for the boys' dorm to gaze at from afar. She was the most soberly beautiful girl I ever saw. In the first year of high school, I sat between her and Yingmao and was the envy of many. Of course, the woman now holding me tightly was not that cool and reserved beauty, and though her eyes had dimmed, she still stood out in a crowd. With her was Yu Yuzhi (who, along with Liu Zhiqi and me, were the three literary friends in the class). They said that Liu Zhiqi was living in Tianjin and in recent years had always said she would be sure to attend a class reunion when Chi Pangyuan showed up. When they were leaving my hotel that evening, I said that I had made the trip specifically for a happy gathering and we would not discuss 1) illness or medicine and 2) returning to the motherland.

The following day, I went to Xing Wenwei's house (after graduating from college, she had married Kang Guojie, a classmate who adored her for his whole life). More than ten people from the same class were there, but we didn't recognize one another when we met, all of us being old women. Only when we mentioned our names was there a startled outburst, but we quickly adjusted the image of ourselves from fifty years before to the reality of today. So many "Do you remember?" questions seemingly explained something that had puzzled me greatly in Taiwan and proved that my youth had indeed been a very happy one. These people and events, the fish pond and plum orchard, had all existed, and though times might have changed, none of it could be destroyed.

Around noon, the doorbell rang. Xing Wenwei called me to the door and said, "Liu Zhiqi has come from Tianjin to see you, but whatever you do, don't say you don't recognize her." The door opened and two young people entered, supporting an old woman. I never could have imagined unyielding Liu Zhiqi being bent over and unable to stand up straight.

Entering the corridor, she embraced me and crying said, "I never thought I'd see you again in this life!" The night before, I had not been told that due to a spinal injury she could not take the train, and that for our gathering her daughter had hired a car so that she could half recline the entire sixty miles from Tianjin to Beijing. Our different fates were sealed when a half century before, she and some friends had gone to the area liberated by the Communists and I had gone to Taiwan alone. Reciting lines from the Qing dynasty poet Gu Zhenguan's "To the Tune of Jinluo qu" was no better than a sob: "Jizi, how are you? Even one day you'd return, all things in this life bear not a look back."

During the summer break of 1946, the various universities were being demobilized after victory and began returning to their original campuses from Sichuan and Yunnan. Classes began in the fall, and Liu Zhiqi left her home in Sichuan with great excitement and went to Beiping. She studied at Yanjing University, which during the war had moved to Huaxiba in Chengdu. Ten of our classmates were there and had one more year to go before graduation. Before I returned to Wuhan to resume classes, she and I met again in Beiping and happily did some sightseeing together. As this was her first time in the north, she was filled with curiosity at the vast spectacle of the politics and culture of the ancient capital. Liu Zhiqi must have been one of the last to personally witness the final days of Yanjing University. Just after liberation the university was categorized as useless because it was an "American imperialist" Christian university. The beautiful campus and famous Weiming Lake (such an inauspicious name!) were forced to become part of the Beijing University campus; those who wrote recollections of student life on the shores of Weiming Lake after 1950 were all students of Beijing University. I'm certain that no one in China in the second half of the twentieth century would dare openly write nostalgically about Yanjing University and its elegant traditions. Political power had thus categorically extinguished a common memory! After fifty years of turbulence, how would that friend of mine who was filled with literary feelings look back on our parting in 1949?

The reunion made me feel more timid the closer I got to home! Every moment was precious, with too much to say about the events of those years and too many old songs to sing. Our voices feeble and memories weak, we sought to rekindle the Nankai spirit. . . . Before parting the following afternoon, they started singing our class song, which I had written as an eighteen-year-old with literary aspirations: "The blossoming plum trees and the morning sun; the western pool and the evening clouds . . . the wind of 1943 is now far away; farewell, alma mater, we know not when we'll return."

In the student movement that was rolling on with full force behind the lines, from demonstrations in the street evolving into full-fledged participation, some of our university classmates went to Yan'an, all of whom had long stories to tell. One of them was Fu Qizhen, who was from Taiyuan in Shanxi Province. She was still big and hearty. I immediately recalled her resonant laughter when we talked at school. It was said that not long after starting college, she and several friends went to Yan'an. In middle school it was nearly impossible to distinguish who was "progressive" and who was "reactionary" because no one revealed themselves! For the last half century the people from Yan'an have been the masters of China, so her lot should have been a fortunate one. (Five years later I received photos in the mail of her during her Nankai days, in one of which she was wearing a PLA uniform, with a note that said: "Entering Taiyuan City with the Army." Her letter said it was not entirely accurate.) There were so many questions I wanted to ask, but at a gathering of more than ten people, I really didn't know how to put those individually vital questions. Now nearly sixty years later, with recalled enthusiasm, we sang song after song from when we were young, our hearts having gone through so many hardships. How can you still remember? Our generation that grew up in wartime Chongqing taking shelter in the desolate outskirts amid the sound of air-raid sirens, our heads were filled with and our imaginations absorbed in the blind love of *Days of Tomorrow* and *Graziella*, but in our lives was there ever a sky-blue bay? Was there ever the possibility of "Black hair blown by the wind, the shadow of a sail passes over my cheeks, as I listen to the fisherman singing at night"? Those who remained in mainland China experienced political turmoil, and some suffered; those who went to Taiwan or abroad always felt uprooted. While we were meeting anew like this, it seemed like a different world. When there was "too much to say" and songs like "The Wind of 1943 is Now Far Away" had been sung repeatedly, memory and oblivion were like two soft strands circling above a roomful of white-haired childhood friends. The elite of the elite in their youth, they lost much time for a normal life due to political disruptions and the demands of marriage, becoming a lost generation, swallowed up in the simple sigh of a "faraway spring breeze," with no desire to remember and no ability to forget.

That afternoon, we left Xing Wenwei's house and walked to the big street at the end of the lane and had lunch at a restaurant. I forgot to ask the name of the street, and all I remember is that it was planted with willow trees or Persian silk trees, and April was the time of flying willow catkins, so thick as to cover the ground. Holding hands, Yu Yuzhi and I brought up the rear. Seeing the heads and shoulders of the seven or eight classmates ahead of us sprinkled with willow catkins, I couldn't help but recall "Water Dragon's Chant," Su Dongpo's lyric about willow catkins that we memorized, which was included in Professor Meng Zhisun's textbook of selected lyrics. Yu said she remembered that it began, "It seems to be a flower, yet not a flower." In relay, we recited: "And no one shows it any pity: let it fall! / Deserting home, it wanders by the road; / When you come to think of it, it must / Have thoughts, insentient as it may be. . . . A pond full of broken duckweed! / Of all the colors of springtime, / Two-thirds have gone with the dust, / And one third with the flowing water! / When you look closely, / These are not willow catkins, / But, drop after drop, tears from people who part!" We stood on that unfamiliar Beijing street amid the white willow catkins, our lives drifting together and apart, and the sadness carpeting the ground that no poem can capture!

Two years later in Taipei, I received a copy of the *43 Newsletter*, which contained the news item: "Xing Wenwei Passes Away." Upon first seeing it, I couldn't believe my eyes, but examining it by lamplight, I found it was true. Even beyond the grief, however, I noticed that her name, Xing Wenwei, was written in simplified characters, which angered me and made me question its veracity. At our age, death draws nearer, but I had no idea she had fallen ill and I could not convey my sympathy! And here was her death announced with this Chinese character I didn't recognize. There were quite a few of us present the last time we met, and each of us was unable to articulate what we had encountered. The singing, the laughter, and the talk were not a complaint about the suffering and regrets of being born at the wrong time—that cup of bitterness had been drained long before—but that gathering nearly sixty years later served to prove that I had been young once.

Gradually, news from my school friends ceased; the spring breeze of 1943 had not only grown distant, it had vanished forever.

After the '43 reunion I went to Chaoyang Gate to meet with Yang Jingyuan, who was two years ahead of me at Nankai and with whom I had once shared a room. When I got to Wuhan University, she was in her third year in the Department of Foreign Languages and Literatures and was an advanced pupil of Zhu Guangqian. At Leshan, I once had New Year's Eve dinner at her house. Her father, Professor Yang Duanliu, was an expert on currency in the Department of Economics, and her mother, Yuan Changying, since returning from Europe in 1929 had taught drama and Shakespeare in the Department of Foreign Languages and Literatures at Wuhan University (I studied with her for two years), and was referred to as one of the "Three Luojia Talents," the other two being Ling Shuhua and Su Xuelin.

Growing up in such a household, Yang Jingyuan was a solid student with depth of thought, and was kind and romantic by nature. During normal times she could have become the writer she longed to be as well as an intellectual capable of doing academic research. However, before graduating from college in 1945, she had already joined the political trend of thought that perplexed most university students. The students who leaned toward Communism referred to themselves as "progressives" and those who were more conservative as "reactionaries." At that time, the Nationalist army that had spent six years fighting the Japanese found itself sunk in the most difficult stage of defending Hunan, Guangxi, and Guizho. Sichuan was too large, and most urban and village dwellers passed peaceful lives, but the refugees from downriver once again found themselves in a panic, thrust again into the proximity of the fighting.

In 2003, Yang Jingyuan published *The Diary of Ranglu*, in which she recounted what attracted her to politics in those early days and the feeling that the government was "thoroughly corrupt" and had to be reorganized. A leftist student loaned her *One Month in Yan'an* and *Random Jottings of Going to the West*, which changed her from a girl who was a diligent student of English and American literature; as she put it: "I had to read it; I had to seize every opportunity to learn about Communism." At the time, her parents earnestly advised her to first finish her studies and not rush into joining a political party: "Politics and love are quite similar, for there is no escaping once you've been together for a while." After she graduated from Wuhan University, her parents did everything in their power to help her pursue advanced study in the English department of the University of Michigan, but swept up in the tide after "liberation" and on account of love, she abandoned her studies without consulting anyone and returned to build the New China. Fifty years later, she published the collection of love letters from two places, *Letters to My Love—1945–1948* (Henan People's Publishing House, 1994). That year in Beijing I saw her and her beloved, Yan Guozhu (Institute of Engineering, Wuhan University, and in the same class as I was for four years), and learned that her life had been happy in love. However, the cruelty of the political persecution her parents had suffered was perhaps difficult to forget. In 2002 she published *The Peacock Flies Home—Yuan Changying* (Beijing People's Publishing House), in which she gives a detailed account of how miserably Professor Yuan was treated late in life: she swept the campus streets and then was banished back to her old home where she found refuge alone with relatives, which she referred to as imprisonment in a "mountain jail," living a solitary existence until she died. It made this student of hers weep to no end.

I also recalled Zhu Guangqian, the professor I visited who had encouraged me to change to the Department of Foreign Languages and Literatures, and who would have been my advisor. Shortly after Taiwan allowed people to return to mainland China for family visits, I read an article in *Luojia*, the Wuhan University newsletter, written by an upperclassman by the name of Wang Zhu titled "Scenes of Professor Zhu Guangqian During the Ten Years of the Great Catastrophe of the

Cultural Revolution," from which I learned that after spending four years in a "cowshed," Professor Zhu was sent back to Beijing University to the United Nations Materials and Translation Section in 1970, and while under continued supervision and reform through labor, he could get his hands on a few books while sweeping and cleaning toilets. One day while he was sweeping up in the Department of Western Languages, he happened to discover his manuscript translation of the second volume of Hegel's *Aesthetics*, which had been taken away as something "feudalistic, capitalistic, and revisionary" when his house was searched and his property confiscated. Once again seeing this manuscript on which he had so painstakingly labored seemed like something from another world. Fortunately, Ma Shiyi, the section chief, took it and hid it. After laboring by day, Professor Zhu worked at pounding out a final draft, word by word, line by line, as well as translating the third volume. His work was published after the Cultural Revolution. Professor Zhu was lucky. In 1989, Qian Mu went to Hong Kong to lecture at the New Asia College and had the chance to meet him again. I too had intended to go to Hong Kong to pay my respects but never did, because when Qian Mu returned to Taipei, he informed me that Professor Zhu scarcely recognized anyone any longer.

Professor Wu Mi's words of hope and encouragement in those days—"The Buddha says, Love is like a torch, though it light ten thousand fires, its light never diminishes"—sustained me for more than sixty years. Under political persecution, he too lost his academic honors. Nearly fifty years later, several students of Professor Wu Mi, now famous scholars, pieced together an outline and his lecture notes for Literature and Life and had them published, and Qian Zhongshu inscribed the title. There were also some handwritten notes in English and Chinese, some of which were written with a brush. One of the editors was retired Professor Wang Minyuan of the Department of Foreign Languages and Literatures at Beijing University, who translated the English into Chinese. He was eighty years old at the time and "sitting and facing the wall for several months, I used a magnifying glass to decipher and study his original handwriting word by word. After translating it, I also added annotations." The book also describes Professor Wu's lifetime dedication to study and teaching, and although he himself led a simple and thrifty life, he never stinted when it came to helping others. However, during the Cultural Revolution, he "came to a bad end." He was not allowed to teach; he was struggled against and criticized, humiliated, forced to write self-criticism, forced to labor, beaten, not allowed to eat, seized by both arms, quickly frog-marched and fell to break his legs, and lost his sight. . . . In the final moments of his life, he lost consciousness, repeatedly calling out, "Give me water, I am Professor Wu Mi. I want to eat, I am Professor Wu Mi." He was persecuted to such an extent because he had the audacity to say at a meeting dedicated to the criticism of Confucius that "Some of what Confucius said is still right." When someone tried to force him to criticize Confucius, his reply was: "I would rather die." In his afterword, Professor Wang writes, "A person who ought to receive respect in any civilized society—I deeply cherish the memory of Professor Wu Mi."

Nearly all of these teachers under whom I studied in the university did not survive, and their bitter experiences are the worst suffered by China's intellectuals in the last century, and all were the result of politics. All the water in the three rivers would not be enough to wash away the anger and resentment.

A HERO'S MEMORIAL

After the reunion in Beijing I went to Nanjing, and there to meet me was Zhang Wen, another member of the class of '43. We were good friends in school, and she was straightforward and kind, never calculating. Her father was in cultural circles, so we had much in common with regard to our attitude toward life and what we talked about. She was one of the earliest to write to me after Taiwan permitted family visits to the mainland. We recognized each other at once the first time we saw each other after fifty years. She was still big and robust and appeared optimistic and dependable, as if she possessed a calm and unhurried poise with regard to aging.

Returning to Nanjing was like returning home. The first day we got together for lunch with four other friends from the same class. I hadn't been all that close to them at Nankai, so we had no intimate talk, and with so few of us, we didn't sing either. Following lunch, and according to my plans, I went to look for our old house on Ninghai Road. I first located Lane 3 on Ninghai Road, where I recognized nothing save the street name. The primary school on Shanxi Road was squeezed between two old buildings, with no playground to speak of. Drum Tower Primary School was just a hundred feet from the Holiday Inn where I was staying. I walked over and back from the hotel but never saw the name of the school above the dark and narrow, dilapidated door. The signs on the stores on either side seemed to block it out. Entering, I simply couldn't believe how small, simple and crude, old and shabby it was. Among primary schools in Nanjing, Drum Tower was one with a history, and if I hadn't see its current state with my own eyes, I never would have believed that such a gap could exist between memory and reality. Before 1937 was the "golden decade" of the capital, but of the Nanjing that underwent the extensive nation-building plan not a trace remained.

The following day, Zhang Fei and her husband, Liu Shousheng, came to show me the Nanjing of today. First we went to see the newly constructed memorial to the Nanjing massacre. Going through the door, we entered into the front courtyard paved with yellow sand, around which stood stone markers inscribed with the names of the dead from the various city districts. Inside the broad and weighty single-story building were related photographs and materials. The deep grief was displayed in the simplest fashion. To this day, I can't remember how I walked out of that building.

The next place I hoped to see was the Sun Yat-sen Memorial. When I was young, when guests arrived from the north, my parents would have me accompany them to climb those seemingly never-ending stone steps. However, when the taxi arrived at the memorial, I saw all kinds of peddlers among the mix of trees, but never the entrance to the stairs. Getting out of the car, I stood looking up at the white stone mausoleum and a few scattered people ascending and descending the stone stairs on four sides, all the while entirely lacking a solemn demeanor. Suddenly I felt disappointed and didn't want to go up. I returned to the car and, recalling the map of Nanjing I had seen the night before, I asked Zhang Fei if she knew where the public cemetery for aviator martyrs was located on Purple Hill. She said she knew where it was and had thought about going to see it. She asked the driver how far it was and if we could go. He said we had to head south around the mountain for about thirty *li*, and that he could take us and would be willing to stay and wait to take us back to the city.

As the car traveled the winding mountain road, I seem to find myself in a dream world. The car stopped at a place where the mountain road widened, and we entered the cemetery through a high and spacious stone gateway and ascended the stone steps. I still had the feeling of being in a dream. What a strange and unexpected journey! Only when we stood facing a large stone tablet on which was inscribed in Sun Yat-sen's hand "Saving the Country by Air," which was situated in a pavilion, did I begin to believe that it was true. Ascending still farther, about halfway up the slope, there was a large white terrace, at the center of which stood a large stone tablet and a pair of stone statues of soldiers in flying gear—one Chinese and one American. On the stone tablet was written: "Memorial for the Aviator Martyrs of the War of Resistance Against Japan." On the first level on the slope was a group of more than seven hundred gravestones for American martyrs. Flowers were placed in front of some of the markers (the brochure about the memorial said that descendants continue to come from America to pay homage). Continuing up the slope, on the second level was row after row of even larger tablets of black granite on which were engraved the more than three thousand names of the Chinese Air Force martyrs. Trees were sparsely planted on the slope behind, and under the early May sun, the large swath of gravestones was in no way gloomy or forbidding. Climbing to the top of the stone steps, I let go of Zhang Fei's hand and quietly said to her that I wanted to be alone and find stone tablet M. Before I left for Beijing, Zhang Dafei's brother had sent me a booklet about the memorial and said his name was located there.

All of this was absolutely true. On stone tablet M were engraved twenty names, and the line for Zhang Dafei was simply written:

> Zhang Dafei Captain, from Yinkou, Liaoning Born 1918—Died in the line of duty 1945

This young man who was determined to be like the hero in the poem: "If the winged general were at the Dragon City, / the enemy horsemen would never cross the Yin mountains" gave his life for his country, and his twenty-six years of life were reduced to a single line. Could this piece of stone and these few words become the refuge of a soul?

That day in May, the sun shown down on me in my seventy-fifth year, and was as warming as his unforgettable voice. Was my visit there something to which he eagerly looked forward? Or was it not completely a matter of chance, like attending the church memorial service on the one-year anniversary of his death in the line of duty? I sat for a long time on the small stone bench in front of the marker, until Zhang Fei took me down the hill and we returned to the city via Xuanwu Lake, which was one of the places I had planned to see. But it was close to sunset, so the water was dark and the color of the trees difficult to distinguish—all the events of my childhood were concealed in the twilight.

Among the rows of large stone markers with no individual characteristics of life and death, I thought of the winter of 1936 and listening to him cry, telling with difficulty how the Japanese had tortured and burned his father to death. That was the first time I understood why my father was frequently not at home and the work that occupied him after returning to the north since the Mukden Incident; and also why with Mother in Beiping and Tianjin, we frequently changed our surname from Wang to Xu to Zhang . . . and finally why the heads of the fathers of the Gai children had been hung on the city wall.

Undertaking the first stage of exile from Nanjing to Hankou, the senior high boys of Sun Yat-sen Middle School became my family's traveling companions, to live or die together. They carried my seriously ill mother and my three baby sisters onto cars and boats. These boys who were not yet twenty, their very existence threatened, grew up to become protectors. Disembarking from the boat in Hankou, the troop of boys shouldered more than a hundred rifles and were settled in a primary school auditorium. One December night, when there was not enough clothing or blankets to stay warm and while the Japanese planes bombed the city and riverside around the clock, a dozen or so boys who were eighteen years old crossed the river to apply for admission to the Central Military Academy. Zhang Dafei applied for the air force. He said that from that point on in life, there would be no tears, just struggle and the defense of the country.

From then on he was totally committed to the new world of the protector. He earnestly undertook military training from winter to summer, which totally transformed him so that now he walked with his chest thrust forward and with great strides. After flight training began, he entered yet another world. On his twentieth birthday, he wrote to my mother, my brother, and me, excited about having read the biography of Gao Zhihang, whose patriotic and idealistic spirit made him increase his own efforts in his studies and gave him more determination to pass the flight-training exam and one day join a pursuit squadron to fight the enemy in the sky and reduce the casualties among his fellow countrymen. "Although pilot Gao Zhihang died, there will be countless others to take his place." He also had to develop steadiness, resourcefulness, and accurate judgment, so that in a dogfight he could use his sharp eyes and quick reflexes to pursue and shoot down enemy aircraft and live to return.

In those youthful days, I worshiped the heroes who flew pursuit fighter aircraft! That kind of hero worship can only exist at a certain age and during wartime. My feelings were pure and sincere, for which propaganda was unnecessary, and which nobody would mock. Those who had fled and took shelter amid the wail of air-raid sirens for years not only worshiped the heroes who beat back death in the sky but also were grateful and ashamed—a feeling of being too beholden. When we on the ground fled and hid from the enemy bombs, they stood at attention and set off into the sky to destroy the enemy planes. While we received a proper education without interruption, they fought not knowing if they would be alive tomorrow.

But in his letters he repeatedly said that in his heart, songs of hero worship made him even more conflicted. He never lost his dream of becoming a military chaplain. When he went for training in Colorado, he frequently kept company with the base chaplains, and attending their gatherings only served to strengthen this idea of his. When he returned to China, he attended church at the Kunming base, where he obtained the warmest feeling of inner peace in his entire life. Later he probably learned that there was no system of military chaplains in the Chinese armed forces, but still the hope sustained him. Not wasting his time with drink and women, he had a hope in life and obtained true spiritual redemption. He was the first person to talk to me about the soul. The Twenty-third Psalm in the Bible is a prayer for safety, and he recited the passage "He restoreth my soul." In the education provided at home and in school in those days, no one discussed the soul, but for my entire life, this has been an overriding issue in my reading.

Among my mother's things I found two photos of Zhang Dafei in military uniform, one taken when he rose to the rank of first lieutenant and the other when he was promoted to the rank of captain. The warm smile on his face was at odds with his stern military dress. For fifty years I had searched war memorials of that age in which he gave his life in the line of duty.

In 1998, his brother sent a story from the Henan *Xinyang Daily News* reporting on the search for where he died: "In May 1945, a plane did, in fact, go down on the riverbank below the old street of Xishuanghe. Quite a few curious people went to have a look at the plane, which lay with one wing upright, the other buried in the sand. A few days later, people were sent by those in authority to dismantle the plane and ship it with the use of salt rafts down the canal to Xinyang."

In an article of three thousand words, not a single word was devoted to the pilot's body. The plane had not caught fire, so his body must have been intact. Where did the local people bury him? No one in the last fifty years seems to know or ever will know if that poor soul, whose family was destroyed and scattered and forced to wander and who lived another ten years after finding religion, will ever really find spiritual rest. Or is his soul still wandering around on the land where it entrusted its body, a bloody wandering ghost with nowhere to return?

Late at night after receiving the copy of the *Xinyang Daily News*, as the clamor of the city gradually subsided, I took down the Bible he had presented to me before he left in 1937, looking for guidance as to how I should view his life after half a century, and my life. I opened it straight to chapter 3 of Ecclesiastes:

> To everything there is a season, and a time to every purpose under the heaven: a time to be born, and a time to die;. . . a time to get, and a time to lose; a time to keep, and a time to cast away; a time to rend, and a time to sew; a time to keep silence, and a time to speak; a time to love, and a time to hate; a time of war, and a time of peace.

All of this seemed to be the last sixty years of my life. With his blessing, I have arrived at the time in life to cast things away. Ecclesiastes reminded me that the happy days of youth were gone and the days of decline and disintegration were now upon me. In my reading, what I most enjoyed were the symbols for that time in which to cast things away:

> While the sun, or the light, or the moon, or the stars, be not darkened, nor the clouds return after the rain . . . and the almond tree shall flourish, and the grasshopper shall be a burden, and desire shall fail: because all men goeth to his long home, and the mourners go about the streets. Or ever the silver cord be loosened, or the golden bowl be broken, or the pitcher be broken at the fountain, or the wheel broken at the cistern. Then shall the dust return to the earth as it was: and the spirit shall return unto God who gave it. Vanity of vanities, saith the preacher; all is vanity.

I read the passage again after returning from Nanjing and having seen the black granite stone on which the name "Zhang Dafei" was inscribed, along with the dates of his birth and death. What was the concrete connection? With a few memories buried in real life, I had been able, with the power of reason, to gradually sum up the wisdom transmitted by the Bible: wisdom is an awakening from all emptiness.

In my heart, Zhang Dafei's life was like a night-blooming cereus, blossoming deep in the night and quickly closing to fall to the ground: such glorious purity, such unspeakable nobility.

ANCHORAGE FOR A SOUL

In early autumn 2001, on the seventieth anniversary of the Mukden Incident, my brother escorted me and my two sisters, Ningyuan and Xingyuan, across the Pacific to Shenyang to attend the opening ceremony of the Chi Shiying Memorial Library at Northeast Sun Yat-sen Middle School, memorializing that generation of drifting souls.

Chi Shiying, who nursed a grievance from 1925, when he accompanied General Guo Songlin at the Juliu River, to 1987 when he was buried in Taiwan, led a wandering life with his wife and children in tow, with no roof overhead and no land underfoot. The family home was demolished and the ancestral graves were plowed under, and the ancestral home of Tieling, Liaoning, that my siblings and I named when filling out forms had become nothing but a homeland on paper.

The fate of the Northeast Sun Yat-sen Middle School from its very founding was rocky. A group of homeless children and teachers were recruited at Baoguo Temple in Beiping to form a large family linked by blood and tears. From Beiping to Nanjing, from Nanjing to Hankou, to Xiangxiang, Guilin, and Huaiyuan, in vehicles when they were available or on foot when not, they traveled and wandered down into Sichuan, finding shelter at Jingning Temple, where the school stayed for eight years, their education never interrupted. After victory in the War of Resistance against Japan, they made their way home, running happily. The school shut down in 1946 and reopened in 1994, pushed for by alums from all over the country and overseas.

On the podium erected for the opening ceremony sat local senior officials, those in charge of the school, and Guo Feng and Li Tao, who had expended the most energy to see the school reestablished. They spoke of the rocky history of the Northeast Sun Yat-sen Middle School since its founding sixty-seven years earlier, and with no little satisfaction they said that due to the efforts of the past few years, it had become one of the important schools of Shenyang, owing to the high-quality teaching. It was a day for alums to return to the school. A new generation of students stood in rows on the playing field, singing a new school song. This was followed by the old alums singing together, which awakened many long-buried memories—the song of my first awakening that accompanied me from Nanjing to Hunan, on the Hunan–Guangxi Road to the Sichuan–Guizhou Road, a distance of eight thousand miles over time; the song of growing up amid that tide of refugees. In the morning breeze in early autumn, standing on the soil of my homeland, these people for whom the school had been family, people now old who had shared in life and death, their white hair fluttering in the wind, wept amid the singing. The water of the Songjiang River still had the clear voice of the Jialing River, but in the sobbing was something indomitable.

> Only the people of Chu have upright men, with merely three families to destroy Qin!
> I come from the north and to the north I will return.

Coming away from the ceremony, I visited the Mukden Incident Memorial and then boarded a train for Dalian alone. The train passed through Yingkou and I thought of the winter of 1925, when my father received orders to go with Brigade Commander Ma to enter and occupy Yingkou. They got off in Goubangzi, across the river fromYingkou, and with Chief of Staff Su Bingwen, they crossed the Liao River with the advance force. The river was not entirely frozen over and filled with floating ice. The troops used small wooden boats and risked being swept out to sea as they made the dangerous crossing. When they came ashore at Yingkou, they were stopped by the Japanese Kwantung Army.

I went to Dalian because I wanted to see the ocean as it flowed toward Taiwan from the coast of my homeland. For two straight days, I went to the seaside park and sat alone on the stone steps and saw the Bohai Bay flow into the Yellow Sea, and farther on into the East China Sea and then into the vast Pacific, two thousand *li* by ship to Taiwan. Rounding the island to Oluanpi at its southern extreme, it flows to the Yakou Sea, a few *li* from the lighthouse, where the bay is deep blue, where it is calm and beautiful and where the waves, it is said, end in silence.

Everything returns to eternal silence.

Index